USING
dBASE III® PLUS

Edward Jones

Osborne **McGraw-Hill**
Berkeley, California

Osborne **McGraw-Hill**
2600 Tenth Street
Berkeley, California 94710
U.S.A.

For information on translations and book distributors outside of the
U.S.A., please write to Osborne **McGraw-Hill** at the above address.

Using dBASE III® PLUS

0 DODO 89

ISBN-0-07-881252-6

Cynthia Hudson, Acquisitions Editor
Fran Haselsteiner, Project Editor
Yashi Okita, Cover Design

To Judie, Nikki, and Jarel

About the Author

Edward Jones of Herndon, Virginia, is a consultant in the area of microcomputer applications and database design. As owner of J.E. Jones Associates, Jones has developed client applications in dBASE for a number of Baltimore–Washington, D.C., area clients, including Lawyers' Committee for Civil Rights, Edison Electric Institute, and American Industrial Arts Students Association. Jones is also a free-lance writer and newspaper columnist. During the past four years his articles have been published in *Lotus* magazine, *Popular Computing*, *Business Computing*, and *Signature* magazine. His newspaper column, written under the "Brian Starfire" pseudonym, appears on a nationally syndicated basis. Before pursuing a full-time consulting and writing career, Jones was employed by IBM and Xerox, where he was involved in training and writing documentation for microcomputer-based products.

Contents

Introduction **xi**

Chapter 1 Introduction to dBASE III PLUS **1**

Relational Databases
How You Will Use dBASE III PLUS
History of dBASE III PLUS
dBASE III PLUS's Improvements
Limitations of dBASE III PLUS
System Requirements

Chapter 2 Database Design **15**

About Data and Attributes
Three Phases of Database Design

Chapter 3 Creating and Displaying a Database With dBASE III PLUS **25**

Making the dBASE III PLUS System
 Disk 1 Self-Booting
Creating a CONFIG.SYS File on Your Hard Disk
Some Important Notes for Hard-Disk Users
Starting dBASE III PLUS
Selecting Options From a Menu
Canceling a Selection
The dBASE III PLUS Dot Prompt
Conventions
Getting Help

Creating a Database
Displaying a Database Structure
The APPEND Command
Viewing a Database
Viewing Selective Data With the
  Assistant Options
Using Multiple Conditions
Searching Within a Field
A Warning About Memo Fields
Keeping Track of Records

Chapter 4   Changing Your Database   **65**

The EDIT Command
The BROWSE Command
Using BROWSE From the Assistant
Deleting Records
Deleting Files
Changing the Contents of a Database
Modifying the Structure of a Database
The Assistant

Chapter 5   Creating Entry Forms With the dBASE III PLUS
Screen Painter   **87**

Creating a Data-Entry Form
Moving Fields
Changing Field Widths
Adding Fields
Deleting Fields
Changing the Display Characteristics of a Field
Using the Picture Function, Picture Template,
  and Range
Drawing Lines and Boxes on a Form

Chapter 6   Sorting and Indexing Your Database   **113**

Sorting
Indexing
When to Index, When to Sort

Chapter 7 Creating Reports   139

Using LIST With Printers
Using LIST With the Assistant
Margin Settings and Page Eject
dBASE III PLUS Report Generator
Creating and Printing Mailing Labels

Chapter 8 More Efficient Searches With Query Files   177

Nesting Expressions Within a Query

Chapter 9 Introduction to dBASE III PLUS Programming   195

Creating Command Files
Programming Concepts
Some Commonly Used Commands
Overview of a Program Design

Chapter 10 Decision Making Within a dBASE III PLUS
Program   225

Going in Circles
IF, ELSE, and ENDIF
The CASE Statement

Chapter 11 File Management   237

The Copy Command
Work Areas and Active Files
CLEAR ALL
Combining Files
Copy Structure
Using UPDATE

Chapter 12 Using the Relational Powers of dBASE III PLUS   259

Using the SET RELATION TO Command
Creating and Using View Files
Creating or Choosing a Catalog
Adding Files to a Catalog

Closing a Catalog
A Note About DOS and Open Files

Chapter 13 Creating and Refining Screen Displays   277

Putting Information on the Screen With
  @ and SAY
Using Format Files
Helpful Hints on Screen Design

Chapter 14 More Programming with dBASE III PLUS   295

Common Functions
More About Memory Variables
Using dBASE III PLUS Macros
Editing Records Under Program Control
Hiding and Showing Variables With
  PRIVATE and PUBLIC
Using the Applications Generator

Chapter 15 Improving Your dBASE III PLUS Programs   325

Speeding Up Your Programs
  With Procedures
Debugging Techniques
Customizing dBASE III PLUS
  Programs with SET Commands
Using a Configuration File

Chapter 16 Interfacing With dBASE III PLUS   353

File Formats
The Data Sharing Options of the APPEND
  and COPY Commands
Some Examples

Chapter 17 Sample dBASE III PLUS Programs   379

A Mailing List
An Inventory System
An Employee Payroll System
A Personnel Tracking System

Chapter 18   The dBASE II to dBASE III PLUS Connection   **405**
Using dCONVERT
Using dCONVERT From DOS

Chapter 19   Using dBASE III PLUS on a Local Area Network   **413**
dBASE and Networks
Requirements for Network Use
Installing dBASE III PLUS on a Network
Starting dBASE on a Network
Network Commands
General Network Hints
Introducing PROTECT
Using PROTECT
General Security Hints
Programming Considerations
Watch Out for the Deadly Embrace...
Where Do I Go From Here?

Chapter 20   Utility Programs for dBASE III PLUS   **453**
dUTIL III PLUS
Compilers

Appendix A   Glossary of dBASE III PLUS Commands   **465**
Glossary Symbols and Conventions

Index   **511**

Introduction

Many changes have taken place in the few years between the introduction of dBASE II and the introduction of dBASE III PLUS. When dBASE II was introduced, microcomputers were largely the province of dedicated hobbyists who were challenged by the task of learning in-depth programming skills. By the time dBASE III PLUS came along, however, thousands of business professionals were using microcomputers in their day-to-day working environment.

These professionals do not all wish to become programmers, but they do have one thing in common: they want to put the power of the personal computer and of software packages like dBASE III PLUS to use. This book is for them.

Using dBASE III PLUS covers the topics that you'll need to know to put dBASE III PLUS to work in your business. Chapters 1 and 2 introduce dBASE III PLUS and the concepts of database design. Creating, changing, and rearranging your database and using entry forms are the topics of Chapters 3, 4, 5, and 6. Chapter 7 shows you how to produce reports of your data. Chapter 8 details the use of Query files to refine your searches. In Chapters 9 through 14 you learn how to use command files to automate many operations that are time-consuming when performed manually. Chapter 15 shows you how to improve your dBASE III PLUS programs. In Chapter 16 you learn to bridge the gap between dBASE III PLUS and other popular software, including Lotus 1-2-3 and WordStar. Samples of programs that you can use with dBASE III PLUS are provided in Chapter 17. Chapter 18 provides information on converting dBASE II databases and programs to dBASE III PLUS formats. Chapter 19 describes the use of dBASE III PLUS on a local area network (LAN). Chapter 20 briefly discusses various utility packages that are included with dBASE III PLUS or are offered by other software distributors. These utility programs can help you write, test, and format your programs. Appendix A provides a glossary of dBASE III PLUS commands.

The best way to learn dBASE III PLUS is to use it. This book presents a series of exercises that explain the various dBASE III PLUS commands and then has you use those commands in a practical application. Using your copy of dBASE III PLUS, you should follow along with the examples.

Introduction to dBASE III PLUS

Chapter 4

Although *database management* is a computer term, it can also apply to the ways in which information is catalogued, stored, and used. At the center of any information management system is a database. Any collection of related information grouped together as a single item, like Figure 1-1, is a *database*. Metal filing cabinets with customer records, a card file of names and phone numbers, and a notebook with a penciled listing of a store inventory are all databases. However, a cabinet or a notebook does not make a database; the way information is organized makes it a database. Objects like cabinets and notebooks only aid in organizing information, and dBASE III PLUS is one such aid.

Information in a database is organized and stored in a table with rows and columns. In Figure 1-1, for example, a mailing list in database form, each row contains a name, an address, a phone number, and a customer number. Each row is related to the others because they all contain the same types of information. And because the mailing list is a collection of information arranged in a specific order—a column of names, a column of addresses, a column of customer numbers—it is a database.

Name	Address	City	State	ZIP	Phone No.	Cust. No.
J. Billings	2323 State St.	Bertram	CA	91113	234-8980	0005
R. Foster	Rt. 1 Box 52	Frink	CA	93336	245-4312	0001
L. Miller	P.O. Box 345	Dagget	CA	94567	484-9966	0002
B. O'Niell	21 Way St. Apt. C	Hotlum	CA	92346	555-1032	0004
C. Roberts	1914 19th St.	Bodie	CA	97665	525-4494	0006
A. Wilson	27 Haven Way	Weed	CA	90004	566-7823	0003

Figure 1-1. A simple database

Rows in a database file are called *records*, and columns are called *fields*. As an illustration, compare a database file to an address filing system kept in a box of 3 × 5 file cards (Figure 1-2). Each card in the box is a single record, and each category of information on a card is a field. Fields can contain any type of information that can be categorized. In the card box, each record contains six fields: a name, address, city, state, ZIP code, and phone number. Since every card in the box has the same type of information, the card box is a database file. Figure 1-3 identifies a record and a field in the mailing-list database.

In theory, any database is arranged in such a way that information is easy to find. In Figure 1-3, for example, names are arranged alphabetically. If you want to find the phone number of a customer, simply locate the name and read across to the corresponding phone number.

You are already interested in how a computerized database management system can make information storage and retrieval more efficient than a traditional filing system, and you will find that dBASE III PLUS offers many advantages. A telephone book,

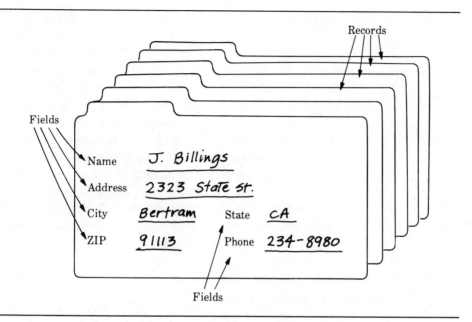

Figure 1-2. Each card represents a record; information is separated into fields

Name	Address	City	State	ZIP	Phone No.	Cust. No.
J. Billings	2323 State St.	Bertram	CA	91113	234-8980	0005
R. Foster	Rt. 1 Box 52	Frink	CA	93336	245-4312	0001
L. Miller	P.O. Box 345	Dagget	CA	94567	484-9966	0002
B. O'Niell	21 Way St. Apt. C	Hotlum	CA	92346	555-1032	0004
C. Roberts	1914 19th St.	Bodie	CA	97665	525-4494	0006
A. Wilson	27 Haven Way	Weed	CA	90004	566-7823	0003

Field

Record

Figure 1-3. Records and fields of a database

for instance, is fine for finding telephone numbers; but if all you have is an address and not the name of the person who lives there, the phone directory becomes fairly useless for finding that person's phone number. A similar problem plagues office filing systems: if the information is organized by name and you want to find all the clients located in a particular area, you could be in for a tedious search. In addition, organizing massive amounts of information into written directories and filing cabinets can consume a great deal of space. A manual database can also be difficult to modify. For example, adding a new phone number to the listing may mean rearranging the list. If the phone company were to assign a new area code, someone would have to search for all phone numbers having the old area code and then replace it with the new one.

When a database is teamed with a computer, many of these problems are eliminated. A computerized database provides speed: finding a phone number from among a thousand entries takes less than two seconds, and sorting a database with a hundred items requires less than two minutes. A computerized database is compact: a database with over 10,000 items can be stored on a small disk. A computerized database is flexible: it has the ability to examine information from a number of angles, so you, for example, could automatically search for a phone number by name or address.

Tasks that would be time consuming to accomplish manually are more practical with the aid of the computer. In principle, a database in a computer is not different from a database recorded on paper and filed in cabinets. But the computer does the tedious work of maintaining and accessing a database, and does it fast. A computerized database that can do all this is known as a database management system, or *DBMS* for short.

RELATIONAL DATABASES

There are a number of ways to store information in a computer, but not all of these are true database management systems.

A word processing program can be used to organize data in the form of a list; however, it will offer only limited flexibility. *You* still have to sort, rearrange, and access the information.

A step above word processing are the simple file managers. File managers are relatively inexpensive programs that use database files to store information. Most file managers can also do sorting and other clerical tasks.

Database managers also store information in database files, but in addition to being more sophisticated than file managers, they can access information from more than two database files simultaneously, whereas a file manager can access only one database file at a time. Being able to work on only one database file can be severely limiting. If the file manager is accessing information from one file, but needs three fields of information from a second file, the file manager can't continue unless the second database file is available. Only after the file manager is finished with the first database file can it proceed to the second database file. But what good is this when the file manager needs information from both database files simultaneously? The only solution is to duplicate the three fields from the second database file into the first database file. Fortunately, this is not a problem with a database manager like dBASE III PLUS.

Suppose the mailing list stores customer information for a warehouse that distributes wholesale kitchen appliances. The warehouse would also have a separate database for customer orders, which would include fields for customer number, merchandise number, price per unit, quantity ordered, and total cost. The mailing list and customer order databases are relational because they have the customer number field in common (Figure 1-4). By searching for the customer number in the mailing list and matching it to the customer number in the order form, the database manager can determine who the purchaser is and where the purchaser is located from one database, and what the purchaser ordered and the total cost of the purchase from the other database. A database manager that draws information from different databases linked by a common field is called a *relational database manager*.

Mailing List

Name	Address	City	State	ZIP	Phone No.	Cust. No.
J. Billings	2323 State St.	Bertram	CA	91113	234-8980	0005
R. Foster	Rt. 1 Box 52	Frink	CA	93336	245-4312	0001
L. Miller	P.O. Box 345	Dagget	CA	94567	484-9966	0002
B. O'Niell	21 Way St. Apt. C	Hotlum	CA	92346	555-1032	0004
C. Roberts	1914 19th St.	Bodie	CA	97665	525-4494	0008
A. Wilson	27 Haven Way	Weed	CA	90004	566-7823	0003

Customer Order

Cust. No.	Merchandise No.	Price per Unit	Quantity	Total Price
0001	15A	1500.00	5	7500.00
0001	15B	1750.00	10	17500.00
0002	311	500.00	3	1500.00
0003	555	1000.00	4	4000.00
0004	69	650.00	7	4550.00
0005	1111	300.00	2	600.00
0006	15A	1500.00	1	1500.00

Figure 1-4. Relationship between databases

To handle this same chore with a file manager would be very difficult, since the file manager cannot access the mailing list when it comes time to find out where the merchandise should be shipped. The only alternative would be to combine the two databases, but this would result in a clumsy and inefficient database.

For example, to represent both of R. Foster's purchases, you would have to duplicate his name, address, and phone number (Figure 1-5). If R. Foster had purchased 100 items instead, the extra typing could take far longer and use up valuable memory space.

Name	Address	Phone No.	Merchandise No.	Price per Unit	Quantity	Total Price
J. Billings	2323 State St. Bertram CA 91113	234-8980	1111	300.00	2	600.00
R. Foster	Rt. 1 Box 52 Frink CA 93336	245-4312	15A	1500.00	5	7500.00
R. Foster	Rt. 1 Box 52 Frink CA 93336	245-4312	15B	1750.00	10	17500.00
L. Miller	P.O. Box 345 Dagget CA 94567	484-9966	311	500.00	3	1500.00
B. O'Niell	21 Way St. Apt. C Hotlum CA 92346	555-1032	69	650.00	7	4550.00
C. Roberts	1914 19th St. Bodie CA 97665	525-4494	15A	1500.00	1	1500.00
A. Wilson	27 Haven Way Weed CA 90004	566-7823	555	1000.00	4	4000.00

Figure 1-5. Combined customer order invoice and mailing list database files. Unnecessary customer number field was eliminated

HOW YOU WILL USE
dBASE III PLUS

Figure 1-6 shows the relationship between the database, the user, and the database software. At the core is the database from which you will retrieve, add, and delete information. The database must somehow be accessible to the user, and that is accomplished by the dBASE III PLUS programming language. The dBASE III PLUS programming language is a collection of commands that give you access to the database via the keyboard. Commands are words that tell the computer what operation you want performed. Whatever you want done to the database has to be communicated to the computer by typing the command on the keyboard. For example, if you wanted to view the database in the computer, you would type the command DISPLAY ALL at your keyboard and the computer would display the database on your monitor. Don't try this command now, since there is no database in the computer yet.

The various commands in the dBASE III PLUS programming language offer you a host of ways to manage information. But among all these commands, you won't find a single command that creates a database, inputs the information into it, and prints the database on the printer. In any application, you probably won't be able to use only one command that will perform the entire task. Instead, you will have to divide the task into smaller chores that dBASE III PLUS commands can handle. For example, to create a mailing list, you will need to perform the following steps:

1. Create the database structure

2. Input information in the database

3. Print the contents of the database.

Even after breaking the problem down this far, you will need to segment the procedure further, since, for example, there is no single command that inputs information into the database. How does one know when the task is divided into sufficient steps for dBASE

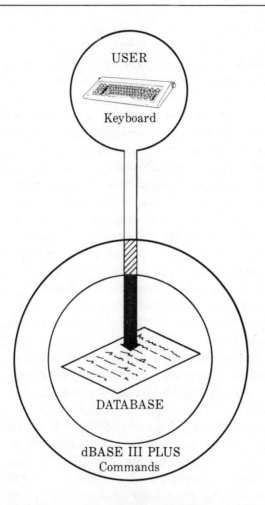

Figure 1-6. Simplified layout of database manager

III PLUS to cope with it? Experience. You have to know the language, and you have to know what you can and can't get away with. And by the end of the book, you will know.

After the commands you will use are determined, it is time to execute them. But you shouldn't execute the commands in random order; you must execute them in the sequence that will achieve the desired results. In the previous example, it would make little sense to print the database first, add information to it, and then create it. Sequence is as important as finding the right commands. Once you have determined the commands and established the correct sequence, you have what is called a dBASE III PLUS program.

Most commands can be entered on the keyboard or selected from a series of menus, and dBASE III PLUS will execute them immediately. This is called *immediate mode* operation. It is possible to do all your work on a database in immediate mode, but there are drawbacks. The most important is that you have to remember the exact form, or syntax, of the command, some of which are complicated. A typing error will result in the computer not accepting the command; and when you want to repeat an operation, you have to remember the list of commands and the sequence you have already used. Fortunately, dBASE III PLUS can store your program on disk for reuse (dBASE III PLUS stores all programs in a *file*, but more about this in Chapter 3). When storing your program on the computer, you still have to type the commands correctly, you still have to use the proper sequence, but you only have to do it once. If you frequently create databases, input information, and print the information, you could save yourself work by entering the operation only once on a file and reusing it as needed.

When you type a sequence of commands to be stored on file, don't expect them to operate immediately. Only after you have finished typing the commands and request the computer to execute the list will the commands be executed. For most applications you will work in *programmed mode*, where a series of instructions are executed together. If you are executing only one or two commands, you will find immediate mode to be more efficient.

HISTORY OF dBASE III PLUS

No introduction to dBASE III PLUS would be complete without a brief look at the program's colorful history.

dBASE III PLUS is an improved version of dBASE III. dBASE III is a successor to dBASE II, the first popular database manager for microcomputers. The program had its beginnings long before the personal computer became popular. Scientists at the Jet Propulsion Laboratory (JPL) at Pasadena, California, were using a database management system on mainframe computers to track information received from JPL's satellites. When early microcomputers were introduced, Wayne Ratliff, a software systems designer for JPL, impressed by the capabilities and features of the mainframe database manager, set to work writing a database system for his micro using the JPL system as a model. After its completion, Ratliff decided to market his database manager and settled on the name Vulcan. (The name was in honor of the home planet of "Star Trek's" Mr. Spock.) Vulcan was a far cry from dBASE III PLUS, or, for that matter, dBASE II. It lacked many of the powerful sorting and indexing commands present in dBASE II and dBASE III PLUS, but despite its limitations, Vulcan was a powerful database language at that time. The program picked up a very small but dedicated following.

One of those followers was George Tate, a software distributor who heard of Vulcan's capabilities. Tate gave Vulcan a try and was sufficiently impressed to contact Ratliff in hopes of distributing the program. Ratliff, who felt far more comfortable as a programmer than as a salesman, turned over Vulcan's marketing to Tate. In turn, Tate signed a contract providing Ratliff with royalties for sales of the program.

Tate used a number of marketing ploys to increase sales of Vulcan. First, the name was dropped in favor of dBASE II—there was no dBASE I, but the II implied a newer version. At a computer show, Tate floated a gas-filled blimp with the name dBASE II emblazoned on its sides over the exhibit booth. And a famous advertisement compared competitors' similar products to a bilge pump in a rather unflattering way. The ads drew sharp criticism from competitors as well as from the bilge-pump maker, but the public noticed the ads and the product. Tate teamed up with Hal Lashlee and formed a company, Ashton-Tate, to distribute dBASE II. (There was no Ashton, but Tate felt that the name had a nice ring to it.)

After years of dBASE II success, competitors began touting products with major advancements over dBASE II. In response, Ratliff and a team of Ashton-Tate designers spent two years working on a new program, dBASE III. Unlike its predecessor, dBASE III was designed to make full use of 16-bit microcomputers and was written in the C programming language. Then, because the need for networking personal computers grew, and because customers expressed the desire for increased user friendliness, dBASE III PLUS was developed. The program offers a significant number of improvements over dBASE II and dBASE III.

dBASE III PLUS'S IMPROVEMENTS

As popular as dBASE II was, the program was not without its faults. dBASE II was limited in the amount of information that it could deal with at any given time. The program could handle a maximum of 1000 characters per record and no more than 32 fields per record. No more than 65,535 records could be in a database, and dBASE II could only sort one field at a time. dBASE II could only open two files at once, a limitation that caused programmers grief with many applications.

With dBASE III PLUS, it appears that Ashton-Tate set out to correct every noticeable flaw that existed in dBASE II. dBASE III PLUS can handle 1 billion records and up to 128 fields per record. As many as 4000 characters can be placed in a single record. It can sort several fields simultaneously and work with as many as 10 database files at the same time. The availability of this much power may well be more impressive than realistic. A few quick calculations will indicate that if a database contained 1 billion records of 128 fields each, it would take your PC more than a month to read through the database once, and the database would occupy some 30 million floppy disks. And sorting data with dBASE III PLUS is fast: a file that took just under 50 minutes to sort with dBASE II takes less than 60 seconds to sort with dBASE III PLUS. If you are already a dBASE II user, you will be glad to know that dBASE III PLUS has a program that converts your dBASE II files and data so they can be used with dBASE III PLUS. dBASE III PLUS allows multiple users to access the program when it is operating on a local area network. The security features of the program can be used with most popular local area networks for the IBM PC and PC-compatibles. Suffice it to say that if your database application outgrows the capabilities of dBASE III PLUS, you should be talking to a mainframe computer salesperson.

LIMITATIONS OF dBASE III PLUS

dBASE III PLUS's limitations are few, but they do exist. The main one is that dBASE III PLUS often requires information stored on disk for many operations. This may slow your programs down as they retrieve information from the disk drives. The delays are more evident on a floppy-based system than on a hard-disk system.

SYSTEM REQUIREMENTS

To use dBASE III PLUS, you will need a 16-bit computer using MS-DOS or PC-DOS, like the IBM PC, COMPAQ, Tandy 1000/1200, Leading Edge, or AT&T PC. Any 16-bit microcomputer that is fully software-compatible with the IBM PC should be able to use dBASE III PLUS. Your computer must have a minimum of 256K of memory (K equals 1000 bytes), and 320K or more is recommended for best use. Memory requirements for machines used on a network are discussed in Chapter 18. You must be using MS-DOS or PC-DOS version 2.0 or newer. Your system should have two floppy-disk drives or one floppy drive and one hard-disk drive. (Because of the size of the files on the dBASE III PLUS system disk, it is impractical to use dBASE III PLUS on a system with only one disk drive.) Any printer that can print at least 80 columns of text can be used.

Database Design

Chapter 2

At this point you're probably anxious to load dBASE III PLUS into your computer and begin using the program. There's an excellent reason for not doing that just yet. Planning is vital to effective database management. Many a purchaser of database management software has gotten started with the software, created a database, and stored data within the database, only to discover later that the database doesn't provide all of the necessary information. And it can become a tedious job to make up for mistakes that were made during the design of a database. To avoid such time consuming mistakes, this chapter will focus on database design.

Database design requires that you think about how the data should be stored and how you and other users will ask for data from the database. During this process, your problem (which dBASE III PLUS was purchased to help solve) will be outlined on paper. Just as one would not haphazardly toss a bunch of files into a filing cabinet without designing some type of filing system, one cannot place information into a computer database without first designing the database. As you do so, you must define the kinds of information that should be stored in the database.

ABOUT DATA AND ATTRIBUTES

Data and *attributes* are two important terms in database design. Data is the information that goes into your database. Attributes are the types of data that make up the database. An individual's last name, Smith, for example, is data. An attribute is another name for a field, so an entire group of names is considered to be an attribute. Names, phone numbers, customer numbers, descriptions, locations, and stock numbers are common attributes that your database might contain.

In addition to thinking about what kinds of information will go into the database, you must give careful consideration to the ways in which information will come out of the database. Information comes from a database in the form of *reports*. When you ask a computer for a list of all homes in the area priced between $50,000 and $100,000, or for a list of all employees earning less than $15 per hour, you are asking for a report. When you ask for John Smith's address, you are also asking for a report. A report is a summary of information. Whether the computer displays a few lines on the screen or hundreds of lines on a stack of paper, it is providing a report based on the data contained in the database. To practice the techniques of database design, you will design a database using a hypothetical example.

ABC Realty Company is a real-estate firm that specializes in managing rental properties. The company manages a number of rental properties in different locations. Each rental unit owned by ABC Realty is currently occupied by a tenant. The company needs a computerized method for tracking all of its rental properties.

The database management system must produce a monthly report of the properties, so that the firm's overall profits can be monitored. The system must also keep listings of tenant information and descriptions of the rental units, such as the number of bedrooms and baths and special features.

At first, ABC Realty is simply interested in getting all relevant information about the properties into a single database. A later goal is to create a system that even a company employee who doesn't know dBASE III PLUS can use to get information and reports out of the database.

THREE PHASES OF DATABASE DESIGN

Database design, whether it is for ABC Realty or your own purposes, involves a three-step process:

1. Data definition (an analysis of existing data)
2. Data refinement (refining necessary data)
3. Establishing relationships between the attributes.

Data Definition

During the first phase, data definition, you must make a list, on a piece of paper, of all the important attributes involved in your application. To do this, you must examine your application in detail to determine exactly what kinds of information must be stored in the database.

ABC Realty maintains 16 rental properties located in two major metropolitan areas: Detroit, Michigan, and Washington, D.C. The Detroit office oversees seven homes that vary in rental costs from $500 to $1200 per month. The Washington, D.C., office oversees one house, four townhouses, and three apartments located in the District of Columbia and the nearby Maryland and Virginia suburbs. Rental costs for these properties range from $450 to $1025 per month.

In discussing the design of the database, the employees of ABC Realty determined that certain items must be known about each property: the name of each tenant; the property address; a description of the property; the date that the lease expires; the number of bedrooms and bathrooms; the size of the property; the rental cost; and amenities such as parking, fireplaces, microwave ovens, and the like. The resulting list of attributes is shown in Figure 2-1.

An important point to remember is that during this phase, database design, you should list *all* possible attributes of your database management system. You may list more attributes than are actually needed by your particular application, but this isn't a problem, as unnecessary attributes will be eliminated during the data refinement phase.

Data Refinement

During this phase, you will refine the attributes on your initial list, so that the attributes form an accurate description of the types of

---

Attributes

1. *Tenant name*
2. *Property address*
3. *Number of bedrooms*
4. *Number of bathrooms*
5. *Lease expiration date*
6. *Type of property (house, townhouse, or apartment)*
7. *Rental cost*
8. *Size of unit (in square feet)*
9. *Parking available?*
10. *Amenities*

Figure 2-1. Initial list of attributes

data that will be needed in the database. At this stage it is vital to include suggestions from as many other users of the database as possible. The people who use the database are likely to be the ones who know what kinds of information they will need to get from the database.

When the employees of ABC Realty took a close look at their list of attributes, they realized that most of the refinements were obvious. The address attribute, for example, should be divided into street address, city, state, and ZIP code. In your own case, some refinements may quickly become evident, and others may not be as evident. But going over your written list of attributes will help make any necessary refinements more obvious. For example, when the employees of ABC Realty further examined the initial attribute list, they discovered that the existing index card file of tenant names contained two occurrences of the name "Robinson." To avoid confusion, the name attribute was divided into last name and first name.

While you are refining the list of attributes, it is a good idea to calculate the amount of space in characters that will be needed to store the longest entry for a particular attribute. Be sure to count blank spaces and punctuation in the character count. For example, 23 Oak St. is ten characters. The longest address, 4205 Park Ave. Apt. 101-C, in abbreviated form is 25 characters, so the field width for addresses should be at least 25 in the example database. dBASE III PLUS will ask you to specify the width of the fields for your data when you first create the database. If you use a field width that is too small, you will have problems when entering data. And if you specify a field width that is unnecessarily large, dBASE III PLUS will reserve the space on your disks whether you use it or not.

Figure 2-2 shows the refined attribute list and the field width of each attribute. Chapter 3 will explain exactly how to determine field widths for such attributes as lease expiration and parking.

Attributes	Field Widths
1. Tenant's last name	15
2. Tenant's first name	15
3. Street address	25
4. City	15
5. State	2
6. ZIP	10
7. Number of bedrooms	2
8. Number of bathrooms	2
9. Lease expiration date	8
10. Parking available?	1
11. Type of property (house, townhouse, or apartment)	10
12. Rental cost	7
13. Size of unit (in square feet)	5
14. Amenities	10

Figure 2-2. Redefined list of attributes and their field widths

Establishing the Relationships

During the third phase, drawing relationships between attributes can help determine which attributes are important and which are unimportant. A way to determine relationships among the attributes is to ask the same question that you will ask your database. If a salesperson wants a listing of townhouses priced over $700 per month, the database system must draw a relationship between type of rental unit (house, townhouse, or apartment) and rental cost.

Relationships can be more complex. The company president might want to know how many apartments with two or more bedrooms rent for less than $300 per month. The database management system must compare attributes for the rental costs with attributes for the number of bedrooms and the type of rental units.

Such questions will help reveal which attributes are unimportant so that they can be eliminated from the database.

When establishing relationships among the variables, you may also discover that an additional attribute is necessary. For example, someone in the company asked how many apartments handled by the D.C. office offer parking; since there was no attribute for the sales office, one was added. After amending the list, ABC Realty then had a final list of attributes and field sizes (Figure 2-3). It is from this list that you will create ABC's database in the next chapter.

During the three design phases, it is important that potential users be consulted to determine what kinds of information they

Attributes	*Field Widths*
1. *Tenant's last name*	*15*
2. *Tenant's first name*	*15*
3. *Street address*	*25*
4. *City*	*15*
5. *State*	*2*
6. *ZIP*	*10*
7. *Number of bedrooms*	*2*
8. *Number of bathrooms*	*2*
9. *Lease expiration date*	*8*
10. *Parking available?*	*1*
11. *Type of property (house, townhouse, or apartment)*	*10*
12. *Rental cost*	*7*
13. *Size of unit (in square feet)*	*5*
14. *Amenities*	*10*
15. *Sales office (Detroit or D.C.)*	*1*

Figure 2-3. Finalized list of attributes

will expect the database to supply. Just what kinds of reports are wanted from the database? What kinds of queries will employees make of the database management system? By continually asking these types of questions, you'll think in terms of your database, and this should help you determine what is important and what is unimportant.

You may have noticed that throughout the entire process, the specific data, such as tenants' names, addresses, and so forth, has not been discussed. It's not necessary to identify any specific data at this point; only the attributes need to be defined.

Keep in mind that even after the third phase, the design of the database is not graven in stone. Changes to the design of a database can be made later if necessary. But if you follow the systematic approach of database design for your specific application, the chances are better that you won't create a database that fails to provide much of the information you need and must then be extensively redesigned. dBASE III PLUS lets you change the design of a database at any time, although such changes are often more inconvenient to make once the database is designed. Here is an example: if you were to create a database using dBASE III PLUS to handle a customer mailing list, you might include attributes for names, addresses, cities, states, and ZIP codes. At first glance this might seem sufficient. You could then begin entering customer information into the database and gradually build a sizable mailing list. But if your company later decides to begin telemarketing using the same mailing list, you may suddenly realize that you have not included an attribute for telephone numbers. Using dBASE III PLUS, you could easily change the database design to include an attribute for phone numbers. But then you would still face the possibly mammoth task of going back and adding a telephone number for every name currently in the mailing list. If this information had been added as you developed the mailing list, you would not face the inconvenience of having to enter the phone numbers as a separate operation.

In later chapters, you will create a database system for ABC Realty. At first you'll use individual commands in immediate mode to perform all the desired tasks. Later in the book, you will automate the tasks by using program files. And as you do so, you'll have a chance to see the development of a complete database management system.

Creating and Displaying
A Database
With dBASE III PLUS

Chapter 3

dBASE III PLUS comes in the form of two manuals and eight disks. The eight disks in your package are System Disk 1, System Disk 1 (Backup), System Disk 2, Administrator 1, Administrator 2, the On-Disk Tutorial, the Sample Programs and Utilities Disk, and the Applications Generator. System Disk 1 and System Disk 2 are used to run the dBASE III PLUS program. The Administrator disks are used with local area networks, and the Applications Generator is used to create menu-driven systems within dBASE III PLUS. The On-Disk Tutorial is a learning aid for new users of dBASE III PLUS. It will not be discussed at length in this text, but you can run it at any time by inserting it in the drive and entering INTRO from the DOS prompt. The Sample Programs and Utilities Disk contains sample dBASE III PLUS databases and programs, and a utility for converting dBASE II files to dBASE III PLUS format. (No conversion is necessary for dBASE III files when using dBASE III PLUS.)

System Disk 1 is copy-protected, so you cannot make an operating copy of this disk. For this reason, Ashton-Tate supplies an extra copy of System Disk 1; you should file away the extra copy for safekeeping. System Disk 2 is not copy-protected. You should make a copy of System Disk 2 and use this copy instead of the original System Disk 2. Use the following procedure to copy the dBASE III PLUS System Disk 2, so that if the copy is damaged or erased, you can make another replacement. You create a copy of System Disk 2 from within the operating system.

1. Format two floppy disks with the operating system's FORMAT command for your system. One disk will become a backup of System Disk 2, and the other will be used to create a working disk for storage of your database files.

2. Use the COPY command to copy all of the files from the dBASE III PLUS System Disk 2 onto the backup disk. You can do this by placing the System Disk 2 in drive A and the backup disk in drive B and entering the following:

   ```
   COPY A:*.* B:
   ```

3. Put the original System Disk 2 in a safe place.

MAKING THE dBASE III PLUS SYSTEM DISK 1 SELF-BOOTING

Perform the following steps to make the dBASE III PLUS System Disk 1 self-booting:

1. Insert your DOS disk in drive A.

2. Insert your System Disk 1 in drive B.

3. From the DOS prompt enter SYS B: and press RETURN.

4. Enter COPY A:COMMAND.COM B: and press RETURN when the DOS prompt reappears.

Your System Disk 1 can now be used to start your computer.

IMPORTANT NOTE: If you plan to use a disk other than System Disk 1 to start your computer before using dBASE III PLUS, you must place a configuration file, called CONFIG.SYS, on that disk. If the disk you plan to use to start your computer already contains a file called CONFIG.SYS, use your word processor to add the following commands to that file:

```
FILES = 20
BUFFERS = 15
```

If the disk does not have a file called CONFIG.SYS, use the DOS COPY command to copy the CONFIG.SYS file present on your System Disk 1 onto the other disk. Refer to your DOS manual for instructions, if needed, about the use of the DOS COPY command.

Hard-Disk Users: If you are using an IBM PC XT or another computer equipped with a hard disk, you can install the dBASE III PLUS program files onto your hard disk. Because the program is copy-protected, you cannot simply copy all the files onto your hard disk; the program will not run. You must use the INSTALL program, contained on System Disk 1, to create a working copy of dBASE III PLUS on your hard disk. If you have an earlier version of dBASE III installed on your hard disk, you must uninstall it (using the uninstall procedure outlined in your dBASE III documentation) before installing dBASE III PLUS.

If you use separate subdirectories, use the appropriate DOS commands to change to the subdirectory that will contain dBASE III PLUS. Next, change the default drive to the A drive by typing A: and pressing RETURN.

Once the A prompt is on the screen, insert your dBASE III PLUS System Disk 1 in drive A and enter the following command:

```
INSTALL C:
```

NOTE: If your hard disk is designated by a letter other than C, use that letter in place of the letter C with the preceding command.

The installation program will load, and you will see the dBASE III PLUS installation screen. Follow the instructions provided on the screen to install dBASE III PLUS on your hard disk.

Once you have finished using the INSTALL program, you may wish to use the DOS COPY command to copy the files from the Applications Generator and On-Disk Tutorial disks onto your hard disk. This step is optional; you may or may not want to take up hard-disk space with these programs and files. You will not need these files on your hard disk for any exercises contained in this text.

CREATING A CONFIG.SYS FILE ON YOUR HARD DISK

For hard-disk users, another important step exists. You must create a CONFIG.SYS file on the root directory of your hard disk (if you start your computer using the hard disk). If you start your computer with a special floppy boot disk, you must place a CONFIG.SYS file on that disk. The CONFIG.SYS file is a DOS text file, so it can be created with any word processor that can create DOS text files. If you have such a word processor, use it now to create a file, called CONFIG.SYS, that contains the following lines:

```
FILES = 20
BUFFERS = 15
```

Once you have created the CONFIG.SYS file, copy that file to the root directory of the hard disk (or to the floppy disk that is used to start your system).

If you do not have a word processor, make sure you are in the root directory of the hard disk (or change the default to the appropriate floppy disk if you use a floppy disk to start your system). Next, type the following command:

```
COPY CON CONFIG.SYS
```

When you press RETURN, the cursor will move to the next line. Enter the following lines, pressing RETURN after each one:

```
FILES = 20
BUFFERS = 15
```

After you have entered these lines, press the F6 key and then press RETURN. You will see the following message:

```
1 File(s) copied.
```

You are now ready to use dBASE III PLUS on your hard-disk system.

SOME IMPORTANT NOTES
FOR HARD-DISK USERS

dBASE III PLUS uses software copy protection called Superlok. Use of the DOS BACKUP or RESTORE command can cause havoc with Superlok-protected files, making your installed version of dBASE III PLUS unusable. You can safely use BACKUP or RESTORE on individual subdirectories. *Never* use the BACKUP or RESTORE command on files in the root directory of your hard disk if dBASE III PLUS has been installed on that hard disk. If you do so, you will damage dBASE III PLUS files, and the program will not operate.

If you ever wish to install dBASE III PLUS on another hard disk, you must first uninstall the program from your existing hard disk. To do this, you can place System Disk 1 in drive A, and enter the command UNINSTAL C: (where C is the letter of your hard disk). Follow the on-screen instructions to uninstall the program. You can also uninstall dBASE III PLUS if you wish to use the DOS BACKUP or RESTORE command safely on your entire hard disk.

STARTING dBASE III PLUS

Start your computer (with System Disk 1 if you use a floppy system, or with your usual procedure if you use a hard disk system). If you use subdirectories on a hard disk, select the subdirectory that contains dBASE III PLUS. Start dBASE III PLUS by entering the command

DBASE

After you have started dBASE III PLUS, you'll see a sign-on notice and a copyright message. At the bottom of the message you'll see this

Press (ret.) to assent to the license agreement and begin dBASE
III+

Press RETURN. If you are using dBASE III PLUS on a floppy disk system, you will be prompted to insert System Disk 2. Remove System Disk 1 and insert System Disk 2 in drive A, and press RETURN to proceed. Hard-disk users will not need to perform this step.

Within a few moments, the dBASE Assistant will appear (Figure 3-1).

The Assistant is a system of menus that dBASE III PLUS provides. Using the Assistant, you can select various choices for creating databases, adding and changing information, printing reports, and performing most functions that can be performed within dBASE III PLUS. The Assistant is just one of three ways that you can use dBASE III PLUS. The other ways, from a prompt called the dot prompt, and from within a command file, will be discussed in more detail later.

The top line of your screen shows the time, along with eight menu choices. This line is the menu bar. Any one of eight menus can be open at a time; currently, the Set Up menu is open. When a menu is open, the appropriate menu choices appear in a rectangular box called a pull-down menu.

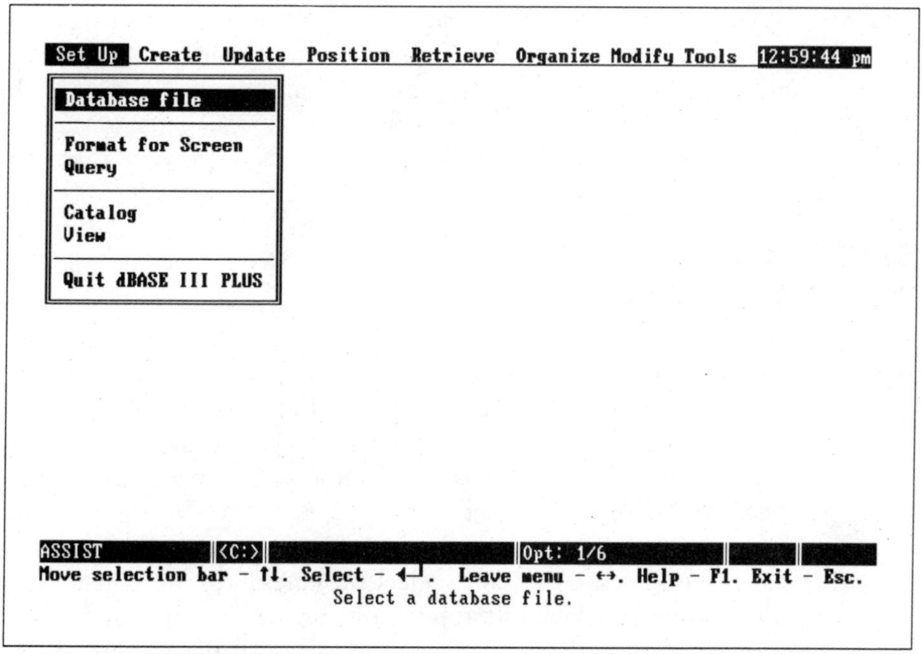

```
 Set Up  Create  Update  Position  Retrieve  Organize Modify Tools  12:59:44 pm
┌──────────────────────┐
│ Database file        │
│                      │
│ Format for Screen    │
│ Query                │
│                      │
│ Catalog              │
│ View                 │
│                      │
│ Quit dBASE III PLUS  │
└──────────────────────┘




ASSIST          <C:>                       Opt: 1/6
Move selection bar - ↑↓. Select - ◄┘. Leave menu - ↔. Help - F1. Exit - Esc.
                       Select a database file.
```

Figure 3-1. dBASE III PLUS Assistant

Near the bottom of the screen is a highlighted bar. This bar is the status bar. It tells you what disk drive you are using, the name of the database you are working with (if any), and the status of the NUM LOCK and CAPS LOCK keys.

Directly below the status bar is the navigation line. This line provides helpful messages that tell you how to move about within the various dBASE III PLUS menus. Below the navigation line is the message line. This line provides various messages as you use the program.

Press the → key once. You'll see the Set Up menu close, and a pull-down menu for CREATE will open. The choices displayed within the pull-down menu apply to creating various files within dBASE III PLUS.

Continue pressing your → or ← key, and note the various menu choices. You can also choose a menu from the menu bar by entering the first character of its name. As an example, press T. The pull-down menu for Tools will open.

SELECTING OPTIONS FROM A MENU

Once a menu has been opened, an option of that menu can be chosen by pressing the ↑ or ↓ key to highlight the option, and pressing RETURN. As an example, press the ↓ key until the Directory choice of the Tools menu is highlighted. Then press RETURN to choose the Directory option.

Another window will appear, showing your system's available disk drives. Press RETURN to select the current drive. When you do this, another window will appear, displaying the types of files you can display in a directory. Press the key until the last option, All Files, is highlighted. Press RETURN to choose this option, and you will see a directory of the disk.

After the directory has been displayed, press any key. The Assistant will reappear.

You can see each of the menu options the Assistant offers. You cannot choose all of the options, however, because you are not yet using a file within dBASE III PLUS. For example, within the Tools menu, you cannot choose the LIST STRUCTURE option, because this option applies to a database that is in use, and you are not yet using a database.

CANCELING A SELECTION

You can use the ESC key from any point in the Assistant to cancel an operation or a menu selection. You should be aware that some operations, like copying files, cannot be canceled once the process has actually begun.

THE dBASE III PLUS DOT PROMPT

As mentioned previously, the Assistant is just one way in which you can use dBASE III PLUS. Another method of use is direct entry of commands from the dot prompt. Press the ESC key now to exit the Assistant. At the bottom of the screen you'll see a period, the message **Command Line** within the status bar, and a message **Enter a dBASE III PLUS Command** within the message line.

The period displayed on the screen, or *dot prompt* as it is commonly known, indicates that dBASE III PLUS is in interactive mode and ready to accept a command. But before you begin, insert the work disk in drive B, if you are using a floppy system.

The first command you'll use will tell dBASE III PLUS which disk drive to examine when searching for a database file. Since the system disk in drive A is near capacity, you will work from drive B, so enter the command

SET DEFAULT TO B:

If you are using a computer with a hard-disk drive, enter

SET DEFAULT TO C:

If you don't use this command, dBASE III PLUS will assume that you want to use drive A. You can also specify a drive by including a drive identifier before the filename, such as USE B:NAMES, and dBASE will use the specified drive for the next command. But drive identifiers are used for only one command, whereas the SET DEFAULT command will remain in effect until another SET DEFAULT command is used. The SET DRIVE option of the Tools menu in the Assistant can also be used to select a default drive.

dBASE III PLUS's basic command structure becomes obvious after you try a few commands. To print information on the screen, you use the question mark. As an example, type

```
? "Using dBASE"

Using dBASE
```

The ? command prints everything between the quotation marks except for the quote marks themselves.

You need not type quotation marks to print numbers on the screen. (The reason other characters require quotation marks will be explained later.)

```
? 23

23
```

dBASE III PLUS performs addition, subtraction, multiplication, division, and square root calculations by using the mathematical operators listed in Table 3-1.

To use dBASE III PLUS as a quick calculator, you enter the question mark after the dot prompt followed by the numbers and appropriate operators. For example:

```
?5*45

225


? 5/15

0.33
```

To clear the entire screen of information, enter

```
CLEAR
```

dBASE III PLUS also accepts commands in abbreviated form. Only the first four letters of any command are necessary, so that you could use CLEA instead of CLEAR to clear the screen. However, all commands in this book will be used in their complete form.

CONVENTIONS

Before you start working with dBASE III PLUS, you need to know some conventions that will be used throughout the book.

All commands are printed in UPPERCASE, but you can type them in either upper- or lowercase. Any part of a command surrounded by the left ([) and right (]) bracket is optional, and any part of a command followed by an ellipsis (...) can be repeated. Parameters in the command are in *italics*. Every command that you enter will be terminated by pressing RETURN (or ENTER). Pressing RETURN indicates to dBASE III PLUS that you are finished typing the command and that you want it to execute. So whenever you are asked to enter a command, finish by pressing RETURN unless otherwise noted.

In this book new terms are printed in *italics*, and messages that the computer displays are printed in **boldface**.

Table 3-1.   dBASE III PLUS Mathematical Operators

Operation	Symbol
Addition	+
Subtraction	−
Multiplication	*
Division	/
Exponentiation	**
Square root	SQRT( )

GETTING HELP

Should you need help, dBASE III PLUS offers brief information on subjects ranging from the dot prompt to creating a database, all of which is stored in a HELP file on the system disk and accessible while in dBASE III PLUS. A series of menus will assist you in finding the information you are searching for. For example, if you are working with dBASE III PLUS and need information on the CLEAR command, you can enter HELP and a main menu of six subjects will appear (Figure 3-2). Pick the subject that best describes your problem; since the sixth choice looks as good as any and you want to know about the CLEAR command, enter 6 by typing it on the keyboard. The Commands and Functions menu

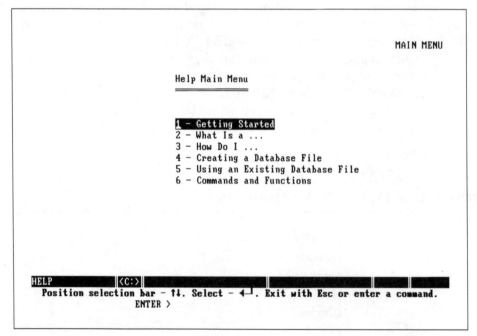

Figure 3-2. Main menu for HELP files

(the name of the menu is posted in the top-right corner) appears
with five more selections (Figure 3-3). Selecting 1, "Commands
(Starter Set)," will print a screenful of commands, including the
CLEAR command. But if you accidentally choose 2, "Commands
(Advanced Set)," you can correct your mistake by pressing PG UP,
which will return you to the previous menu, and then select 1. The
menus have helped guide you to the information on CLEAR
because the Starter Command menu has CLEAR as the sixth
entry (Figure 3-4). Select 6 and a description of the CLEAR command, along with the command's syntax usage and its variations,
is displayed on screen (Figure 3-5). If you already know the name
of the command, you can circumvent the menus and go directly to
the explanation by entering HELP followed by the command
name, such as HELP CLEAR.

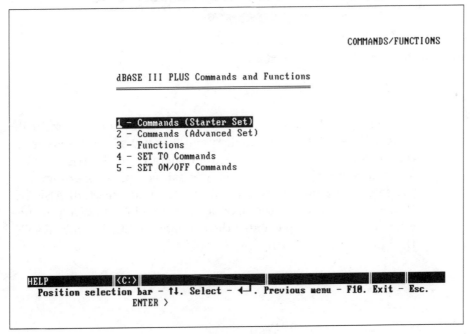

Figure 3-3. Commands and Functions menu

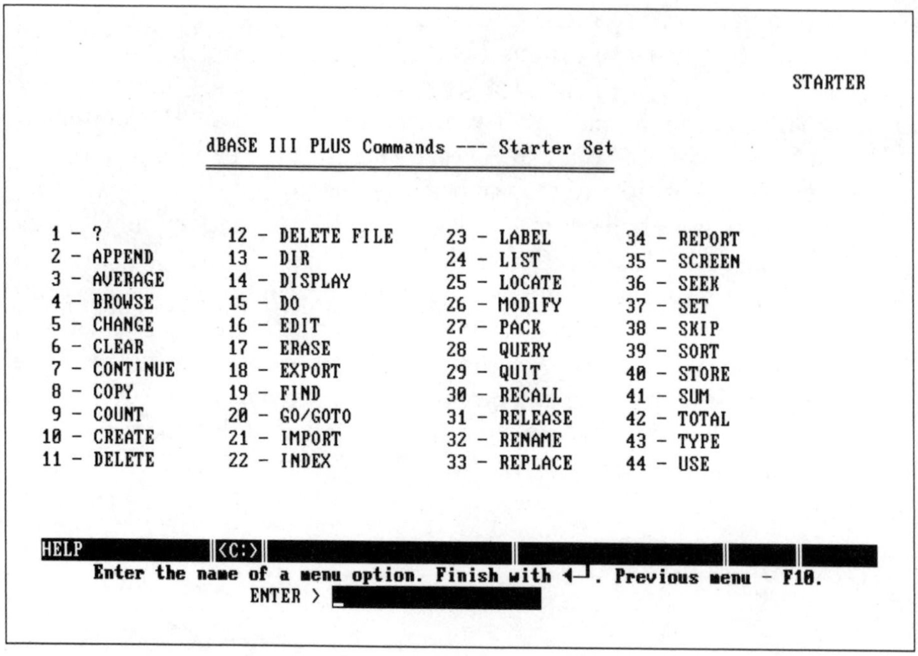

```
                                                              STARTER

              dBASE III PLUS Commands --- Starter Set
              ════════════════════════════════════════════

  1 - ?          12 - DELETE FILE   23 - LABEL     34 - REPORT
  2 - APPEND     13 - DIR           24 - LIST      35 - SCREEN
  3 - AVERAGE    14 - DISPLAY       25 - LOCATE    36 - SEEK
  4 - BROWSE     15 - DO            26 - MODIFY    37 - SET
  5 - CHANGE     16 - EDIT          27 - PACK      38 - SKIP
  6 - CLEAR      17 - ERASE         28 - QUERY     39 - SORT
  7 - CONTINUE   18 - EXPORT        29 - QUIT      40 - STORE
  8 - COPY       19 - FIND          30 - RECALL    41 - SUM
  9 - COUNT      20 - GO/GOTO       31 - RELEASE   42 - TOTAL
 10 - CREATE     21 - IMPORT        32 - RENAME    43 - TYPE
 11 - DELETE     22 - INDEX         33 - REPLACE   44 - USE


 HELP         <C:>
      Enter the name of a menu option. Finish with ←┘. Previous menu - F10.
                    ENTER >
```

Figure 3-4. Starter Command menu

dBASE III PLUS will offer you help, even if you don't ask for it. If dBASE III PLUS can't understand how you are trying to use a command, it will ask if you need any help from the HELP files. You can refuse by pressing N, or you can accept by pressing Y. If you entered a command that is only partially incorrect, dBASE III PLUS will read the correct part as a clue and try to give you specific help. For example, enter the command CLOSE, and dBASE III PLUS responds with

```
Unrecognized phrase/keyword in command
    ?
close

Do you want some help?  (Y/N)
```

dBASE III PLUS looked at the incomplete command and decided that you need help with the CLOSE command. To discover what was missing from the command, press Y and the screen in Figure 3-6 appears.

The HELP file is quite extensive, so by all means take some time and rummage through it, view the different commands, and understand how the file is set up. Knowing where to locate information about a command can be a great aid when you work with some of the more difficult operations later in the book. When you are done, press ESC to exit the HELP files.

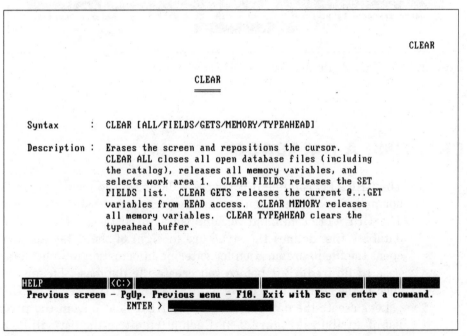

Figure 3-5. HELP file for the CLEAR command

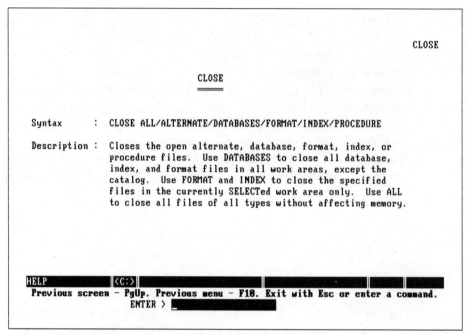

Figure 3-6. HELP file for the CLOSE command

CREATING A DATABASE

The CREATE command prepares a database file for use. This is normally done once, when you are beginning to create a database. The CREATE command accomplishes three tasks: it creates a database file, defines the structure (design) of the database, and opens the file in preparation for entering information into the database (if desired). But before you create the database, be sure to specify the correct disk drive with SET DEFAULT TO B: (or C:).

Let's create the database needed by ABC Realty from the final list of attributes (Figure 2-3). Each attribute in the list will be a specific field.

First, return to the Assistant. To do this, enter ASSIST at the dot prompt. The dot prompt will disappear, and the familiar Assistant menu will return.

To create a database, you must highlight the Create menu. Remember, you can open menus by using the cursor keys, or by pressing the first letter of the desired menu name (in this case, C for Create).

After opening the Create menu, press RETURN to accept the Database File option. A window displaying your available disk drives will appear; the drive that you have previously selected with the SET DEFAULT TO command will be highlighted. Press RETURN to accept this choice. dBASE III PLUS will respond with

```
Enter the name of the file:
```

Each database file must have a name. A filename consists of letters, numbers, or the underscore; however, a filename must begin with a letter and cannot contain more than 8 characters. Violate any of these rules, and dBASE III PLUS will ask you to try again. dBASE III PLUS automatically assigns an extension of .DBF to the name because it only searches for files with the .DBF (*database file*) extension.

Enter ABC1 for the name of the file. Within a few seconds, dBASE III PLUS will display a screen with highlighted blocks for the entry of field names, types of fields, field widths, and numbers of decimal places (Figure 3-7). When naming a field, use a name that best describes the contents of the field. Like filenames, field names can be made of letters, numbers, and underscores but must start with a letter. Unlike filenames, though, field names can contain 10 characters. If a field name is too long or contains illegal characters (such as symbols), dBASE III PLUS will trim the excess or illegal characters from the field name.

The first attribute on the list is tenant's last name, so enter LASTNAME for the field name. Once you press the RETURN key, the cursor will automatically move to the field-type block. dBASE III PLUS allows for the entry of five types of fields. They are

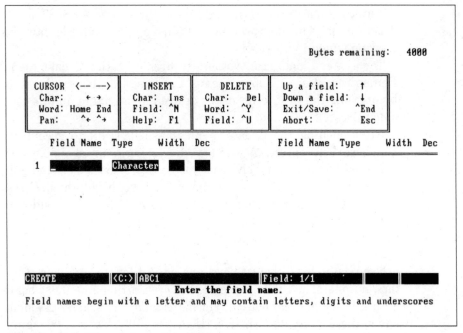

Figure 3-7. Entry form for field names

- Character/Text Fields: These are used to store any characters, including letters, numbers, any special symbols, or blank spaces. A character/text field has a maximum size of 254 characters.

- Date Fields: You'll use the date field to store dates. The normal format for entering dates is MM/DD/YY. dBASE III PLUS automatically inserts the slashes as you enter the date into a date field.

- Numeric Fields: These use numbers with or without decimal places. Only numbers and the minus sign (the hyphen) can be entered; dBASE does *not* use commas in numbers larger than 1000. dBASE III PLUS is accurate to 15 digits, so unless you are performing scientific calculations, you shouldn't have a problem with numerical accuracy.

- Logical Fields: These consist of a single letter representing a true or false value. The letter T or Y represents true, and F or N represents false. The ABC Realty database will use a logical field to denote whether private parking is available for tenants since there are only two possibilities—either you have it or you don't.

- Memo Fields: dBASE III PLUS can store large blocks of text for each record in the form of memo fields. Up to 4000 characters can be stored in a memo field.

Most fields in a database are of the character or numeric type, although there are times when you will need all of the different types of fields that dBASE III PLUS offers.

dBASE III PLUS is still waiting for you to define the field type. Try pressing the spacebar. Each time you press the spacebar, dBASE III PLUS will display one of the five choices for field type, and an accompanying description will be shown at the bottom of the screen. You can choose a field type in either of two ways. You can continue to press the spacebar until the appropriate choice appears, and then press RETURN; or you can type the first letter of the field type—C for Character/Text, D for Date, N for Numeric, L for Logical, or M for Memo. Since the entries for LASTNAME will consist of letters, enter C for Character/Text.

dBASE III PLUS now asks for the field width. Character fields can be up to 254 characters in length, while numeric fields are limited to 19 digits. Earlier, in Chapter 2, ABC Realty calculated that the longest last name would be no more than 15 characters, so enter 15 for the field width. Logical fields are fixed at 1 character (T or F), and the date field is fixed at 8 characters. Once you have pressed RETURN, the highlighted block moves to the second field definition, again asking for a field name. The dec (decimal) column was ignored by dBASE III PLUS because you selected the character/text field type.

For the second item on the attribute list, the tenant's first name, enter FIRSTNAME. Again, when the cursor moves to the field-type prompt, type C for Character/Text and enter 15 for the field width. Once you have entered the field width, the cursor will move to the next field definition.

Moving down the list, enter ADDRESS for the third field definition, C for Character/Text, and 25 for the field width. For the fourth field enter CITY, type a C in response to the field-type prompt, and enter 15 for the field width. For the next field enter STATE, type a C in response to the field-type prompt, and enter 2 for the field width.

The next field will be the ZIP code. Before going on, what do you think the field type for ZIP codes should be? ZIP codes consist of numbers, so at first it might make sense to use a numeric field. However, this is not really practical. New 9-digit ZIP codes are coming into use, and each code is divided by a hyphen. If two numbers are separated by a hyphen (which happens to be the mathematical subtraction symbol), dBASE III PLUS will attempt to subtract the two parts of the ZIP code, which could result in erroneous ZIP codes. You'll never use a ZIP code in a numerical calculation, so it makes no sense to store it as a number. To prevent such a problem from ever occurring, you will specify a character/text field for the ZIP codes stored in the ABC Realty database. The character/text field will accept any number that you enter, though it considers each digit as a character. A number stored as a character cannot be used in a numerical calculation.

Enter the word ZIP as the field name. Enter a C to denote a character/text field, and enter 10 for width (remember, 9 digits plus a hyphen). Once you have entered the width, the cursor will move to the next field description.

For this field name enter BEDROOMS. For field type enter N (for Numeric), and for field width enter 2. This will create a numeric field with a maximum width of 2 digits. You will be able to store numbers from 0 to 99 in this field. (ABC Realty assumes it will never rent homes with more than 99 bedrooms.) Since you specified a numeric field, the cursor now moves to the decimal heading. You could, if desired, specify a number of decimal places for the numeric field. Since you are using whole numbers to describe the number of bedrooms, simply press RETURN to bypass the decimal entry.

For the next field name enter BATHROOMS. For field type enter N for Numeric. For field width enter 2. Again you will create a numeric field with a maximum width of 2 digits. Press RETURN to bypass the decimal choice.

You may recall from Chapter 2 that one of the attributes takes the form of a date; that is the "expiration date" of the lease. dBASE III PLUS lets you use date fields to enter dates.

Enter EXPDATE and type D for Date. dBASE III PLUS automatically assigns a width of 8 characters for the date format MM/DD/YY, where MM represents the month, DD represents the day, and YY represents the year.

PARKING is a logical field so enter PARKING as the field name, and type L to define this as a logical field. The width is automatically defined as 1 for the true (T) or false (F) character.

Enter the remaining information as shown for the next four fields:

Field Name	Type	Width	Decimal
PROPTYPE	C	10	
RENTAMT	N	7	2
SIZE	N	5	
EXTRAS	M		
SALESOFF	C	2	

In the table RENTAMT has a field width of seven digits, of which one digit is for the decimal point, two are for decimals (so RENTAMT can include cents), and the remaining four digits are for the dollar amount. Rent at any ABC-owned location cannot be more than $9999.99. Whenever you include decimal amounts, allow one digit for the decimal; and if you are working exclusively with decimal numbers, include one digit so the decimal point can be preceded by a zero (for example, 0.1). Thus, the minimum field width for a decimal number is 3.

```
                                          Bytes remaining:   3871

 ┌─────────────────┬──────────────┬──────────────┬──────────────────────┐
 │ CURSOR  <-- -->  │  INSERT       │  DELETE       │ Up a field:     ↑    │
 │  Char:    ← →    │  Char:  Ins   │  Char:   Del  │ Down a field:   ↓    │
 │  Word: Home End  │  Field: ^N    │  Word:   ^Y   │ Exit/Save:     ^End  │
 │  Pan:   ^← ^→    │  Help:  F1    │  Field:  ^U   │ Abort:          Esc  │
 └─────────────────┴──────────────┴──────────────┴──────────────────────┘

     Field Name  Type     Width Dec          Field Name  Type      Width Dec
    ──────────────────────────────          ──────────────────────────────
  1  LASTNAME    Character  15           9  EXPDATE     Date        8
  2  FIRSTNAME   Character  15          10  PARKING     Logical     1
  3  ADDRESS     Character  25          11  PROPTYPE    Character  10
  4  CITY        Character  15          12  RENTAMT     Numeric     7    2
  5  STATE       Character   2          13  SIZE        Numeric     5    0
  6  ZIP         Character  10          14  EXTRAS      Memo       10
  7  BEDROOMS    Numeric     2    0     15  SALESOFF    Character   2
  8  BATHROOMS   Numeric     2    0

 ┌───────────────────────────────────────────────────────────────────────┐
 │MODIFY STRUCTURE│<C:>│ABC1                      │Field: 7/15│    │    │   │
 └───────────────────────────────────────────────────────────────────────┘
                        Enter the field name.
  Field names begin with a letter and may contain letters, digits and underscores
```

Figure 3-8. Listing of fields, including types and widths

Depending upon the property, the EXTRAS attribute may need to store a lengthy list of items. The most economical way of storing any large group of information is to use a memo field, and so EXTRAS should be designated as a memo field. After you have entered the field name EXTRAS and the memo field type, dBASE III PLUS will automatically supply 10 as a field width.

While you are creating the database, notice the statistic listed at the top of the screen. In the right corner is the number of available bytes remaining in the current record. This number is calculated by adding the numbers in the field width column and subtracting the sum from the allotted 4000 bytes (characters) per record. The status bar at the bottom of the screen indicates the number of fields created so far. Both figures, the number of bytes remaining and number of fields, will change as you add fields to the database. At the left side of the status bar is the name of the file, and the letter indicating which disk drive the database will be saved on.

To tell dBASE III PLUS that you have finished defining the database structure, position the cursor on an empty field and press the RETURN key. The screen will display the message **press ENTER to confirm — any other key to resume.** Your list of defined fields should now look like Figure 3-8.

Press RETURN again, and dBASE III PLUS will store the database structure on disk. Within a few moments, you'll see this at the bottom of the screen:

```
Input Data Records Now? (Y/N)
```

You could begin entering the records for ABC Realty at this time. However, let's first display a list of database files on disk. To do this, press N and dBASE III PLUS will return to the Assistant.

Choose the Tools menu, and select the Directory option. Press RETURN to accept the default disk drive when it is displayed, and a window of file types will appear.

The Directory option of the Assistant lets you choose the type of files you wish to display. You want to display only those files that are databases, so press RETURN to accept the Database Files choice. ABC1 is, of course, the only database file in the list.

```
ABC1.DBF

1024 bytes in  1 files.
9015296 bytes remaining on drive.
```

The display also shows the available disk space on the disk you are currently using. Press any key, and you will return to the Assistant menus.

DISPLAYING A DATABASE STRUCTURE

The LIST STRUCTURE command can be used to examine the structure of a database. LIST STRUCTURE will show the name of the file being used, the number of records in the file, the last date any item was changed, and the field definitions for all of the database fields.

Choose the LIST STRUCTURE option of the Tools menu. dBASE III PLUS will ask if you wish to print the results on your printer. Press N to answer no to this option, and the screen in Figure 3-9 will appear.

Notice that the number of data records is shown as 0. The database exists but it is empty. You'll use another command, APPEND, to add information to the database. Press any key to return to the Assistant.

THE APPEND COMMAND

The APPEND command is used to put information into an existing database. (If the database already contains information, any new data is appended to it.)

Open the Update menu, and select the APPEND option. The screen clears, and the silhouette of a fill-in form for record 1 of the database appears (Figure 3-10). The cursor is flashing in the LASTNAME field. For each field in the record, enter the following information, pressing RETURN after each entry is completed.

```
LASTNAME:    Morse
FIRSTNAME:   Marcia
ADDRESS:     4260 Park Avenue
CITY:        Chevy Chase
STATE:       MD
ZIP:         20815-0988
BEDROOMS:    4
BATHROOMS:   2
EXPDATE:     03/01/85
PARKING:     Y
PROPTYPE:    HOUSE
RENTAMT:     750.00
SIZE:        1345
```

```
 Set Up  Create  Update  Position  Retrieve  Organize Modify Tools  01:10:49 pm
Structure for database: C:abc1.dbf
Number of data records:      9
Date of last update   : 03/23/86
Field  Field Name  Type      Width   Dec
    1  LASTNAME    Character    15
    2  FIRSTNAME   Character    15
    3  ADDRESS     Character    25
    4  CITY        Character    15
    5  STATE       Character     2
    6  ZIP         Character    10
    7  BEDROOMS    Numeric       2
    8  BATHROOMS   Numeric       2
    9  EXPDATE     Date          8
   10  PARKING     Logical       1
   11  PROPTYPE    Character    10
   12  RENTAMT     Numeric       7      2
   13  SIZE        Numeric       5
   14  EXTRAS      Memo         10
   15  SALESOFF    Character     2
** Total **                   130

ASSIST          <C:> ABC1                    Rec: 9/9
            Press any key to continue work in ASSIST._
```

Figure 3-9. Complete listing of ABC database

As you fill in the various fields, dBASE III PLUS will occasionally cause the computer to beep. This occurs whenever you enter
data that fills the field. This is normal, but you can turn off the
beep if it is annoying (how to do so will be discussed later in this
book). Once you have entered all of the information shown, the cursor should be at the start of the memo field.

Entering Data
In a Memo Field

Entering data in a memo field is quite different from the way data
is entered in other fields. You'll notice that the word *memo*, which

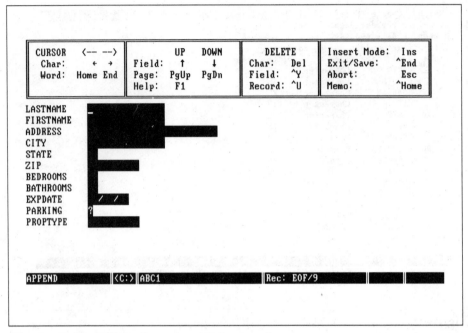

Figure 3-10. Fill-in form for ABC record

was supplied by dBASE when you indicated the memo field type, already appears in the field. Whenever the cursor is in a memo field (as it is now), you are at the entry point for a "memo slip" that can hold as many as 4000 characters. To get to the memo slip, press the CONTROL key and then the PG DN key. The Append screen will vanish, and a Help screen with the heading **Edit:EXTRAS** will appear in its place. You are now in the dBASE word processor. The dBASE word processor lets you type text as you would with any word processing software. It isn't necessary to press the RETURN key at the end of every line; the word processor will automatically move the cursor to the next line. The BACKSPACE key will erase any mistakes, and you can use the arrow keys to move the cursor around the screen for editing. As an example, type the following.

Pool, sauna room, carpeted bedrooms and microwave oven.

When you have finished typing the text, you'll need to get back to the Append screen. To do so, press CONTROL-END. The Append screen will reappear. Press the RETURN key to move to the next field.

Finally, for the SALESOFF field, type the letters DC (for District of Columbia). Notice that once the record is completely filled, dBASE III PLUS automatically stores the record and advances to the next blank record.

Editing on the Append Screen

If you make a mistake during data entry, use the BACKSPACE key to erase the character to the left of the cursor. (The only instance

Table 3-2. Editing Functions With APPEND

Key	Action
← or CONTROL-S	Cursor back one character
→ or CONTROL-D	Cursor forward one character
↑ or CONTROL-E	Cursor up one field
↓ or CONTROL-X	Cursor down one field
INS or CONTROL-V	Insert mode on/off
DEL	Delete character
BACKSPACE	Delete character to left of cursor
CONTROL-Y	Delete to end of field
CONTROL-Q	Abort screen operation; don't add record to database
ESC	Abort screen operation; don't add record to database
CONTROL-T	Delete word or all characters until next blank
END or W	Saves record and adds to database

in which this is not done is when you type the last character of the final field. If you do this, dBASE III PLUS automatically moves on to the next record. If you then want to edit the record, you must then press the ↑ key until dBASE III PLUS returns to the previous record.) You can also use the arrow keys to move left, right, up, or down in the form. To insert new characters between existing characters, press the INS key and then type the correction. Pressing INS again takes you out of the insert mode. When not in insert mode, any characters that you type will write over existing characters. A more complete list of dBASE III PLUS editing keys used with APPEND is shown in Table 3-2. these editing keys also work with the word processor in the memo slip.

Before finishing the APPEND process, add the remaining records for the Washington, D.C., area to the ABC Realty database.

```
Levy
Carol
1207 5th Street S.E.
Washington
DC
20003
3
2
04/12/85
N
townhouse
875.00
1345
Close to  Metrorail station.  Bright, airy den and
bedrooms  with large closets.
DC


Jackson
David
4102 Valley Lane
Falls Church
VA
22044
1
1
09/30/85
Y
condo
525.00
980
Efficiency condo with combo den/bedroom.  Near commuter bus.
DC
```

Westman
Andrea
4807 East Avenue
Silver Spring
MD
20910-0124
2
1
12/23/85
Y
condo
570.00
1250
2 blocks from Silver Spring metro station. Covered assigned
parking. Den/loft overlooks wooded area. Has heat pump and
central air.
DC

Mitchell
Mary Jo
617 North Oakland Street
Arlington
VA
22203
5
3
12/25/85
Y
house
990.00
2350
Lots of trees; quiet street. Panelled rec room and private study.
DC

Hart
Edward
6200 Germantown Road
Fairfax
VA
22025
3
2
12/20/85
N
townhouse
680.00
1670
Near shopping mall and interstate. Many extras including
built-in cabinets and patio.
DC

```
Robinson
Shirley
270 Browning Ave #3C
Takoma Park
MD
20912
1
1
12/20/85
N
condo
425.00
870
Efficiency condo with combined bedroom and den.  Airy views of
quiet street.
DC


Robinson
William
1607 21st Street N.W.
Washington
DC
20009
3
1
05/20/86
N
townhouse
920.00
1400
Close to Kennedy Center and within walking distance of Watergate.
Two big levels with redone kitchen.
DC



Jones
Jarel
5203 North Shore Drive
Reston
VA
22090
3
3
04/15/85
Y
townhouse
1025.00
2230
Spectacular lakeside view, 3 large levels, rec room in basement,
two fireplaces.
DC
```

After the last record has been entered, press RETURN to save the records and return to the Assistant.

VIEWING A DATABASE

You can use the LIST and DISPLAY commands to examine the contents of a database. Typing the LIST command by itself will show the entire contents of a database, but you can limit the display to certain fields by including the field name after LIST. If you specify more than one field, separate them by a comma. For example, press ESC to return to the dot prompt. Then enter the following:

```
LIST LASTNAME, RENTAMT
```

dBASE III PLUS shows only the last names and rental amounts contained in the database.

```
Record#   LASTNAME        RENTAMT
      1   Morse            750.00
      2   Levy             875.00
      3   Jackson          525.00
      4   Westman          570.00
      5   Mitchell         990.00
      6   Hart             680.00
      7   Robinson         425.00
      8   Robinson         920.00
      9   Jones           1025.00
```

The DISPLAY command lets you view selected information. With the DISPLAY command you must tell dBASE III PLUS exactly what you would like to see displayed. Enter the following:

```
GO 3
DISPLAY
```

You should see the third record in the database. This happens to be the location in the file that dBASE III PLUS is currently viewing. Enter the following:

```
GO 2
DISPLAY NEXT 3
```

You should now see three records, beginning with record number 2. To see the entire database, enter

```
DISPLAY ALL
```

There is one significant difference between DISPLAY and LIST. If the database is large, the LIST command will cause the contents to scroll up the screen nonstop. (You can use CONTROL-S to start and stop the scroll.) If you use the DISPLAY command, the screen will pause after every 20 lines, and you can press any key to resume scrolling.

The DISPLAY command can also be used to search for specific information if it is followed by a specific condition. As an example, you could find rental homes that are priced at $1025 per month by entering

```
DISPLAY FOR RENTAMT = 1025
```

VIEWING SELECTIVE DATA WITH THE ASSISTANT OPTIONS

The Assistant menus provide simple but effective ways to search for specific information contained in a database. To see these options, enter ASSIST to return to the Assistant menus and then open the Retrieve menu.

Among the options shown in the menu are LIST and DISPLAY. These options will perform the same functions as those performed by the LIST and DISPLAY commands when you used them from the dot prompt. But there are a number of additional ways to use the LIST and DISPLAY commands. If you are entering the commands from the dot prompt, you must know these commands from memory (or look them up in the manual). If you use the Assistant, however, these additional choices will be displayed for you. As an example, select the DISPLAY option of the Retrieve menu now. You will see five additional choices in a new window (Figure 3-11).

The first choice, "Execute the command," will cause the DISPLAY command to be carried out. The "Specify scope" option lets you choose a display of all records, a specific number of records, or an individual record number. The "Construct a field list" option lets you choose what fields will be shown by the DISPLAY com-

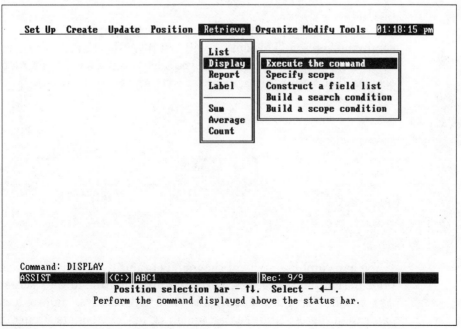

Figure 3-11. Menu options

mand. "Build a search condition" lets you identify one or more conditions to search for records. "Build a scope condition" lets you further refine your searches to display or print records while those records continue to meet specific criteria.

As an example, if you wanted to display all tenants that live in Maryland, you could use "Build a search condition" to accomplish this task. To try this, select "Build a search condition." A window displaying the names of the fields in the database will appear. You want to search for a specific state, so use the cursor keys to highlight the STATE field. Then press RETURN to choose this option.

A new window will appear, showing your comparison options. dBASE III PLUS provides six comparison options: "Equal To," "Less Than Or Equal To," "Less Than," "Greater Than," "Greater Than Or Equal To," and "Not Equal To." In this case, you want all states equal to "MD," so choose the "Equal To" option. Enter "MD" in response to the prompt to enter a character string.

Another window will appear, asking if any other conditions are desired. In this case, no more conditions are necessary, so press RETURN.

Finally, use the cursor keys to again highlight the "Execute the command" option. This option will tell dBASE III PLUS to carry out the selective command that you have created with the menu choices. The result will appear on your screen as follows:

```
Record#  LASTNAME       FIRSTNAME      ADDRESS                    CITY
    STATE  ZIP        BEDROOMS BATHROOMS EXPDATE  PARKING PROPTYPE  RENTAMT  SIZE
EXTRAS  SALESOFF
       1  Morse          Marcia            4260 Park Avenue        Chevy Chase
    MD     20815-0988        4          2 03/01/85 .T.     house     750.00  1600
Memo    DC
       4  Westman        Andrea            4807 East Avenue        Silver Spring
    MD     20910-0124        2          1 12/23/85 .T.     apartment 570.00  1250
Memo    DC
       7  Robinson       Shirley          270 Browning Ave #3C     Takoma Park
    MD     20912             1          1 12/20/85 .F.     apartment 425.00   870
Memo    DC
```

You can combine many of the menu options to obtain the precise information that is needed, without adding clutter to your screen. As an example, you might wish to show only the last names, lease expiration dates, and rental amounts of all tenants living in

Washington, since the city government is about to pass a rent control law, and you want to determine the number of ABC Realty tenants that will be affected by the law. First, choose the DISPLAY option of the Retrieve menu. You'll want to see specific fields, so select the "Construct a field list" option.

With this option, you can mark all fields that are to be displayed by moving the cursor to that field, and pressing the RETURN key. Since you want to see only the last names, expiration dates, and rental amounts, move the cursor to each of these fields and press RETURN after highlighting each field.

Notice the message at the bottom of the screen: it indicates that you can leave the menu with the ← or → key. You've selected the fields to be displayed, so press the ← or → key now. Next, you'll want to build a search condition that tells dBASE III PLUS to select those records where the state is "DC". Choose the "Build a search condition" option, and highlight the STATE field. Select the "Equal To" choice for your comparison, and enter "DC" in response to the prompt. Choose "No More Conditions" at the next menu.

Before you choose the "Execute the command" option, examine the command shown just above the status bar at the bottom of the screen. This command, which dBASE III PLUS is about to execute, is a dBASE command that you have built by choosing the various menu options. You could type this command in at the dot prompt and accomplish the same results. Once you become familiar with the commands that you will use most often, you may prefer to save time by entering those commands directly from the dot prompt instead of using the menu choices of the Assistant.

To see the results of your command, select the "Execute the command" choice. The last names, lease dates, and rental amounts of the Washington, D.C., tenants will appear on your screen.

USING MULTIPLE CONDITIONS

You can use multiple conditions to further refine a search. For example, if you wanted a list of all properties in Virginia with more than two bathrooms, you could use the "Combine With AND" option when the Assistant offers that menu choice. To try this, choose the DISPLAY option of the Retrieve menu, and select "Build a search condition." You want only those properties in Virginia, so select STATE from the list of field names. From the comparison menu that appears, choose "Equal To." Enter "VA" in response to the character string prompt.

The next menu that appears offers a choice of what dBASE III PLUS calls logical operators. Logical operators compare values with other values and make true or false decisions based upon those values. The operators provided by the Assistant are AND and OR. Using these operators, you can search for information using an AND combination, such as all records where the state is Virginia AND the property has more than two bathrooms. You could also use an OR combination, such as all records where the city is Falls Church OR the city is Arlington.

In this case you want to use the AND condition, so select "Combine With AND" from the menu. The list of field names will again appear. Select BATHROOMS, and a comparison menu will again appear. Choose "Greater Than" for your comparison operator. You want only those homes with more than two bathrooms, so enter 2 in response to the prompt for a numeric value. Finally, select "No More Conditions"; then select "Execute the command." The result, which follows, shows the specific records that met both conditions you specified.

Record#	LASTNAME	FIRSTNAME	ADDRESS	CITY		
	STATE ZIP	BEDROOMS BATHROOMS	EXPDATE PARKING PROPTYPE	RENTAMT	SIZE	
	EXTRAS SALESOFF					
5	Mitchell	Mary Jo	617 North Oakland Street	Arlington		
	VA 22203	5	3 12/25/85 .T. house	990.00	2350	
	Memo DC					
9	Jones	Jarel	5203 North Shore Drive	Reston		
	VA 22090	3	3 04/15/85 .T. townhouse	1025.00	2230	
	Memo DC					

SEARCHING WITHIN A FIELD

There may be occasions when you want to search for information that is contained within a field, but you know only a portion of that information. This can cause problems, because dBASE III PLUS does not search "full text," or within a field, unless you give it specific instructions to do so. To demonstrate the problem: If one of ABC Realty's sales agents calls and asks for full details on the property on North Shore Drive, how do you find that data? The agent can't recall the entire address, and to make matters worse, the agent isn't sure what town the property is in. Try searching for a property on North Shore Drive by performing the following steps: Choose the DISPLAY option of the Retrieve menu. Select "Build a search condition," and choose ADDRESS for the field. Select "Equal To," and enter "North Shore Drive" in response to the prompt for a character string. Choose "No More Conditions," and then choose "Execute the command."

Don't feel that you've done something wrong when the record does not appear. dBASE normally begins a search by attempting to match your characters with the first characters of the chosen field. In our database, there is no record that begins with the characters "North Shore Drive" in the address field. As a result, dBASE III PLUS failed to find the data.

To get around this problem, you can search within a field. Unfortunately, this cannot be done from within the Assistant menus; you must perform this type of search from the dot prompt. The normal layout, or syntax, for the necessary command is

```
DISPLAY FOR 'search text' $ FIELDNAME
```

where 'search text' are the actual characters that you want to look for, and FIELDNAME is the name of the specific field that you wish to search. To try an example, press ESC to exit the Assistant and return to the dot prompt. Then enter the following command:

```
DISPLAY FOR 'North Shore Drive' $ ADDRESS
```

This time dBASE III PLUS will find the desired information.

A WARNING ABOUT MEMO FIELDS

dBASE III PLUS stores memo fields in a manner that is different from the way it stores other database information. Because of this difference, you cannot search for information contained within a memo field. For example, choose the DISPLAY option of the Retrieve menu, and try to build a search condition based on the memo field, EXTRAS, contained within the ABC Realty database. You will find that the Assistant will not let you choose the memo field. There is no way to search the memo field from the dot prompt either. Keep this limitation in mind if your databases make use of memo fields. You can display and print information contained in the memo fields, but you cannot search or use conditions on memo fields.

KEEPING TRACK OF RECORDS

Whenever dBASE III PLUS looks at a database, it examines one record at a time. Even when you list all records in the database, dBASE III PLUS starts with the first record in the file and then examines each subsequent record one by one. The program keeps track of its location by means of a pointer. Whenever you are using a database, the dBASE III PLUS pointer is always pointing to a particular record (Figure 3-12).

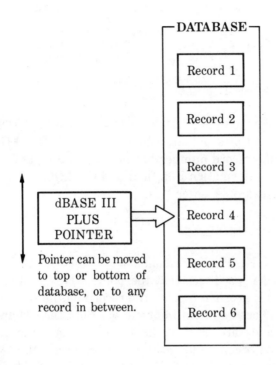

DATABASE

Record 1

Record 2

Record 3

dBASE III PLUS POINTER → Record 4

Pointer can be moved to top or bottom of database, or to any record in between.

Record 5

Record 6

Figure 3-12. dBASE III PLUS record pointer

You can move the pointer to a record with the GO command. Press ESC until the dot prompt appears. Then enter GO TOP and then DISPLAY. The pointer will be at the first record in the file.

```
Record#  LASTNAME     FIRSTNAME      ADDRESS ...............
      1  Morse        Marsha         4260 Park Avenue........
```

To move the pointer to the fourth record, enter GO 4. Enter DISPLAY, and you will see the fourth record.

```
LASTNAME  FIRSTNAME ADDRESS          CITY          STATE
Westman   Andrea    4807 East Avenue Silver Spring MD

   ZIP       BEDROOMS BATHROOMS EXPDATE  PROPTYPE
20910-0124 2         1         04/30/85  apartment


RENTAMT  SIZE EXTRAS PARKING SALESOFF
   570.00 1250 Memo    .T.      DC
```

You can go to the first record by entering GO TOP, or you can go to the end of a database by entering GO BOTTOM. If you don't know the record number but need to find a particular record, you can use information in a field and the LOCATE command to find it. For example, enter this:

```
LOCATE FOR RENTAMT = 875
```

dBASE III PLUS responds with **Record**=2. If you now enter DISPLAY, you'll see that the pointer is repositioned at record 2. LOCATE does not display the record on the screen; it only finds a record based on field information. Both the GO and the LOCATE commands are also available from within the Assistant. These commands can be found in the Position menu.

To exit from dBASE III PLUS, use the QUIT command. From the dot prompt, enter QUIT. Or, from the Assistant, open the Set Up menu, and choose QUIT dBASE III PLUS. When you enter QUIT, the database is automatically saved to disk and you return to the operating system.

Changing Your Database

Chapter 4

dBASE III PLUS has a number of commands that you can use to change records and fields. You can edit information in a record, such as a person's name or phone number on a mailing list, and you can change the structure of a database, adding fields for items that you didn't plan for or deleting fields that you no longer use. You can also expand or shorten the width of a field. Let's begin by editing records in the ABC1 file.

THE EDIT COMMAND

First, let's get into the database. Until now, you have been relying on the Assistant to execute most dBASE III PLUS commands. Beginning with this chapter, you will make increasing use of commands entered directly from the dot prompt. The Assistant may seem like the simpler, less confusing way to use dBASE III PLUS, and it usually is. But there are many complex functions of dBASE III PLUS that cannot be executed from the Assistant. For these functions, it pays to have a working knowledge of the use of commands from the dBASE dot prompt. Load and start dBASE

III PLUS if you haven't done so, and place your working disk in drive B if you are using a floppy system. Press ESC to get to the dot prompt, and remember to tell dBASE III PLUS to use the correct drive by entering

`SET DEFAULT TO B: (OR TO C:)`

Activate the ABC Realty database with

`USE ABC1`

The USE command has the same result as the Database File option of the Set Up menu in the Assistant. Both will tell dBASE III PLUS to use a particular database.

See that the file is all there by entering LIST. You should see the list of tenants entered in Chapter 3.

Let's assume that David Jackson has had a rent increase, and you need to edit his record to change RENTAMT. Notice that Mr. Jackson is listed in record number 3 of the database.

To edit any record, you type the command EDIT, followed by the record number; or you enter GOTO 3 and then EDIT. From the Assistant you would choose GoTo Record from the Position menu; then you would choose Edit from the Update menu. EDIT displays a single record at a time for editing. The record is shown in the same manner as with the APPEND command. In this case, from the dot prompt enter

`EDIT 3`

and you'll see the record for Mr. Jackson displayed on the screen, as shown in Figure 4-1.

At this point you are in editing mode, a mode of operation during which you can make changes to the data contained within the chosen record. The cursor is flashing underneath the first character of the first field in the record. Try pressing the ↓, ↑, ←, and → keys a few times, and notice that each keypress moves the cursor

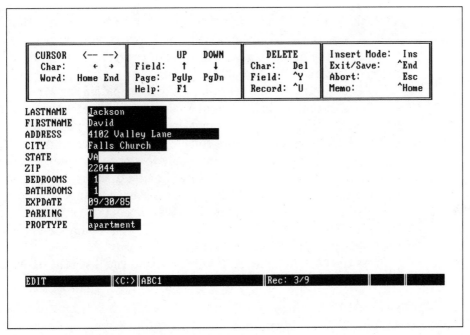

Figure 4-1. Editing screen for record 3

either one character or row at a time. If you keep pressing the ↑ key, you'll see that dBASE III PLUS takes you to the preceding record in the file, while pressing the ↓ key repeatedly will take you to the next record in the file. You can use the arrow keys to move the cursor to any location in the database. Try pressing F1 repeatedly. Doing so will hide and display the Help screen that shows the editing commands. Press F1 until the Help screen is no longer visible.

While in the editing mode, you can also use the PG UP and PG DN keys to move around the database. The PG DN key takes you one record forward, while the PG UP key moves you one record back. If you are at record 1, the PG UP key will take you out of editing mode and back to the dot prompt. If you are at the last record, PG DN will also take you out of editing mode and back to the prompt. If the Help screen is not displayed, PG UP and PG DN will immediately take you to the preceding or next record, regardless of where in a record the cursor is located at that time.

Get back to the record containing the information for Mr. Jackson. Move the cursor to the rental amount and type 570; then press RETURN. At this point the change isn't stored and you're still in edit mode. Whenever you have finished editing a record, press the CONTROL and END keys simultaneously to store your changes and leave edit mode. (If you were making changes to many records, you would not have to press CONTROL-END after each change; you could make all the necessary changes and then press CONTROL-END.) To leave the edit mode without any changes, you would press ESC, assuming you haven't moved to another record.

Press the CONTROL and END keys now, and you'll see the dBASE III PLUS prompt reappear. Enter

```
GO 3
DISPLAY
```

and record 3 is displayed with the new RENTAMT.

THE BROWSE COMMAND

Another command for editing information in a record is the BROWSE command. BROWSE displays more than one record on the screen, so you can conveniently access a number of records for editing. To use BROWSE, first go back to the top of the database by entering GO TOP. Then enter the command

```
BROWSE
```

and you'll see a screen of records (Figure 4-2).

BROWSE displays as many fields as will fit on the screen and can display 23 records in horizontal format. If there are more fields in a record than will fit on a screen, BROWSE only shows the first fields. This is the case with the ABC Realty database.

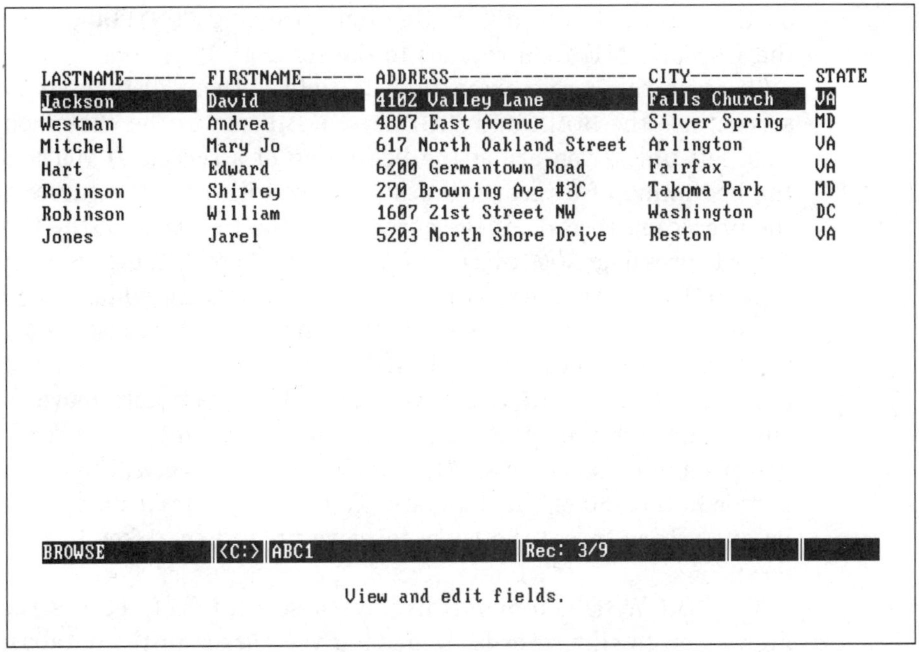

```
LASTNAME-------- FIRSTNAME------- ADDRESS------------------- CITY----------- STATE
Jackson          David            4102 Valley Lane           Falls Church    VA
Westman          Andrea           4807 East Avenue           Silver Spring   MD
Mitchell         Mary Jo          617 North Oakland Street   Arlington       VA
Hart             Edward           6200 Germantown Road       Fairfax         VA
Robinson         Shirley          270 Browning Ave #3C       Takoma Park     MD
Robinson         William          1607 21st Street NW        Washington      DC
Jones            Jarel            5203 North Shore Drive     Reston          VA




















BROWSE          <C:> ABC1                         Rec: 3/9
                        View and edit fields.
```

Figure 4-2. Display of database with the BROWSE command

Fields after the STATE field are not visible. All that BROWSE can show you is the LASTNAME, FIRSTNAME, ADDRESS, CITY, and STATE fields. The other fields are to the right of the display. BROWSE lets you scan across the database to bring the other fields into view by using the combinations CONTROL-← and CONTROL-→.

Hold CONTROL and press the → key once. The fields shift from right to left on the screen, with the LASTNAME field disappearing off the left side of the screen and the ZIP field appearing on the right side of the screen. If you press the CONTROL and → keys repeatedly, fields on the screen will disappear as the remaining fields come into view, until you reach the last field, which is SALESOFF.

Press CONTROL-← and you'll notice the opposite effect. The fields that disappeared at the left of the screen reappear while the fields on the right side disappear. Continue pressing CONTROL-← until the LASTNAME field returns to the screen.

To move the cursor from field to field without disturbing the screen, use the HOME and END keys. HOME moves the cursor one field left unless you are at the beginning of a record. If you're at the beginning of a record, the HOME key will move the cursor to the preceding record. (If the cursor is at the first field of the first record, pressing HOME has no effect.) END moves the cursor one field right, unless the cursor is at the last field, in which case it moves to the following record (if the cursor is on the last field of the last record, nothing happens).

Try using the PG UP and PG DN keys. These two keys move the cursor through the database one screenful at a time. Since ABC's list of tenants is rather short, pressing PG DN once will move the cursor to the end of the database. To move the cursor up or down by one record, press the ↑ key to move up and the ↓ key to move down.

The BROWSE command displays a screenful of records that allows you to edit records by moving the cursor in the database. You can type changes in a field, and they will take effect just as they did when you were using the EDIT command. But since BROWSE displays a screenful of records, not just one record at a time, it is easier to access a particular field with BROWSE.

If you want to add records while in BROWSE mode, press the ↓ key until the last record in the database is highlighted, press the ↓ key again, and dBASE III PLUS will display

```
Add new records?  (Y/N)
```

at the bottom of the screen.

Press Y to tell dBASE III PLUS that you wish to add another record. Now add the following record, pressing the RETURN key after entering each field:

LASTNAME	FIRSTNAME	ADDRESS	CITY	STATE
Smith	Bob	2612 Lee Highway	Vienna	VA

Notice that after you enter data for the STATE field, the highlighted cursor moves to the next record, which is blank, rather than moving to the right to display the ZIP field. To add data to the ZIP field, you display the field on screen by pressing CONTROL-→. Since you will delete this record later in the chapter, it is not necessary to add more information now.

If BROWSE is so all-powerful, why must you bother with the EDIT command? The reason is that the EDIT command, though not as fast as BROWSE, always shows you the complete record. BROWSE, on the other hand, shows you only those fields that fit on the screen. If your database contains many fields, BROWSE will have to display it in small pieces.

After changing or adding information with the BROWSE command, press CONTROL-END to save the record and return to the dot prompt. There are options that can be specified along with the BROWSE command. These options provide ways to lock certain fields in place so that they are not lost from view when you pan with the control and cursor keys. The options also let you show or edit selected fields when using BROWSE.

The FIELDS option of the BROWSE command lets you name the fields that you want to display with BROWSE. This option is particularly helpful when you want to edit specific information while using BROWSE. The syntax for this form of the command is

```
BROWSE FIELDS (field1, field2, field3)
```

As an example, you might wish to change the rental amounts to reflect new leases among some ABC Realty tenants. You wish to see only the names, addresses, and rental amounts. From the dot prompt, try this command:

```
BROWSE FIELDS LASTNAME, FIRSTNAME, ADDRESS, RENTAMT
```

The resultant display (Figure 4-3) shows only those fields that you named within the command. Since these are the only fields

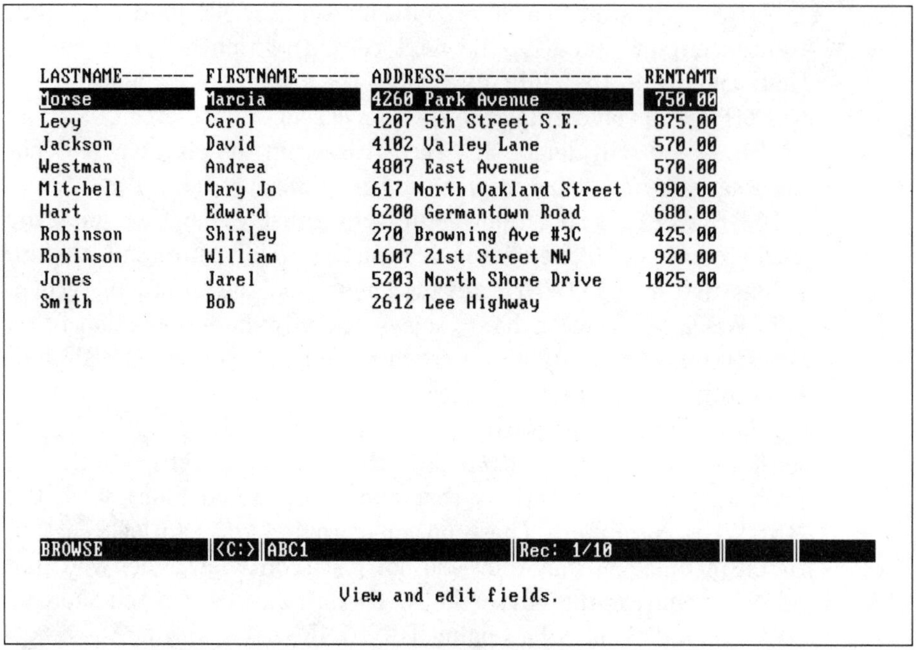

```
LASTNAME-------- FIRSTNAME------- ADDRESS------------------- RENTAMT
Morse           Marcia           4260 Park Avenue            750.00
Levy            Carol            1207 5th Street S.E.         875.00
Jackson         David            4102 Valley Lane            570.00
Westman         Andrea           4807 East Avenue            570.00
Mitchell        Mary Jo          617 North Oakland Street     990.00
Hart            Edward           6200 Germantown Road         680.00
Robinson        Shirley          270 Browning Ave #3C         425.00
Robinson        William          1607 21st Street NW          920.00
Jones           Jarel            5203 North Shore Drive      1025.00
Smith           Bob              2612 Lee Highway



BROWSE          |<C:>|ABC1                        |Rec: 1/10
                        View and edit fields.
```

Figure 4-3. Selected fields within BROWSE

that are displayed, these are the only fields that can be edited at the present time.

The LOCK option of the BROWSE command locks a field at the left side of the screen. The locked field will then remain stationary when you use the control and cursor keys to pan left or right. This option can prove very helpful when editing the entire database. By keeping an important field such as the last name locked, it is visually easier to tell where in the database you are at any point in time. The normal syntax for the command with this option is

```
BROWSE LOCK (X)
```

where X is a numeric value that tells dBASE III PLUS how many fields should be locked. To lock the first two fields of the ABC Realty database, try the following command:

```
BROWSE LOCK 2
```

Use the CONTROL-← and CONTROL-→ keys to pan across the database. Notice that the LASTNAME and FIRSTNAME fields of the database remain locked, while the other fields pan across the screen.

The FREEZE option of the BROWSE command lets you limit any editing to a specific field. All fields are displayed, but only the specified field can be changed. The normal syntax for the command is

```
BROWSE FREEZE (fieldname)
```

To try the effect of this option, enter BROWSE FREEZE RENT-AMT. You will see that you can pan across all fields, but only the RENTAMT field can be edited.

You can use the options of the BROWSE command in combination with each other. As an example, this command,

```
BROWSE FIELDS LASTNAME, FIRSTNAME, ADDRESS, CITY, STATE, RENTAMT,
EXPDATE, SALESOFF LOCK 2 FREEZE RENTAMT
```

would result in a display with the LASTNAME and FIRST-NAME fields locked, the RENTAMT field available for editing, and the other fields named in the field list displayed (but not available for editing).

USING BROWSE
FROM THE ASSISTANT

Most BROWSE options are also available from the Assistant. To see the options, you must access a Browse menu bar that is available by pressing F10 after choosing BROWSE. To see how this works, press ESC to return to the dot prompt. Then enter ASSIST to choose the Assistant. Open the Update menu and choose BROWSE.

Once the BROWSE display appears, press F10. The Browse menu bar will appear at the top of the screen (Figure 4-4).

The options provided by the Browse menu bar are Bottom, Top, Lock, Record Number, and Freeze. The Lock and Freeze options perform the same functions as when they are used with the BROWSE command from the dot prompt. The Bottom option moves the dBASE III PLUS pointer (and therefore the cursor) to the end of the database. The Top option moves the pointer to the beginning of the database. The Record Number option moves the pointer to a specific record in the database. You select a choice as you would select any Assistant menu choice: highlight the desired option and press RETURN.

Try using the various menu options along with BROWSE. When you are done, press CONTROL-END to return to the Assistant menu. Then press ESC to leave the Assistant and return to the dot prompt.

Now let's consider some commands that remove records from a database.

DELETING RECORDS

dBASE III PLUS uses a combination of two commands to delete a record: DELETE and PACK. DELETE prepares a record for deletion but doesn't actually delete the record. What DELETE does is place an asterisk (*) next to the record, indicating that it is a candidate for deletion. You can delete as many records as you wish at one time. By identifying records in this way, DELETE provides a built-in safeguard: you have the opportunity to change your mind with the RECALL command, which will be discussed later in this section.

```
┌──────────────────────────────────────────────────────────────────────┐
│ ▐Bottom▌      Top      Lock      Record No.       Freeze ▐08:47:37 pm▌ │
│ LASTNAME------- FIRSTNAME------ ADDRESS------------------ CITY---------- STATE │
│ ▐Morse        ▌▐Marcia        ▌▐4260 Park Avenue         ▌▐Chevy Chase  ▌▐MD▌ │
│ Levy           Carol           1207 5th Street S.E.       Washington      DC  │
│ Jackson        David           4102 Valley Lane           Falls Church    VA  │
│ Westman        Andrea          4807 East Avenue           Silver Spring   MD  │
│ Mitchell       Mary Jo         617 North Oakland Street   Arlington       VA  │
│ Hart           Edward          6200 Germantown Road       Fairfax         VA  │
│ Robinson       Shirley         270 Browning Ave #3C       Takoma Park     MD  │
│ Robinson       William         1607 21st Street NW        Washington      DC  │
│ Jones          Jarel           5203 North Shore Drive     Reston          VA  │
│ Smith          Bob             2612 Lee Highway           Vienna          VA  │
│                                                                        │
│                                                                        │
│                                                                        │
│                                                                        │
│                                                                        │
│ ▐BROWSE     ▌║<C:>║ABC1             ║Rec: 1/10  ║       ║     ║        │
│         Position selection bar with ↔.   Select with ↵.               │
│                   Go to end of the file.                               │
└──────────────────────────────────────────────────────────────────────┘
```

Figure 4-4. Browse menu bar

Let's say that the record you just added, Bob Smith, is to be removed from the database. You first have to move the pointer to the record. Since you just appended the record, you'll find it at the bottom of the file in record 10. You can move the pointer to record 10 in two ways. One, you can visually search the database, find the name and record number, and enter GOTO followed by the record number; but this method is impractical if there are hundreds of records. Two, you can search for a record with the LOCATE command, which instantly brings you to the desired record no matter how large the database. The format for LOCATE is

```
LOCATE FOR LASTNAME="Smith"
```

If you use the Assistant, the LOCATE command can be found in the Position menu. From the dot prompt enter LOCATE FOR LASTNAME = "Smith". If you entered the command correctly, you'll see **RECORD**=10. Enter DISPLAY, and record 10 will be displayed on the screen. However, if you see something like

```
VARIABLE NOT FOUND
?
```

or

```
SYNTAX ERROR
```

recheck your typing and enter the command again.

Since record 10 is the one you want to remove, enter

```
DELETE
```

and you'll see the confirmation, **1 record deleted.**

If you know the record number, you can specify the DELETE RECORD *number*, where *number* is the number of the record to be deleted. Suppose that Shirley Robinson, listed in record 7, also needs to be removed from the list. Enter the command

```
DELETE RECORD 7
```

Again, the **1 record deleted** message appears. Now enter LIST, and you'll see that records 7 and 10 haven't been removed from the database. They have been marked with an asterisk (*) beside the first field, indicating that these records are marked for deletion.

If you decide that deleting a record is not the thing to do, you can use the RECALL command to undo the damage. For example, enter the command to restore the seventh record:

```
RECALL RECORD 7
```

The confirmation, **1 record recalled**, appears. Now enter LIST, and the database will show that only record 10 is still marked for deletion. You can remove all delete marks with the command RECALL ALL.

When a record has been marked for deletion it remains in the database, and various operations, such as COUNT and SUM (which will be discussed later), will still use the record in calculations as if it had never been deleted. To avoid displaying and using records that have been marked for deletion, you can use the SET DELETED command. Enter

```
SET DELETED ON
```

Now enter LIST, and you will see that the record marked for deletion is no longer visible. To make the record visible again, enter

```
SET DELETED OFF
```

When you enter LIST again, the record marked for deletion is again displayed in the database.

There is no need to delete records one by one with the DELETE command. You can mark more than one record for deletion by specifying the number of records to be deleted. For example, enter the command

```
GO 5
DELETE NEXT 2
LIST
```

GO 5 moves the pointer to record 5; then DELETE NEXT 2 marks record 5 and 6 for deletion.

The RECALL command can be used in the same manner. Enter

```
GO 5
RECALL NEXT 2
LIST
```

and records 5 and 6 will be unmarked.

The PACK command makes the deletion process final. This command removes all marked records from the database, and it renumbers the remaining records to fill any empty spaces created by the deleted records. Enter the command

```
PACK
```

and when the prompt reappears, enter LIST. You will see that Mr. Smith's record has been removed from the ABC Realty database.

DELETING FILES

You can delete files from within dBASE III PLUS with another variation of the DELETE command. For example,

```
DELETE FILE NAMES2.DBF
```

will erase the file NAMES2.DBF from the disk. Use the DELETE FILE command with care, because once a file has been deleted, there is no way you can recall it.

CHANGING THE CONTENTS OF A DATABASE

Suppose that you wanted to replace the five-digit ZIP code with the new nine-digit ZIP codes for all tenants in Washington, D.C. You can change the ZIP code for every Washington, D.C., entry with the CHANGE command. However, you only need to use CHANGE once because it is a *global* command. A global command performs the operation of the command on the entire database, not just a single record.

The CHANGE command consists of a two-step process: first, CHANGE finds the proper field, and then it asks you to enter the correction. The format of the command is CHANGE FIELD *fieldname* FOR *keyfield* = '*keyname*'. *Fieldname* is the field where you want the changes to occur, and *keyfield* is the field where CHANGE searches for the occurrence of *keyname*. Single quotes must surround *keyname*.

In the following example you will use the CHANGE command to "change the field ZIP for each occurrence in the database that has the word 'Washington' within the CITY field." Enter the following:

```
CHANGE FIELD ZIP FOR CITY = 'Washington'
```

Record 2 is the first record containing Washington. Notice that dBASE only displays the field that will be changed.

The cursor is flashing at the first character, so you can enter 20003-0298 as the new ZIP code for record 2. After you have pressed the RETURN key, you'll see record 8. Enter 20009-0101 and the prompt will reappear. To see the results, enter

```
LIST LASTNAME,CITY,ZIP
```

and the new ZIP codes for the Washington, D.C., tenants will be displayed.

Record#	lastname	city	zip
1	Morse	Chevy Chase	20815-0988
2	Levy	Washington	20003-0298
3	Jackson	Falls Church	22044
4	Westman	Silver Spring	20910-0124
5	Mitchell	Arlington	22203
6	Hart	Fairfax	22025
7	Robinson	Takoma Park	20912
8	Robinson	Washington	20009-0101
9	Jones	Reston	22090

REPLACE operates very much like CHANGE except that REPLACE won't ask you to type in the change after it finds the field; instead you specify the change within the command and it

will be made automatically. The format of the command is
REPLACE [*scope*] *fieldname* WITH *'field-replacement'* FOR *key-field = 'keyword'*. *Scope* is optional and is used to determine how
many records REPLACE will look at. If ALL is used as the *scope*,
REPLACE will look at all records; but if NEXT 5 is used as the
scope, REPLACE will look at only the next 5 records from the
pointer's current position. NEXT is always followed by the
number of records REPLACE will look at. *fieldname* is the field
where the change will occur, and *'field-replacement'* is what will be
inserted if *keyfield*, which is the field REPLACE is searching for,
matches *'keyword'*. There is plenty going on with REPLACE, so it
might be best described by an example. Enter the following:

```
REPLACE ALL CITY WITH 'Miami' FOR CITY = 'Washington'
```

This means "Search for all city fields containing the word
'Washington' and then replace those fields with the word 'Miami'."
When the prompt reappears, enter

```
LIST LASTNAME,CITY
```

You'll see that all of the Washington residents have been relo-
cated to Miami. They probably would not enjoy the commute to
work, so let's move them back. Enter the command

```
REPLACE ALL CITY WITH 'Washington' FOR CITY = 'Miami'
```

Again enter

```
LIST LASTNAME,CITY
```

Now the CITY field is correct. As you work with dBASE III
PLUS, you'll find that REPLACE is a handy command for changing area codes, ZIP codes, and other similar applications. But you
should be careful: REPLACE has the potential to wreak havoc on a
database if used improperly. If you doubt whether REPLACE will

have the desired effect, make a copy of the database file under a different name and experiment on the copy instead of the original. REPLACE can be selected from the Update menu of the Assistant. CHANGE, however, is not available from the Assistant; the CHANGE command must be executed from the dot prompt.

MODIFYING THE STRUCTURE
OF A DATABASE

You'll often use a database for a while and then decide to enlarge a field, delete a field, or add a field for another category. You can make these changes in the structure of a database. From the dot prompt this is done with the MODIFY STRUCTURE command. From the Assistant menus this is done by selecting the Database File option of the Modify menu. When you change the structure of a database, dBASE III PLUS copies the entire database into a temporary file and then modifies the database according to your instructions.

Before you use this command, be sure that there is room on the disk for a copy of the database. With dBASE II it was necessary to copy the file into another file manually, modify the structure, and then copy the new file back into the original file. dBASE III PLUS does all of this automatically.

If ABC Realty's manager suddenly decides that the database should include the tenants' telephone numbers, you can add a field for them. To make this change, from the dot prompt first enter

```
MODIFY STRUCTURE
```

or, from the Assistant, choose Database File from the Modify menu, and you will see the structure of the ABC Realty database (Figure 4-5).

The first field in the structure is highlighted, indicating that dBASE III PLUS is ready to modify it. Since you want to add a

```
                                                    Bytes remaining:    3871

       Field Name  Type    Width  Dec      Field Name  Type    Width  Dec

   1  LASTNAME   Character  15
   2  FIRSTNAME  Character  15
   3  ADDRESS    Character  25
   4  CITY       Character  15
   5  STATE      Character   2
   6  ZIP        Character  10
   7  BEDROOMS   Numeric     2      0
   8  BATHROOMS  Numeric     2      0
   9  EXPDATE    Date        8
  10  PARKING    Logical     1
  11  PROPTYPE   Character  10
  12  RENTAMT    Numeric     7      2
  13  SIZE       Numeric     5      0
  14  EXTRAS     Memo       10
  15  SALESOFF   Character   2

 MODIFY STRUCTURE <C:> ABC1                  Field: 1/15
                        Enter the field name.
   Field names begin with a letter and may contain letters, digits and underscores
```

Figure 4-5. Modify the database structure

field, move the highlight past the sixth field with the ↓ key. You will enter the field name, type, and width exactly as you did when you created the database in Chapter 3, but before you do, press the F1 key. Pressing F1 displays a Help screen at the top of the display. The Help screen shows you that you can use CONTROL-N to insert a new field. Press CONTROL-N now, and a new field 7 will appear.

Since you want to enter phone numbers, the word "phone" would be a good title for the field. Enter PHONE. Once you press RETURN, the cursor will move to the type category. You want to choose C for character, so enter C. (You don't want to use N for numeric because phone numbers contain hyphens and dBASE III PLUS would try to subtract the suffix from the prefix; besides, phone numbers never figure in numeric calculations.) At the width category, enter 12. This will leave room for a ten-digit phone number plus two hyphens.

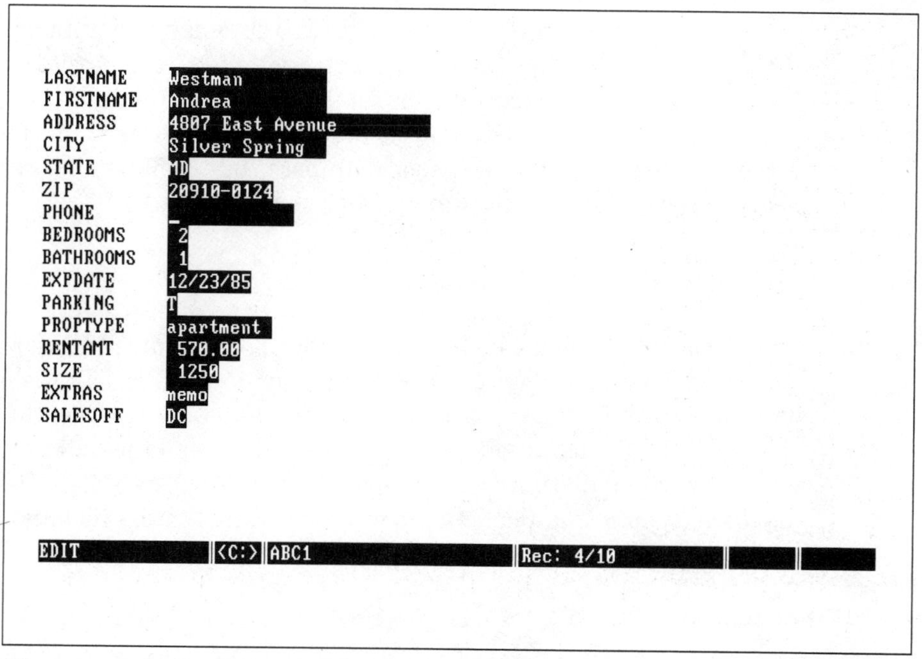

```
    LASTNAME     Westman
    FIRSTNAME    Andrea
    ADDRESS      4807 East Avenue
    CITY         Silver Spring
    STATE        MD
    ZIP          20910-0124
    PHONE
    BEDROOMS     2
    BATHROOMS    1
    EXPDATE      12/23/85
    PARKING      T
    PROPTYPE     apartment
    RENTAMT      570.00
    SIZE         1250
    EXTRAS       memo
    SALESOFF     DC




    EDIT              <C:> ABC1                    Rec: 4/10
```

Figure 4-6. Modification of ABC Realty's database includes field phone
number

The command will return the data from the fields in the temporary file to the fields in the modified database only if the field
types and names match. If you rename a field or change the type of
a field, dBASE III PLUS may not restore the data in that particular field since it doesn't always know where to find the data or how
to convert the data type. When you press CONTROL-END to save the
modified structure in this situation, you'll see the following message
at the bottom of the screen:

```
Press ENTER to confirm--any other key to resume.
Database records will be APPENDED from backup fields of the
same name only!!
```

This indicates that dBASE III PLUS is ready to copy the data
from the temporary file. Press the RETURN key, and after a short

delay (during which time dBASE III PLUS automatically rebuilds the database), you should see the dot prompt or the Assistant menu. Press ESC (if necessary) to return to the dot prompt.

Enter LIST, and the database should return to its original form. You now have a space for phone numbers, but none are shown because you haven't entered any. Enter the command

```
EDIT 4
```

This time the edit fields include a field for phone numbers (Figure 4-6). Use the arrow keys to move the cursor to the PHONE field and enter 202-525-1234. Next, press CONTROL-END to save this change and get back to the prompt. Enter LIST, and the database will show the added phone number in record 4. To complete the database, type in the phone numbers for the rest of the tenants.

```
Record#      Phone Number
1            202-525-6678
2            202-538-2916
3            202-848-8778
5            202-252-9234
6            202-634-9338
7            202-525-9144
8            202-585-4356
9            202-575-5017
```

Had this field been planned in advance during Chapter 2, you wouldn't have the inconvenience of returning to each record to type a phone number.

THE ASSISTANT

When you're on your own and don't have this book at hand, you can always call on the dBASE III PLUS Assistant to help you. Most of the Assistant's commands that relate to changing your files are contained in the Update menu. To modify the structure of a data-

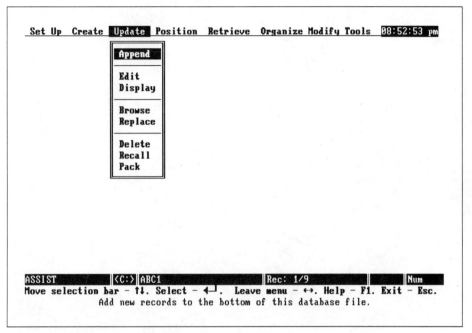

Figure 4-7. Update menu

base, you use the Database File option of the Modify menu. From the dot prompt enter

ASSIST

The Set Up menu will be highlighted. Since you want Update, press U to open the Update menu. You will see that the Update menu provides menu access to the same BROWSE, EDIT, DELETE, RECALL, PACK, and REPLACE commands that you have been using throughout this chapter (Figure 4-7).

Try selecting the various options within the Update menu, to get a feel for the use of the Assistant when changing a database. When you are done, choose QUIT from the Set Up menu to exit dBASE III PLUS.

Creating Entry Forms
With the dBASE III PLUS
Screen Painter

Chapter 5

When adding data with APPEND or making changes to a database with EDIT, you were presented with a simple on-screen entry form that listed the various fields, along with highlighted areas that contained the actual data. For the purposes of demonstrating how to add or change data within a database, this was sufficient. But there can be problems with such a straightforward approach to adding data to a database. One drawback is the unfriendly screen that this presents to the computer user. If an ABC Realty employee does not know what is meant by the word "SALESOFF" on the screen, the help screens or the dBASE manual won't offer any assistance. Another drawback is the lack of editing control offered by the EDIT command. If for any reason you wish to prevent the editing of a particular field, you cannot do so with EDIT.

To overcome such limitations, dBASE III PLUS provides a flexible entry-form builder called Screen Painter. An entry form is simply a form that appears on the screen that is used for data display and data entry. Using Screen Painter, you can build forms that resemble the printed forms commonly used in an office. You can also restrict entry by omitting certain fields while including other fields in the data-entry form; and you can tell dBASE III PLUS to use a specific form when working with a database, so that the form automatically appears when you use the APPEND and EDIT commands. Forms created with the Screen Painter can be used for the entry or the display of data in a database.

If you're not already in dBASE III PLUS, load the program and move to the Assistant menu. Choose the Database File option from the Set Up menu, and select the ABC1 database.

CREATING A DATA-ENTRY FORM

Data-entry forms can be created from the same Create menu that is used for creating a database. (From the dot prompt you can also use the CREATE SCREEN command. For the purpose of illustration, we will use the Assistant menus.) Open the Create menu, and choose the Format option.

Press RETURN to accept the chosen disk drive. dBASE III PLUS will now prompt you for the name of the file. This filename will be stored on the disk; therefore, you must follow the standard DOS rules for filenames (8 characters or less and no spaces).

Enter ABCFORM. Once you have entered the name for the form, the Screen Painter menus will replace the Assistant menu (Figure 5-1).

The Screen Painter uses a menu bar and pull-down menus similar to those used by the Assistant. The first menu, Set Up, is currently open. The Screen Painter offers four menus: Set Up, Modify, Options, and Exit. The Set Up menu lets you choose the database that will be used by the form. You can also create new databases, or load fields from the database into the form with the Set Up menu.

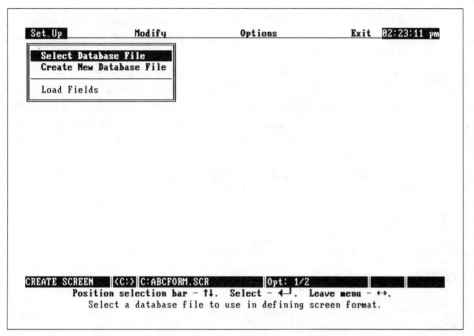

Figure 5-1. Screen Painter menus

The Modify menu allows field changes and additions to an existing form and its associated databases. The Options menu lets you add lines or boxes to a form, or create an image of the form as a text file. The Exit menu is used to save the completed form and to exit from the Screen Painter.

The first step in the process of building the form is to tell the Screen Painter which database file you will use with the form. If no database existed, you could choose the "Create New Database File" option of the Set Up menu. This option would cause dBASE III PLUS to display the same database definition screen that was used in Chapter 3 to create a new database. In this case, the database already exists; therefore, defining a new one isn't necessary.

Choose "Select Database File" from the Set Up menu. A list of available database files contained on the disk will appear. Select

ABC1. Once you have chosen the database, the next step is to load those fields that you want displayed in the form. For this, you will select the Load Fields option of the Set Up menu. A list of the fields in the ABC Realty database will appear (Figure 5-2).

The next step is to mark the fields that you wish to include within the form. Marking a field is accomplished by placing the cursor on the field name and pressing RETURN. The first field in the database, LASTNAME, is already highlighted by the cursor, so press RETURN.

The triangular symbol that appears after you've pressed RETURN

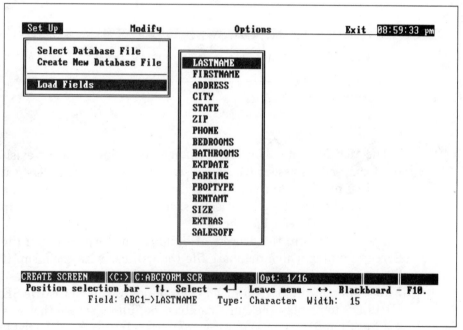

Figure 5-2. Fields for loading

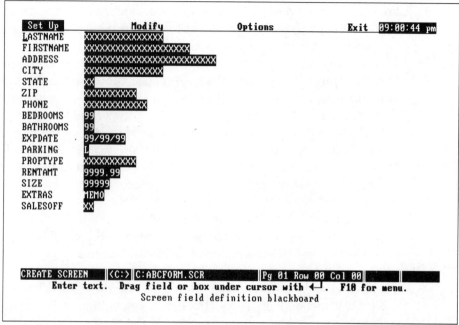

```
 Set Up              Modify           Options           Exit  09:00:44 pm
LASTNAME    XXXXXXXXXXXXXX
FIRSTNAME   XXXXXXXXXXXXXXXXXXX
ADDRESS     XXXXXXXXXXXXXXXXXXXXXXXXX
CITY        XXXXXXXXXXXXXX
STATE       XX
ZIP         XXXXXXXXXX
PHONE       XXXXXXXXXXX
BEDROOMS    99
BATHROOMS   99
EXPDATE   · 99/99/99
PARKING     L
PROPTYPE    XXXXXXXXX
RENTAMT     9999.99
SIZE        99999
EXTRAS      MEMO
SALESOFF    XX




CREATE SCREEN    <C:> C:ABCFORM.SCR        Pg 01 Row 00 Col 00
      Enter text.  Drag field or box under cursor with ◄┘.  F10 for menu.
                    Screen field definition blackboard
```

Figure 5-3. Screen Painter Blackboard

indicates that the field is marked for inclusion within the form.
For this example, you want to mark all of the fields for inclusion
within the entry form. Therefore, move the cursor to each field
name, and press RETURN until all of the fields have been marked.

The message shown on the message line at the bottom of the
screen indicates that you can press the ← or → key to leave the
menu, once all of the desired fields have been marked. Press the ←
or → key once. The selected fields, plus areas for data entry, will
now appear on a screen known as the Blackboard (Figure 5-3).

The Blackboard is a work area where you can draw your desired
entry form. Fields can be moved around, lines and borders can be

added, and more descriptive names can be entered to describe the fields. You can move back and forth between the Blackboard and the Screen Painter menus by pressing F10.

When you first load fields into a form and begin using the Screen Painter Blackboard, the field names appear at the left side of the screen. The highlighted areas that appear to the right of the field names represent the actual fields. It is important to recognize the difference between actual fields and field names, as the Screen Painter's Modify menu offers options that apply only to the fields. On your screen, the word "LASTNAME" is a field name, not a field. The first highlighted letter X to the right of the LAST-NAME label marks the start of the actual field. The characters in these highlighted areas represent the types of data that will appear in those fields when you use the completed form. The letter X is used to indicate a character field; the number 9 is used to indicate a numeric field; the number 9 with a slash indicates a date field; the letter L indicates a logic field; and the word "memo" indicates a memo field. The status bar at the bottom of the screen tells you the row and column position of the cursor while you are working within the Blackboard. Cursor movement is performed with the same editing keys used by the APPEND and EDIT functions.

Try pressing the INS (INSERT) key repeatedly. As you do so, note that the word "Ins" appears and disappears from the status bar. Pressing the INS key moves you in and out of insert mode. When you are in insert mode, all characters that you type are added to the existing text at the cursor location. When you are out of insert (and in the overwrite mode), all characters that you type replace any existing characters.

The cursor is currently at the L in LASTNAME. The form would look less cluttered if there were open space at the top of the screen, so press the INS key until you are in the insert mode. Then, press RETURN three times to insert three blank lines at the top of the screen. This step will provide space at the top of the form for a descriptive title later.

Move the cursor to the letter B in the field name BEDROOMS, and press RETURN once to insert a blank line between the phone and bedrooms fields.

Next, let's use the Screen Painter to add a descriptive title to our form. Move the cursor to row 1, column 20. (Remember, the position of the cursor is indicated by the status bar.) Then enter the title: ABC Realty Company Data Entry Form.

MOVING FIELDS

The form is already starting to look better, but there are further changes that would improve its appearance. A sensible arrangement would be to place the last and first names of tenants on the same line. You can easily move a field by placing the cursor at the beginning of the field, pressing RETURN, placing the cursor in a new location, and pressing RETURN again. For example, place the cursor at the start of the FIRSTNAME field (the first letter X within the highlighted block). Once the cursor is at the first character within the field, press RETURN. The message below the status bar now indicates that you can use the cursor keys to reposition the cursor. Press RETURN to complete the movement of the field.

Move the cursor to row 3, column 50. This location will leave sufficient room to add the field name. Press RETURN and the field will be moved to the new location (Figure 5-4). When moving fields to new locations, you must be careful to measure whether there is sufficient room to fit the entire field at the screen location that you choose. If, for example, you attempt to place a field that is 20 characters long at column 62, the Screen Painter will cut off the display of the last two characters, because the screen ends at the 80th character position.

A field name is needed for the repositioned field, so place the cursor at row 3, column 40. Press the INS key until you are in overwrite mode, and type FIRSTNAME. Then move the cursor to

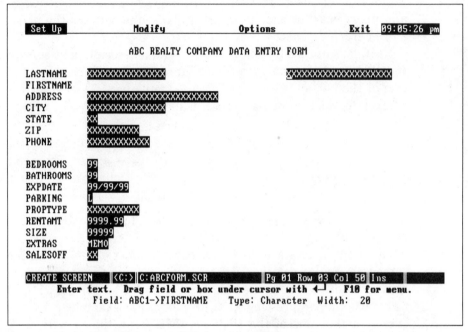

Figure 5-4. New location of firstname field

the start of row 4 and use the DEL (DELETE) key to delete the earlier FIRSTNAME field name.

To reduce the visual clutter still present in the form, let's move the memo field, EXTRAS, to the right side of the form. Place the cursor at the start of this field (the letter M in "MEMO") and press RETURN. Then move the cursor to row 10, column 50, and press RETURN again to reposition the field.

To add a field name, move the cursor to row 10, position 40. Press the INS key until you are in overwrite mode, and type the word "EXTRAS". Then move the cursor to the previous field name, EXTRAS, and use the DEL key to remove that name.

One benefit of the Screen Painter is its ability to add descriptive messages to a form. ABC Realty employees may not instinctively understand how to enter data in the memo field. To add an explanation, move the cursor to row 11, column 30, and type the following message:

```
(Control-PgDn to add text; Control-End saves.)
```

Finally, some of the field names could use clarification. It may not be clear to new users what the names EXPDATE, SALES-OFF, and PROPTYPE refer to. The Screen Painter lets you change the labels that refer to the names of the fields. Changing these labels does not change the actual names of the fields within the database. To change the labels on the form, you can type over them (when in the overwrite mode), or you can use the DEL key to delete the labels and type in new ones (when in the insert mode).

Press the INS key until you are in the insert mode. (In this case, this is done as a precaution to avoid accidentally overwriting a field when you are typing new names.) Next, move the cursor to the start of the field name EXPDATE. Type the words "EXPIRATION DATE". Then, use the DEL key to delete the previous field name.

Using the same process as outlined in the previous paragraph, replace the field name PROPTYPE with the words "PROPERTY TYPE", the field name RENTAMT with the words "RENTAL AMOUNT", and the field name SALESOFF with the words "SALES OFFICE".

That looks better, but the lower half of the form is still somewhat cluttered. In the insert mode, you can use the spacebar to push the field names and the fields to the right; conversely, the BACKSPACE key will remove spaces, pulling the field names and fields to the left. Make sure that you are in the insert mode, and place the cursor at the start of the words "EXPIRATION DATE". Press the spacebar 30 times to move the name and the accompanying field to the right side of the screen.

Next, place the cursor at the "P" in "PARKING". Press the spacebar until the letter P in PARKING is aligned underneath the letter E in EXPIRATION.

Place the cursor at the "S" in "SIZE". Press the spacebar until the letter S in SIZE is aligned underneath the letter P in PARKING.

Finally, place the cursor at the "S" at the beginning of the word "SALES". Press the spacebar until the letter S in SALES is aligned with the letter S in SIZE. Your screen should now resemble the one shown in Figure 5-5.

Our entry form is ready for use. At the bottom of the screen, the message beneath the status bar indicates that you can use the F10 key to leave the Blackboard and return to the Screen Painter menus. Press F10, and the menus will reappear.

The choices provided within the Modify menu, which should now be on your screen, will be discussed in more detail later. For now, press E to open the Exit menu. Then, choose the Save option. The form will be saved on the disk, and the Assistant menus will reappear.

All that remains is to tell dBASE III PLUS that you want to use the form when adding and editing data. A screen form can be selected from the Set Up menu. Open the Set Up menu, and select the "Format for Screen" option. Press RETURN to accept the default disk drive, and select ABCFORM as the desired form.

Once you have made the selection, there will be no noticeable immediate change; you will be returned to the Set Up menu. From this point on, however, your custom form will be used for all functions of the APPEND and EDIT commands (until you tell dBASE III PLUS not to use that form). To see the results of your work, open the Position menu and choose the GoTo Record option. Choose this option to tell dBASE III PLUS to go to a specific record in the database. Enter 3 in response to the prompt for a numeric value. This choice will move you to record number 3 in the ABC Realty database.

Now, open the Update menu, and choose EDIT. Instead of the standard append/edit form, you will be greeted with the record displayed within the custom form that you designed with the Screen Painter. Try pressing the PG UP and PG DN keys to move around in the database. Changes can be made to any of the records with the same editing keys that are used in the APPEND and

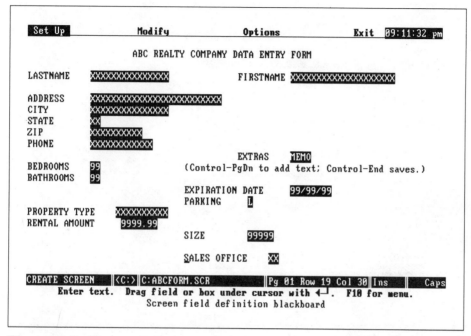

Figure 5-5. Form containing moved fields and new field labels

EDIT functions. When you are done examining the effects of the entry form, press ESC to leave the form and return to the Assistant menus.

CHANGING FIELD WIDTHS

It is possible to change field widths, on a form and within a database, from the Screen Painter. To do so, you place the Blackboard's cursor at the start of the field to be changed, and press F10 to return to the Screen Painter menu. Then you fill in the desired field widths. As an example, ABC Realty employees have been complaining that the first name field in the database is too short.

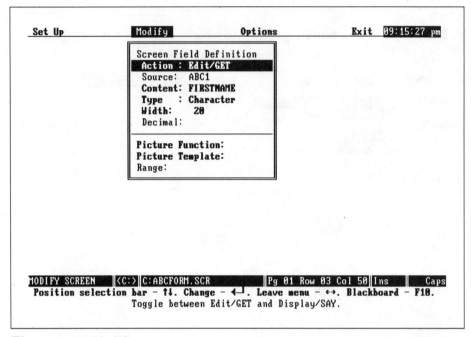

Figure 5-6. Modify menu

You want to change the width of the field, in both the entry form and in the database.

First, get back into the Screen Painter using either of these two methods. From the dot prompt, you can enter the command MODIFY SCREEN, and then respond to the prompt for the screen file-name by entering ABCFORM, the name of the form. Or, from the Assistant, open the Modify menu and select Format. Press RETURN to accept the default disk drive, and choose ABCFORM as the form to modify.

Get to the Blackboard by pressing F10. Place the cursor at the start of the FIRSTNAME field, and press F10 to return to the Screen Painter menu. The Modify menu will be open on the screen (Figure 5-6).

The Modify menu shows a number of options. All of these options are available only when the Blackboard cursor is placed on a field. The Action option indicates whether the field can be edited on the form by the user or only displayed. You can change this action by pressing RETURN. When this option is set to Edit/GET, users of the data-entry form can make changes to the data contained in the field. When this option is set to Display/SAY, users of the form can see the data, but they cannot make any changes.

The Source indicates the name of the database in use, and the Content shows the name of the chosen field. Type, Width, and Decimal show the characteristics of the field. Picture Function, Picture Template, and Range let you control how characters are entered or displayed in the field; these options will be discussed in further detail later.

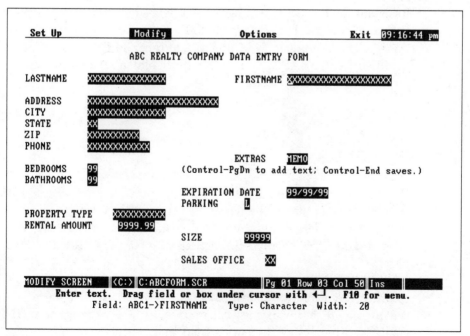

Figure 5-7. Entry form with new field width

In this case, you want to increase the width of the LASTNAME field. Select the width by highlighting the Width option and pressing RETURN. The triangular symbol will appear next to the Width option. Enter 20 for a new field width, then press F10 to return to the Blackboard. The screen now displays the longer width of the field (Figure 5-7). Once you save the changes to the form with the Save option of the Exit menu (don't do this yet), the field width will be changed within the database.

A Warning

The Modify menu of the Screen Painter can modify a database, just as the MODIFY STRUCTURE command (from the dot prompt) and the Modify/Database File menu options (from the Assistant menus) do. If you decrease a field's width, you will cut off any existing data that is too large to fit in the new, smaller field. If the field is a numeric field and the number is too large for the modified field, dBASE III PLUS will display a series of asterisks in place of the actual data.

ADDING FIELDS

You can also add fields to a form and its associated database. This is possible by entering the name for the new field, using the Content option of Screen Painter's Modify menu. As an example, you need to add a field called SALESREP to the ABC Realty database.

First, place the cursor at row 6, column 50. This empty area contains room for the placement of a new field. Where you place the cursor on the form does not matter, as long as there is sufficient room to display the entire field that you plan to add.

Press F10 to call up the Screen Painter's Modify menu. Since the Blackboard's cursor is not presently located at the start of any field, the field type and width descriptions contain no information.

Choose the Content option of the menu. After you press RETURN, a list of the fields will appear. Select NEWFIELD to tell Screen Painter that you want to create a new field.

Enter SALESREP as the new field name. dBASE III PLUS will modify the database, adding the new field. For field type, dBASE III PLUS will add a character field, with a width of one character. One character won't store any names of ABC's sales representatives, so you will want to change this width. Select the Width option, and enter 15 for the width of the field. Your screen should resemble Figure 5-8.

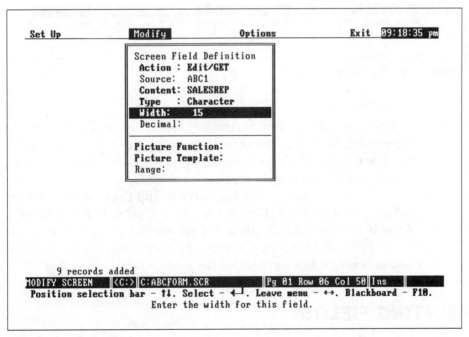

Figure 5-8. Screen field definition

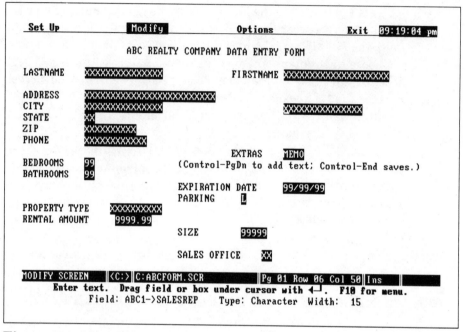

```
   Set Up          Modify          Options          Exit  09:19:04 pm
                ABC REALTY COMPANY DATA ENTRY FORM

   LASTNAME    XXXXXXXXXXXX          FIRSTNAME  XXXXXXXXXXXXXXXXXX

   ADDRESS     XXXXXXXXXXXXXXXXXXXXXXXXXX
   CITY        XXXXXXXXXXXXX               XXXXXXXXXXXXX
   STATE       XX
   ZIP         XXXXXXXXX
   PHONE       XXXXXXXXXXX
                                EXTRAS     MEMO
   BEDROOMS    99         (Control-PgDn to add text; Control-End saves.)
   BATHROOMS   99
                                EXPIRATION DATE    99/99/99
                                PARKING       L
   PROPERTY TYPE    XXXXXXXXX
   RENTAL AMOUNT    9999.99
                                SIZE       99999

                                SALES OFFICE    XX

   MODIFY SCREEN   <C:> C:ABCFORM.SCR        Pg 01 Row 06 Col 50 Ins
        Enter text.  Drag field or box under cursor with ←┘.  F10 for menu.
            Field: ABC1->SALESREP    Type: Character  Width:  15
```

Figure 5-9. New field on form

The Type option shows "character" as the field type. Since this is acceptable, leave it unchanged. If you wished to change the type of field, you could select the type and press the RETURN key to choose among the available field types.

Press F10 to return to the Blackboard, and the new field will be displayed on the form (Figure 5-9). At this point, the addition of a label is all that would be needed if you wanted to use the new field with the form. In this case, there is no need to add a label, because you will delete this field under the next topic.

DELETING FIELDS

Screen Painter provides the ability to delete unwanted fields. You are given the choice of removing the field from the form only or removing it from both the form and its associated database. Deleting a field is done by placing the Blackboard cursor on the field, and pressing CONTROL-U.

Since the cursor is presently positioned on the new field, press CONTROL-U now. dBASE III PLUS will ask:

```
Do you wish to also delete field from database? [Y/N]
```

In this case, you wish to remove the field from both the form and the database, so confirm your choice by pressing Y. dBASE III PLUS will delete the field from the form and the database. Obviously, this is a potentially destructive choice of commands that should be used with care. Once you remove a field from a database, any existing data contained within that field is lost.

Press F10 to return to the menu, and select Exit. Choose Save to save your modified form (remember, it does have a changed field width for the FIRSTNAME field). To see the difference in the field width, open the Update menu and choose Edit; the new form will appear, containing a record in the ABC Realty database.

CHANGING THE DISPLAY
CHARACTERISTICS
OF A FIELD

Using the Modify menu of Screen Painter, you can change the manner in which data is displayed in a field. You can also limit the user's ability to edit particular fields. These changes are possible with the Action, Picture Function, Picture Template, and Range options of the Modify menu.

The Action option indicates whether the field can be edited on the form by the user or is a display-only field. You can change this action by pressing RETURN when Action is highlighted. To see how this option is used, consider this example: All employees of ABC Realty shouldn't be permitted to make changes to the address of a rental property. Tenants may change, but houses and condos move only under the most unusual circumstances. If a house is sold, you want to be able to remove it from the database, but you want to restrict access to address changes. The Action option provides an ideal way to do this.

If necessary, press ESC to return to the Assistant. Open the Modify menu and select Format. Press RETURN to accept the default disk drive, and choose ABCFORM as the form to modify. Press F10 to return to the Screen Painter Blackboard.

Place the cursor on the ADDRESS field, and press F10. The Action option on the Modify menu should be highlighted. Pressing RETURN will switch the option between Display/SAY and Edit/GET, so press RETURN until Display/SAY appears (Figure 5-10).

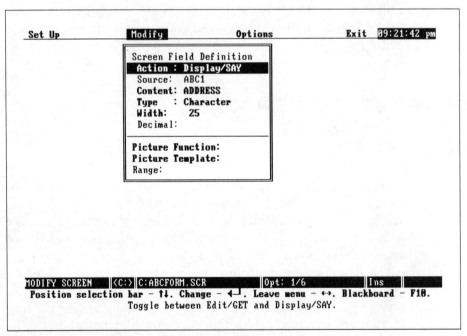

Figure 5-10. Modify menu with Display/SAY option selected

Press F10 to return to the Blackboard. You will see that the ADDRESS field is shown, but not highlighted. This means that users of the entry form will be able to see the data in the ADDRESS field, but they will not be able to edit that data.

Move the cursor to the CITY field, and press F10. Again, change the Action option to Display/SAY; then press F10 to return to the Blackboard. Repeat these steps for the STATE and ZIP fields.

To see the result, press F10 until the Screen Painter menu appears. Choose Exit and then Save, to save the modified form. When the Assistant reappears, open the Update menu and choose Edit. A record will appear, but you will not be able to edit the ADDRESS, CITY, STATE, or ZIP fields within that record. Press ESC when you're done, to return to the Assistant.

USING THE PICTURE FUNCTION, PICTURE TEMPLATE, AND RANGE

The Picture Function and Picture Template options are used to format the manner in which data is displayed on the form. With these options, you can display all characters as uppercase letters, or you can display dates in American or European date format. You can also use these options to restrict the way data can be entered into the system. You can accept letters only or numbers only; and with numeric fields, you can specify a range of acceptable numbers.

The Picture Function option is used to restrict entry to letters, to identify any lowercase to uppercase conversion of data from the database, and to format an entry (when used in combination with the Picture Template option). For example, you might wish to convert all characters entered in the LASTNAME field to uppercase letters. Open the Modify menu, choose Format, accept the disk drive, and select ABCFORM to get back to the Screen Painter. Press F10 to get to the Blackboard.

Move the cursor to the start of the LASTNAME field, and press

F10 to return to the Screen Painter's Modify menu. Choose Picture Function. Another menu appears (Figure 5-11), highlighting the available choices. The choices identified are explained in Table 5-1. The ! choice is used to tell dBASE III PLUS that all characters entered into this field will be converted to uppercase.

Type an exclamation point (!) and press RETURN to choose the uppercase conversion option of Picture Function. Next, you will choose an option for Picture Template.

Picture Template lets you choose what types of data users of the form will see and be allowed to enter. Picture Template also lets you format a field by adding special characters, as described in Table 5-1. As an example, you could use Picture Template to cause all phone numbers in a database to be displayed with a parenthesis

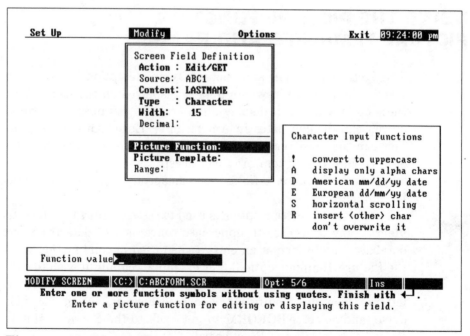

Figure 5-11. Picture Function options

and a hyphen, such as (202)555-1212. The parentheses and hyphens would not be contained in the database, but they would appear within the form. To try using Picture Template, select the Picture Template option now. Another menu appears (Figure 5-12), displaying the available choices with Picture Template. (These options are also described in Table 5-1.) The "A" choice allows entry of letters only. For a field that is to contain only names, this sounds

Table 5-1. Functions and Templates Used With Picture From Assistant

		Functions
Symbol		**Meaning**
!		Converts letters to uppercase
A		Displays alphabetic characters only
D		Displays American date format
E		Displays European date format
S		Allows horizontal scrolling of characters
R		Allows entry into a field without overwriting special characters contained in an associated picture template

		Templates
Symbol		**Meaning**
A		Allows only letters
L		Allows only logical data (true/false, yes/no)
N		Allows only letters and digits
X		Allows any character
Y		Allows Y or N
#		Allows only digits, blanks, periods, and signs
9		Allows only digits for character data, or digits and signs for numeric data
!		Converts letters to uppercase
other		Used to format the entry, such as with hyphens and parenthesis to format a phone number [example: (999)999-9999]

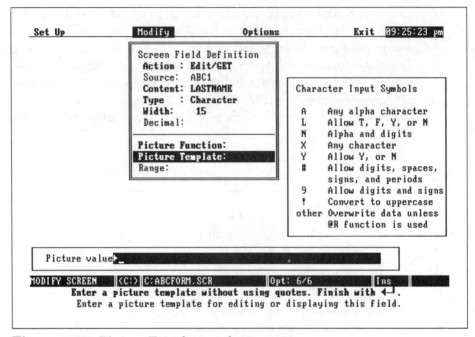

Figure 5-12. Picture Template options

reasonable; therefore, create a template for the entry of letters only by entering the letter A, 15 times. (When creating a template, the template character must be entered once for each desired position in the field; hence, you will need the letter A in each of the 15 spaces.)

Press F10 to return to the Blackboard, and move the cursor to the RENTAMT field. You will use the Range option to specify the dollar amounts that will be accepted as a minimum rental amount.

Press F10 to return to the Modify menu, and select the Range option. A window appears (Figure 5-13), asking you to specify a lower and upper limit for the range of acceptable numbers. Press RETURN to select the lower limit option. ABC Realty management has decided to rent no property for under $400 per month, so enter 400. Then choose the upper limit option, and enter 2000. Finally, press ESC to finish specifying your Range options.

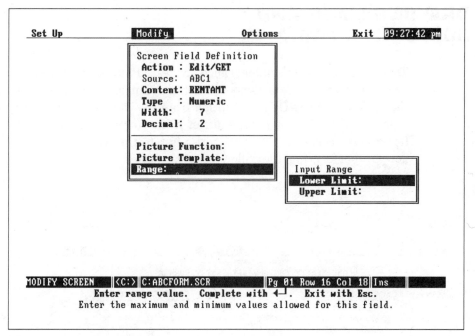

Figure 5-13. Range options

Select Exit from the Screen Painter menu, and choose Save to save the modified form. When the Assistant reappears, open the Update menu and choose Edit. You will note that all letters in the LASTNAME field are stored and displayed as uppercase letters. For the sake of uniformity, this use of Picture Template can be a noticeable help when using dBASE III PLUS. dBASE III PLUS is case-specific, meaning that it considers uppercase letters to be a value different from lowercase letters. Rather than risk having some users of a database enter data in all lowercase letters while others enter the data in uppercase letters, you can design an entry form that forces all users to add character data in uppercase letters only.

Try entering an amount of $350.00 for the monthly rent. An error message showing the acceptable range will be displayed in the message line when you try to do this. Press ESC when you are finished, to cancel the changes and return to the Assistant.

DRAWING LINES AND
BOXES ON A FORM

To improve a form's appearance, Screen Painter allows you to draw lines and borders composed of lines. This is done by selecting the "Draw Window Or Line" option from the Options menu and by marking the left and right sides of a line (or the upper-left and lower-right corners of a box). Add a box to the ABC Realty form now by performing the following steps: Open the Modify menu,

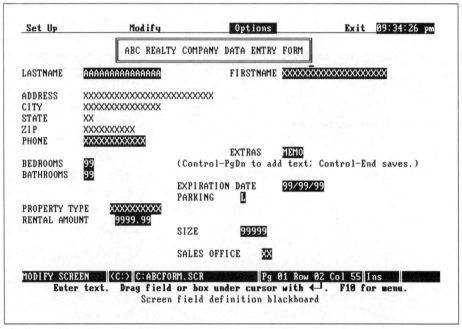

Figure 5-14. Heading with border

choose Format, accept the disk drive, and select ABCFORM to get back to the Screen Painter. Next, open the Options menu, and choose the Double Bar option underneath the "Draw a Window or Line" selection.

The message in the message line now asks you to position the cursor at the box corner. Place the cursor just above and to the left of the heading, "ABC Realty Company Data Entry Form". Press RETURN to mark this corner of the box.

The message line now asks you to position the cursor at the other corner. Place the cursor below and to the right of the word "Form" in the heading, and press RETURN to mark this corner. A double-line border will appear surrounding the heading (Figure 5-14).

To draw a line, you would simply place the cursor on the same line when marking the corners, and a single line instead of a box would then be drawn by the Screen Painter. If you decide that you don't like the appearance of a box or a line, you can delete it by placing the cursor on any part of the line and by pressing CONTROL-U. Press F10 now to leave the Blackboard. Then, select Exit from the Screen Painter menu, and choose Save to save the modified form and return to the Assistant.

A Note About Boxes, Lines And Your Printer

If you use the SHIFT-PRTSCR key to print screen images to your printer, any form containing lines or boxes created by Screen Painter may not print out as you might expect. In most cases, the lines on the form will print as alphabetic characters on your printer. Only printers that can print the IBM Extended Graphic Character set will print these lines as they actually appear on a form.

A Note About Files

Screen Painter builds two files for each form that you create. One file has an extension of .SCR. dBASE III PLUS uses this file to build the actual form. The other file has an extension of .FMT. This file can be used within a dBASE III PLUS program or command file, a subject that will be discussed in a later chapter. If you choose the "Generate Text File Image" option from the Screen Painter's Options menu, Screen Painter will create a file with a .TXT extension. This file is a text file, containing the field definitions and screen locations for the form. This file can be read, edited, and printed by most word processors.

Sorting and Indexing
Your Database

Chapter 6

After a database is built, you may need to arrange it in different ways. In the ABC1 database, for example, ABC's real-estate agents might want to refer to the listing by rental cost. The accounting department might desire a list in alphabetical order by last names, while the billing department might need the list in order of ZIP codes, as the Post Office offers discounts for mail presorted by ZIP codes. You can arrange a database in a number of different ways by using the SORT and INDEX commands.

In this chapter, most commands will be executed from the dot prompt, rather than through the Assistant. Not all sorting and indexing commands are available from the Assistant. While you will be using commands from the dot prompt through most of this chapter, alternative methods of use with the Assistant will also be described.

SORTING

When dBASE III PLUS sorts a database, it creates a new file with a different filename. If you were to sort a database of names in alphabetical order, the new file would contain all the records that were in the old file, but they would be arranged in alphabetical order (Figure 6-1).

The format for the SORT command is SORT ON *fieldname* [A/D] TO *new-filename*. First, load the program and get to the dot prompt. Then, set dBASE III PLUS to use the appropriate drive (SET DEFAULT TO B: or C:) and then open ABC1 (USE ABC1). The SORT command then creates a new file by the name of *new-filename*, sorted by the field that you specify. If you specify the A option, SORT will sort character fields in alphabetical order (capital letters have a higher order than their counterparts), or numeric fields in numerical order. If you use the D option, SORT will sort character fields in descending order — Z to A — or numeric fields from highest to lowest. You can specify A or D but not both. If you do not use either A or D, dBASE III PLUS assumes that ascending order is your preference. If you sort on date fields, they will appear in chronological order. You cannot sort on logical fields or memo fields.

Use the SORT command to alphabetize the ABC Realty database by tenants' last names. Press ESC, if necessary, to get to the dot prompt. Before you begin to sort, make sure that dBASE III PLUS uses the appropriate drive (SET DEFAULT TO B: or C:) and that ABC1 is open (USE ABC1). Since you want the names in alphabetical order, you'll want to sort on the LASTNAME field. Enter

```
SORT ON LASTNAME TO RENTERS
```

After a few seconds dBASE III PLUS responds with the message **100% sorted**. To see the results, list the LASTNAME field in the new file with the following:

```
USE RENTERS
LIST LASTNAME
```

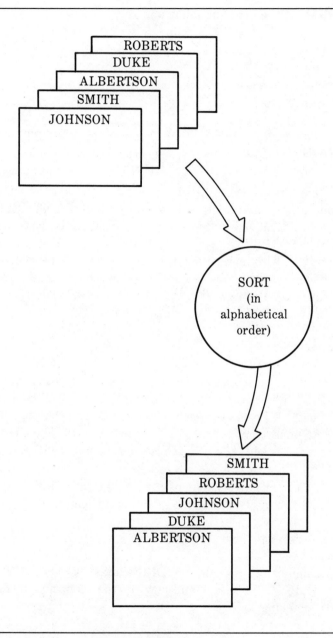

Figure 6-1. Sorting records in a database

You will then see the following:

```
Record#  lastname
      1  Hart
      2  Jackson
      3  Jones
      4  Levy
      5  Mitchell
      6  Morse
      7  Robinson
      8  Robinson
      9  Westman
```

The old file, ABC1, still exists in its unchanged form. The SORT operation has added a new file (called RENTERS) that is in alphabetical order. Remember, a file cannot be sorted unto itself in dBASE III PLUS: each time SORT is executed, a new file must be created. This new file can be temporary if desired; to save disk space, you can copy the sorted file back to the old file, and then you can erase the new file. All of this can be done without leaving dBASE III PLUS. For example, enter

```
COPY TO ABC1
```

You'll see a message warning you about overwriting the existing ABC1 file. Answer yes by pressing Y. The COPY command says, in effect, "Take the contents of the entire file that is in use (RENTERS) and copy it to the file named ABC1." The COPY operation erases the old ABC1 database file, replacing it with the RENTERS file.

Now you have two identical files, so let's eliminate the RENTERS file by using the DEL command. Enter

```
DELETE FILE RENTERS.DBF
```

Remember to include the .DBF extension.

Enter USE ABC 1 and now try the /D option on LASTNAME by entering

```
SORT ON LASTNAME /D TO RENTERS
```

To see the results, you need to list the new file you created. Enter this:

```
USE RENTERS
LIST LASTNAME
```

The results should be

```
Record#   lastname
      1   Westman
      2   Robinson
      3   Robinson
      4   Morse
      5   Mitchell
      6   Levy
      7   Jones
      8   Jackson
      9   Hart
```

Return to ABC 1 and, as an example of numerical sorting, enter

```
SORT ON RENTAMT TO RENT2
```

When the sorting process is completed, copy the temporary file back to the ABC1 file by entering

```
USE RENT2
COPY TO ABC1
```

Answer yes to the warning message about overwriting the file by pressing Y. Be sure to delete RENT2 from the disk with the DEL command and then enter

```
USE ABC1
LIST LASTNAME,RENTAMT
```

You should then see the following:

```
Record#   lastname        rentamt
      1   Robinson         425.00
      2   Jackson          570.00
      3   Westman          570.00
      4   Hart             680.00
      5   Morse            750.00
      6   Levy             875.00
      7   Robinson         920.00
      8   Mitchell         990.00
      9   Jones           1025.00
```

Now the LASTNAME field is sorted by rental costs.

When using the Assistant, the SORT command is available from the Organize menu. When you choose SORT from the menu, a list of fields will appear (Figure 6-2). You can select the field to sort on from this list. Once you have selected a field, you can press the ← or → key, and the Assistant will ask for the name of the disk drive to store the sorted file on. After the disk drive is selected, the Assistant will ask for the name of the new file. Note that the Assistant does not provide a choice of ascending or descending order. All sorts done with the Assistant will be in ascending order.

You can also copy and delete files from the Assistant. These options can be found within the Tools menu; the copy option is called Copy File, and the delete option is called Erase.

Sorting on Multiple Fields

Sometimes you may need to sort on more than one field. For example, if you alphabetize a list of names that is divided into FIRSTNAME and LASTNAME fields, you would not be able to sort only on the LASTNAME field if there were three people with the last name of Williams. You would also have to sort on the FIRSTNAME field to find the correct ordering of the three Williamses. Fortunately, dBASE III PLUS can sort on more than

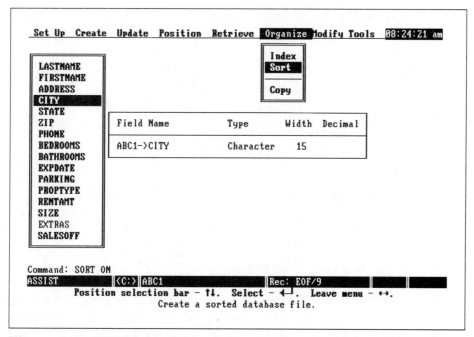

Figure 6-2. SORT from the Assistant menu

one field. From the dot prompt, this can be done by listing the fields as part of the SORT command, separating them by commas. The field that is sorted first would be listed first. From the Assistant, this is done by selecting more than one field when prompted for a choice of field to sort on.

dBASE III PLUS can also sort on both numeric and character fields at the same time. As an example, if the ABC1 database needs to be sorted by state and then for each state by rental price in descending order, you would enter

```
USE ABC1
SORT ON STATE,RENTAMT /D TO RENTERS
```

(Answer yes to the warning message about erasing the existing file.)

When the sort is complete, enter

```
USE RENTERS
COPY TO ABC1
USE ABC1
LIST STATE,LASTNAME,RENTAMT
```

The result is

```
Record#   state lastname        rentamt
      1   DC    Robinson         920.00
      2   DC    Levy             875.00
      3   MD    Morse            750.00
      4   MD    Westman          570.00
      5   MD    Robinson         425.00
      6   VA    Jones           1025.00
      7   VA    Mitchell         990.00
      8   VA    Hart             680.00
      9   VA    Jackson          570.00
```

In this sort, STATE is the *primary field*. A primary field is the field that will be sorted first by the SORT command. After the database has been sorted by the primary field, if there is any duplicate information in the first field, SORT will sort the duplicate information by the second field listed in the command. This field is known as the *secondary field*. It is possible to sort further with additional secondary fields; you can, in fact, sort with all fields in the database. As an example, try these commands:

```
USE ABC1
SORT ON STATE,CITY,LASTNAME,RENTAMT TO MASTER
```

This will create a database called MASTER that will alphabetize records by state. Inside each group of states, cities and then tenants' last names will be sorted in alphabetical order. If there are any duplicate entries at this point, the rental amounts are sorted from highest to lowest. In this example, STATE is a primary field, while CITY, LASTNAME, and RENTAMT are all secondary fields. When the sort is complete, enter this:

```
USE MASTER
LIST STATE,CITY,LASTNAME,RENTAMT
```

The database with STATE, CITY, LASTNAME, and RENTAMT
fields will be displayed (Figure 6-3).

Sorting With Qualifiers
On a Subset of a Database

You can add a qualifying FOR statement to a SORT command.
Using this technique, you can produce a sorted file that contains
only a specific subset of the records in the database. The format for
the SORT command when used in this manner is

```
SORT ON fieldname [A/D] TO new-filename FOR condition
```

```
Record#  state  city          lastname    rentamt
   1     DC     Washington    Levy         875.00
   2     DC     Washington    Robinson     920.00
   3     MD     Chevy Chase   Morse        750.00
   4     MD     Silver Spring Westman      570.00
   5     MD     Tacoma Park   Robinson     425.00
   6     VA     Arlington     Mitchell     990.00
   7     VA     Fairfax       Hart         680.00
   8     VA     Falls Church  Jackson      570.00
   9     VA     Reston        Jones       1025.00
```

Figure 6-3. Alphabetized ABC1.DFB by LASTNAME and FIRSTNAME

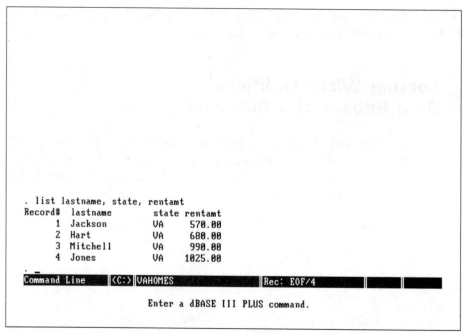

```
. list lastname, state, rentamt
Record#  lastname      state rentamt
      1  Jackson       VA     570.00
      2  Hart          VA     680.00
      3  Mitchell      VA     990.00
      4  Jones         VA    1025.00
. _
```

Command Line |<C:>|VAHOMES |Rec: EOF/4 | | |

Enter a dBASE III PLUS command.

Figure 6-4. Results of a conditional SORT

As an example, to produce a new database sorted by rental
amounts and containing only those records with Virginia addresses,
try the following commands:

```
SORT TO VAHOMES ON RENTAMT FOR STATE = "VA"
USE VAHOMES
LIST LASTNAME, STATE, RENTAMT
```

The display (Figure 6-4) shows the result of using a qualifying
FOR condition. The new database contains only the records of rentals located in Virginia.

More examples of conditional use of the SORT command include

```
SORT TO RENTS ON LASTNAME, RENTAMT FOR RENTAMT <= 600

SORT TO SPECZIP ON ZIP FOR ZIP <= "30000"
```

You cannot perform this type of conditional sort from the Assistant.

Why Sort?

Now that you've learned all about sorting with dBASE III PLUS, you should know why you should not sort a database, at least not very often. Sorting with dBASE III PLUS is relatively fast and provides a great improvement in speed over dBASE II. Still, sorting can be very time consuming, particularly when you are sorting large files. Sorting uses a lot of disk space. Each time a sort occurs, dBASE III PLUS creates a new file that will be as large as the original. For this reason, you must limit the database to no more than half the space on disk if you are going to sort it. This may not be a big problem for hard-disk users, but for floppy disk users it can severely limit file size.

Adding records to the database merely complicates matters. After you add records, chances are that the database must be sorted to maintain the desired order. If you are sorting multiple fields, the sorting time can become noticeable. But there is a more efficient way of arranging a database alphabetically, numerically, or chronologically—by using the INDEX command.

INDEXING

An *index file* consists of at least one field from a parent database. The field is sorted alphabetically, numerically, or chronologically, and with each entry in the field is the corresponding record number from the parent database. The record number is used to reference the record in the parent database (Figure 6-5). In effect, an index file is a virtual sort of the parent database, since none of the records in the parent database are sorted. Just as a book index is a separate section that indicates where information is located, a dBASE III PLUS index file is a separate file that contains informa-

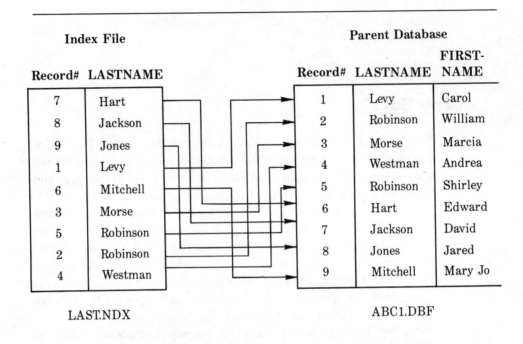

Figure 6-5. Index file alphabetized by LASTNAME (LAST.NDX) and parent directory that is organized by ZIP code

tion regarding the location of individual records in the parent database. When the database file is opened along with the index file, the first record to be retrieved is not the first record in the parent database; instead, it is the first record listed in the index. The next record retrieved will be the second record listed in the index, and so on. Remember, indexing does not affect the order of the parent database.

From the dot prompt, the general format of the INDEX command is similar to the format of the SORT command: INDEX ON *fieldname* TO *filename*. dBASE III PLUS appends the suffix .NDX to all indexed files; however, if you use the DIR command to list a directory of files on disk, index files will not be listed unless you have supplied the .NDX extension or have chosen the .NDX extension from the appropriate Assistant menu.

Suppose that you need to arrange the tenant list in alphabetical order for ABC Realty. You can create an index file with this command:

```
USE ABC1
INDEX ON LASTNAME TO NEW
```

Enter LIST LASTNAME and you will see the result of the new index file:

```
Record#  lastname
      8  Hart
      9  Jackson
      6  Jones
      2  Levy
      7  Mitchell
      3  Morse
      1  Robinson
      5  Robinson
      4  Westman
```

Notice that the record numbers are not in order.

It's good practice to name index files after the field that has been indexed. This helps you and others keep track of how the file was indexed and what field was used.

From the Assistant, the INDEX command is available within the Organize menu. Once you choose INDEX, you will be prompted for an index key. This is usually the name of the field that you wish to index on, but it can be a combination of fields. After entering a response, the Assistant asks for a drive name and the name of the index file, in a manner similar to the SORT command under the Assistant.

Indexing on Multiple Fields

You can index files based on several fields. The process is similar to sorting on multiple fields. There is a limitation, however; you cannot directly index multiple fields that are not of the same field type. For example, you could not index by LASTNAME and RENTAMT, because RENTAMT is a numeric field while LAST-NAME is a character field. There is a way to do this using special operations known as functions. This technique will be discussed later.

To see how indexing on multiple fields works and to be sure the LAST index file that you created earlier is active, look at the LASTNAME and FIRSTNAME fields by entering LIST LAST-NAME, FIRSTNAME. Now notice that Shirley Robinson is listed after William Robinson, which is not correct. Because you indexed the file on last names only, the order of first names was ignored. To rectify this situation, enter

```
INDEX ON LASTNAME+FIRSTNAME TO ALLNAMES
```

In the index file ALLNAMES, records having the same last name are now indexed by last names and then by first names. To see the results, enter

```
LIST LASTNAME,FIRSTNAME
```

The listing should be as follows:

Record#	lastname	firstname
8	Hart	Edward
9	Jackson	David
6	Jones	Jarel
2	Levy	Carol
7	Mitchell	Mary Jo
3	Morse	Marcia
5	Robinson	Shirley
1	Robinson	William
4	Westman	Andrea

You can use this multiple index technique to create an index file on any number of fields within a record. The plus (+) symbol is always used with the INDEX command to tie the fields together. For example, this INDEX command,

```
INDEX ON ZIP+LASTNAME+FIRSTNAME TO TOTAL
```

would result in a database that is indexed three ways: by ZIP codes, by last names for records having the same ZIP code, and by first names for records having the same last name. As you might expect, multiple indexes are valuable aids when you are dealing with a large database and must organize it into comprehensible subgroups.

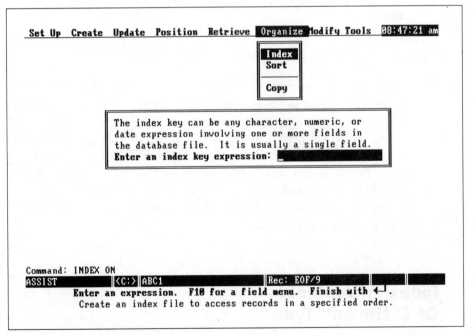

Figure 6-6. INDEX from the Assistant menu

Indexing on Multiple Fields
With the Assistant

You will need to use the same plus (+) symbol to build a list of multiple index fields if you use the Assistant to index your files. To see how this works, enter

```
ASSIST
```

and open the Organize menu. Select INDEX, and note the prompt that appears (see Figure 6-6).

What this doesn't tell you (at least, not in a clear fashion) is that in addition to entering the name of a single field, you can enter multiple fields, separated by plus signs. For example, enter the following:

```
ZIP + LASTNAME + FIRSTNAME
```

Notice that, as you enter a long character string, the characters in the window move to make room for the complete string. Once you have pressed RETURN to complete the entry, you are prompted for a disk drive on which to store the index file. Press RETURN to accept the default drive, and enter SAMPLE as the name of the index file. The new index file, sorted on the fields that you specified, will be created. You can examine the results with the List option of the Retrieve menu. When you're done, press ESC to return to the dot prompt.

Indexing on Fields
Of Different Types

One limitation of the basic use of the INDEX command, as noted earlier, is the inability to index directly on combinations of fields that are of different types. For example, you cannot index on a combination of the last name and rental amount fields in the ABC Realty database. To see the problem, at the dot prompt, try either of the following commands:

```
INDEX ON LASTNAME + RENTAMT TO TEST

INDEX ON LASTNAME + EXPDATE TO TEST
```

The resulting error message, **data type mismatch**, tells you that dBASE III PLUS cannot index on a combination of fields that are of differing data types (such as date and character fields). The secret to indexing on fields that are not of the same type is to use functions to convert fields that are not character data into character data. Functions are used to perform special operations that supplement the normal dBASE III PLUS commands. Functions will be explained in greater detail in Chapter 9. For now, it is sufficient to know about two functions: the DTOC (Date-To-Character) function and the STR (String) function. The DTOC function will convert the contents of a date field into a string of characters. The STR function will convert the contents of a numeric field into a string of characters. You can use the DTOC and STR functions in combination with your index commands to accomplish the result of indexing on combinations of different types of fields. The normal format for an index command, when combined with these functions, would be

```
INDEX ON character field + STR(numeric field) + DTOC(date field)
```

As with all index commands, you can use a combination of additional fields, in whatever order you prefer to build the index. As an example of the use of these functions, to build an index file that is indexed in alphabetical order by state, and in chronological order by date within each group of states, enter this command:

```
INDEX ON STATE + DTOC(EXPDATE) TO TEST
```

Enter LIST LASTNAME, STATE, EXPDATE to see the results of the index file. Note that you can also use these functions within the Assistant, by entering the functions along with the field names when the Assistant prompts you for the index key expression.

Using SET INDEX

In many cases you'll create and work with more than one index file for a database. But you can only work with one index file at a time, and before you can work with an index file, it must be *active*. A file that has just been created is active, and the SET INDEX command makes a dormant file active. You can only display and process data in the parent database file from the active index file.

Suppose that you need three lists from the ABC1 database. One must be selected by rental cost, another by last name, and a third by ZIP codes. You can create index files from these three fields with the following commands:

```
INDEX ON LASTNAME TO NAME
INDEX ON RENTAMT TO RENT
INDEX ON ZIP TO ZIP
```

These commands create three files on your working disk: NAME.NDX, RENT.NDX, and ZIP.NDX. Each file contains only the appropriate field from each record and the corresponding record numbers. NAME, for example, contains last names in alphabetical order and the matching record numbers for each last name. Since ZIP.NDX was the last index file created, it is the active file. By using the SET INDEX command you can activate any index file. For example, to activate and display the database organized by rental cost instead of by ZIP code, enter

```
SET INDEX TO RENT
LIST LASTNAME,RENTAMT
```

The display should appear as follows:

```
Record#  lastname          rentamt
      5  Robinson           425.00
      4  Westman            570.00
      9  Jackson            570.00
      8  Hart               680.00
      3  Morse              750.00
      2  Levy               875.00
      1  Robinson           900.00
      7  Mitchell           990.00
      6  Jones             1025.00
```

Note that you do not have to specify the .NDX extension when using the SET INDEX command.

Now try the same method to activate and display the ZIP file:

```
SET INDEX TO ZIP
LIST LASTNAME,ZIP
```

The display should appear as follows:

```
Record#  lastname          zip
      2  Levy              20003-0298
      1  Robinson          20009-0101
      3  Morse             20815-0988
      4  Westman           20910-0124
      5  Robinson          20912
      8  Hart              22025
      9  Jackson           22044
      6  Jones             22090
      7  Mitchell          22203
```

Remember, ZIP codes are stored as characters, so they will be indexed "alphabetically," not numerically, which explains why the nine-digit ZIP code is not always on the bottom of the list.

Open Files

Although you can only have one index file active at a time, you can have seven *open files*. If an index file is open, any changes you make to the parent database will automatically be updated in the index file. For example, adding a record to ABC1.DBF will place the LASTNAME field of the new record and the record number in NAME.NDX and then re-alphabetize the file, provided that NAME.NDX is open. You can open an index file with either of two commands: the USE INDEX command and the SET INDEX command. List the index files that you want opened after the USE INDEX command. For example, USE INDEX NAME,RENT will open the NAME and RENT index files. SET INDEX TO NAME, RENT will also open the NAME and RENT index files if they are not already open. You do not have to supply the .NDX extension in the command. An active index file is also an open index file, so using SET INDEX will open a file. If you list more than one file with SET INDEX, all files will be opened but only the first will be active. For example, enter

```
SET INDEX TO RENT,NAME
```

The two index files are open. Now enter LIST LASTNAME, RENTAMT and the display shows that the first index file specified (RENT) is the active file but NAME.NDX is also open. This is important if you append or edit the database, because as long as the index files are open, they will be updated automatically. See how this works by entering

```
APPEND
```

When the blank fields appear, enter the following data:

```
Roberts
Charles
247 Ocean Blvd.
Vienna
VA
22085
703-555-1234
3
2
05/01/86
N
Condo
520.00
1100
memo      (no memo: just press ENTER)
DC
```

To save the new record, press CONTROL-END after entering the data for the last field. Now enter this command again:

```
LIST LASTNAME,RENTAMT
```

The index file now includes the new entry. This brings up an important point: whenever you make changes or add records to a database, dBASE III PLUS will automatically update all open index files, and this may slow down the entire operation, particularly if more than one index file is open at once. If you wish, you can close all open index files with the CLOSE INDEX command.

Using **REINDEX**

If you changed a database and didn't remember to open an index file, you can update the index file with the REINDEX command. You will want to do this with the ZIP index file, for example; because you did not open the ZIP index file, it does not include the newly added record. You can verify this by using the ZIP index and looking at the names in the database. Enter the following:

```
SET INDEX TO ZIP
LIST LASTNAME
```

As you can see, the name Roberts does not appear in the database because the ZIP index file was not open when you added the record:

```
Record#    lastname
      2    Levy
      1    Robinson
      3    Morse
      4    Westman
      5    Robinson
      8    Hart
      9    Jackson
      6    Jones
      7    Mitchell
```

To update an index that was not open at the time you added or edited records, you must use the REINDEX command. Try the command now by entering the following:

```
REINDEX
```

To display the updated result, enter LIST LASTNAME.

```
Record#   lastname
     2    Levy
     1    Robinson
     3    Morse
     4    Westman
     5    Robinson
     8    Hart
     9    Jackson
    10    Roberts
     6    Jones
     7    Mitchell
```

The Roberts entry is now in the indexed ZIP file. Mr. Roberts is no longer needed in the database. Enter DELETE RECORD 10 and PACK to remove him from the list. Since the ZIP index file is open, Roberts' ZIP code will be removed.

Using **CLOSE INDEX**

If you decide that you do not want to use any index file, the CLOSE INDEX command will close the index file, while leaving the associated database open. To execute the command from the dot prompt, you enter

```
CLOSE INDEX
```

Note that the REINDEX and CLOSE INDEX commands are not available through the Assistant menus. To reindex an index file from the Assistant, you could choose the INDEX option of the Organize menu and create a new index file with the same name as the old index file. (On large databases, this is slower than using REINDEX from the dot prompt.) To close an index file, you could choose the Database File option of the Set Up menu and open the same database file a second time. But this time, you would answer "N" for no to the "Is the file indexed?" prompt. This would cause dBASE III PLUS to reopen the database without opening any associated index files.

Searching for Specifics

You can use two additional dBASE III PLUS commands with indexed files: FIND and SEEK. These commands quickly find information in an indexed file. Both commands operate only on an active index file. The format for FIND is FIND *character-string*, where *character-string* is a group of characters that do not have to be surrounded by quote marks. The format for SEEK is SEEK *expression. expression* can be a number, a character string (which must be surrounded by either single or double quotes), or a variable (variables are discussed in Chapter 9).

FIND and SEEK will search the active index file and find the first record that matches your specifications. The record itself will not be displayed; the FIND and SEEK commands will simply locate the record pointer at the desired record. If no match is found, dBASE III PLUS will respond with a **No find** error message. To try the FIND command, enter

```
SET INDEX TO NAME
FIND Westman
DISPLAY
```

The result is

```
Record#  LASTNAME      FIRSTNAME      ADDRESS...
     4   Westman       Andrea         4807 East Avenue...
```

To try the SEEK command, enter

```
SET INDEX TO RENT
SEEK 920
DISPLAY
```

The result is

```
Record#  LASTNAME      FIRSTNAME      ADDRESS...
     2   Robinson      William        1607 21st Street NW
```

The FIND and SEEK commands offer the advantage of speed over the LOCATE command (as discussed in Chapter 4). LOCATE is simple to use, but slow. In a database containing thousands of records, the LOCATE command can take several minutes. The FIND or SEEK command can accomplish the same task in a matter of seconds. You should keep in mind that the FIND command searches for an exact match, in terms of the character string entered. For example, if the ABC Realty database index is set to NAME, the following commands:

```
FIND Wes
```

```
FIND Westman
```

would both find the record for Westman. However, the following command:

```
FIND wes
```

would not find the record, because dBASE III PLUS considers uppercase and lowercase letters to be different characters. As far as dBASE III PLUS is concerned, "Westman" and "westman" are different names. One way of preventing problems with the case significance of dBASE III PLUS is to design entry forms with the Screen Painter that store your character data in all uppercase letters. Another method is to use a dBASE III PLUS function known as the UPPER function. The use of this function will be discussed in a later chapter.

WHEN TO INDEX, WHEN TO SORT

Sorting and indexing are commonly used to examine and set up files for the best retrieval of data by dBASE III PLUS programs. Sorting a file always creates a rearranged copy of the active database file. Sorting has two advantages over indexing. First, files can be sorted in either ascending or descending order, while indexes are always sorted in ascending order. Second, multiple fields of different field types can be sorted, while indexing with multiple fields works only when field types are the same or when special functions are used within the commands. One of the advantages of indexing is that it creates much smaller files than sorting does, and no rearranging of the database is necessary.

Creating Reports

The information you retrieve from a database is generated in the form of a report. dBASE III PLUS offers two ways of printing reports on paper: one is to use dBASE III PLUS's sophisticated built-in report generator to create custom reports; the other uses a combination of the LIST and DISPLAY commands to print specific information. Both methods will be explored in this chapter. Before going any further, be sure that your printer is turned on and ready; otherwise, you may lock up your system when trying to print.

USING LIST WITH PRINTERS

The LIST command is useful for printing data as well as examining data on the screen. The SET PRINT command directs all output to the printer as well as the screen for all subsequent LIST commands, while SET PRINT OFF stops output from being sent to the printer. To use these commands, use the ABC1 file on the appropriate drive (SET DEFAULT TO B: or C: and USE ABC1) and from the dot prompt enter

```
SET PRINT ON
LIST LASTNAME
```

Anything that you type with SET PRINT on will be directed to the printer, including all commands that you type and any error messages. Enter

```
SET PRINT OFF
```

to turn off the output to the printer.

A more precise method of directing output to the printer is to use the TO PRINT option with the LIST command. The normal format of the command is LIST *fieldname* TO PRINT. Enter

```
LIST LASTNAME TO PRINT
```

to print all last names in the ABC1 database. Even if you specify conditions within the LIST command, you can still send output to the printer with TO PRINT. For example,

```
LIST LASTNAME, FIRSTNAME, CITY FOR LASTNAME = "Robinson" TO
PRINT
```

prints the last names, first names, and cities of Shirley Robinson and William Robinson. The command

```
LIST LASTNAME, CITY, STATE, RENTAMT FOR RENTAMT > 600 TO PRINT
```

provides a printed list of last names, cities, states, and rent of tenants living in units priced at over $600 per month.

```
Record#  lastname      city          state  rentamt
      1  Morse         Chevy Chase    MD     750.00
      2  Levy          Washington     DC     875.00
      5  Mitchell      Arlington      VA     990.00
      6  Hart          Fairfax        VA     680.00
      8  Robinson      Washington     DC     920.00
      9  Jones         Reston         VA     950.00
```

USING LIST WITH THE ASSISTANT

You can use the LIST command with the Assistant menus to list specific information on the printer. The LIST option of the Retrieve menu is used in the same manner as described in earlier chapters, with one difference: when asked if the output should be directed to a printer, you answer "Y" for yes. This response will produce the equivalent of the TO PRINT specification for any choices made with the Assistant menus.

As an example, to print a list of all tenant last names, cities, states, and rent amounts where the state is Maryland or D.C., you can perform the following steps. First, enter ASSIST from the dot prompt to return to the Assistant menus. Open the Retrieve menu, and choose LIST. You wish to list only four specific fields, so choose the "Construct a Field List" option. Select the LASTNAME, CITY, STATE, and RENTAMT fields, then press the ← or → key to leave this menu.

You also wish to add a search condition, so select the "Build a Search Condition" option. Choose STATE, then select "equal to," and enter MD in response to the prompt. Another condition is desired, so select "Combine with .OR." from the next menu that appears. Again, select STATE, choose "equal to," and this time, enter DC in response to the prompt.

Choose "No more conditions" to complete the command, and finally, choose the "Execute the command" option. A prompt asking whether output should be directed to the printer will appear (Figure 7-1). Enter Y, and the desired report will be printed, with the following result:

```
Record#  lastname        city            state  rentamt
      1  Robinson        Washington      DC     920.00
      2  Levy            Washington      DC     875.00
      3  Morse           Chevy Chase     MD     750.00
      4  Westman         Silver Spring   MD     570.00
      5  Robinson        Takoma Park     MD     425.00
```

When the printing of the report is completed, press any key, and the Assistant menus will reappear.

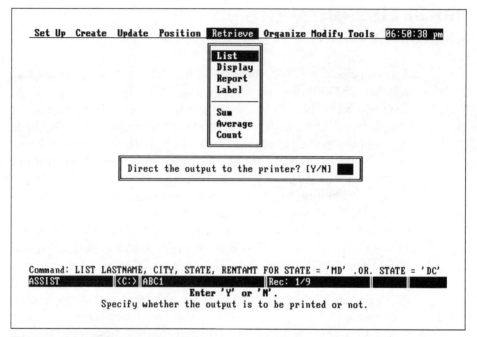

Figure 7-1. Printer prompt

MARGIN SETTINGS
AND PAGE EJECT

You can change the printer's left margin with the SET MARGIN command. dBASE III PLUS normally defaults to a printer margin value of zero. Entering SET MARGIN TO 12, for example, would cause the printer to indent 12 spaces at the beginning of each line. (This command affects only the left margin. The right margin cannot be set with a command in dBASE III PLUS.) The EJECT command causes the printer to perform a form feed, to advance to the top of the next sheet. The SET MARGIN and EJECT commands are not available from the Assistant; both must be entered from the dot prompt.

dBASE III REPORT GENERATOR

dBASE III PLUS has an automatic report generator for creating custom reports. If you have used the dBASE II or dBASE III report generator, you should take a closer look at this new version; it is quite different from the earlier versions. The dBASE III PLUS report generator has its limits, but if your reports have a fairly simple format, it can save you time and programming. Reports that consist primarily of database listings with numeric totals and simple titles and headings are the best candidates for the report generator.

The most significant limitation of the report generator is that it formats pages only one way. The page number followed by the date will always appear at the top of the page. The third through sixth lines of the report contain the heading, and the actual report begins on line 7. While subtotals can appear within the body of the report, any totals appear at the bottom of the page. A sample report created by the report generator is shown in Figure 7-2. If a report requires a complex format, it will have to be created with command files, a subject discussed in later chapters.

Planning the Report

Before starting the report generator, you should plan the design of the report. This may mean asking the other users of the database what information will actually be needed from the report. In the case of ABC Realty, you would consider what information the managers need from the report and how the report should look.

It is usually best to outline the report contents and format on paper. ABC Realty, for example, needs an income report that will display the tenant's last name, the city and state of the property, and the rental cost of the property. For state tax purposes the managers would find it helpful if the report were organized by state—Maryland properties in one group, Virginia properties in a second group, and District of Columbia properties in a third

```
Page No.       1
12/07/84
                   Metropolitan Washington Income Report
                          ABC Realty, Inc.
                          Rental Properties

Tenant              City            State         Rental
Occupying           Of              Of            Amount
Property            Property        Property


** Income by state DC
 Levy               Washington      DC             875.00
 Robinson           Washington      DC             920.00
** Subtotal **
                                                  1795.00


** Income by state MD
 Morse              Chevy Chase     MD             750.00
 Westman            Silver Spring   MD             570.00
 Robison            Takoma Park     MD             425.00
** Subtotal **
                                                  1745.00


** Income by state VA
 Jackson            Falls Church    VA             570.00
 Mitchell           Arlington       VA             990.00
 Hart               Fairfx          VA             680.00
 Jones              Reston          VA            1025.00
** Subtotal **
                                                  3265.00

*** Total ***
                                                  6805.00
```

Figure 7-2. Sample report for ABC Realty

group. Once the report has been designed, your outline should resemble the actual report that will be produced by the report generator (Figure 7-3).

Before deciding what database fields you want to include in the report, print the field names from the database as a reminder of the fields used. This can be done by entering LIST STRUCTURE

ABC Realty
Income Report

Tenant's Last Name	City	State	Rent Amount	
				Subtotal: D.C.
				Subtotal: Maryland
				Subtotal: Virginia
				Total

Figure 7-3. Designing ABC Realty's report

TO PRINT after the database file has been selected with the USE command.

Creating the Report

Once you have designed the report on paper, you use the CREATE REPORT command to start the report generator. The format of the command is CREATE REPORT *filename*, when issued from the dot prompt. From the Assistant, you can choose the REPORT option of the Create menu.

The report generator creates a special file called a *report format file*. The command will assign the extension of .FRM to *filename*. You will not normally see this file listed if you use dBASE III PLUS's directory command (DIR), but the directory will show it if you enter the DIR *.FRM command. You can produce the report at any time by using the report format file.

To start the report generator for ABC Realty, first be sure that you have ABC1 in use. Get to the dot prompt, and then enter

```
CREATE REPORT INCOME
```

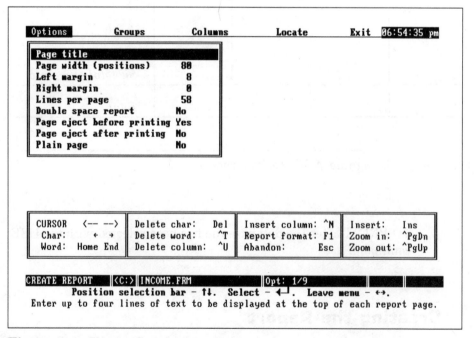

Figure 7-4. Report Generator menu

and you will see the Report Generator menu (Figure 7-4). The Report Generator menu works in a fashion similar to the Screen Painter and Assistant menus. You can open a menu by highlighting that menu's name and pressing RETURN or by pressing the first letter of the name of the menu (that is, the letter C for Columns). As you select options, various submenus will appear to guide you through the process of the creation of the report. The lower half of the screen displays a help screen listing the actions of various editing keys. Try pressing F1 repeatedly, and you will see this menu alternate with a display of the report format for the report you will create.

There are five menus within the report generator: Options, Groups, Columns, Locate, and Exit. The Options menu controls various printing specifications. The Groups menu lets you group records by particular fields within the report. The Columns menu is used to control the content and locations of the actual columns in the report. The Locate menu provides a fast way to recall a particular column within the Column menu, and the Exit menu lets you save changes to the report and exit from the report generator.

First, consider the Options menu, which is currently open. The Options menu displays the "Page title" and the formatting specifications: page width, margin settings, lines per page, and spacing (see Table 7-1). The "Page title" describes the contents of your report. It can be up to four lines in length and will always appear at the top of the printed report, unless you tell the report generator not to print it with the "Plain page" option.

The first thing you will do to the report is enter the title. Press RETURN to select the "Page title" option, and a window for the page title will appear (Figure 7-5).

The cursor is at the beginning of the "Page title" area. Enter the following, pressing the RETURN key after each line. To correct errors, use the BACKSPACE and arrow keys.

```
Metropolitan Washington
Income Report
ABC Realty, Inc.
Rental Properties
```

Table 7-1. Options

Option	Description
Page title	A descriptive title that appears at the top of the report. Up to four lines of text can be entered in the title. The title can print at the top of every report or at the top of the first page only.
Page width (positions)	Maximum characters that will appear on a printed line. The standard (default) is 80, which works with most standard-width printers. For most wide printers, use 132. Acceptable values are from 1 to 500.
Left margin	Spaces from the left side of the page to the first character. The standard (default) is eight characters.
Right margin	Spaces from the right side of the page to the last character. The standard (default) is zero characters.
Lines per page	The number of printed lines per page. When this number is reached, a PAGE EJECT command will be sent to the printer to feed a new sheet of paper. The standard (default) value is 58. Acceptable values are from 30 to 300.
Double space report	Allows printing of one extra line between each record. The standard (default) value is single spacing.
Page eject before printing	When turned on, this option sends a PAGE EJECT command to the printer. As a result, a blank sheet will feed before the report starts.
Page eject after printing	When turned on, this option sends a PAGE EJECT command to the printer upon completion of the report. As a result, a blank sheet will feed after the report is completed.
Plain page	If this option is set to "yes," page numbers and the system date are not printed at the top of each page. Also, the page title will print on the first page only. When this option is set to "no," the date, page number, and report title are printed at the top of each page. The standard (default) value is "no."

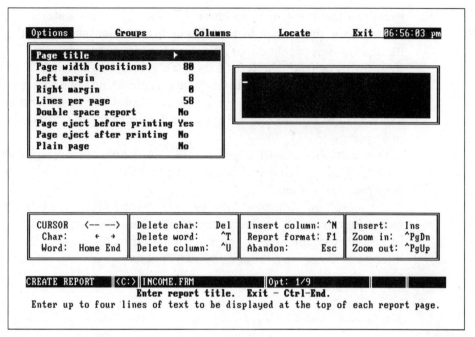

Figure 7-5. "Page title" window

Pressing RETURN on the fourth line will complete the entry for "Page title," and the window will close. You are now ready to proceed to the printing specifications.

The report generator allows you to set different printing specifications for page widths, left and right margins, number of lines per page, single or double spacing, whether page ejects should be included, and whether printing of the system date and page numbers should be included. dBASE III PLUS supplies default values for these specifications; if these values are acceptable, you can simply leave the default value unchanged for each choice.

For the sake of an example, let's change the left and right margins (default values of 8 and 0). Press the ↓ key to move the highlighted cursor to the "Left margin" option, and press RETURN to select the option. You would like a left margin of 10 instead of 8 spaces to the right of 0, so enter 10. Once you have entered the value, move the cursor to the "Right margin" option, and press RETURN to select this option. You want a right margin of no less than 5 spaces from the left of the 80th column, so enter 5. Next, you decide that 64 lines of information would fit nicely on a single page. Therefore, move the cursor to the "Lines per page" option, and press RETURN to select this option. Enter 64 for the number of lines per page.

The next option asks if you would like double spacing on this report. Single spacing will be fine, so press the ↓ key twice to proceed past this option.

The next two options, "Page eject before printing" and "Page eject after printing," specify whether a form-feed command will be sent to your printer at the start and end of the report. In the interest of saving your paper, set both options to "no." You set these

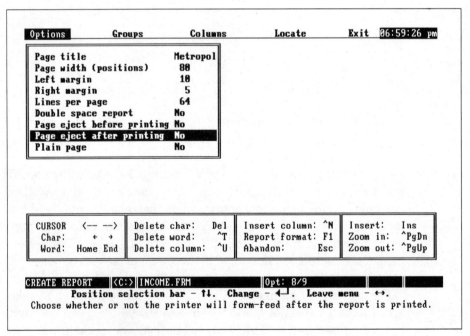

Figure 7-6. Options selected

options by highlighting the option and pressing RETURN until the word "No" appears beside the option.

The last option, "Plain page," specifies whether the report will contain page numbers and the system date at the top of the report. If this option is set to "No," the date and page numbers will appear on every page. If this option is set to "Yes," no date appears, and the title appears on the first page only. For now, leave this option set to the default (no) position. Your screen should resemble the one shown in Figure 7-6.

Once you have finished entering the printing specifications, you are ready to proceed to the Groups menu. Press the → key once to move the Groups menu (Figure 7-7). The Groups menu identifies various choices for "Group on expression" and "Subgroup on expression." These options will be used to group the records in the report, within groups identified by the name of a field that has

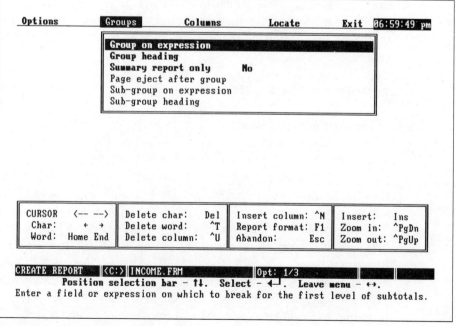

Figure 7-7. Groups menu

been indexed. Both "Group on expression" and "Subgroup on expression" are options that can be bypassed by leaving them blank.

These choices on the Groups menu specify how your report will group information and subtotal numeric data. Groups can be made from any field in your database. For example, the ABC Realty report will be grouped by states based on the STATE field in the database. In addition, each state group will have a subtotal for rental costs. The "Subgroup on expression" specification will be used to create subgroups for cities within the state groups. The report will also include subtotals for the city subgroups.

Both the state subtotals and the city subtotals are character fields; however, the actual data producing the subtotals is numeric, since it is obtained from the RENTAMT field.

The highlighted cursor is now on the "Group on expression" option. Press RETURN to select this option. Since you need subtotals of income by state, enter STATE, the field name in the database.

After you have entered the field name, move the cursor down to the next option, "Group heading." This is a printed heading that will appear at the start of each group in the report. Press RETURN to choose this option. Since the report will be grouped by states, enter

```
Income By State
```

The next option, "Summary report only," lets you choose from a full report or a summary report. A full report lists the individual items that make up the subtotals. A summary report includes the subtotals but does not list individual items. Since a full report is desired, you can leave this option set to the default value of "N," which is no.

The next option, "Page eject after group," causes a new page to begin after each subtotal when the option is set to "Yes." This isn't necessary here. So again, the default value of "No" is sufficient. The last options, "Subgroup on expression" and "Subgroup heading" will be used later. For now, you will bypass these options by pressing the → key to open the Columns menu (Figure 7-8).

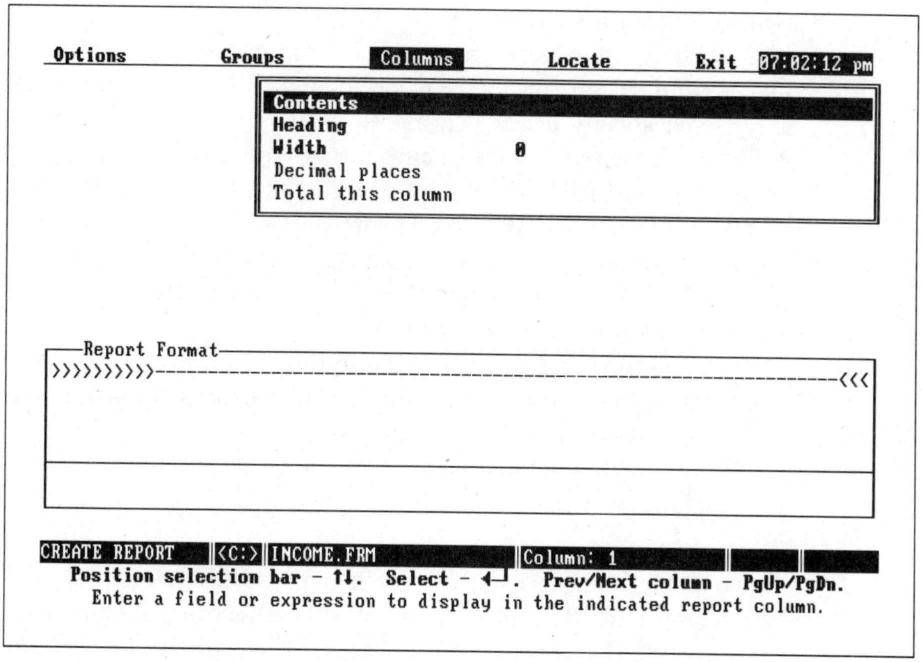

```
 Options          Groups        Columns          Locate        Exit  07:02:12 pm
                           ┌─────────────────────────────────────────┐
                           │ Contents                                 │
                           │ Heading                                  │
                           │ Width              0                     │
                           │ Decimal places                          │
                           │ Total this column                       │
                           └─────────────────────────────────────────┘




    ┌─Report Format────────────────────────────────────────────────────────┐
    │>>>>>>>>>──────────────────────────────────────────────────────────<<< │
    │                                                                        │
    │                                                                        │
    │                                                                        │
    │                                                                        │
    └────────────────────────────────────────────────────────────────────────┘
  CREATE REPORT    <C:> INCOME.FRM                Column: 1
       Position selection bar - ↑↓.  Select - ↵.  Prev/Next column - PgUp/PgDn.
       Enter a field or expression to display in the indicated report column.
```

Figure 7-8. Columns menu

You are now at the Columns menu, which is used to specify the
fields that will make up the columns of your report. The report
will contain four columns displaying the tenants' last names, cities,
states, and rental costs. The "Column: 1" notation in the status bar
at the bottom of the screen indicates that you are choosing the first
field. Because the report will have four columns, you will step
through four screens, one screen for each field. The Contents
option will identify the field that is to be placed within the particular column of the report. The Heading option is used to specify a
heading that will be placed at the top of the column; each heading
can be four lines. The Width option is used to set the width of the
column. Columns in a report can be wider or narrower than the
actual field within the database. If the column is narrower, infor-

mation within a field that is too long to fit in the report column will wrap onto succeeding lines of the report. The "Decimal places" and "Total this column" options within the menu are used only if you specify a numeric field.

The highlighted cursor should be on the Contents option. To select the field for the first column in the report, press RETURN and enter LASTNAME. The report generator checks the list of fields within the database to make sure that you have entered the field name correctly. LASTNAME has a field size of 15, so the width automatically defaults to 15.

Move the cursor to the Heading option, and press RETURN to select the option. When a window for the heading appears, enter

```
Tenant
Occupying
Property
```

Press RETURN after each word; then press RETURN to skip the fourth line and complete the entry of the heading. At this point, you have all the specifications that are needed for this column. Since this is not a numeric field, decimal places and totals will not be used. You could change the width of the column, if desired. In this case, 15 characters is plenty for this report. Note that the message line indicates that you can select the next column by pressing the PG DN key. Press PG DN now to move to the next column. When you do so, a set of blank options will appear.

Notice that below the menus is the header that you just selected for the first column, along with a row of X's. This information represents the current design of the report. As you continue to enter new columns, dBASE III PLUS will display the headers and characters representing the data to give you an idea of the final report's appearance. The second column will contain the name of the city. Press RETURN to choose the Contents option, and enter CITY. Then select the Heading option. When the heading window appears, enter

```
City
Of
Property
```

Press RETURN to skip the blank line and to complete the entry of the heading. Again, the default width of 15 (the same as the field width) is fine. Press the PG DN key to proceed to the next column.

Press RETURN to select the Contents option. Until now, you have been entering the names of the desired fields directly. However, there is another way to enter the fields, by selecting a field from a menu. Note that the message line indicates that the F10 key can be used to display a list of fields.

Press F10 now, and a field list will appear (Figure 7-9). Since STATE is the desired field for this column, highlight STATE and press RETURN. Then, press RETURN once more to accept this choice as the desired option.

Select the Heading option. When the heading window appears, enter

```
State
Of
Property
```

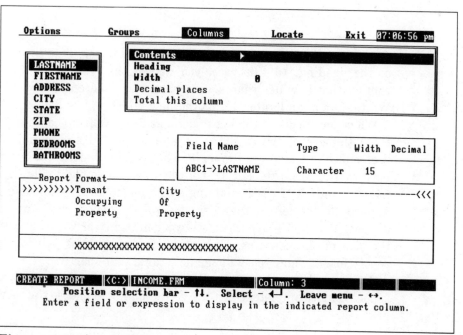

Figure 7-9. List of fields

Press RETURN to skip the last line and to complete the entry of the heading. Note that the width has taken on a value of 8. This value was assumed because, while the actual field is only two characters wide, the heading that you just entered is going to take a width of at least eight characters. If a heading is larger than the field, dBASE III PLUS defaults to the width of the heading. Press the PG DN key to proceed to the last column.

The last column will contain the rental amounts. Press RETURN to choose the Contents option, and enter RENTAMT. Notice that after you have entered RENTAMT, default values for the "Decimal places" and the "Total this column" options appear automatically. This occurs because RENTAMT is a numeric field, and you are given the options of choosing the number of decimal places to appear and of having totals appear. Since you are using dollar amounts and desire a total of the rents, leave these options set at the default values of 2 for decimal places and "Yes" for totals.

Select the Heading option. When the Heading window appears, enter

```
Rental
Amount
```

Press RETURN twice to skip the last line and to complete the entry of the heading. In this case, you decide that you would like a column that is wider than seven characters. Therefore, select the Width option, and enter 10 for the new width.

When you specified the left margin as 5 spaces from column 0 on the Title screen, the report generator displayed a > symbol for each space in the unused margin. That is why there are 4 > symbols starting from the left side of the screen. The right side shows five < symbols. If the remaining space for columns (indicated by hyphens to the left of the < symbols) isn't enough, you have two options. You can reduce the size of your margins, or you can reduce the size of the columns. Either choice would mean editing the report format, and you will see how to do that shortly.

Since you have identified all four columns, the design of your report is now complete. Open the Exit menu, and choose the SAVE option to save this report. The reports form will be saved on disk as INCOME.FRM. But before using the report, you need to perform one additional step. You may recall that you asked for subtotals by state. Whenever you request subtotals for a group in a report form, you must index the field on which the group is based. In this case, you must index on the STATE field. To do this, enter

```
INDEX ON STATE TO STATES
```

Once the file has been indexed, the REPORT FORM *filename* command can be used to produce the report. Enter

```
REPORT FORM INCOME
```

Note that you don't have to add the .FRM extension to the command. A report like the one shown in Figure 7-10 will be generated on the screen.

The same printing commands used to print data can be used along with the REPORT FORM command. As an example, REPORT FORM INCOME TO PRINT will result in the full report being printed (Figure 7-10).

Using Conditionals With Report Commands

You can also use additional statements within the REPORT FORM command to get specific information from the report. Try the following command:

```
REPORT FORM INCOME FOR STATE = "MD" TO PRINT
```

In response, a report form with only those properties located in Maryland will be printed.

```
Page No.       1
12/07/84
                   Metropolitan Washington Income Report
                          ABC Realty, Inc.
                          Rental Properties

Tenant            City            State           Rental
Occupying         Of              Of              Amount
Property          Property        Property


** Income by state DC
  Levy            Washington      DC               875.00
  Robinson        Washington      DC               920.00
** Subtotal **
                                                  1795.00


** Income by state MD
  Morse           Chevy Chase     MD               750.00
  Westman         Silver Spring   MD               570.00
  Robison         Takoma Park     MD               425.00
** Subtotal **
                                                  1745.00


** Income by state VA
  Jackson         Falls Church    VA               570.00
  Mitchell        Arlington       VA               990.00
  Hart            Fairfx          VA               680.00
  Jones           Reston          VA              1025.00
** Subtotal **
                                                  3265.00

*** Total ***
                                                  6805.00
```

Figure 7-10. Report including group and subtotal

Now enter

REPORT FORM INCOME FOR RENTAMT > 700 TO PRINT

A report showing only those properties with a rental cost of over $700 per month will be printed.

You can use the DTOC function, introduced in Chapter 6, to convert a date field into a string of characters. That string of characters can then be used to form a conditional command for printing a report. This is a handy tool for printing activity reports that indicate activity within a certain time period. As an example, the command

```
REPORT FORM INCOME FOR DTOC(EXPDATE) <= "10/01/85" TO PRINT
```

will produce a report of all records with expiration dates earlier than November 2, 1985. A report of all rentals with expiration dates within a particular month could be produced with a command like this one:

```
REPORT FORM INCOME FOR DTOC(EXPDATE) > "07/31/85" .AND.
DTOC(EXPDATE) < "09/01/85" TO PRINT
```

If you use this trick to create reports that span across differing years, be careful. You can get into trouble with the date-to-character conversion function, because the year makes up the last two characters of the converted string, and dBASE will consider the month more important. As far as dBASE is concerned, 05/15/86 is less than 07/09/85. Within your commands, this would cause 05/15/86 to appear as an earlier date than 07/09/85, even though this is clearly not the case. If you perform a great deal of database work with dates, you can solve this problem by using the command

```
SET DATE ANSI
```

This command will set the date formatting of dBASE III PLUS to year/month/day, and dates used as character strings will be calculated correctly.

Producing Reports
From the Assistant

The REPORT FORM command can be accessed through the Retrieve menu of the Assistant. To try this, enter ASSIST to get the Assistant menus on the screen. Open the Retrieve menu, and select Report. Press RETURN to accept the default disk drive.

Choose INCOME.FRM (the name that you assigned the report with the CREATE REPORT command). You will next see the familiar Conditional menu of the Assistant (Figure 7-11). Note that you cannot choose the "Construct a field list" option. Since

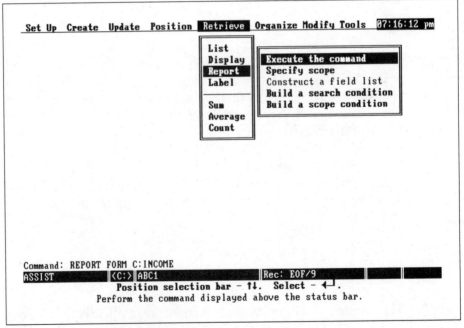

Figure 7-11. Conditional menu

reports contain previously specified columns of fields, it would not make sense to try to specify a field list here. All other options of this menu are available.

Choose the "Build a search condition" option. For this example, ABC Realty needs all properties with more than 1300 square feet of living space. Select the SIZE field, then choose the "Greater than or equal to" option. Enter 1300 for a value, then choose "No more conditions." Next, choose the "Execute the command" option. Answer "N" to the "Output to printer" option, and the report will appear on the screen. When the report completes its display, press any key to return to the Assistant. Then, press ESC to return to the dot prompt.

Editing the Report

Reports can be changed with the MODIFY REPORT command. From the dot prompt, the format of this command is MODIFY REPORT *filename*, where *filename* is the name of the report that you want to change. (You can also use the CREATE REPORT command. When you use CREATE REPORT with an existing report, there is no difference between the CREATE REPORT command and the MODIFY REPORT command.) When you modify a report, its parent database should be in use. To modify a report from the Assistant, you can select the Report option of the Modify menu.

The managers at ABC Realty would like the income report to include total rents for individual cities as well as total rents for individual states. This is where Subgroup/sub-subtotal can be used. You've already chosen the STATE field as the group to provide subtotals; you can now choose the CITY field as a group for sub-subtotals. To begin this editing process, enter

MODIFY REPORT INCOME

The Report Generator menu will again appear, with the Options menu presently open. Press the → key once to open the Groups menu. To edit the "subgroup on expression" option, press the ↓ key four times.

You want to provide subgroup subtotals for cities, so press RETURN to select the option, and enter CITY as the field name. Once you have entered the name, select the "Subgroup heading" option. Enter the heading

```
Income by city
```

Once you have pressed RETURN, the entry will be accepted as a heading for the subgroup. The managers at ABC Realty have one more change to suggest: they would like the CITY column in the

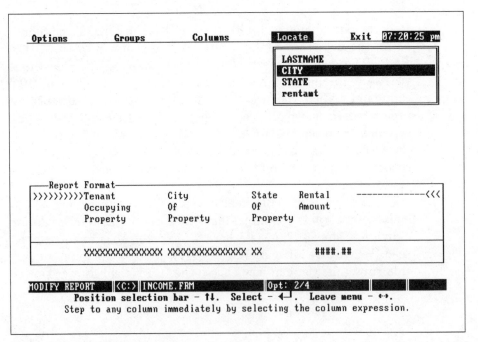

Figure 7-12. Locate menu

report widened to 20 characters. You can easily move to any column with the Locate menu.

Open the Locate menu (Figure 7-12). Within the Locate menu are the names of all columns presently in your report. You want to change the width of the CITY column, so select CITY. Upon pressing RETURN, the Columns menu will open, with the CITY field displayed (Figure 7-13). Select the Width option, and enter 20 for the new width. The change will be displayed by the widening of the simulated field in the Report Format window on the lower half of the screen.

These are all of the changes to the report that are necessary. To save the new report form, open the Exit menu, and select the SAVE option.

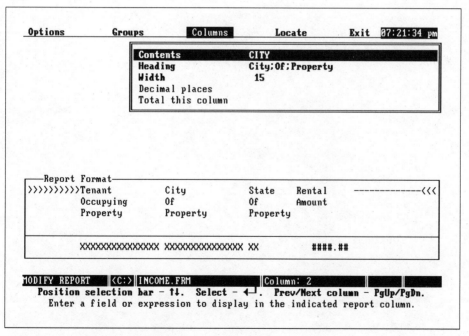

Figure 7-13. Editing the CITY column

Since you are creating a report that uses states for groups and cities for subgroups, you will need to index the database on both the STATE and CITY fields. Enter

```
INDEX ON STATE + CITY TO LOCATION
```

To print the new report (be sure the index file is active), enter

```
REPORT FORM INCOME TO PRINT
```

The report, complete with subgroup/sub-subtotals by city, will be printed (Figure 7-14).

```
Page No.      1
12/07/84
                Metropolitan Washington Income Report
                       ABC Realty, Inc.
                       Rental Properties

Tenant           City            State          Rental
Occupying        Of              Of             Amount
Property         Property        Property


** Income by state DC
* Income by city Washington
 Levy            Washington      DC               875.00
 Robinson        Washington      DC               920.00
* Subsubtotal *
                                                 1795.00
** Subtotal **
                                                 1795.00

** Income by state MD

* Income by city Chevy Chase
 Morse           Chevy Chase     MD               750.00
* Subsubtotal *
                                                  750.00
```

Figure 7-14. Report including subgroup/sub-subtotal

```
* Income by city Silver Spring
  Westman          Silver Spring   MD            570.00
* Subsubtotal *
                                                 570.00


* Income by city Takoma Park
  Robison          Takoma Park     MD            425.00
* Subsubtotal *
                                                 425.00

** Subtotal **
                                                1745.00


** Income by state VA

* Income by city Arlington
  Mitchell         Arlington       VA            990.00
* Subsubtotal *
                                                 990.00


* Income by city Fairfx
  Hart             Fairfx          VA            680.00
* Subsubtotal *
                                                 680.00


* Income by city Falls Church
  Jackson          Falls Church    VA            570.00
* Subsubtotal *
                                                 570.00


* Income by city Reston
  Jones            Reston          VA           1025.00
* Subsubtotal *
                                                1025.00

** Subtotal **
                                                3265.00


        Page No.        2
        12/07/84
                Metropolitan Washington Income Report
                        ABC Realty, Inc.
                        Rental Properties

        Tenant          City            State           Rental
        Occupying       Of              Of              Amount
        Property        Property        Property


        *** Total ***
                                                6805.00
```

Figure 7-14. Report including subgroup/sub-subtotal (*continued*)

Displaying Text Within a Report

If you want to include a description of properties from the memo field (or any information from any memo field) within the report, you can do so by naming that field as a column. A major improvement of the dBASE III PLUS report generator over the report generator contained in previous versions of dBASE is in its ability to display large amounts of text in columnar form, with word wrap. You can display memo fields or large character fields within a column of the report. You do this by intentionally limiting the width of the field in the report. If, for example, you limit the width of a column containing a memo field to 30 characters, the contents of the memo field will print on successive lines within that 30-character boundary.

To see how this works, let's modify the ABC Realty report. Instead of using the last column to display rental amounts, you will use it to display the contents of the memo fields. To modify the report, enter the command

```
MODIFY REPORT INCOME
```

When the Report Generator menu appears, open the Locate menu. You want to change the RENTAMT column, so select RENTAMT. Upon pressing RETURN, the Columns menu will open, with the RENTAMT field displayed.

Select the Contents option, use the BACKSPACE key to erase the RENTAMT field name, and enter EXTRAS for the new field name. Next, select the Heading option, and change the heading from "Rental Amount" to "Description of Extras". Press RETURN to skip the last line and complete the heading entry.

Note that the Width option has assumed a width of 18 characters. This amount has been allotted automatically, because it is as wide as the column can possibly be with the margins, page width, and other columns existing within the report. At this time, you can make the memo field column narrower, but not wider, than 18 characters. You could, as an option, narrow the width of other columns and of the margins to allow more room for the memo field. For now, leave the width at the value of 18 characters.

To save the new report form, open the Exit menu, and select the SAVE option. To see the results, enter the command

```
REPORT FORM INCOME TO PRINT
```

The report will include a neatly-formatted display of the memo fields, as shown in Figure 7-15.

Remember that because memo fields are different in design from other dBASE III PLUS fields, you cannot use conditionals

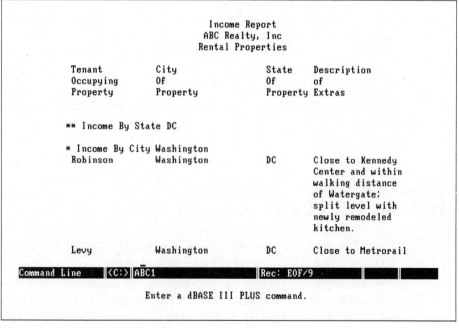

Figure 7-15. Report including memo fields

with the memo fields. As an example, the command

```
REPORT FORM INCOME FOR EXTRAS = "Near commuter bus" TO PRINT
```

will produce an error message.

As mentioned earlier in the chapter, there are limitations to the report generator. If you wanted to print information in horizontal rather than columnar format, you could not do so with the Report Generator. Only two levels of grouping are provided, so you could not break down a large report by states, then by cities, and then by ZIP codes within the cities. You also could not print today's date at the top of each page while leaving out the page heading.

Whenever you cannot use the report generator to produce the kind of report you need, you must turn to other methods. These will be discussed beginning with the next chapter. Before going on, however, you should experiment with the report generator. Try creating a different report with groups of various categories. Can you create a report that is divided by types of properties (town-houses, houses, and apartments)? If you have a printer that can print on wide (132-column) paper, try changing margins and page widths, and see how many additional columns of information you can place in a report. Experimenting with the dBASE III PLUS report generator is the best way to determine its capabilities and limitations.

CREATING AND PRINTING MAILING LABELS

dBASE III PLUS provides three commands, CREATE LABEL, MODIFY LABEL, and LABEL FORM *filename* that are the mailing-label equivalent of the CREATE REPORT, MODIFY REPORT, and REPORT FORM commands. These commands allow the menu-assisted design and printing of mailing labels. dBASE offers five predefined label sizes that match most sizes of office mailing labels, including the popular Cheshire binder and Xerox copier format. If you don't like any of the standard sizes, you can create your own label size by entering the various dimensions. You can also print the labels in the common "three-across" format, where the labels are placed on the label sheet in rows of three labels each.

Creating the Label Form

From the dot prompt, you use the CREATE LABEL command to start the design of the label. The format of the command is CREATE LABEL *filename*. (Label files are stored on disk with an .LBL extension.) To create labels from the Assistant, you can select the Label option of the Create menu.

Enter the command

```
CREATE LABEL ABCMAIL
```

The Label menu will appear (Figure 7-16).

In appearance and operation, the Label menu is similar to the Report Generator menu. There are three choices: Options, Contents, and Exit. The Options menu, which is currently open, displays the predefined size and the formatting specifications: label width, label height, margin settings, lines and spacing between labels, and number of labels across the page (see Table 7-2). You can use the Options settings in one of two ways: you can select from one of five predefined sizes, or you can manually enter your own specifications in the options below the "Predefined size" option.

The "Predefined size" option is currently highlighted. Press RETURN repeatedly to view the five predefined sizes that you can select. The measurements shown are in inches. The first number indicates the width of the label, while the second number indicates the label's height. The third value indicates the number of labels

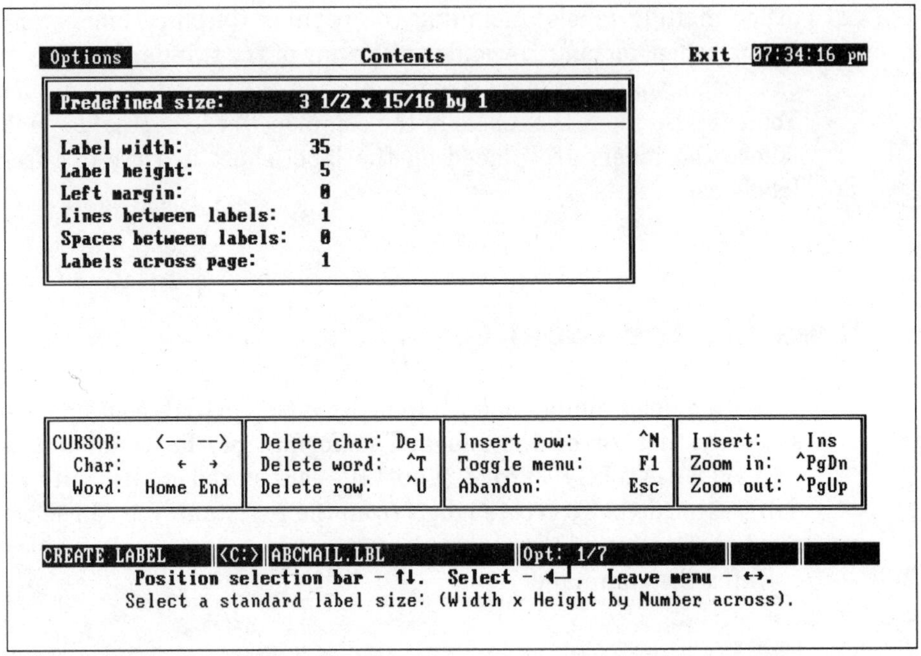

```
 Options             Contents                Exit  07:34:16 pm
 ┌────────────────────────────────────────────────────────┐
 │ Predefined size:      3 1/2 x 15/16 by 1                │
 ├────────────────────────────────────────────────────────┤
 │ Label width:          35                                │
 │ Label height:         5                                 │
 │ Left margin:          0                                 │
 │ Lines between labels: 1                                 │
 │ Spaces between labels: 0                                │
 │ Labels across page:   1                                 │
 └────────────────────────────────────────────────────────┘



 ┌──────────────────┬──────────────────┬──────────────┬──────────────────┐
 │ CURSOR:  <-- -->  │ Delete char: Del │ Insert row:  ^N │ Insert:     Ins  │
 │ Char:     ← →     │ Delete word: ^T  │ Toggle menu: F1 │ Zoom in:  ^PgDn  │
 │ Word:  Home End   │ Delete row:  ^U  │ Abandon:    Esc │ Zoom out: ^PgUp  │
 └──────────────────┴──────────────────┴──────────────┴──────────────────┘

 CREATE LABEL    <C:> ABCMAIL.LBL              Opt: 1/7
      Position selection bar - ↑↓.  Select - ↵.  Leave menu - ↔.
      Select a standard label size: (Width x Height by Number across).
```

Figure 7-16. Label menu

across a page. Note that as you press RETURN, the default sizes
displayed below the "Predefined size" option change to show the
specifications used for that particular label size.

Press RETURN until the 3 1/2 by 15/16 by 2 value appears. For
our sample label, you will use this option. The option will produce a
printout that matches mailing labels that are 3 1/2 by 15/16 inches,
two across to a page.

Next, press the → key to leave the Options menu, and open the
Contents menu (Figure 7-17). The Contents menu is used to tell
dBASE III PLUS what you would like to place in the labels. You
can enter the name of a field or combinations of fields. Press
RETURN to select the first line.

Table 7-2. Label Options

Label Option	Description
Predefined size	Pressing RETURN while in this option displays one of five available predefined label sizes.
Label width	Maximum width for any line on the label. Acceptable values are 1 to 120.
Label height	Number of lines contained on each label. Acceptable values are 1 to 16.
Label margin	Number of characters from the left side of the paper to the first character printed. Acceptable values are 0 to 250.
Lines between labels	Number of lines separating rows of labels. Acceptable values are 0 to 16.
Spaces between labels	Number of spaces between the columns of labels. Acceptable values are 0 to 120.
Labels across page	Number of labels on a row across the label page. Acceptable values are 1 to 15.

For the first entry, the name of the tenant is desired. Names are made up of a combination of two fields from the ABC Realty database: the FIRSTNAME field and the LASTNAME field. To place both names on the same line of the label, you will enter both names on this line.

Enter FIRSTNAME,LASTNAME and press RETURN (Figure 7-18). Note the presence of the comma between the FIRSTNAME and LASTNAME fields. A comma tells dBASE III PLUS to trim any extra spaces in the name fields, so that the names format neatly. With the comma, instead of a line on the label that reads

```
Carol        Levy
```

you will get a line that reads

```
Carol Levy
```

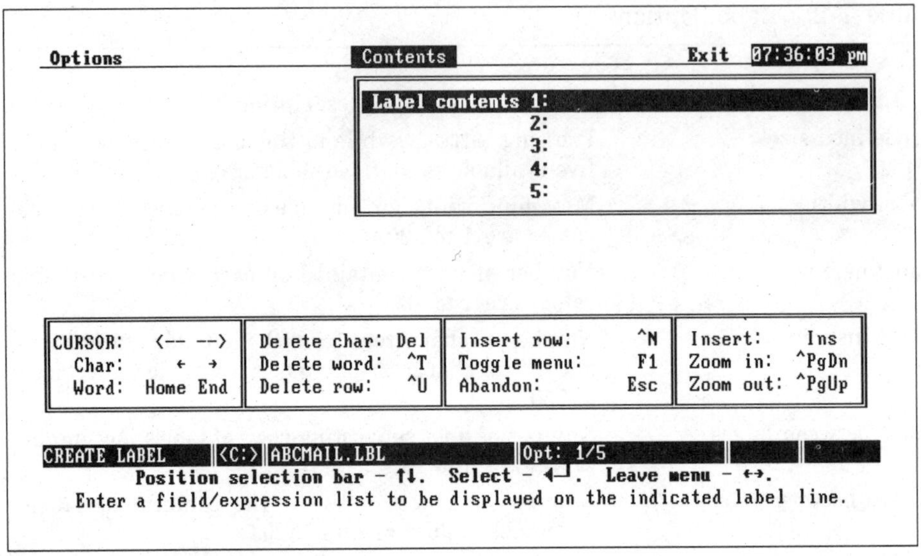

```
┌──────────────────────────────────────────────────────────────────────────┐
│  Options                    ▐Contents▌                    Exit ▐07:36:03 pm▌│
│                        ┌────────────────────────────────────────┐          │
│                        │ Label contents 1:▐                    ▌│          │
│                        │               2:                       │          │
│                        │               3:                       │          │
│                        │               4:                       │          │
│                        │               5:                       │          │
│                        └────────────────────────────────────────┘          │
│                                                                            │
│  ┌─────────────────┬─────────────────┬─────────────────┬─────────────────┐│
│  │ CURSOR:  <-- -->│ Delete char: Del│ Insert row:   ^N│ Insert:     Ins ││
│  │ Char:     ← →   │ Delete word: ^T │ Toggle menu:  F1│ Zoom in:  ^PgDn  ││
│  │ Word: Home End  │ Delete row:  ^U │ Abandon:     Esc│ Zoom out: ^PgUp  ││
│  └─────────────────┴─────────────────┴─────────────────┴─────────────────┘│
│  ▐CREATE LABEL   ▌▐<C:>▌▐ABCMAIL.LBL      ▌   ▐Opt: 1/5▌                    │
│              Position selection bar - ↑↓.  Select - ◄┘.  Leave menu - ↔.   │
│          Enter a field/expression list to be displayed on the indicated label line.│
└──────────────────────────────────────────────────────────────────────────┘
```

Figure 7-17. Contents menu

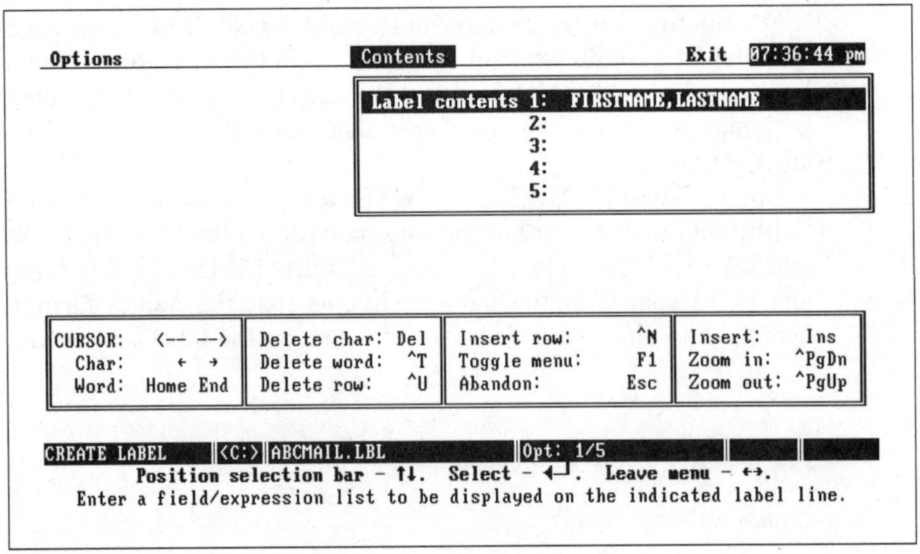

```
┌──────────────────────────────────────────────────────────────────────────┐
│    Options                  ▐Contents▌                    Exit ▐07:36:44 pm▌│
│                        ┌────────────────────────────────────────┐          │
│                        │ Label contents 1:  FIRSTNAME,LASTNAME  │          │
│                        │               2:                       │          │
│                        │               3:                       │          │
│                        │               4:                       │          │
│                        │               5:                       │          │
│                        └────────────────────────────────────────┘          │
│                                                                            │
│  ┌─────────────────┬─────────────────┬─────────────────┬─────────────────┐│
│  │ CURSOR:  <-- -->│ Delete char: Del│ Insert row:   ^N│ Insert:     Ins ││
│  │ Char:     ← →   │ Delete word: ^T │ Toggle menu:  F1│ Zoom in:  ^PgDn  ││
│  │ Word: Home End  │ Delete row:  ^U │ Abandon:     Esc│ Zoom out: ^PgUp  ││
│  └─────────────────┴─────────────────┴─────────────────┴─────────────────┘│
│  ▐CREATE LABEL   ▌▐<C:>▌▐ABCMAIL.LBL      ▌   ▐Opt: 1/5▌                    │
│              Position selection bar - ↑↓.  Select - ◄┘.  Leave menu - ↔.   │
│          Enter a field/expression list to be displayed on the indicated label line.│
└──────────────────────────────────────────────────────────────────────────┘
```

Figure 7-18. Label contents with FIRSTNAME,LASTNAME

You can, as an option, replace the comma with a plus sign. This will tell dBASE III PLUS not to trim the spaces from the contents of the fields.

Highlight line 2 and press RETURN to select the line. Enter ADDRESS, and press RETURN. Highlight line 3 and press RETURN to select the line. As with the report generator, you also have the option of choosing fields from a list. Press F10 now, and a list of fields will be displayed (Figure 7-19).

Highlight CITY and press RETURN once. The field name, CITY, will be entered into the "Label contents" window. The cursor is flashing at the end of the line. This position lets you add commas or plus signs, to include additional fields.

Type a comma, then press F10 again. When the Fields menu appears, highlight STATE and press RETURN. The STATE field name will be entered into the contents window.

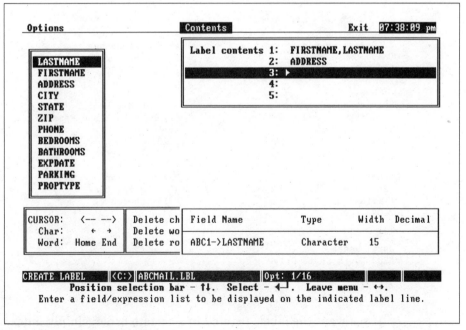

Figure 7-19. Fields list

Press RETURN to accept the contents for line 3. Then, press the ↓ key to move to line 4, and press RETURN to select the line. Enter ZIP and press RETURN. This is all that is needed for our label. Open the Exit menu, and choose SAVE to save the label form.

Once the form has been saved, the LABEL FORM command is used to print the mailing labels. The format for this command is

```
LABEL FORM (label filename) (FOR CONDITION) (TO PRINT)
```

Try the LABEL FORM command now by entering the command

```
LABEL FORM ABCMAIL TO PRINT
```

The results should resemble the following listing:

```
William Robinson              Carol Levy
1607 21st Street NW           1207 5th Street S.E.
Washington DC                 Washington DC
20009-0101                    20003-0298


Marcia Morse                  Andrea Westman
4260 Park Avenue              4807 East Avenue
Chevy Chase MD                Silver Spring MD
20815-0988                    20910-0124


Shirley Robinson              Mary Jo Mitchell
270 Browning Ave #3C          617 North Oakland Street
Takoma Park MD                Arlington VA
20912                         22203


Edward Hart                   David Jackson
6200 Germantown Road          4102 Valley Lane
Fairfax VA                    Falls Church VA
22025                         22044


Jarel Jones
5203 North Shore Drive
Reston VA
22090
```

If you want the labels printed in a certain order, simply index or sort the database first, as desired. Then use the LABEL FORM command. It is usually wise to print a test run of your labels on plain paper first and to visually align the printout with a sheet of blank labels. If the alignment looks correct, you can proceed to print on the label sheets themselves.

You can combine conditional FOR clauses to print specific labels, just as you did with reports. For example, the command

```
LABEL FORM ABCMAIL FOR STATE = "VA" TO PRINT
```

will print mailing labels for properties located in Virginia. The command

```
LABEL FORM ABCMAIL FOR DTOC(EXPDATE) > "07/31/87" .AND.
DTOC(EXPDATE) < "09/01/87" TO PRINT
```

will print only those labels for properties where the lease expiration date falls in the month of August, 1987.

Labels can be printed from the Assistant, by opening the Retrieve menu and selecting Label. Search conditions can be executed from the menus in the same manner as previously demonstrated with the report generator.

Using MODIFY LABEL

The MODIFY LABEL command is used to make changes to an existing label format. From the Assistant, you can access this command by opening the Modify menu, and choosing Label. From the dot prompt, you can enter the command, MODIFY LABEL *filename*. Get to the dot prompt now, and enter the command

```
MODIFY LABEL ABCMAIL
```

Within a moment, the Label menu will reappear. This time, you will use the individual options within the Options menu to change from a predefined size to a unique size of your own making.

Select the "Label width" option, and enter 25 for a new label
width. In a similar manner, change "Label height" to 6, "Left
margin" to 5, "Lines between labels" to 8, and "Labels across page"
to 3. Then, open the Exit menu, and choose SAVE to save the modified label form. Finally, print the new design of the labels with the
command

```
LABEL FORM ABCMAIL TO PRINT
```

The revised form of the labels probably won't be an exact fit for
any labels on the market. But these options demonstrate the ease
with which you can customize the labels to fit an odd size that may
be in use at your office. When making your own labels and reports,
you may find it necessary to experiment with the various margins
and size specifications, until you find values that work best for
your applications.

More Efficient Searches With Query Files

Chapter **8**

Throughout the previous chapters, you have made use of the various conditional powers of the dBASE III PLUS commands to find and print reports for records that meet various conditions. Some of the examples have also demonstrated that commands for such searches and retrievals can grow quite complex. If you need to perform such searches regularly, you may find yourself entering the same complex command or menu choice sequences over and over again.

With dBASE III PLUS, there is an easier way. You can use a query file, a special type of dBASE III PLUS file that filters a database to display or report on only those records that meet specific criteria. A query file identifies a set of conditions and in effect pulls only those records that meet the conditions from within the database. You can use the editing commands of dBASE III PLUS, such as the EDIT and BROWSE commands, with a query file limiting the available records. You can also use stored report formats, created with the report generator in combination with query files, to print reports containing records that meet the conditions of the query file.

Query files are designed and stored using a menu called the Query menu. In appearance and operation, it is much like the Report Generator and Label menus that you have used in previous chapters. Once you have created and stored a query file, you can recall that file at any time to view a database or to print reports. If you have varying sets of conditions that you wish to use regularly, you can create multiple query files, one for each set of conditions.

As an example, you may regularly want to use the BROWSE command to examine only those ABC Realty tenants who live in Virginia and whose rental payments are greater than $600. (This is a rather simple set of conditions, but you'll see how to build query files for more complex conditions later.) To perform this task regularly, you'll store the described conditions in a query file, to be named VAHOMES.

First, get into dBASE III PLUS, if you're not in it already. Select the ABC1 database (from the dot prompt or from the Assistant, your preference). It isn't necessary to choose an index file, although you could do this if you desired to view the records in a certain order.

Once the ABC1 database is in use, you must tell dBASE III PLUS to begin the creation of a query file. From the dot prompt, you use the CREATE QUERY *filename* command, where *filename* is the name of the query file you wish to create. If you are at the dot prompt, enter the command

```
CREATE QUERY VAHOMES
```

If you are using the Assistant, open the Create menu and choose the Query option. Press RETURN to accept the default disk drive, and enter VAHOMES as the name of the query file.

In a moment, the Query menu will appear (Figure 8-1). As with other dBASE III PLUS menus, you can open a menu by pressing the first letter of the menu's name or by highlighting the menu and pressing RETURN. The lower half of the screen displays a table called the query form. The query form will display the conditions that you specify as the query file is being built.

The Query menu offers four options: Set Filter, Nest, Display,

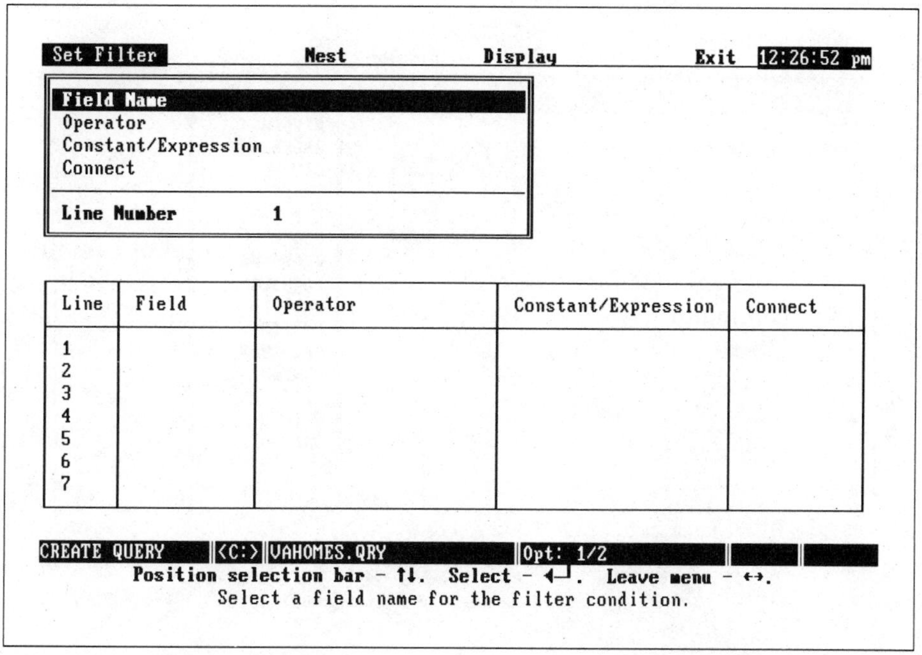

```
┌────────────────────────────────────────────────────────────────────────┐
│ Set Filter          Nest           Display          Exit 12:26:52 pm     │
│ ┌──────────────────────────────────────────┐                            │
│ │ Field Name                                │                            │
│ │ Operator                                  │                            │
│ │ Constant/Expression                       │                            │
│ │ Connect                                   │                            │
│ │                                           │                            │
│ │ Line Number          1                    │                            │
│ └──────────────────────────────────────────┘                            │
│                                                                          │
│  ┌──────┬─────────┬──────────────┬──────────────────────┬────────────┐  │
│  │ Line │ Field   │ Operator     │ Constant/Expression  │ Connect    │  │
│  │      │         │              │                      │            │  │
│  │  1   │         │              │                      │            │  │
│  │  2   │         │              │                      │            │  │
│  │  3   │         │              │                      │            │  │
│  │  4   │         │              │                      │            │  │
│  │  5   │         │              │                      │            │  │
│  │  6   │         │              │                      │            │  │
│  │  7   │         │              │                      │            │  │
│  └──────┴─────────┴──────────────┴──────────────────────┴────────────┘  │
│                                                                          │
│ CREATE QUERY      <C:> VAHOMES.QRY          Opt: 1/2                      │
│     Position selection bar - ↑↓.  Select - ◄┘.  Leave menu - ↔.          │
│         Select a field name for the filter condition.                    │
└────────────────────────────────────────────────────────────────────────┘
```

Figure 8-1. Query menu

and Exit. The Set Filter menu is used to select the actual conditions that the query file will use to filter your database. The Nest menu will be used to add parentheses that will affect the operation of complex conditions (more on that topic later). The Display menu lets you apply the conditions of the filter in any query you are designing to the database in use. You can use this option to see whether the query works as you want it to before you save it. The Exit menu lets you save the completed query file and return to the Assistant or to the dot prompt.

Before building a query file, it is a good idea to outline the conditions you wish to use on paper, particularly if those conditions are complex. In this case, you want all records in which the state is Virginia and the rental payments are greater than $600.

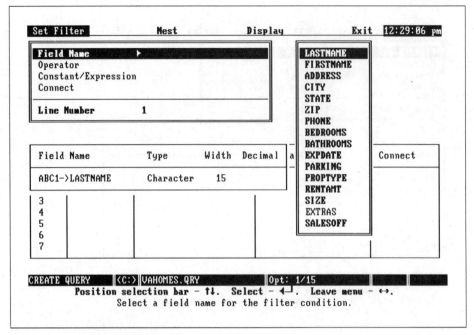

Figure 8-2. Field names

With the Set Filter menu already open, you are ready to begin building the query. The first choice in the Set Filter menu is Field Name. Press RETURN to choose the Field Name option, and a menu of field names from the ABC1 database will appear (Figure 8-2).

You want to select all states equal to Virginia; therefore, select the STATE field from the menu. Once you press RETURN, STATE will be automatically entered as the first field name for the query, and the highlighted cursor will move to the Operator selection. The Operator selection lets you choose the operator (less than, equal to, and so on) that you wish to apply to the condition you are building. Press RETURN to select Operator, and a menu of appropriate comparison operators will appear (Figure 8-3).

The comparison operators displayed will change, depending on the type of field you specified in the Field Name option. The

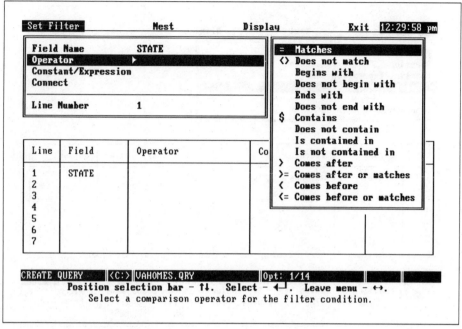

Figure 8-3. Comparison operators

choices that you see now apply to a character field, but would not be entirely appropriate for a logical or date field. When you enter those types of fields as field names, you will view different menus for the comparison operators.

You want states that match Virginia, so press RETURN to select the Matches option. The highlighted cursor will move to the Constant/Expression option. The meaning of the terms "constant" and "expression" will be covered in greater detail in the next chapter. For now, it is sufficient to understand that a constant is any value that does not change (such as 5672 or "VA"), while an expression can be a combination of one or more fields or constants.

Press RETURN to select the Constant/Expression option. The message line at the bottom of the screen indicates **Enter a field name or an expression.** Since you want to evaluate records that

```
┌──────────────────────────────────────────────────────────────────────────┐
│                                                                            │
│  Set Filter              Nest            Display          Exit  12:31:37 pm│
│  ┌──────────────────────────────────────────────────┐                     │
│  │ Field Name         STATE                          │                     │
│  │ Operator           Matches                        │                     │
│  │ Constant/Expression "VA"                          │                     │
│  │ Connect                                           │                     │
│  │                                                   │                     │
│  │ Line Number        1                              │                     │
│  └──────────────────────────────────────────────────┘                     │
│                                                                            │
│  ┌──────┬─────────┬────────────┬─────────────────────┬──────────┐         │
│  │ Line │ Field   │ Operator   │ Constant/Expression │ Connect  │         │
│  ├──────┼─────────┼────────────┼─────────────────────┼──────────┤         │
│  │  1   │ STATE   │ Matches    │ "VA"                │          │         │
│  │  2   │         │            │                     │          │         │
│  │  3   │         │            │                     │          │         │
│  │  4   │         │            │                     │          │         │
│  │  5   │         │            │                     │          │         │
│  │  6   │         │            │                     │          │         │
│  │  7   │         │            │                     │          │         │
│  └──────┴─────────┴────────────┴─────────────────────┴──────────┘         │
│                                                                            │
│  CREATE QUERY      <C:> VAHOMES.QRY            Opt: 4/5                     │
│        Position selection bar - ↑↓.  Select - ↵.  Leave menu - ↔.          │
│        Select a logical connector for the filter condition.                │
└──────────────────────────────────────────────────────────────────────────┘
```

Figure 8-4. Query form

contain "VA" in the previously-named field, enter "VA" and include the quotation marks. Quotation marks are needed around strings of characters whenever they are used in a query expression.

If you examine the query form on the lower half of the screen, you can see the query taking shape (Figure 8-4). Line 1 shows "STATE Matches VA", which is the condition that you have constructed so far. At this point, you could halt the process and save the query form; but if you did that, it would only filter those records in which the State field contains "VA". You want to go a step further and limit access to records with a rental amount greater than $600. To add more conditions to the filter, you will use the Connect option. Press RETURN to select Connect. A window will appear, showing the available Connect choices (Figure 8-5).

From the design of the search previously laid out on paper, you

```
┌────────────────────────────────────────────────────────────────────┐
│ Set Filter            Nest         Display          Exit 12:32:12 pm │
│ ┌──────────────────────────────────┐ ┌─────────────────────────────┐│
│ │ Field Name        STATE          │ │ No combination              ││
│ │ Operator          Matches        │ │ Combine with .AND.          ││
│ │ Constant/Expression "VA"         │ │ Combine with .OR.           ││
│ │ Connect              ►           │ │ Combine with .AND..NOT.     ││
│ │                                  │ │ Combine with .OR..NOT.      ││
│ │ Line Number       1              │ └─────────────────────────────┘│
│ └──────────────────────────────────┘                                │
│ ┌──────┬───────┬──────────┬─────────────────────┬──────────┐        │
│ │ Line │ Field │ Operator │ Constant/Expression │ Connect  │        │
│ ├──────┼───────┼──────────┼─────────────────────┼──────────┤        │
│ │ 1    │ STATE │ Matches  │ "VA"                │          │        │
│ │ 2    │       │          │                     │          │        │
│ │ 3    │       │          │                     │          │        │
│ │ 4    │       │          │                     │          │        │
│ │ 5    │       │          │                     │          │        │
│ │ 6    │       │          │                     │          │        │
│ │ 7    │       │          │                     │          │        │
│ └──────┴───────┴──────────┴─────────────────────┴──────────┘        │
│ CREATE QUERY      <C:> VAHOMES.QRY          Opt: 1/5                 │
│      Position selection bar - ↑↓.  Select - ◄┘.  Leave menu - ↔.    │
│      Select a logical connector for the filter condition.           │
└────────────────────────────────────────────────────────────────────┘
```

Figure 8-5. Connect choices

know that you want all records with State = "VA" AND all records with RENTAMT > 600. This calls for an AND condition, so select "combine with .AND." from the menu. The Set Filter menu will clear, and the Line Number option will indicate that you are now on line 2 of the query.

Press RETURN to select Field Name, and choose RENTAMT from the menu of fields that appears. Then, select Operator. (Note that the Operator menu for a numeric field offers choices different from the ones offered by the Operator menu for a character field.)

Choose the "More than or equal" option. Then, select Constant/Expression, and enter a value of 600 for the rental amount.

Choose Connect. No further conditions are desired, so choose the No Combination option. The query that is displayed in the query form, "STATE Matches VA .AND. RENTAMT More than or equal

600", is the filter that the query file will apply to the ABC Realty database.

The Nest and Display menu choices will be considered shortly. For now, open the Exit menu, and choose SAVE to save the completed query. The query will be saved, and you will be returned to the Assistant or to the dot prompt.

The final step is to tell dBASE III PLUS to use the query file as a filter for the database. If you're in the Assistant, open the Set Up menu, choose the Query option, and press RETURN to accept the default disk drive. Then, select VAHOMES, open the Update menu, and choose BROWSE.

If you're at the dot prompt, enter the following commands:

```
SET FILTER TO FILE VAHOMES
GO TO TOP
BROWSE
```

Try to move up and down within the database, and you'll find that as far as dBASE III PLUS is concerned, you have just three records in the entire database. The query file is filtering all other records that do not meet the conditions you specified.

Press ESC until you are at the dot prompt, then generate a report by entering the command

```
REPORT FORM INCOME
```

As the report scrolls up your screen, you will again see only those records that meet the filter conditions. When the dot prompt reappears, enter the command

```
EDIT
```

and try using the PG UP and PG DN keys to move through the database. Using a query file in the manner you have just demonstrated, you could effectively limit access to selected records, whether you are using EDIT or BROWSE or are printing reports.

NESTING EXPRESSIONS WITHIN A QUERY

More complex expressions in a query file can create a problem. Before describing why the problem can occur, it's helpful to see what the problem is. Let's modify our existing query file, to widen the filter to include homes from Maryland. Modifying an existing query file can be done with the MODIFY QUERY *filename* command (from the dot prompt) or by opening the Assistant's Modify menu and choosing Query.

From the dot prompt, enter the command

```
MODIFY QUERY VAHOMES
```

and the Query menu will appear. You can edit any line of the query by moving the cursor to the Line Number option and pressing RETURN to select the option to enter a new line number.

In this case, let's begin by editing the first line. You want to change the query to select states that are "VA" OR "MD", so select the Connect option, and choose "Combine with .OR." from the menu. The Set Filter menu will now display the existing contents of line number 2.

For this line of the query, you want states that contain "MD". So, select Field Name, and choose STATE from the Field menu. Then, press RETURN to choose Operator, and select Matches. Finally, press RETURN to choose Constant/Expression, and enter "MD" (don't forget the quotation marks).

As it exists, the query will filter the database for records in Virginia and Maryland. However, a condition of rental amounts greater than $600 is still desired. So, choose Connect, and select the "Combine with .AND." option.

For line number 3, select Field Name, and choose RENTAMT from the Field menu. Select Operator, and choose "More than or equal". Choose Constant/Expression, and enter 600 for the rental value. Choose Connect and select No Combination to end the query.

Looking at the query form at the bottom of the screen, you might get the impression that this query will provide all records in Virginia and Maryland, where the rental amounts are greater than $600. In actuality, that's not quite what happens. To see what you will get, try using the Display menu.

The Display menu lets you see the results of a query without saving the form and leaving the Query menu. Highlight the Display menu now, and press RETURN. Notice that a database record appears, in a format similar to that used by the EDIT command (Figure 8-6). Pressing F1 repeatedly will show and hide the query form. Press F1 now until the query form disappears, so that you can see the entire record.

Try using the PG UP and PG DN keys to view the database through the filter. You'll notice that the record for David Jackson is

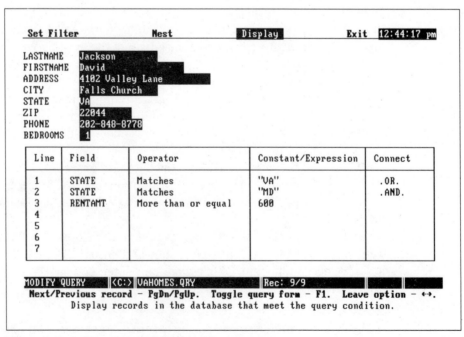

Figure 8-6. Results of Display Menu option

visible through the query filter. If you look closely, you'll see a problem here. The rent amount on Mr. Jackson is $570.00 per month. Yet, you distinctly asked the query file to limit access to records with rental amounts of $600 or more. Or, did you?

If you examine all of the records through the filter, you will see that the Virginia records are not limited in rental amounts, while the Maryland records are limited to those with rental amounts over $600. This illustrates the problem hinted at in the beginning of this subheading. When dBASE III PLUS evaluates complex conditions, it follows certain rules known as "rules of precedence." Logical operators such as .AND. and .OR. are used as a part of the conditions in the query file. The rules of precedence for these operators state that an .AND. operator is taken into account before an .OR. operator. Therefore, when dBASE III PLUS evaluates your existing query, it is interpreting the command in this manner:

```
STATE matches "VA" (OR STATE matches "MD" AND RENTAMT >= 600)
```

while what you really want is for the program to interpret the command in this manner:

```
(STATE matches "VA" OR "MD") AND RENTAMT >= 600
```

The only difference between the above two statements is in where the parentheses have been placed. Such use of parentheses to control how an expression is evaluated is known as nesting. Nesting is common in complex math and in most programming languages (including dBASE III PLUS). You can use the Nest menu to add parentheses to statements and to control how those statements are evaluated. Since you know that what you prefer is

```
(STATE matches "VA" OR "MD") AND RENTAMT >= 600
```

use the Nest menu to add the parentheses in the desired locations. Open the Nest menu (Figure 8-7).

The Nest menu lets you add a parenthesis to the start and end of any line number in your query. A starting parenthesis will appear

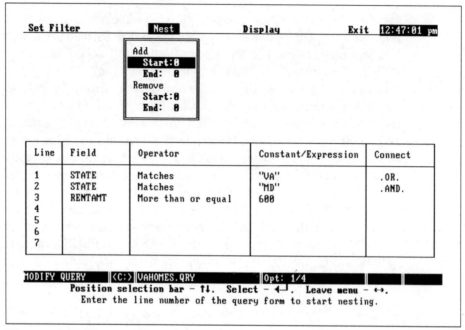

Figure 8-7. Nest menu

at the beginning of the field, while an ending parenthesis will appear at the end of the constant or expression. You want to surround line 1 and line 2 in parentheses, so select the Start option on the menu. Enter 1, to tell dBASE III PLUS to add the parenthesis at the start of line 1. Press RETURN after entering 1, and you will see the parenthesis added in the query form on the lower half of the screen (Figure 8-8).

You also need an ending parenthesis on line number 2, so select the End option of the menu. Enter 2 for this option, and the ending parenthesis will appear in the query form (Figure 8-9). In this case, these are all the parentheses that will be needed. In the case of more complex statements, you can enter more than one parenthesis on a single line, and you can use the Remove options of the Nest menu to remove any parentheses that you no longer want included in the statement.

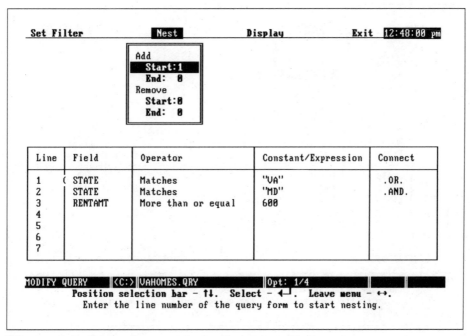

Figure 8-8. Query form with starting parenthesis

Open the Exit menu, and choose SAVE to save the modified query file. Then, choose BROWSE from the Update menu of the Assistant, or enter BROWSE from the dot prompt. This time, the records meeting the desired conditions will be the only records displayed.

You may want to try a more complex case in order to see the additional levels of nesting that may be required when you filter a database based on a number of rules. As an example, ABC Realty needs to see how lease expiration dates compare with the deadline for rent control laws in the three states containing its properties. The problem is that the rent control laws in the Virginia and Maryland counties affected take effect on December 1st, while the law for the District of Columbia takes effect on January 1st. You want a filter to show all Virginia and Maryland properties with expiration dates greater than 12/01/85 and all D.C. properties

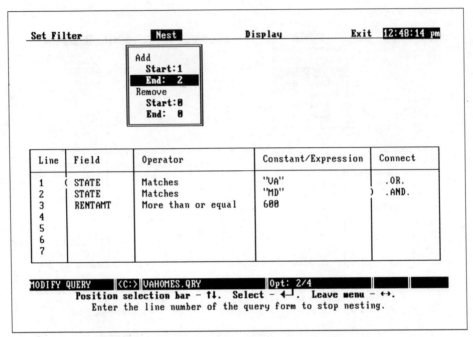

Figure 8-9. Query form with both parentheses

with expiration dates greater than 01/01/86. To be assured of getting the precedence right, the expression needs to be evaluated by dBASE III PLUS like this:

```
((STATE matches "VA" OR "MD") AND EXPDATE >= 12/01/85) OR
(STATE matches "DC" AND EXPDATE >= 01/01/86)
```

Get to the dot prompt, and enter the command

```
MODIFY QUERY VAHOMES
```

The Query menu will appear. Open the Nest menu, and select the Start option. Enter 1, to tell dBASE III PLUS to add another starting parenthesis to the beginning of line 1. The parenthesis will appear in the query form at the bottom of the screen.

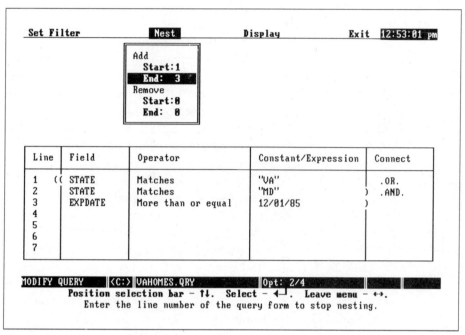

Figure 8-10. Query form

We already have an ending parenthesis at the end of the second line. However, the third line needs editing. Open the Set Filter menu, and select the Line Number option. Enter 3 to move to the third line of the query.

We want this line to read, "EXPDATE >= 12/01/85"; therefore, select the Field Name option, and choose EXPDATE from the list of fields. Next, select Operator, and choose "More than or equal." Then, select Constant/Expression, and enter 12/01/85. (No quotation marks are needed, because the comparison is between data contained in a date field and not in a character field.)

For proper precedence, a closing parenthesis is needed at the end of this line. Therefore, open the Nest menu, and select the End option. Enter 3 to place a closing parenthesis on line 3. At this point, your query form should resemble the one shown in Figure 8-10.

Open the Set Filter menu again, and choose Connect. The next step is to combine with an OR statement for the D.C. homes. Choose the "Combine with .OR." option, and Line Number 4 will appear in the Set Filter menu.

Select Field Name, and choose STATE from the menu. Select Operator, and choose the Matches option. Select Constant/Expression, and enter "DC" (with the quotes). Then select Connect, and choose the "Combine with .AND." option. Line Number 5 will appear in the Set Filter menu.

Select Field Name, and choose EXPDATE from the list of fields. Select Operator, and choose "More than or equal." Select Constant/Expression, and enter 01/01/86. Finally, choose Connect, and select the No Combination option.

All that's needed is one more parenthesis, around lines 4 and 5. Open the Nest menu, and select Start. Enter 4 for the starting parenthesis. In a similar manner, select End, and enter 5 for the line with the ending parenthesis. Your query form should now look like the one shown in Figure 8-11.

Open the Exit menu, and choose SAVE to save the query. Get to the dot prompt, and enter the following command:

```
LIST LASTNAME, FIRSTNAME, STATE, EXPDATE
```

You will see a list of only those homes meeting the conditions specified: expiration dates greater than 12/01/85 in Maryland and Virginia, and expiration dates greater than 01/01/86 in D.C.

Record#	lastname	firstname	state	expdate
1	Robinson	William	DC	05/20/86
4	Westman	Andrea	MD	12/23/85
5	Robinson	Shirley	MD	12/20/85
7	Mitchell	Mary Jo	VA	12/25/85
8	Hart	Edward	VA	12/20/85

You can cancel the filtering effects of a query file by entering the SET FILTER TO command, without specifying any query filename. For example, enter the following commands:

```
SET FILTER TO
LIST LASTNAME, FIRSTNAME, STATE, EXPDATE
```

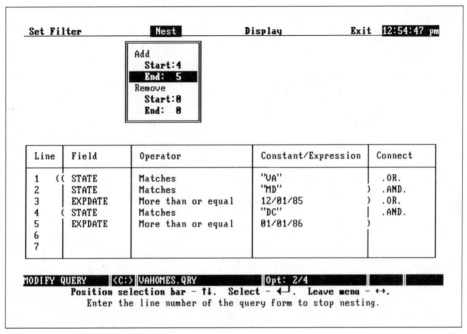

Figure 8-11. Completed query form

The list that appears shows all records in the database.

When working with complex queries like the one just described, errors may crop up. One common form of error is a misplaced or missing parenthesis. If the query contains an error, dBASE III PLUS will display an **Invalid Filter** message and won't display any records. You can then go back into the Query menu and correct the problem.

Introduction
To dBASE III PLUS
Programming

Chapter 9

While you may not have purchased dBASE III PLUS with the intent of becoming a computer programmer, you'll find that programming with dBASE III PLUS is not as difficult as you might expect. As you will see in this chapter, you program in dBASE through the use of *command files*. Using programs that automate the way dBASE III PLUS works for you is well worth the effort spent in designing and writing command files.

Any computer program is simply a series of instructions to a computer. These instructions are commands that cause the computer to perform specific tasks. The commands are written in a file contained on a disk, and they are performed each time the file is retrieved from the disk.

A dBASE III PLUS command file is made up of dBASE III PLUS commands. Each time you use a command file, dBASE III PLUS will execute the list of commands in sequential order, unless you request otherwise.

Let's look at an example using the ABC Realty database. If an ABC Realty employee wanted a printed listing of tenants' last names, rental amounts, and cities and states of the properties, that employee could enter commands, like those you have learned to use, to produce the listing. This may not seem like a complex task; in fact, it could be done with the following two commands:

```
USE ABC1
LIST LASTNAME, RENTAMT, CITY, STATE
```

If, however, the employee needed to reprint this list frequently, typing these same commands over and over would be a waste of time. Instead, you can place these commands inside of a command file, and then the user would only type one command to execute all the commands in the file.

Two characteristics of command files make them a powerful feature of dBASE III PLUS:

- Any series of dBASE III PLUS commands entered from the keyboard can be stored in a command file. When the command file is run, the dBASE III PLUS commands present in the file are executed just as if they had been entered from the keyboard.

- One command file can call and execute another command file. Information can be transferred between command files. This means that complex systems can be efficiently designed by creating a series of smaller command files for individual tasks.

Using command files, you can create a system that relies on menus that appear on the screen. An example of a menu screen is shown in Figure 9-1. Rather than using individual commands, the user simply makes choices from the menu to retrieve and manipulate information in the database. Such a *menu-driven system* can easily be learned and used by people unfamiliar with dBASE III PLUS commands.

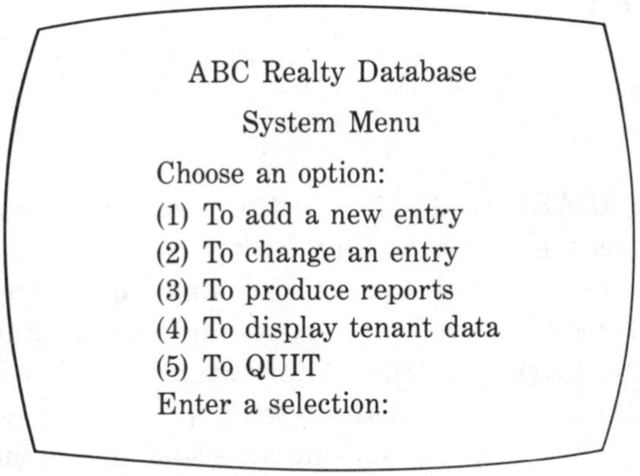

```
ABC Realty Database
System Menu
Choose an option:
(1) To add a new entry
(2) To change an entry
(3) To produce reports
(4) To display tenant data
(5) To QUIT
Enter a selection:
```

Figure 9-1. Sample menu for ABC Realty

CREATING COMMAND FILES

You can create command files with the MODIFY command. The format is MODIFY COMMAND *filename*. This command must be entered from the dot prompt; it is not available from the Assistant. Entering MODIFY COMMAND along with a filename brings up the dBASE III PLUS word processor. You then use the word processor to type commands that will be stored as command files. All files stored by the dBASE III PLUS word processor will have an extension of .PRG (for "program") unless you specify otherwise. If the filename you enter already exists on the disk, it will be recalled to the screen. If the filename does not exist, a help screen with the heading EDIT: "filename.PRG" is displayed on the top.

Let's create a command file now. Enter SET DEFAULT TO B: or C:, so that the file will be placed on the appropriate disk drive. Then enter

```
MODIFY COMMAND TEST
```

The dBASE III PLUS word processor appears, and the rest of the screen is blank (except for the help screen at the top of the page). At this point, the screen is like a blank sheet of paper. You type the commands that you wish to place in your command file, pressing RETURN as you complete each line. If you make any mistakes, you can correct them with the arrow keys and the BACK-SPACE or DEL key. The editing keys available in the word processor are listed in Table 9-1. When using the dBASE III PLUS's word processor, any characters you type will overwrite any existing characters in the same position unless you are in insert mode. You can get in and out of insert mode by pressing INS. When you are in insert mode, Ins. appears at the top of the screen, and any characters to the right of the cursor will be pushed to the right as you type new characters.

Type the following series of commands now, pressing RETURN after you complete each line; only one command should appear on each line. (If you don't have a printer on your system, omit the SET PRINT ON and SET PRINT OFF commands.)

```
SET PRINT ON
LIST LASTNAME, FIRSTNAME, CITY, RENTAMT FOR STATE = "MD"
LIST LASTNAME, FIRSTNAME, CITY, RENTAMT FOR STATE = "VA"
LIST LASTNAME, FIRSTNAME, CITY, RENTAMT FOR STATE = "DC"
SET PRINT OFF
```

Whenever you finish editing with the dBASE III PLUS word processor, press CONTROL-END to save the command file. (If you want to leave the dBASE III PLUS word processor without saving the file, you can press the ESC key to get back to the dot prompt.)

The simple command file that you have created will print a listing of each property, state by state, including tenant names, city

Table 9-1. Editing Keys in the dBASE III PLUS Word Processor

Key	Function
↑ or CONTROL-E	Move cursor up one line
↓ or CONTROL-X	Move cursor down one line
→ or CONTROL-D	Move cursor one character forward
← or CONTROL-S	Move cursor back one character
CONTROL-N	Insert a blank line
CONTROL-T	Delete word beginning at the cursor to the next word
CONTROL-Y	Delete line
INS or CONTROL-V	Turn insert mode on or off
DEL	Delete character at the cursor position
BACKSPACE	Delete character to the left of the cursor
PG UP or CONTROL-R	Scroll screen upward
PG DN or CONTROL-C	Scroll screen downward
CONTROL-END	Save file on disk
ESC	Exit the word processor without saving

names, and rental amounts. Make sure that your printer is turned on; then, to see the results of your work, enter

```
USE ABC1
DO TEST
```

The commands in the file will be carried out in sequential order, just as if you had entered them individually. (Remember, before you execute the file, the database that you will use must be active.)

```
Record#  LASTNAME      FIRSTNAME     CITY           RENTAMT
      1  Morse         Marcia        Chevy Chase     750.00
      4  Westman       Andrea        Silver Spring   570.00
      7  Robinson      Shirley       Takoma Park     425.00
Record#  LASTNAME      FIRSTNAME     CITY           RENTAMT
      3  Jackson       David         Falls Church    525.00
      5  Mitchell      Mary Jo       Arlington       990.00
      6  Hart          Edward        Fairfax         680.00
      9  Jones         Jarel         Reston         1050.00
Record#  LASTNAME      FIRSTNAME     CITY           RENTAMT
      2  Levy          Carol         Washington      875.00
      8  Robinson      William       Washington      920.00
```

You can also create a command file by using other word processing programs. While the dBASE III PLUS word processor is convenient, it may not offer as many text manipulation commands as other word processing programs. The most noticeable limitation is that the dBASE III PLUS word processor cannot handle files containing more than 4000 characters. This is usually not a problem, but if you plan to write large and complex dBASE III PLUS command files, you may find that 4000 characters is not enough.

Any word processor that can save files as ASCII text can be used to create a dBASE III PLUS command file. This includes Word, MultiMate, WordStar, and NewWord. The important thing to remember is to use the .PRG extension when naming the file; otherwise, dBASE III PLUS won't recognize the file as a command file.

PROGRAMMING CONCEPTS

There are various concepts associated with programming that you should know about before delving into the topic of dBASE III PLUS command files: constants, variables, expressions, operators, and functions.

Constants

A constant is data that does not change. There are numerical, character, or logical constants. For example, 5.05 might be a numerical constant, while "a" might be a character constant. All character constants must be surrounded by quotes.

Memory Variables

A memory variable ("variable" for short) is a memory location within the computer that is used to store constants. A variable's precise location in the computer isn't important—what is important is the name given to the variable. A variable name must be 10 or fewer characters. It must consist of letters, numbers, and underscores only, and it must start with a letter. You cannot use names of commands; it is advised not to use field names. Because the contents of a memory variable are stored apart from the contents of a database, memory variables are useful for temporary processing of values and data within a dBASE program. Data can be stored in the form of memory variables, to be recalled for use by the program at a later time.

The STORE command is commonly used to assign data to a variable. The format is

STORE *expression* TO *variable-name*

dBASE III PLUS allows four types of variables: character, numeric, date, and logical variables. Character variables store strings of characters, which can be letters, numbers, or a combination of both. Numbers in a character variable are treated as characters. Numeric variables contain whole or decimal numbers. Date variables contain dates written in date format (for example, 12/16/84). Logical variables contain a logical value of T (true) or F (false), or Y (yes) or N (no). You do not have to designate the type when creating a variable—just assign the value you will be using. Use a descriptive name to help you remember what is stored in the variable. For example, the following STORE command assigns a numeric value of 18 to the variable LEGALAGE:

```
STORE 18 TO LEGALAGE
```

You can change the value by using the STORE command again.

```
STORE 21 TO LEGALAGE
```

The contents of a field can be stored to a memory variable. As an example, the command STORE LASTNAME TO ROSTER would store the contents of the LASTNAME field to a memory variable named ROSTER. When a list of characters is stored in a variable, the list of characters, known as *character string*, must be surrounded by single or double quote marks. For example, the command

```
STORE "BILL ROBERTS" TO NAME
```

would store the character string BILL ROBERTS in the variable NAME.

Surround the logical variable T, F, Y, or N with periods to distinguish it from a regular character: while .T. has a logical value of true, "T" is simply the letter T. Logical values can also be stored in variables with the STORE command. The following command would assign a logical value of false to the variable CHOICE:

```
STORE .F. TO CHOICE
```

In addition to STORE, other commands assign values to variables. These commands will be discussed in later chapters. To display a list of the variables you have used and their values, type the command DISPLAY MEMORY.

Expressions

An expression can be a combination of one or more fields, functions, operators, memory variables, or constants. As an example, Figure 9-2 shows a print statement combining a field, a memory variable, and a constant to form a single expression. This statement calculates total rent over a period of months, deducting 5% for estimated utilities (water, garbage, and so on). Each part of an expression, whether that part is a constant, a field, or a memory variable, is considered an element of the expression. All elements of an expression must be of the same type. You cannot, for example, mix character and date fields within the same expression. If you try to mix different types of fields within an expression, dBASE III PLUS will display a **data type mismatch** error message.

The most common type of expression found in dBASE programs is the math expression. Math expressions contain the elements of an expression (constants, fields, memory variables, or functions), linked by one or more math operators (+, −, *, /). Examples of math expressions include

```
RENTAMT * 12

BEDROOMS + BATHROOMS

RENTAMT + (RENTAMT * .05)

HOURLYSAL * 40

637.5/HOURLYSAL

82
```

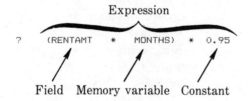

Figure 9-2. An example of an expression

Character expressions are also quite common in dBASE III PLUS programs. Character expressions are used to manipulate character strings or groups of characters. Examples of character expressions include

```
"Bob Smith"

"Mr." + FIRSTNAME + LASTNAME + "is behind in rent payments."
```

Operators

Operators, which are represented by symbols, work on related values to produce a single value. Operators that work on two values are called *binary operators;* operators that work on one value are called *unary operators.* Most of dBASE III PLUS's operators are binary operators, but there are a couple of unary operators. dBASE III PLUS has four kinds of operators: mathematical, relational, logical, and string operators.

Mathematical Operators   Mathematical operators are used to produce numeric results. Besides addition, subtraction, multiplication, and division, dBASE III PLUS has operators for exponentiation and unary minus. The symbols for math operators are as follows:

Operation	Symbol
Unary minus	$-$
Exponentiation	** or $^\wedge$
Division	/
Multiplication	*
Subtraction	$-$
Addition	$+$

If an expression contains more than one math operator, dBASE III PLUS executes the operations in a prescribed order: unary minus will be issued to the number first, followed by exponentiation; then multiplication or division is calculated, and then addition or subtraction. In the case of operators with equal precedence — division and multiplication, subtraction and addition — calculation will be from left to right. You can alter the order of operations by grouping them with matched pairs of parentheses. For example, the parentheses in $(3 + 6) * 5$ force dBASE III PLUS to add $3 + 6$ first and then multiply the sum by 5. You can group operations within operations with *nested* parentheses. dBASE III PLUS begins with the innermost group and calculates outward, as in the case of $((3 + 5) * 6) \wedge 3$, where $3 + 5$ is added first, multiplied by 6, and then raised to the power of 3.

Relational Operators Relational operators are used to compare character strings with character strings and numbers with numbers. The values you compare can be constants or variables. The relational operators are

Operation	Operator
Less than	$<$
Greater than	$>$
Equal to	$=$
Not equal to	$<>$ or #
Less than or equal to	$<=$
Greater than or equal to	$>=$

The simple comparison $6 < 7$ would result in .T. The result of $6 <$ NUMBER depends on the value of NUMBER. You can also compare such character strings as "canine" $<$ "feline" because dBASE III PLUS orders letters and words as in a dictionary. However, uppercase letters come before lowercase letters; so "Z" $<$ "a" even though a comes before Z in the alphabet.

Logical Operators Logical operators compare values of the same type to produce a logical true, false, yes, or no. The logical operators are

```
.AND.
.OR.
.NOT.
```

Table 9-2.   Truth Table for Logical Operators .AND., .OR., and .NOT.

First Value	Operator	Second Value	Result
.T.	.AND.	.T.	.T.
.T.	.AND.	.F.	.F.
.F.	.AND.	.T.	.F.
.F.	.AND.	.F.	.F.
.T.	.OR.	.T.	.T.
.T.	.OR.	.F.	.T.
.F.	.OR.	.T.	.T.
.F.	.OR.	.F.	.F.
.T.	.NOT.	N.A.	.F.
.F.	.NOT.	N.A.	.T.

Table 9-2 lists all possible values produced by the three logical operators. .AND. and .OR. are binary operators, while .NOT. is a unary operator.

String Operators   The only string operator you will use in dBASE III PLUS is the plus (+) sign. The plus sign is used to combine two or more character strings. This is known as *concatenation*. For example, "Orange" + "Fox" would be combined as "OrangeFox" (remember, a blank is a character). Strings inside variables can also be concatenated; for example, if ANIMAL = "Fox" and COLOR = "Orange", then COLOR+ANIMAL would result in "OrangeFox".

Functions

Functions are used in dBASE III PLUS to perform special operations that supplement the normal dBASE III PLUS commands. dBASE III PLUS has 70 different functions that range from calculating the square root of a number to finding the time. To discuss all of dBASE III PLUS's functions would require a detailed explanation of programming, which is not the purpose of this book.

However, you should know about two functions that are commonly used in command files: the EOF (End Of File) and BOF (Beginning Of File) functions.

The EOF function indicates when the dBASE III PLUS record pointer has reached the end of a database file. The normal format of the function is simply EOF( ). To see how EOF( ) is set to true when the pointer is *past* the last record, enter

```
GO BOTTOM
```

This moves the pointer to the last record. Now enter

```
DISPLAY
```

and you will see that you are at record 9, the final record in the database. Next enter

```
? EOF()
```

to display the value of the EOF function. dBASE III PLUS tells you .F. (false), meaning that the value of the EOF function is false because you are not yet at the end of the file. Now enter

```
SKIP
```

to move the pointer past the last record. (The SKIP command, discussed shortly, is used to move the dBASE III PLUS record pointer.) Next enter

```
? EOF()
```

The .T. (true) value shows that the pointer is now at the end of the file.

The BOF function is the opposite of the EOF function. The value of BOF is set to true when the beginning of a database file is reached. The format is BOF( ). To see how BOF operates, enter

```
GO TOP
```

The pointer moves to the first record. Now enter

```
DISPLAY
```

and the first record in the database is displayed. Next enter

```
? BOF()
```

to display the value of the BOF function, which is .F. (false) because the pointer is at the first record and not at the beginning of the file. Enter

```
SKIP -1
```

to move the pointer above record 1. Then enter

```
? BOF()
```

The .T. (true) value shows that the pointer is at the beginning of the file.

SOME COMMONLY USED COMMANDS

Some dBASE III PLUS commands are often used within command files but rarely elsewhere. Since you will be using command files with increasing regularity through the rest of this book, these commands deserve a closer look. At the end of this chapter, you will begin using the commands to design a program.

SET TALK

SET TALK ON displays on-screen execution of the commands within a command file. When SET TALK OFF is executed within a command file, visual responses to the dBASE III PLUS commands will halt until a SET TALK ON command is encountered. When you begin a session with dBASE III PLUS, SET TALK is on.

SKIP

The SKIP command moves the record pointer forward or backward. The format of the command is SKIP [+/− *integer*]. The integer specified with SKIP will move the pointer forward or backward by that number of records. For example, entering SKIP 4 moves the record pointer forward by four records. Entering SKIP −2 moves the record pointer backward by two records. Entering SKIP without an expression moves the pointer one record forward.

The values can be stored in a memory variable, which can then be used as part of SKIP. For example, entering STORE 4 TO JUMP assigns 4 to JUMP; then the command SKIP JUMP moves the record pointer forward by four records. If the record pointer is moved beyond the end of the file or above the beginning of the file, an error message will result.

RETURN

The RETURN command is used to halt the execution of a command file. When a RETURN command is encountered, dBASE

III PLUS will return to the dot prompt. If the RETURN command is encountered from within a command file that has been called by another command file, dBASE III PLUS will return to the command file that called the file containing the RETURN command.

ACCEPT and INPUT

Two dBASE III PLUS commands display a string of characters and then wait for the user to enter a response that is then stored in a variable. These commands are ACCEPT and INPUT. The ACCEPT command stores characters; the INPUT command stores values. The format for ACCEPT is ACCEPT *"prompt"* TO *variable-name;* for INPUT the format is INPUT *"prompt"* TO *variable-name.*

The order of the commands is the same whether you are dealing with characters or numbers. You enter the command, followed by the question or message that is to appear on the screen (it must be enclosed in single or double quotes), followed by the word TO, followed by the memory variable you want to store the response in. For example, let's use this format with the ACCEPT statement to store a name in a memory variable. Enter the following:

```
ACCEPT "What is your last name?" TO LNAME
```

When you press RETURN, you'll see the message **What is your last name?** appear on the screen. dBASE III PLUS is waiting for your response, so enter your last name. When the prompt reappears, enter the following:

```
? LNAME
```

You'll see that dBASE III PLUS has indeed stored your last name as a character string within the memory variable LNAME.

The same operation is used for numbers, but you use the INPUT statement instead. For example, enter

```
INPUT "How old are you?" TO AGE
```

and in response to the prompt, enter your age. Next, enter

```
? AGE
```

You'll see that the memory variable, AGE, now contains your response.

COUNT

The COUNT command is used to count a number of occurrences of a condition within a database. One condition might be to search for the name "Robinson" from a field of last names, another to search for rental units that are townhouses. The general format is COUNT FOR *fieldname* = *condition* TO *variable-name*. *Fieldname* is the field where COUNT will search for the occurrence of *condition;* thus, *condition* should match the field type of *fieldname* (if *condition* is a character string, it should be enclosed in quotes). The number of occurrences of *condition* will be stored in *variable-name*. The variable can then be used in another part of the program for calculations or for printing. For example, the command

```
COUNT FOR LASTNAME = "Robinson" TO NAMECOUNT
```

would count the occurrences of the last name, Robinson, in the LASTNAME field of ABC 1. That count would then be stored as a memory variable, NAMECOUNT.

SUM

The SUM command provides the total for any numeric field. The basic format of the command is SUM [*scope*][*fieldlist*] [FOR *fieldname condition*] TO [*variablelist*].

SUM can be used with or without conditions, in a number of ways. *scope* identifies the magnitude of the summation; that is, if *scope* is absent, all records will be checked; if *scope* is the word NEXT followed by an integer, then only the specified number of records below the pointer will be summed, or if *scope* is ALL, all records are summed, which is the same as when no *scope* is specified. If *scope* is the word RECORD, only the current record will be summed (which is rather ridiculous, since there is nothing to add). *fieldname* is a list of the numeric fields to be summed by the SUM command. The memory variable list assigns the memory variables that the values produced by SUM will be stored in. For example, entering SUM without any specifics will cause dBASE III PLUS to add and display the totals of all the numeric fields within the database. Entering SUM RENTAMT TO TOTAL will store the total of the RENTAMT field in a memory variable called TOTAL. SUM RENTAMT, SIZE TO C,D stores the total of the RENTAMT field in variable C and the total of the SIZE field in variable D. SUM RENTAMT FOR LASTNAME = "Hart" TO E would store rent totals from the name Hart in variable E.

AVERAGE

The AVERAGE command calculates the average value of a numeric field. The basic format is AVERAGE [FOR *fieldname*, . . .] WHILE *fieldname=condition* TO [*variable*, . . .]. *fieldname* must be numeric (there can be more than one *fieldname*). The average of each *fieldname* will be stored in *variable*.

The command AVERAGE RENTAMT TO F would store average rental amounts in variable F.

@, ?, ??, and TEXT

Four commands are used to display or print text: @, ?, ??, and TEXT. The ? and ?? commands will display a single line of text at a time. If ? is used, a linefeed and carriage return occur before the display. A ?? does not include the linefeed and carriage return operation before the display. If the ? or ?? command is preceded by a SET PRINT ON command, output is also routed to the printer. An example is shown in the following command file:

```
SET PRINT ON
? "Choose a selection."
?
?
? 1500*3
SET PRINT OFF
```

For more selective printing or display, the @ command will move the cursor to a specific location on the screen, and when combined with SAY, will display the information there. dBASE III PLUS divides the screen into 24 rows by 80 columns. The top left coordinate is 0,0, while the bottom right coordinate is 23,79. The general format of the command is

@ row,column [SAY *character-string*]

To try this, enter

```
CLEAR
@ 12,20 SAY "This is a display"
```

Using the @ command with the SAY option, you can generate report headings or statements at any required location. Screen formatting with the @ command will be covered in greater detail in Chapter 10.

The TEXT command is useful for displaying large amounts of text. TEXT is commonly used to display operator warnings, menu displays, and notes that appear during various operations of the program. TEXT is followed by the text to be displayed, and then ended with ENDTEXT. The text does not need to be surrounded by quotes. Everything between TEXT and ENDTEXT is printed. The following example will erase the screen with CLEAR and then display a copyright message:

```
CLEAR
TEXT
*************************************************************
        dBASE-III Copyright (C) 1984 Ashton-Tate
Payroll System Copyright (C) 1984 J Systems and Programming
For technical support, phone our offices at (703) 555-5555
*************************************************************
ENDTEXT
DO MENU
(rest of program)
```

The TEXT command must be used from within a command file. Any attempt to use TEXT as a direct command will cause the keyboard to lock up, requiring a restart of the computer.

OVERVIEW OF A PROGRAM DESIGN

Programming involves more than entering commands and statements into the computer correctly—in fact, that's the simplest part. Programming requires careful planning of the code and rigorous testing afterward. How do you start to write a program, and after it is operational, how do you determine whether the program is efficient? Unfortunately, there is no one correct way to write a program or determine when it is efficient or good. But most programmers have a natural tendency to follow five steps in the design of a program:

1. Defining the problem

2. Designing the program

3. Writing the program

4. Verifying the program

5. Documenting the program.

As these steps imply, the process of good programming is more than just writing a series of commands to be used in a particular command file. It is somewhat similar to the process of designing a database (outlined in Chapter 2), but because you are designing a program and not a database, you must think about how the program will use information in the source database, how the program will produce reports, and how the program can be designed so that it is easy to use.

Defining the Problem

The first step is to define the problem that the program is intended to solve. This step is too often skipped, even by professional programmers, in the rush to create a program. The problem may be as simple as wanting to automate a task; but in the process of defining it, you should query the people who will be using the program and find out just what they expect the program to do. Even if you will be the only user, you should stop to outline what the program must provide before you begin writing it.

Output Requirements Output, the information the program must produce, should be considered. Output is most useful in the form of a printed report, so defining what type of output is needed is often similar to the process of defining what is needed in a report. What types of output must the program produce? What responses to queries do the users expect? What must the reports look like? Sample screen displays or reports should be presented to the users for suggestions and approval. This may sound like a time-consuming process (and it often is), but the time saved in unnecessary rewrites of an inadequate program is worth the initial effort.

In the case of ABC Realty, asking the employees to list the kinds of reports they needed revealed two specific output needs. The first is a printed summary report that shows the tenants' names, the cities and states of the rental properties, and subtotals of rental amounts by state. This information was extracted by the report generator in Chapter 6. The second is a way to find and display all of the information about a particular tenant. You want to be able to display information so that it appears organized and is easy to read and visually pleasing.

Input Requirements Input, the ways in which the program can be used to place data into the database, also should be considered during the problem-definition process. This examination asks the question, "How will the information used by the program be entered?" A logical method for getting all of the information into the computer must be devised. For example, someone must key in all of the information for an inventory that is being placed on the computer system for the first time. It's easy to think, "Why not just use the APPEND command to enter a record, and let personnel type in all the data they might ever need?" There are two reasons against this haphazard approach. First, it can be inefficient: some of the data entered may never be used by the program. Second, if the data-entry screens aren't easy to understand and logically designed, and if verification of the data isn't performed, chances are you'll have a database full of errors. Good design comes from using program control to make the data-entry process clear and straightforward.

ABC Realty's employees have identified two specific input needs. The first is a way to add new records to the database. You will do this by using not only the APPEND command, but also other

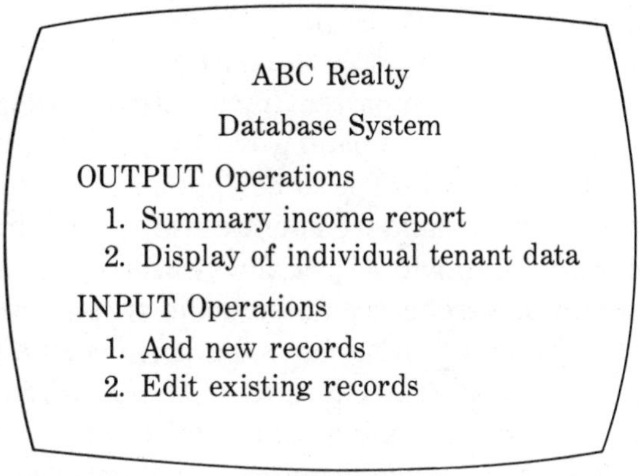

```
                ABC Realty
              Database System
         OUTPUT Operations
            1. Summary income report
            2. Display of individual tenant data
         INPUT Operations
            1. Add new records
            2. Edit existing records
```

Figure 9-3. Input and output operations for ABC Realty database system

commands that will make the screen display visually appealing and easy to read. The second is a way to select and edit a particular record in the database. If you outline the output and input requirements of ABC Realty, the list might look like Figure 9-3.

Designing the Program

Most well-designed programs are a collection of smaller programs, often referred to as *modules*, each performing a specific function. For example, a payroll accounting program is thought of as one program, but most such programs consist of at least three smaller programs. One module handles accounts receivable, the process of tracking incoming funds; the second module handles accounts payable, the process of paying the bills; and the third module handles the general ledger, a financial balance sheet that shows the funds on hand (Figure 9-4).

Small modules help tackle large programming tasks in small steps, which is an important principle of good program design. Many tasks worth performing with a database management system are too large in scope to be done in one simple operation. An inventory system is an excellent example. At first glance, such a system may appear to be just a way of keeping track of the items on hand in a warehouse. Scratch the surface, though, and you'll find that there are numerous modules in such a system. The first module in the system adds items to the inventory as they are received; a second module subtracts inventory items as they are shipped; a third module monitors inventory levels; and if the quantity of an item falls below a specific point, a fourth module alerts

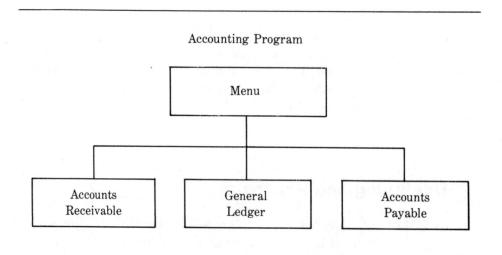

Accounting Program

Figure 9-4. Modules of an accounting program

the user by printing a message on the screen. Modules will inter-
act and exchange information with other modules in the system,
but they share one pool of information—the database itself.

In addition, finding errors in the program is easier if the program is divided into modules, since the problem can be traced to
the modules performing the tasks that may be in error. It is during
the design phase that the general and subsidiary functions of the
program are outlined in detail. It cannot be overemphasized that
any program worth writing is worth outlining on paper. The
designer should resist the urge to begin writing programs at the
keyboard without first outlining the steps of the program. The outline will help ensure that the intended program design is followed
and that no steps are accidentally left out. Outlines are of great
help in identifying the smaller tasks to be done by your system.

You'll find that it's best to list the general steps first and then
break the general steps into smaller, more precise steps. Let's use
the ABC Realty database system as an example. The system
should perform these tasks:

1. Allow new records (rental properties) to be added

2. Allow existing records to be changed (edited)

3. Display data from a record

4. Produce reports on all rental properties.

This simple outline shows what is basically required of the database management system. You then add more detail to the outline
as in Figure 9-5.

With so much to think about during the process of designing a
program, you can easily overlook how the user will use it. Good
program design considers users by including menus. Menus provide the user with a simple way of selecting what he would like to
do. In a way, they are like a road map of the system; they guide the
user through the steps in performing a task. For that reason,

Outline of Program Design

1. Allow new entries to be added—APPEND
2. Change (edit) existing entries
   - Show all record numbers and names on the screen
   - Ask the user for number of the record to be edited
   - Edit the selected record
3. Display data regarding a chosen entry
   - Ask the user for name of tenant
   - Search for that name in the database
   - If name is found, print the information contained in all fields of the record
4. Produce reports of all properties
   - Use the REPORT FORM *filename* command to produce a report

Figure 9-5. Rough outline of ABC Realty program

menus should be easy to follow, and there should always be a way out of a selection if the user changes his mind. In addition, the program should not operate abnormally or *crash* (stop running) in the event that the user makes an error when entering data.

Writing the Program

Now it's time to write the program. Since most applications typically begin with a menu of choices, the menu module should be written first. Each selection within the menu should then lead to the part of the program that performs the appropriate function. For example, a choice of "RUN REPORT" from a menu could result in a REPORT FORM command being issued to print a report. An "ADD NEW ENTRIES" choice could result in an APPEND command that adds data to the database. When you design your own systems, you'll find it helpful to design the menu first and then use it as a starting point for the other modules in the program. In this example, however, you will design the menu module of the program in the next chapter because it will use various commands that will be explained there.

It often helps, particularly if you are new to designing programs, to use *pseudocode*. Pseudocode is the English equivalent to the dBASE III language. You write the program in pseudocode and then convert it into actual code. For instance, the process that would allow users to display a list of names and edit a particular name would look like this in pseudocode:

1. Clear screen.

2. List all names in the database.

3. Ask user for number of record to be edited, and store that number as a variable.

4. Edit specified record.

5. Return to main menu.

When you know what steps are needed to perform the task, you store the corresponding commands in a command file. As an example, enter

```
MODIFY COMMAND CHANGES
```

to create a new command file called CHANGES.PRG. When dBASE WORD PROCESSOR appears, enter the following commands and then press CONTROL-END to save the command file:

```
CLEAR
LIST LASTNAME, FIRSTNAME
INPUT "Edit what record?" TO RECNO
EDIT RECNO
RETURN
```

Verifying the Program

Any errors in the program are corrected during this step. The program is also examined to see if the needs of all the users have indeed been met; if not, you may need to make changes or additions to some modules. In addition, you should now make any improvements that can speed up the system or minimize user confusion. The best way to find errors in a program is to use the program, so verify the program's operation by entering

```
DO CHANGES
```

The program will display a list of all tenant names. The corresponding record numbers will be shown to the left of the names:

```
Record#  LASTNAME      FIRSTNAME
      1  Robinson      William
      2  Levy          Carol
      3  Morse         Marcia
      4  Westman       Andrea
      5  Robinson      Shirley
      6  Jones         Jarel
      7  Mitchell      Mary Jo
      8  Hart          Edward
      9  Jackson       David
Edit what record?
```

The program now asks for the number of the record that you wish to edit. In response to the prompt, enter 8 (for record 8). If the program works as designed, the Edit screen for record 8 should appear. Change the rental amount for Edward Hart to $720 and save the change by pressing CONTROL-END. (Later, as a convenience for the user unfamiliar with dBASE III PLUS, you may want to display a message explaining how to save changes.) You should return to the dBASE III PLUS prompt, and for now, that is all that is expected of the program.

Documenting the Program

Documentation of a program takes one of two forms—written directions (like a manual) explaining how the program operates, and comments within the program itself about how the program is designed. The use of clear and simple menus and instructions within the program can help minimize the need for written documentation. A few sentences on how to start dBASE III PLUS and run the command file that displays the menu may be sufficient. As for directions and remarks within the program, dBASE III PLUS lets you put comments, in the form of text, at any location in a command file. Comments are preceded by an asterisk (∗) or by the NOTE command. When dBASE III PLUS sees a line beginning with an asterisk or the word NOTE, no action is taken by the program. Comments are simply an aid to you or any other person who modifies your command files. For example, this short command file documents the program with NOTE and the asterisk (∗):

```
CLEAR
NOTE Display the tenants' names
LIST LASTNAME, FIRSTNAME
NOTE Ask for a record number and store it.
INPUT "Edit What Record?" TO RECNO
EDIT RECNO
*Edit the record
RETURN
```

This file may seem somewhat overabundant in comments, because it does not need elaboration. If a command file consists of dozens of commands, the need for comments becomes more necessary. Not only do they make the program easier to understand, but if any other person must make changes to your dBASE III PLUS program, the task will be much easier.

Decision Making Within a dBASE III PLUS Program

The ability of command files to automate the storing and retrieval of records provides even more flexibility when you use decision-making conditions from within a command file. A condition can prompt the user for a response, and the user's response determines what the program does next. To program a condition, you'll need a way to evaluate user responses, and based on those responses, cause dBASE III PLUS to perform certain actions. In this chapter you'll use the IF, ELSE, ENDIF, DO WHILE, and ENDDO commands to perform these operations within a program.

GOING IN CIRCLES

There will be many times when your program will need to perform the same task repeatedly. dBASE III PLUS has two commands, DO WHILE and ENDDO, that are used as a matched pair to repeat a series of commands for as long as is necessary. The commands that you wish to repeat are enclosed between the DO WHILE and the ENDDO commands. The DO WHILE command always begins the loop, and the ENDDO command normally ends the loop. The series of commands contained within the DO WHILE loop will continue to execute until the condition, specified immediately next to the DO WHILE command, is no longer true. You determine when the loop should stop by specifying the condition; otherwise, the loop could go on indefinitely. The format is

> DO WHILE *condition*
> > [commands...]
>
> ENDDO

As long as *condition* within the DO WHILE is true, the commands between the DO WHILE and the ENDDO commands are executed. Whenever the ENDDO is reached, dBASE III PLUS evaluates *condition* to see if it is still true. If *condition* is true, dBASE III PLUS executes the commands within the loop again; if the condition is not true, dBASE III PLUS jumps to the command following the ENDDO command. If *condition* is false when the DO WHILE command is first encountered, none of the commands in the loop are executed, and the program proceeds to the first command that follows the ENDDO command.

You could use the DO WHILE and ENDDO commands in a command file that will print the names and addresses in the ABC Realty database with triple line spacing between them. Get to the dot prompt, and open a command file and call it TRIPLE by entering

```
MODIFY COMMAND TRIPLE
```

When the dBASE III PLUS word processor comes up, enter the following command file. Note that if you use a hard disk, you should change the second line of the program to indicate the appropriate letter of your hard disk drive.

```
SET TALK OFF
SET DEFAULT TO B:
USE ABC1
GO TOP
SET PRINT ON
DO WHILE .NOT. EOF()
        ? FIRSTNAME + LASTNAME
        ? ADDRESS
        ? CITY + STATE + " " + ZIP
        ?
        ?
        ?
        SKIP
ENDDO
? "Triple report completed."
SET PRINT OFF
```

Before you save this command file, take a brief look at its design. After such preliminaries as setting the default drive to B and activating the ABC1 file, the program sets the pointer to the top of the file and then begins the DO WHILE loop. The condition for the DO WHILE is .NOT. EOF( ), which simply means, "As long as the end of the file (EOF( )) is not reached (.NOT.), continue the DO WHILE loop." The first statement in the loop prints the name and address from the current record. The next three question marks print the three blank lines between each name and address. SKIP moves the pointer down a record each time the body of the DO WHILE loop is executed. If this command were absent, the pointer would never reach the end of the file, the condition would never be false, and the program would never leave the loop. The ENDDO command is then reached, so dBASE III PLUS returns to the DO WHILE loop to evaluate the condition. If the pointer hasn't reached the end of file, the loop is repeated. Once the end of file has been reached, dBASE III PLUS proceeds past the ENDDO command. The final two commands in the program are executed, and you are returned to the dot prompt.

Indenting the commands between DO WHILE and ENDDO will help you identify the body of the loop. This is especially helpful if you have *nested* DO WHILE loops—a DO WHILE loop within a DO WHILE loop.

After entering the commands in the file, press CONTROL-END to save the command file to disk; then make sure your printer is on, and enter DO TRIPLE. The command file will print the names and addresses, triple line spacing each, on your printer.

IF, ELSE, AND ENDIF

In many command files, dBASE III PLUS will need to perform different operations depending on the user's response to a condition option from a previous calculation or operation. For example, if the user has a choice of editing or printing a record in a main menu, the program must be able to perform the chosen operation. dBASE III PLUS uses the IF ELSE and ENDIF commands to branch to the part of the program where the chosen operation is performed. Much like the DO WHILE-ENDDO loop, the IF and ENDIF commands are used as a matched pair enclosing a number of commands. The ELSE command is optional and is used within the body of IF-ENDIF as another decision step. The IF ELSE command, followed by various commands including the IF command, and the ENDIF command can be used to decide between actions in a program. The format of the command is

```
IF condition
    [command...]
[ELSE]
    [command...]
ENDIF
```

This decision-making command must always start with IF and end with ENDIF. The commands that you place between the IF and ENDIF commands determine exactly what will occur if *condition* is true, unless an ELSE is encountered. A good way to write IF and ELSE commands is to write them in pseudocode first and then compare them.

Pseudocode	dBASE III PLUS
If last name is Cooke, then print last name.	IF LASTNAME="Cooke" ? LASTNAME ENDIF
If monthly rent is less than $300, then print "Reasonably priced."	IF RENTMONTH < 300 ? "Reasonably priced" ENDIF

Using IF and ENDIF alone will work fine for making a single decision. But if you wish to add an alternative choice, you'll need the ELSE statement.

Pseudocode	dBASE III PLUS

If last name is Cooke, then print last name; or else print "There is no one by that name in this database."	IF LASTNAME="Cooke"
	    ? LASTNAME
	ELSE
	    ? "There is no one by that name in this database."
	ENDIF

dBASE III PLUS will evaluate the condition following the IF command to see if any action should be taken. If no action is necessary, dBASE III PLUS will simply move on to the next command after the ENDIF command. In this example,

```
IF RENTAMT=850
        STORE RENTAMT TO MATCH
ENDIF
```

if RENTAMT is not 850 the STORE command will not be executed, and dBASE III PLUS will proceed to the command following ENDIF.

You can also use multiple IF-ENDIF commands along with ELSE if you need to have the program make more than one decision.

```
? "Enter 1 to print mailing labels or 2 to edit a record."
INPUT "What is your choice?" TO CHOICE
IF CHOICE = 1
        DO TRIPLE
ELSE
IF CHOICE = 2
        DO CHANGES
ENDIF
```

The answer that the user types will be stored in a variable called CHOICE. One of two things can happen then, depending on whether the user types a 1 or a 2 in response to the question. If CHOICE equals 1, the TRIPLE program will be run from disk. If CHOICE equals 2, the CHANGES program will be run. If CHOICE does not equal 1 or 2, the program will proceed to the next command after the ENDIF command.

Again, indenting the commands within the body of IF-ENDIF will make the flow of the program easier to follow.

You can use these commands in the RENTALS command file to search for and display the data regarding a specific entry in the database. If you want to find the rental occupied by a person named Mitchell, you can use the ACCEPT and IF-ENDIF commands to search for the record. (This operation can be done with SEEK, but for demonstration purposes a combination of IF and DO WHILE will be used.) First, let's use pseudocode to outline what needs to be done:

```
USE ABC1 database

GO to the top of the database

ACCEPT the last name

BEGIN the DO-WHILE loop

IF the last name field = the ACCEPT variable;

PRINT (on the screen) name, address,
monthly rent, property type, number of bedrooms
and bathrooms, and expiration date.

END the IF test
```

SKIP forward one record

END the DO-WHILE loop

RETURN to the dBASE-III PLUS prompt

Now create a command file by entering

MODIFY COMMAND SHOW

When the dBASE III PLUS word processor appears, enter the following command file:

```
*This command file finds and displays the data in a record.
USE ABC1
SET TALK OFF
CLEAR
GO TOP
* Begin loop that contains commands to display record.
ACCEPT "Search for what last name? " TO SNAME
DO WHILE .NOT. EOF()
     IF LASTNAME=SNAME
     ? "last name is "
     ? LASTNAME
     ? "first name is "
     ? FIRSTNAME
     ? "address is "
     ? ADDRESS
     ? CITY + STATE + " " + ZIP
     ?
     ? "rent per month is "
     ? RENTAMT
     ? "unit type is "
     ? PROPTYPE
     ? "number of bedrooms is"
     ? BEDROOMS
     ? "number of bathrooms is"
     ? BATHROOMS
     ? "lease expires on "
     ? EXPDATE
     ?
     ENDIF
     SKIP
ENDDO
WAIT
RETURN
```

When the prompt reappears, try the program by entering DO SHOW. In response to the last-name prompt that appears on the screen, enter Mitchell, and dBASE III PLUS will search the database for the record containing Mitchell.

This search you used the ACCEPT, IF, and ENDIF commands. The ACCEPT command stored the name that you entered into the memory variable SNAME. The IF loop began a decision-making process that stated the condition, "If the memory variable SNAME contains the same name as the LASTNAME field, then execute the commands that follow the IF command."

There is no limit to the number of commands that you can place between IF and ENDIF in the loop. You can also link multiple IF-ENDIF and ELSE commands if multiple choices are needed within a program.

THE CASE STATEMENT

Your program may need to make more than two or three decisions from a single response. A series of IF-ENDIF statements could do the job, but using more than three IF-ENDIFs to test one procedure is unwieldy. There is an easier way: the CASE statement. With the CASE statement, the IF-ENDIF tests are made into cases, and dBASE III PLUS then chooses the first case, second case, or another case. The CASE statement is a matched pair of DO CASE and END CASE. All choices are declared between DO CASE and END CASE. OTHERWISE is treated exactly like the ELSE in an IF-ENDIF statement. The general format is

```
DO CASE
     CASE condition
     [commands...]
     [CASE condition...]
     [command...]
     [OTHERWISE]
     [commands...]
END CASE
```

Whenever dBASE III PLUS encounters a DO CASE command, it will examine each case until it finds a *condition* that is true; then it will execute the commands below the CASE until it encounters the next CASE statement or ENDCASE, whichever comes first. If you want to create a menu that offers to display a record, print labels, edit a record, or add a record, you could create a command file like

```
? "1. Display a record"
?
? "2. Print the database"
?
? "3. Change a record"
?
INPUT "Choose a selection" TO SELECT
DO CASE
        CASE SELECT = 1
                DO SHOW
        CASE SELECT = 2
                DO TRIPLE
        CASE SELECT = 3
                DO CHANGES
ENDCASE
```

In this example, dBASE III PLUS will query the user for a selection with the INPUT statement (the SHOW file for the first selection was created in the last chapter). When the user enters the choice, it is stored in the variable SELECT. Then, in the DO CASE series, dBASE III PLUS will examine the SELECT variable for each CASE until it finds one that matches the value of SELECT. Once a match has been found, no other CASE statement will be evaluated. If no match is found, dBASE III PLUS proceeds to the next statement after the ENDCASE command. Like IF-ENDIF, the DO CASE-ENDCASE commands are used in pairs. You must always end a CASE series with an ENDCASE command.

You should use DO CASE if you have more than three choices. For example, if you wanted to offer the same three selections from the last program using IF-END and ELSE, the command file might look like this:

```
? "1. Display a record"
?
? "2. Print the database"
```

```
        ?
        ? "3. Change a record"
        ?
INPUT "Choose a selection" TO SELECT
IF SELECT = 1
        DO SHOW
ELSE
IF SELECT = 2
        DO TRIPLE
ELSE
IF SELECT = 3
        DO CHANGES
ENDIF
```

Using IF-ENDIF and ELSE is more complex than DO CASE as the number of choices increases.

Let's use a CASE statement to create a main menu for the users of the ABC Realty database. Enter MODIFY COMMAND MENU, and when the dBASE III PLUS word processor appears, enter the following command file:

```
USE ABC1
SET TALK OFF
STORE 0 TO CHOICE
DO WHILE CHOICE < 5
      CLEAR
      * Display the menu.
      ? "ABC Realty Database System Menu"
      ?
      ? " 1. Add a new entry to the database."
      ? " 2. Change an existing entry."
      ? " 3. Produce the rentals report."
      ? " 4. Display data regarding a particular tenant."
      ? " 5. Exit this program."
      INPUT "Enter selection: " TO CHOICE
            DO CASE
                  CASE CHOICE=1
                  APPEND
                  CASE CHOICE=2
                  DO CHANGES
                  CASE CHOICE=3
                  REPORT FORM INCOME
                  CASE CHOICE=4
                  DO SHOW
                  CASE CHOICE=5
                  RETURN
            ENDCASE CHOICE
ENDDO
```

There are five choices, and the INPUT command stores the response in the corresponding CHOICE variable. When dBASE III PLUS finds a matching choice, it executes the command that follows that choice.

Save this command file by pressing CONTROL-END. When the prompt reappears, enter DO MENU. Choose 1 to add new entries to the database, and the APPEND screen will appear. It's time to add a few records to the Detroit records of ABC Realty, so enter the following:

```
Drummond
Rick
9030 Jacob Way
Detroit
MI
64702
313-555-7062
3
1
10/04/87
Y
house
810
1412
memo        (press RETURN to bypass description)
DT          (abbreviation for Detroit)


Andrews
Robin
417 State Plaza
Highland Park
MI
67690
313-555-4139
4
3
03/07/87
Y
house
1010.00
2020
memo        (press RETURN to bypass description)
DT
```

```
Turner
Mitchell
117 Coral Drive
Detroit
MI
67551
313-555-2820
3
2
09/15/87
Y
house
875.00
1850
memo        (press RETURN to bypass description)
DT
```

When you are finished entering the records for the Detroit office, press RETURN to save the additions and leave append mode. Notice that instead of being returned to the dot prompt, you are returned to the menu. Try some of the other menu choices on your own to see how the system operates.

File Management

Chapter 11

This chapter explains how to copy files, combine files, and use more than one file at a time with dBASE III PLUS. These operations are often called *file management*.

You can perform these operations within dBASE III PLUS, without returning to the operating system. You can also transfer information between files—all the data in a file or selected data. dBASE III PLUS lets you set various conditions, like those you have been using, to transfer files. In addition, you can open and work with more than one file at once. The use of multiple files is a common programming method in dBASE III PLUS; and you will find that they are a virtual necessity for performing some types of tasks, such as inventory and complex accounting functions. You'll be using multiple files shortly.

THE COPY COMMAND

The COPY command is used to copy parts or all of a file. The format is COPY TO *filename*, where *filename* is the name of the new file that you want the records copied to. You must first use the

USE command to open the file that you want to copy from. For example, if you now enter

```
USE ABC1
COPY TO FILE1
USE FILE1
LIST
```

all of the records in the ABC1 database are copied to the new file FILE1.

The COPY command offers significant flexibility when you choose to copy specific fields. To select fields to be copied, use the format

COPY TO *filename* FIELDS *field-list*

By adding the word FIELDS after *filename* and then adding a list of fields, you tell dBASE III PLUS to copy the fields that you place in the list to the new database. Copy just the LASTNAME, FIRSTNAME, CITY, and STATE fields in FILE1 by entering

```
COPY TO FILE2 FIELDS LASTNAME,FIRSTNAME,STATE,ZIP
USE FILE2
LIST
```

Only these fields in FILE1 are copied to FILE2.

You can also use FOR to select specific data from a database. FOR is an optional phrase that indicates that the COPY command will apply to every record in the database for which the specified condition is true. The format of the COPY command with FOR is

COPY TO *filename* FIELDS *field-list* FOR *condition*

Using the FOR phrase as part of the COPY command, you can copy LASTNAME and RENTAMT fields from FILE1 for all records in which rental cost is less than $700. To do this, enter

```
USE FILE1
COPY TO FILE3 FIELDS LASTNAME,RENTAMT FOR RENTAMT < 700
```

The FOR condition specified before the RENTAMT field resulted in the new FILE3 containing only those rentals priced at less than $700 per month. To see the results, enter

```
USE FILE3
LIST
```

This kind of selective copying will prove useful later in this chapter, when you will merge two databases with slightly different fields of data.

You can use the Tools menu of the Assistant to copy files, although your choices are more limited than with the COPY FILE command. You cannot selectively copy fields or add conditions when using the Assistant; you must copy the entire database. You must also remember to copy the associated file containing the memo fields, if your database uses memo fields. To see what we mean, enter ASSIST to open the Assistant menus. Open the Tools menu, and select the COPY FILE option. Press RETURN to accept the default disk drive, and a menu of files from which to copy will appear (Figure 11-1).

You can use the PG UP and PG DN keys to move quickly among a large list of files. Select the ABC1 database file, ABC1.DBF. Then, press RETURN to accept the default disk drive, and you will be asked to provide a name for the copied file.

Enter FILE4.DBF and press RETURN (be sure to include the period and the "DBF" extension). This highlights a disadvantage of using the Assistant to copy a database; you must include the extension, or the Assistant will store the file without the DBF extension. If the file were stored without the DBF extension, dBASE III PLUS would produce an error message when you tried to open the file.

Once the file has been copied, press any key to return to the Assistant menus. Open the Set Up menu, select the Database File option, press RETURN to accept the default disk drive, and choose FILE4 for the name of the database. Answer N for "no" to the **Is the file indexed** question.

dBASE III PLUS will try to open the file. It will not be successful, and you will see an error message indicating that the memo

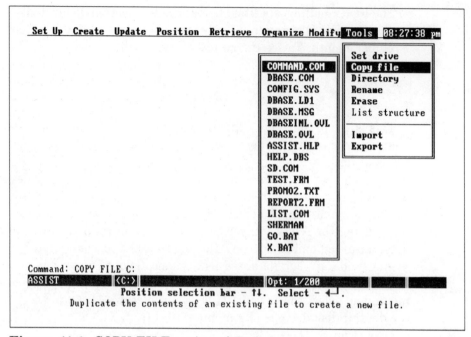

```
Set Up  Create  Update  Position  Retrieve  Organize Modify Tools  08:27:38 pm
                                                          Set drive
                                    COMMAND.COM           Copy file
                                    DBASE.COM             Directory
                                    CONFIG.SYS            Rename
                                    DBASE.LD1             Erase
                                    DBASE.MSG             List structure
                                    DBASEINL.OVL
                                    DBASE.OVL             Import
                                    ASSIST.HLP            Export
                                    HELP.DBS
                                    SD.COM
                                    TEST.FRM
                                    PROMO2.TXT
                                    REPORT2.FRM
                                    LIST.COM
                                    SHERMAN
                                    GO.BAT
                                    X.BAT

Command: COPY FILE C:
ASSIST              <C:>                         Opt: 1/200
              Position selection bar - ↑↓.  Select - ↵.
         Duplicate the contents of an existing file to create a new file.
```

Figure 11-1. COPY FILE option of Tools menu

field file (DBT file) cannot be opened. This illustrates the second disadvantage of copying a database file through the Assistant; the Assistant does not automatically make a copy of the associated .DBT file, which contains the memo fields. Whenever you specify the use of memo fields within a database, dBASE III PLUS creates two files: one containing the database, and the other containing the text of the memo fields. Both files must be on a disk before you can use a database. Therefore, we must copy the associated .DBT file, ABC1.DBT, to a new file called FILE4.DBT before we can open the database called FILE4.

Open the Tools menu, and select the COPY FILE option. Press RETURN to accept the default disk drive. From the menu of files that appears, select the ABC1 memo field file, ABC1.DBT. Then press RETURN to accept the default disk drive. Enter FILE4.DBT and press RETURN (be sure to include the period and the "DBT" extension).

When the file has been copied, press a key to return to the Assistant menus. Open the Set Up menu, and choose Database File. Press RETURN to accept the default disk drive, and select FILE4 from the list of files that appears. Enter N in response to the question regarding indexing. This time, dBASE III PLUS will be able to successfully open the database.

Considering the steps you must remember, you may well conclude that copying databases is one task that is better left to the COPY TO command from the dot prompt than to the Assistant. If you use the COPY TO command, you do not have to include extensions (dBASE III PLUS remembers them for you), and any associated memo files are copied automatically.

Before leaving the subject of copying files, the combination of database (.DBF) and memo field (.DBT) files can cause an associated problem that you should know how to get around. If you ever accidentally erase a memo field file, dBASE III PLUS will not let you open the associated database. With a large database, this could pose a disastrous problem. Fortunately, there is a simple solution. dBASE III PLUS doesn't really care if the information contained in the memo field file is accurate; it simply looks for two files with the same filename and differing extensions of .DBF and .DBT. You can create another small "test" database with one memo field, store a few words in that memo field, and then rename the .DBT file produced by that database so that it has the same filename as the database that lacks the memo field file. dBASE III PLUS will then let you open the file, and you can manually reenter the memo field information into the memo fields.

WORK AREAS
AND ACTIVE FILES

dBASE III PLUS can access any database file that is *open*. Basically, opening a database file amounts to telling dBASE III PLUS,

"I am ready to work with a database file that is stored on disk; now go get it." You can tell this to dBASE III PLUS ten times, because it allows you to have ten open database files at any given time. dBASE III PLUS can read any information in the database from an open database file, but that is all. If you want to change, add, or delete any information in a database, the database file not only must be open, but it must be *active* as well. Commands like EDIT, APPEND, and DELETE can only operate on active database files. dBASE III PLUS allows only one active database file at a time; so out of a possible ten open database files, only one can be active.

Open database files will be discussed later in more detail, but let's now create a small database file, called REPAIRS, that lists the total cost of repairing any damaged rental unit beginning in 1984. LASTNAME and FIRSTNAME fields will be included from ABC1 so as to match the repair cost to the rental unit. Enter CREATE REPAIRS, and define the database structure as follows:

```
Structure for database : b:REPAIRS.DBF
Number of data records :        0
Date of last update    : 12/20/84
Field  Field name  Type       Width   Dec
    1  COST        Numeric       7      2
    2  LASTNAME    Character    15
    3  FIRSTNAME   Character    15
** Total **                     38
```

Once you have saved the new file by pressing CONTROL-END, respond to the **Input data records now?** prompt by pressing Y and entering the following data:

```
Record#        COST LASTNAME    FIRSTNAME
    1         45.00 Jackson     David
    2        123.45 Mitchell    Mary Jo
    3         67.89 Hart        Edward
```

Press CONTROL-END to save the information. The REPAIRS database is now ready to be worked on, but for the purposes of this discussion, assume that the database is on the disk but not in the computer.

Opening a database file from disk requires that it be assigned to a *work area*. No database file can be open unless it resides in a work area, and assigning a database file to a work area is essentially opening it, too. As you might have guessed, there are ten work areas in dBASE III PLUS, numbered from 1 to 10. Assigning a database file to a work area—or opening a database file—is a two-step process: you tell dBASE III PLUS what work area you want the file to be placed in, and then you load the file into the work area. The SELECT command enables you to choose the work area, and the USE command loads the file. For example, if you wanted to open ABC1 in work area 2, you would first select the area by entering

```
SELECT 2
```

To load ABC1 into the current work area, which is 2, you would enter

```
USE ABC1
```

If you had specified a different filename, for example REPAIRS instead of ABC1, REPAIRS would have been loaded into work area 2. In fact, any database file that you now load with the USE command will be directed into work area 2 until you use the SELECT command to change the direction to a different work area.

The last database file loaded into a work area is also the *active database file*. As an example, open REPAIRS in work area 1 and ABC1 in work area 2 by entering the following commands:

```
SELECT 1
USE REPAIRS
SELECT 2
USE ABC1
```

ABC1 is the active database because area 2 was the last work area selected; thus dBASE III PLUS is pointed to ABC1. dBASE III

PLUS can now change or access any information in ABC1, but can only access information from the REPAIRS database. If you want REPAIRS to be the active file, after opening both database files you would enter

```
SELECT 1
2
DISPLAYCOST
```

The active database file switches from ABC1 to REPAIRS, although ABC1 remains open. When you start a session, dBASE III PLUS selects work area 1 as the default work area. This is why in the other chapters you did not have to use the SELECT command first in order to load ABC1.

Up until now you've worked with only one database file, ABC1, so when referencing a field you didn't need to include the filename because ABC1 was the active file. But if you need information from a neighboring open database file, it is then necessary to include the filename with the field. For example, to inspect the COST field in REPAIRS in work area 1 while ABC1 is active in work area 2, enter

```
SELECT 2
?REPAIRS -> COST
```

The hyphen (-) and the greater-than sign (>) are combined to form the extension for the field name. If you want to list COST, FIRSTNAME, and LASTNAME, include the filename for all three.

```
?REPAIRS -> COST, REPAIRS -> FIRSTNAME, REPAIRS -> LASTNAME
```

Listing the filename when referencing a neighboring work area can be tedious, especially if the filename is long or difficult to remember. To alleviate part of the problem, you can give a shorter, or more descriptive, *alias* to a file when you assign it to a work area. In fact, dBASE III PLUS assigns the default alias of A to work area 1, B to work area 2, C to work area 3, and so on. So instead of entering LIST REPAIRS → COST, you can enter LIST A → COST and the same listing will appear. If you're dissatisfied

with the default names, you can name your own alias when loading
a database file into a work area by including the ALIAS option
with the USE command. Even if you are satisfied with A, B, and
C as aliases, you should still declare them in the USE command
because they are not always reliably assigned when you reference
a field. The format for assigning an alias is USE *filename* ALIAS
aliasname. The same naming conventions for *filename* apply to
aliasname, but the .DBF file extension will not be included with
aliasname. The following command will give the alias RP to the
REPAIRS database file in work area 1.

```
SELECT 1
USE REPAIRS ALIAS RP
```

CLEAR ALL

Another command that you will use often is the CLEAR ALL
command. CLEAR ALL closes all database files and index files,
and returns dBASE III PLUS to work area 1. Enter

```
CLEAR ALL
```

to close all of the files that you have opened with SELECT.

COMBINING FILES

dBASE III PLUS lets you transfer records from one database file
to another with a variation of the APPEND command used earlier
to add new records to the database. However, the format of the
command is somewhat different when it is used for transferring
records from another database. Instead of simply entering
APPEND, you must enter the command in the format APPEND
FROM *filename*, where *filename* is the name of the file from which

you wish to transfer records. The file to which you are adding records must be the active database file. You can, for example, transfer records from the newly created FILE3 database to the FILE2 database. To do so, you should first activate FILE2. Enter

```
USE FILE2
```

You can append the records to FILE2 with

```
APPEND FROM FILE3
```

When you list the database to see the appended records, your display should resemble Figure 11-2. One characteristic of the APPEND FROM command becomes apparent by examining the list—namely, only the fields having the same names in both databases will be appended. Remember, you gave different structures to these files as a result of selective use of the COPY command. FILE2 contains the LASTNAME, FIRSTNAME, STATE, and ZIP fields, while FILE3 contains only LASTNAME and RENTAMT. When you appended from FILE3 to FILE2, dBASE III PLUS found just one field common to the two files— LASTNAME. However, even if the field name is the same, dBASE III PLUS won't append the field if the field type is different. And if the field being copied has a field size larger than the field receiving the record, character data will be truncated and asterisks will be entered for numeric data.

The file that you append from does not have to be a dBASE III PLUS database file. The APPEND FROM command is also commonly used when you want to transfer data from other programs, such as spreadsheets or word processors. This aspect of using dBASE III PLUS will be detailed more thoroughly in Chapter 15.

There are times when APPEND FROM simply doesn't do enough for a particular task. One limitation may already be obvious—if the databases to be combined contain different field types, APPEND FROM just won't be of much help. In such cases you can create a new database file that contains the combined

Record#	LASTNAME	FIRSTNAME	STATE	ZIP
1	Morse	Marcia	MD	20815-0988
2	Levy	Carol	DC	20003-0298
3	Jackson	David	VA	22044
4	Westman	Andrea	MD	20910-0124
5	Mitchell	Mary Jo	VA	22203
6	Hart	Edward	VA	22025
7	Robinson	Shirley	MD	20912
8	Robinson	William	DC	20009-0101
9	Jones	Jarel	VA	22090
10	Drummond	Rick	MI	64702
11	Andrews	Robin	MI	67690
12	Turner	Mitchell	MI	67551
13	Jackson			
14	Westman			
15	Robinson			

Figure 11-2. Results of APPEND FROM command

records of the database files. You do this with the more powerful JOIN command. The format of the JOIN command is JOIN WITH *aliasfile* TO *newfile* FOR *condition* [FIELD *fieldname*].

If no field names are listed, dBASE III PLUS assigns all of the fields from the active database (which is not listed in the command) and then all of the fields from the *aliasfile* (you can either use the alias or the original name) to *newfile*. Since dBASE III PLUS has a limit of 128 fields per database, if the JOIN process results in this limit being reached, no additional fields will be joined. Instead of combining all fields from both files, you can select individual fields with the FIELDS *fieldname* option. Fields from the *aliasfile* need the alias, or filename, and the -> symbol attached to each field.

When the joining process begins, dBASE III PLUS sets its record pointer at the beginning of the active file. Every record in the *aliasfile* is then evaluated to see whether the FOR *condition* is true. If *condition* is true, a new record with the combined information will be added to *newfile*. This process is repeated for each record in the active file. Let's use a PARTS database and an ORDERS database to demonstrate JOIN. The PARTS database contains part numbers, part descriptions, and prices per part. Create the following database wtih the name PARTS:

```
Structure:
Field Name      Type        Width       Dec
PARTNO          N           4           0
DESCRIPT        C           15
COST            N           6           2

Contents:
    PARTNO              DESCRIPTION       COST
    1001                keyboard          175.80
    1002                disk drive        192.55
    1003                memory chip         6.15
    1004                power supply      128.32
    1005                microprocessor     24.74
```

The ORDERS database file contains the customer numbers and names, part numbers, and the quantity of items ordered. Create the following database and name it ORDERS.

```
Structure:
Field Name      Type        Width       Dec
CUSTNO          N           4           0
CUSTNAME        C           10
PARTNO          N           4           0
QUANTITY        N           2           0

Contents:
    CUSTNO              CUSTNAME        PARTNO          QUANTITY
    0001                Smith           1003            9
    0002                Johnson         1005            2
    0003                Mills           1002            2
    0004                Reynolds        1001            1
```

In this example, Smith ordered nine memory chips, Johnson ordered two microprocessors, Mills ordered two disk drives, and

Reynolds ordered a keyboard. If you wanted to print an invoice
report showing all of this information, APPEND FROM wouldn't
help because, with the exception of PARTNO, the PARTS database
and the ORDERS database use different field names. You could,
however, use the SELECT command to open and work with both
files at the same time, and you could use the JOIN command to join
the files so that the new file contains CUSTNAME, PARTNO,
QUANTITY, COST, and DESCRIPTION. The following commands would join the database files in this manner, creating a new
file with the desired information.

```
CLEAR ALL
SELECT 2
USE ORDERS
SELECT 1
USE PARTS
JOIN WITH ORDERS TO FINALS FOR PARTNO = ORDERS ->PARTNO FIELDS
ORDERS->CUSTNAME, ORDERS->PARTNO, ORDERS->QUANTITY, PARTS->COST,
PARTS->DESCRIPT
```

Here the JOIN command says, "Join the active database PARTS
with the specified database ORDERS to form a new database,
called FINALS." Fields from the second file are indicated by the
alias, followed by the symbol -> (a hyphen immediately followed by
the greater-than symbol), followed by the field name used for the
condition. Since a condition is a comparison between two or more
items, in this example the matching condition will be the PARTNO
field. Whenever PARTNO in both databases match, a record will
be generated for the new database and that record will contain the
field for CUSTNAME, PARTNO, QUANTITY, COST, and DE-
SCRIPTION. So if you were to carry out these commands and then
list FINALS, you would see

CUSTNAME	PARTNO	QUANTITY	COST	DESCRIPTION
Smith	1003	9	6.15	memory chip
Johnson	1005	2	24.75	microprocessor
Mills	1002	2	192.55	microprocessor
Reynolds	1001	1	175.80	keyboard

JOIN can be time consuming because it examines one record in a database at a time, comparing that record to all of the records in the other database. For this reason, if you are working with large databases JOIN should be used only when necessary. Alternatives to using JOIN to retrieve data from multiple databases will be presented in the next chapter.

Now comes the opportunity to put some of your file management tools to actual use. ABC Realty has just run headlong into a typical problem. The company, based in the United States, is merging with a similar operation in Canada. A new database must be created to serve the new needs of the company. You cannot use the ABC1 database without any changes because some of the fields differ. U.S. ZIP codes differ in format from Canada's postal codes; and while both money amounts are in dollars, Canadian dollar values differ from U.S. dollar values. To make matters more complicated, the company president wants a monthly report that shows all rentals with Canadian amounts converted into U.S. dollars. This calls for three separate databases: one for U.S. operations, another for Canadian operations, and a third that will serve as a master file for the international report. The third database will be created whenever the international report is needed, by combining information from the U.S. and Canadian databases. You must also store the rental amounts from the Canadian properties in a separate file, convert those amounts to U.S. dollars, and then merge those amounts with the proper records in the master database.

COPY STRUCTURE

You can use the COPY STRUCTURE command to create the Canadian database without defining its complete design. COPY STRUCTURE copies only the structure of the active database file to the new name that you specify. Let's copy the ABC1 database structure for the Canadian database called ABC2. Enter the following:

```
USE ABC1
COPY STRUCTURE TO ABC2
USE ABC2
```

If you now enter LIST STRUCTURE, you see this:

```
Structure for database: C:abc2.dbf
Number of data records:       0
Date of last update   : 07/30/87
Field  Field Name  Type       Width   Dec
    1  LASTNAME    Character     15
    2  FIRSTNAME   Character     15
    3  ADDRESS     Character     25
    4  CITY        Character     15
    5  STATE       Character      2
    6  ZIP         Character     10
    7  PHONE       Character     12
    8  BEDROOMS    Numeric        2
    9  BATHROOMS   Numeric        2
   10  EXPDATE     Date           8
   11  PARKING     Logical        1
   12  PROPTYPE    Character     10
   13  RENTAMT     Numeric        7      2
   14  SIZE        Numeric        5
   15  EXTRAS      Memo          10
   16  SALESOFF    Character      2
** Total **                     142
```

The new database, ABC2, has the same structure as the original ABC1 database, but there are two problems. First, the field for ZIP codes is a ten-character field, while the Canadian postal code uses six characters. Second, the STATE field has two characters, but you will need three characters for the Canadian provinces. To accommodate these differences, you can use the MODIFY STRUCTURE command. You may recall from Chapter 4 that the MODIFY STRUCTURE command lets you change the design of an existing database.

Enter MODIFY STRUCTURE. Use the ↓ key to move the highlighted block to the STATE field. Enter PROVINCE and press RETURN and the cursor will move to Type. Here your original selection of character/text will be highlighted. This is fine, so press RETURN to accept the selection. The cursor now moves to the Width selection. Your previous choice of 2 won't be enough for Canadian provinces, so type 3 and press RETURN. The highlighted block will move down to the ZIP field.

For field name, enter POSTAL and the cursor will move to the Type category. Again, the previous selection of character/text is fine for postal codes, so press RETURN. The cursor moves to the Width category. Type 6 and press RETURN again. This will complete the necessary changes to the database, so press CONTROL-END and then RETURN to confirm the changes. When the dot prompt returns, enter LIST STRUCTURE again, and the new database structure will reflect the changes:

```
Structure for database : b:abc2.dbf
Number of data records :        0
Date of last update    : 12/10/84
Field   Field name   Type       Width    Dec
    1   LASTNAME     Character     15
    2   FIRSTNAME    Character     15
    3   ADDRESS      Character     25
    4   CITY         Character     15
    5   PROVINCE     Character      3
    6   POSTAL       Character      6
    7   PHONE        Character     10
    8   BEDROOMS     Numeric        2
    9   BATHROOMS    Numeric        2
   10   EXPDATE      Date           8
   11   PROPTYPE     Character     10
   12   RENTAMT      Numeric        6      2
   13   SIZE         Numeric        5
   14   EXTRAS       Memo          10
   15   PARKING      Logical        1
   16   SALESOFF     Character      2
** Total **                       136
```

Now let's enter the rentals for the new database. Enter APPEND. Since the database is currently empty, the entry screen for the first record appears. Enter the following information:

```
Belange
Mario
4719 Oak Hill Dr
Montreal
QUE
3K6M4E
514-555-1234
3
1
07/30/85
house
830.00
1525
memo       (press RETURN to bypass memo entry)
Y
TR         (abbreviation for Toronto sales office)


Clarke
Joe
87 Prosperity Way
Toronto
ONT
5L7G9A
613-947-2000
3
2
09/30/86
house
905.00
1780
memo       (press RETURN key to bypass memo entry)
Y
TR


Robinson
Linda
1142 Mountain Blvd.
Toronto
ONT
5H4M6B
613-888-3535
2
2
02/02/86
condo
610.00
1100
memo       (press RETURN key to bypass memo entry)
N
TR
```

After completing the last entry, press CONTROL-END to save the entries in the database.

You now have two databases with different structures for U.S. and Canadian operations. You still need a third database for the combined report; for this you can modify the structure of the existing Canadian database. Enter COPY STRUCTURE TO WORLDWIDE. This will create a new database called WORLD-WIDE that you will use as a master file. When the dot prompt reappears, enter

```
USE WORLDWIDE
```

Then enter

```
MODIFY STRUCTURE
```

Since the master file must contain states and provinces, you need to insert a new field for states. Move the highlighted cursor to PROVINCE, field 5, and press CONTROL-N to insert a new field. In the new field enter STATE. Character is fine for the field type, so press RETURN and then enter 2 for the field width. Move the highlighted block down to field 7, POSTAL. You won't need this field for the master report, so press CONTROL-U to delete the entire field. The president of ABC Realty is not concerned with numbers of rooms, descriptions of properties, and the like, so move the highlighted block down to field 8, BEDROOMS. In a similar fashion, press CONTROL-U twice to delete BEDROOMS and BATHROOMS. Next move the cursor down to the SIZE field, and press CONTROL-U three times to delete the SIZE, EXTRAS, and PARKING fields from this database structure. Press CONTROL-END and then RETURN to save the changes. List the WORLDWIDE structure with the LIST STRUCTURE command. Now enter

```
SELECT 1
USE ABC1
SELECT 2
USE ABC2
```

This will open both the ABC1 and ABC2 databases in two separate work areas. Enter SELECT 1 and then enter LIST. You'll see the contents of the U.S. database. Enter SELECT 2 and then LIST, and the contents of the Canadian database will appear.

To combine both databases, you'll make use of the APPEND command to add the desired data to the WORLDWIDE database. Remember, you deleted some fields to make WORLDWIDE simpler in design. So let's add the data for those fields from both databases. Enter

```
CLEAR ALL
USE WORLDWIDE
APPEND FROM ABC1
APPEND FROM ABC2
```

Now if you enter LIST, you'll see that records for all of the rental locations are combined in a single database.

There is still one nagging problem: the dollar amounts of the Canadian properties must be converted to U.S. values for the final report. This is a simple enough task if you use COPY to selectively copy the dollar amounts from the Canadian (ABC2) database to another database, named CURRENCY, for temporary storage. You'll then multiply the dollar amounts contained in the CURRENCY file by the current exchange rate, and use another command (the UPDATE command) to replace the amounts in the WORLDWIDE database with the updated amounts. First enter

```
USE ABC2
COPY TO CURRENCY FIELDS LASTNAME, PHONE, RENTAMT
```

COPY TO will create a new database named CURRENCY and will contain only LASTNAME and RENTAMTS from the Canadian database. (The reason that LASTNAME was included will be discussed in "Using UPDATE.") Next, change the dollar amounts. To do this, you will need to use the REPLACE command. You may recall from Chapter 6 that the REPLACE command is used to change the contents of specific fields in a database. Assuming an exchange rate of 80% of U.S. dollars, enter

```
USE CURRENCY
REPLACE ALL RENTAMT WITH RENTAMT * .8
```

And if you enter LIST, you will see

```
Record#  LASTNAME      RENTAMT
      1  Belange        664.00
      2  Clarke         724.00
      3  Robinson       488.00
```

The listing of the database shows that the dollar amounts have been changed to 80% of their Canadian value. All that remains of this task is to replace the values in the WORLDWIDE database with these new values. For that, UPDATE will come in handy.

USING UPDATE

The UPDATE command can be used to replace records in a database file, based on information contained in a source file. The general format of the command is UPDATE ON *keyfield* FROM *alias-file* REPLACE *field* WITH *expression* (UPDATE has been joined with the "create" version of the REPLACE command). To make replacements, dBASE III PLUS matches records in both database files on a key field common to both databases. This is why the database file CURRENCY was given the LASTNAME field: it will serve as a key with the WORLDWIDE database. dBASE III PLUS then replaces the data field in the active file with the data field from another open file.

Before UPDATE can be used, the database to be updated must be the active database file in the selected work area. The source file is the *aliasfile*, though you don't have to use the alias of the file. In addition, both files must be sorted or indexed on the key field, so you must index the WORLDWIDE database on the LAST-NAME field before you update the dollar amounts in the RENTAMT fields. To do so, enter the following:

```
CLEAR ALL
SELECT 2
USE CURRENCY
INDEX ON PHONE TO NAME
SELECT 1
USE WORLDWIDE
INDEX ON PHONE TO NEWNAME
```

The INDEX command puts the database in the proper order for using UPDATE. Now enter

```
UPDATE ON PHONE FROM CURRENCY REPLACE RENTAMT WITH
CURRENCY -> RENTAMT
```

This format of the UPDATE command says, "Update the database in use (WORLDWIDE), using LASTNAME as a key field and CURRENCY as a source database. Whenever LASTNAME matches, replace RENTAMT with the RENTAMT contained in the CURRENCY database." You used LASTNAME as a key field simply to have a common key field that both databases were indexed on. For your purposes, you could have chosen another field as the key field as long as the key field was the same field in both databases.

To see the fruits of your labors, enter

```
LIST LASTNAME, CITY, RENTAMT
```

And you should see this:

Record#	LASTNAME	CITY	RENTAMT
11	Andrews	Highland Park	950.00
13	Belange	Montreal	664.00
14	Clarke	Toronto	724.00
10	Drummond	Detroit	810.00
6	Hart	Fairfax	680.00
3	Jackson	Falls Church	525.00
9	Jones	Reston	950.00
2	Levy	Washington	875.00
5	Mitchell	Arlington	990.00
1	Morse	Chevy Chase	750.00
7	Robinson	Takoma Park	488.00
8	Robinson	Washington	920.00
15	Robinson	Toronto	488.00
12	Turner	Detroit	875.00
4	Westman	Silver Spring	570.00

Now you have a single database listing U.S. and Canadian properties, and all amounts are adjusted for U.S. dollar values. At this point, it would be a simple matter to produce the desired report for ABC Realty's president. You could turn on the printer with the SET PRINT ON command and then list any desired information. Of course, if you were going to produce this report on a regular basis, you would want to automate the entire process by placing all of the commands that you just used inside of a command file. The command file could be called up from an appropriate choice on the database system menu.

Most file management commands cannot be performed from the Assistant. The JOIN, SELECT, CLEAR ALL, and APPEND FROM commands are not available from the Assistant. You can rename and erase files from the Assistant; these selections are available from the Tools menu.

Using the Relational
Powers of dBASE III PLUS

Chapter 12

As mentioned in the first chapter, dBASE III PLUS is a relational database manager. Relational commands of dBASE III PLUS offer the ability to use more than one file at a time and the ability to define a relationship between two or more files. This chapter will describe a number of ways you can take advantage of the relational capabilities of dBASE III PLUS. Using the SET RELATION TO command, you can link multiple databases by means of a common field that exists in each database. Using view files, you can store a permanent record of these types of relationships between files. And using data catalogs, you can store an associated group of database files, index files, view files, query files, and form files. Then, when you use that catalog, only those files will be accessible through the directories of the Assistant. This chapter makes extensive use of the PARTS and ORDERS databases described in the previous chapter. Therefore, if you did not create those databases as outlined earlier, do so now before proceeding.

USING THE SET RELATION TO COMMAND

The PARTS and ORDERS databases are typical examples of databases that benefit from the use of relational commands. The PARTS database, as shown by its structure, contains part numbers, descriptions, and the costs of each part.

```
Structure for database: C:parts.dbf

Field  Field Name  Type        Width    Dec
    1   PARTNO      Numeric        4
    2   DESCRIPT    Character     15
    3   COST        Numeric        6       2
**  Total **                     26
```

The ORDERS database, on the other hand, contains the names and customer numbers of the customers who order parts, as well as the part numbers and quantities of the parts that have been ordered.

```
Structure for database: C:orders.dbf

Field  Field Name  Type        Width    Dec
    1   CUSTNO      Numeric        4
    2   CUSTNAME    Character     10
    3   PARTNO      Numeric        4
    4   QUANTITY    Numeric        2
**  Total **                     21
```

Using two separate databases is a better solution than using a single database in this case, because a single database would require unnecessary duplication of information. If you had a single database with all of the fields present in these two databases, each time one customer ordered a part number that had been previously ordered by another customer, you would have to duplicate the part description and part cost. To avoid such duplication, you can use two databases and link the databases together with the SET RELATION TO command. The SET RELATION TO command will link the files together by means of a common field. A common field is a field, present in both databases, that has the same field name, field type, width, and contents. In the example, you will draw a relation between the PARTS database and the ORDERS database, by linking the common PARTNO field (Figure 12-1). Then, whenever you move to a record in the ORDERS database, the record pointer in the PARTS database will move to the record that contains the same part number that is in the record in the ORDERS database.

The format of the SET RELATION TO command is SET RELATION TO *key expression* INTO *alias*. The *key expression* is

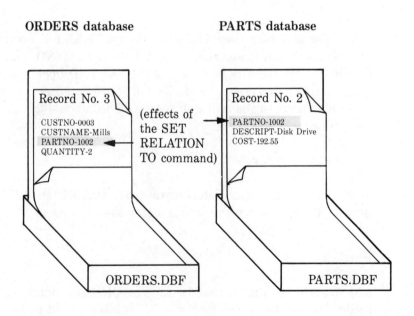

ORDERS database

PARTS database

Record No. 3

CUSTNO-0003
CUSTNAME-Mills
PARTNO-1002
QUANTITY-2

(effects of the SET RELATION TO command)

Record No. 2

PARTNO-1002
DESCRIPT-Disk Drive
COST-192.55

ORDERS.DBF

PARTS.DBF

Figure 12-1. Concept of SET RELATION

the common field present in both databases. The *alias* is the name of the other database that the active database is to be linked to. One important requirement of this command is that you must index the file that will be linked on the common field. In this case, the PARTS database must be indexed on the PARTNO field.

Get to the dot prompt if you're not there already, and set the default drive to the appropriate drive containing your databases. Close the ABC rentals files (if open), and open the PARTS and ORDERS files, complete with index files, by using the following commands:

```
CLEAR ALL
SELECT 1
USE PARTS
INDEX ON PARTNO TO PARTINDX
SELECT 2
USE ORDERS
INDEX ON PARTNO TO ORDINDX
```

You now have both the PARTS and the ORDERS files open, and both files are indexed on the common field of PARTNO. It is now possible to link the files by means of the PARTNO field, using the SET RELATION TO command. The ORDERS database is now the active database, so you will link the PARTS database to it. Enter the following:

```
SET RELATION TO PARTNO INTO PARTS
```

No changes are immediately visible, but dBASE III PLUS has linked the files. To see the effects, enter the commands

```
GO 3
DISPLAY
```

and you will see the third record in the ORDERS database. The record indicates that the customer Mills has ordered two of part number 1002. To see exactly what was ordered, enter these commands:

```
SELECT 1
DISPLAY
```

The PARTS database will become the active database, and the record pointer will be at record 2, showing that part number 1002 is a disk drive and costs $192.55. Get back to the ORDERS database with these commands:

```
SELECT 2
GO 2
DISPLAY
```

Again, you can see that the relation has found a matching part number in the PARTS database by entering these commands:

```
SELECT 1
DISPLAY
```

Wherever you move in the ORDERS database, the record pointer will try to find a matching part number in the PARTS database. If dBASE III PLUS cannot find a match according to the relation that you have specified, the record pointer will be positioned at the end of the database.

CREATING AND USING VIEW FILES

If you must often draw the same relationships between files, you can speed up this process by creating view files. View files let you identify the relationships between files and store those relationships for future use. Relationships are not all that is contained in a view file. View files contain database files, with any desired index files and work areas; relations between the files; one format file, if desired; selected fields from each database; and a "filter" condition, a topic that will be described later. You create view files with the View menu, a system of menus that resembles those you've already used for creating reports, labels, and forms.

The View menu can be opened in one of two ways. From the dot prompt, you can enter the command, CREATE VIEW *filename*. From the Assistant, you can open the Create menu, and choose the View option.

Enter CLEAR ALL from the dot prompt now, to close the files.
Then enter the command

```
CREATE VIEW PARTVIEW
```

This step will create a view file called PARTVIEW and open the
View menu (Figure 12-2). dBASE III PLUS will normally supply
an extension of .VUE to any view file that is created.

    The View menu provides five menus: Set Up, Relate, Set Fields,
Options, and Exit. The Set Up menu is used to choose the database
and associated index files that will be contained in the view. The
Relate menu is used to draw relationships between the files. The
Set Fields menu is used to select fields from each database file.

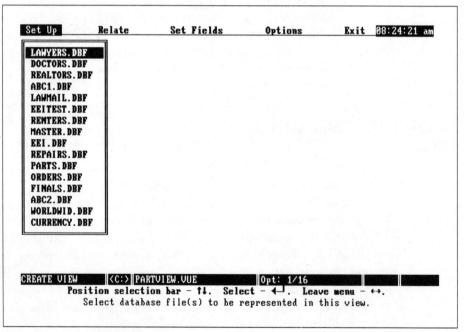

Figure 12-2. View menu

Normally, all fields are available from a database that you select with the Set Up menu. However, you can use the Set Fields menu to "hide" particular fields from use when the view is chosen.

The Options menu lets you select one screen format file, previously created with the Screen Painter, to view databases. You can also enter a Filter from the Options menu; a Filter is an expression that will filter records in the view. Finally, the Exit menu is used to save the completed view file and to return to the Assistant or to the dot prompt.

In this case, the view file will contain the PARTS and ORDERS databases, the index files for both databases, and the relation between the ORDERS and the PARTS databases. Select ORDERS from the Set Up menu now. Once you have selected the ORDERS

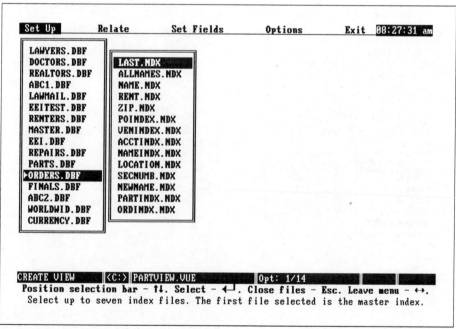

Figure 12-3. Index File menu

database, a window displaying the available index files will appear (Figure 12-3).

Select ORDINDX from the menu (use the PG DN key, if necessary, to see all of the index files). Then press the ← or → key to leave the menu of index files.

You also want to include the PARTS database in this view; therefore, select PARTS from the list of available databases. When the menu of index files appears, select PARTINDX from the list (Figure 12-4). Press the ← or → key to leave the menu of index files. Open the Relate menu, and you will see the names of both databases that you have identified for this view (Figure 12-5).

Note that the message in the message line at the bottom of the screen indicates that you should select the database that will

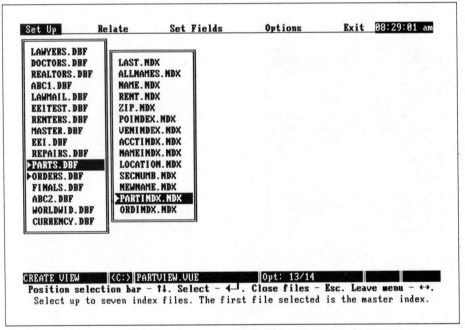

Figure 12-4. PARTS database with PARTINDX index file selected

initiate the relation. The first file selected by the Relate menu is the "initial file," or the file that will initiate the relation. All other files will be linked to the initial file.

Select ORDERS from the menu now. Another menu appears, and the message line says that you should **Select the database that will accept the relation.** The other database, PARTS, is the only database visible in the menu. If you had selected additional databases from the Set Up menu, they would now be visible. In this case, only the PARTS database is needed.

Press RETURN to select the PARTS database. A message at the bottom of the screen indicates that you should enter an expression to link the databases. Press F10 now to display a list of fields (Figure 12-6).

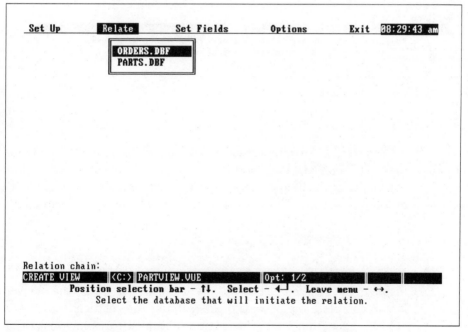

Figure 12-5. Relate menu

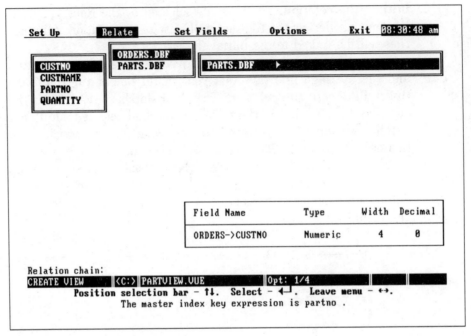

Figure 12-6. Fields list

In this case, the databases are to be linked by the PARTNO field, so select PARTNO. Press RETURN again to accept PARTNO within the menu, and notice the message above the status bar at the bottom of the screen. The message shows the following information:

```
Relation chain: ORDERS.DBF->PARTS.DBF
```

As you use the Relate menu to build a relation, dBASE III PLUS displays the relation at the bottom of the screen. Press the ← or → key to complete the process of identifying the relation.

Next, open the Set Fields menu. The menu displays both the ORDERS and PARTS databases present in this view (Figure 12-7). Normally, all fields are included for display in a view. You can use the Set Fields menu to limit access to a particular field when using the view. For example, select the PARTS database from the

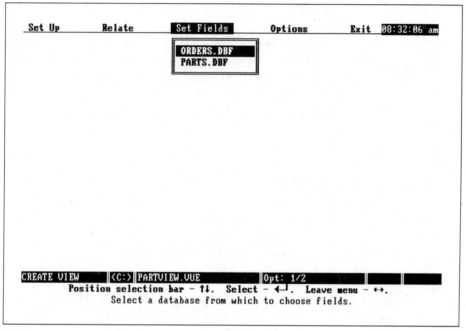

Figure 12-7. Set Fields menu

Set Fields menu now. A window of fields will appear; the triangle
next to each field name indicates that the fields have been automatically selected for inclusion in the view.

The PARTNO field is already highlighted. You don't really need
to see this field, since it is also present in the ORDERS database,
and the databases are linked by the choices made in the Relate
menu. Press RETURN once, to remove the PARTNO field from this
view. Then, press the ← or → key to close the menu.

In this example, the Options menu will not be used; but its available choices are worth discussion. The Filter selection lets you
specify a condition for the records that will be included within the
view file. For example, an expression of "PARTNO <= 1200"
would cause only those records with part numbers of 1200 or less
to be included in the view. The Format selection lets you choose a
format file, to display the fields in a custom screen format. You

must first use Screen Painter to create a format file before selecting this option.

Our view is now ready to be saved. Open the Exit menu, and choose the SAVE option to save the view file. When dBASE III PLUS saves a view file, it also automatically opens that view file and its associated contents.

To see the effects of the view file, enter the following command:

```
LIST
```

and you will see this display:

```
Record#   CUSTNO CUSTNAME   PARTNO QUANTITY DESCRIPT          COST
      4        4 Reynolds     1001        1 keyboard        175.80
      3        3 Mills        1002        2 disk drive      192.55
      1        1 Smith        1003        9 memory chip       6.15
      2        2 Johnson      1005        2 microprocessor   24.74
```

Note that fields from both databases are displayed. The relation specified in the view file provides the desired link between the ORDERS and the PARTS databases. The relational capabilities of dBASE III PLUS, including the use of view files, can be a powerful tool for working effectively with multiple files.

To turn off the effects of a view file, you can use the CLEAR ALL command. Enter these commands now:

```
CLEAR ALL
USE ORDERS
LIST
```

This time, the LIST command shows only the data present in the ORDERS database.

If you have used commands from the dot prompt to open database and index files in work areas and to set relations, you can save this information in a view file without using the View menu. To do this, you can use the CREATE VIEW *filename* FROM ENVIRONMENT command. This command will store any open database and index files, current relations between files, and one open format file.

CREATING OR CHOOSING A CATALOG

dBASE III PLUS lets you store an associated group of database files, index files, view files, query files, and form files in a special file known as a catalog. When using that catalog, only those files will be accessible for use by dBASE III PLUS. This feature comes in particularly handy if you use a hard disk. By placing various files in different catalogs, you do not have to search through excessively long lists of files in a directory. Any new files that you create while a particular catalog is open will be added to that catalog. dBASE III PLUS stores the information that makes up a catalog in a special kind of database that is assigned a .CAT extension. When you open a catalog, either from the Assistant with the Catalog option of the Set Up menu, or from the dot prompt with the SET CATALOG TO *filename* command, dBASE III PLUS looks into the special database to find the files associated with that particular catalog. The relationship of files stored within a catalog is illustrated in Figure 12-8.

You cannot create a catalog from the Assistant; you must use the SET CATALOG TO command to create a catalog. If the catalog exists, this command will select that catalog. If the catalog does not exist, this command will create a new catalog.

As an example, you can create a catalog that contains specific databases, index files, and screen formats for ABC Realty. The first step in doing so is to create a catalog that will contain the files. For this, you use the SET CATALOG TO *filename* command. Enter the command

```
SET CATALOG TO ABC
```

and dBASE III PLUS will ask if you wish to create a new catalog. Enter Y for yes, and dBASE III PLUS will next ask

```
Enter title for file ABC.CAT:
```

This title is used to describe the contents of the catalog. You can

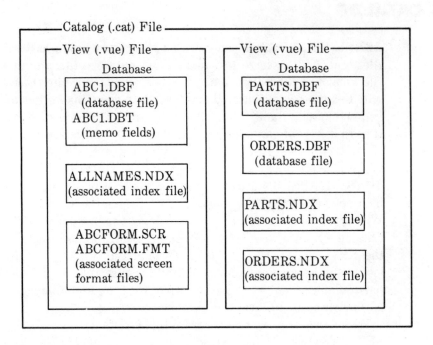

Figure 12-8. Concept of catalogs

enter any message up to 80 characters in length. In this case, enter

```
Catalog contains ABC1, ABC2, WORLDWIDE databases, and other files.
```

Once you have entered the catalog title, dBASE III PLUS will respond with a message indicating that the catalog is presently empty. This is expected, as you have not yet added any files to the catalog.

ADDING FILES TO A CATALOG

Once a new catalog has been created or an existing catalog has been selected, you can add files to that catalog with a number of dBASE III PLUS commands. The commands (and their Assistant menu equivalents) that will add files to an open catalog include the following:

```
CREATE                        (database files)
CREATE/MODIFY LABEL           (label files)
CREATE/MODIFY REPORT          (report form files)
CREATE/MODIFY SCREEN          (screen format files)
CREATE/MODIFY VIEW            (view files)
USE                           (database files)
INDEX, SET INDEX TO           (index files)
SET FILTER TO                 (query files)
SET VIEW TO                   (view files)
COPY TO                       (database files)
COPY STRUCTURE                (database files)
COPY STRUCTURE EXTENDED       (database files)
```

You want to include the ABC1, ABC2, and WORLDWIDE databases in this catalog. You'll also include the ALLNAMES index file created earlier, as well as the ABCFORM entry form created with Screen Painter. To do this, enter the following commands. Note that upon entering each command (with the exception of the INDEX command), dBASE III PLUS will ask for a title for the file. This title will be stored as a helpful description within the catalog.

```
USE ABC2              (enter "ABC2 database" as a title)
USE WORLDWIDE         (enter "Worldwide database" as a title)
USE ABC1              (enter "ABC1 database" as a title)
SET INDEX TO ALLNAMES
SET FORM TO ABCFORM   (enter "data entry form" as a title)
```

To see the results of the catalog, enter ASSIST to open the Assistant menus. Choose the Database File option of the Set Up menu. Note that the menu of available databases shows only those files that are in the catalog, rather than all the various database

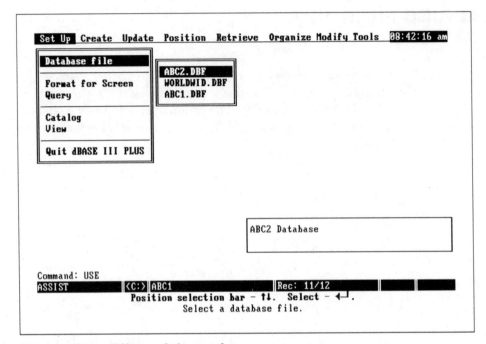

Figure 12-9. Effects of the catalog

files that by now actually exist on your disk. Also note that the lower-right corner of your screen contains a window with a helpful description of the file that you entered earlier (Figure 12-9).

Select ABC1 for the database to open, and answer Y to the **Is the file indexed** prompt. Again, only the index files present in the catalog will be displayed. Press RETURN, then exit the menu by pressing the ← or → key once.

CLOSING A CATALOG

You can close a catalog by selecting another catalog, with either the SET CATALOG TO command or the Catalog option of the Set

Up menu in the Assistant. The CLEAR ALL and QUIT commands will also close any open catalogs.

Press ESC to return to the dot prompt, and enter CLEAR ALL. Then, enter the Assistant, and try using the Database File option of the Set Up directory. All of the databases present on the disk will be visible in the menu, because no catalog is open to restrict those files.

A NOTE ABOUT DOS AND OPEN FILES

Because a catalog is a kind of database, it must be open when in use. Any catalog that you open is normally in work area 10. This means that dBASE III PLUS's normal limit of ten databases open at once is reduced to nine databases when you use a catalog. Also, keep in mind that the standard CONFIG.SYS file that you added to your system disk, hard disk, or start-up DOS disk in Chapter 3 contains the message **FILES** = 20. This CONFIG.SYS file tells DOS to set aside 20 files for the use of your software and your system. Your computer, DOS, and the dBASE III PLUS program will use five of these files. That leaves a maximum of 15 for your use. That may seem like more than enough, but remember that your view files and your catalogs may contain several database files, several index files, and possibly some format and query files. If you run programs, each program file (command file) that is read also counts as another open file. If the combined number of open files reaches 15, and you try to open another file, dBASE III PLUS will display a **Too many files are open** error message. You must then close one of the files before you can open another. If this problem occurs often, you may want to change the CONFIG.SYS file so that more files are open. (You must then restart your system before any changes made to CONFIG.SYS will take effect.) As an example, you could change the line in the CONFIG.SYS file that reads

```
FILES = 20
```

to instead read

```
FILES = 30
```

Keep in mind that the more files you set aside in the CONFIG.-SYS file, the less memory you will have left for programs. Increasing the files to a large number could cause other problems, particularly if you use memory resident software such as Borland's SideKick along with dBASE III PLUS.

Creating and Refining
Screen Displays

Chapter 13

dBASE III PLUS can help you design screen displays that won't confuse the people who use your database management system. The appearance of screen displays may at first seem like a minor point of importance. But if you were a new dBASE III PLUS system user, which of the following two screen displays would be easier to use: the top screen (Figure 13-1a) or the bottom screen (Figure 13-1b)?

Obviously, the bottom screen will make more sense to the novice user of dBASE III PLUS because it is clearer and less cluttered than the top screen. As you will see in this chapter, you can easily create well-designed screens by storing various screen-display commands within a dBASE III PLUS command file. You'll use the @, SAY, and GET options to place prompts and information at selected locations on the screen, and the READ command to allow responses to the prompts displayed by the system. You'll also examine how the Screen Painter can provide most of the commands needed for the formatting of screens.

```
B>type txfig10-
ABC Realty Database System
Choose A Selection Below:
Choose 1 to add entry to the database.
Choose 2 to change an existing entry.
Choose 3 to produce the income summary.
Choose 4 to display data regarding a tenant.
Choose 5 to exit this program.
Enter selection:

B>-
```
a.

```
=====ABC Realty Database System=====

        Choose a selection shown below:


1. Add new entries        3. Produce income summary

2. Change existing entries   4. Display tenant data


            5. Exit this program



    Enter selection: ▮▮▮▮▮▮▮▮▮0
```
b.

Figure 13-1. Two screen displays

PUTTING INFORMATION ON THE SCREEN WITH @ AND SAY

The @ command (commonly referred to as the "AT" command) tells dBASE III PLUS where to place the cursor on the screen. The dBASE III PLUS screen is divided into 25 lines and 80 columns (Figure 13-2).

Rows are numbered from 0 to 24, while columns are numbered from 0 to 79. Row 0, column 0 is in the upper-left corner. Row 24, column 79 is in the lower-right corner of the screen. The cursor can be placed in any screen position.

Once the cursor has been placed in the proper position with the @ command, you can print a message with the SAY option. The SAY option causes the text or the contents of a string variable that follows the command to appear on the screen. The SAY option can be used, along with the @ command, in one of two possible ways: @*row,column* SAY *"message"* or @*row,column* SAY *varname*. In the first format, SAY is followed by one or more characters, which must be enclosed by double or single quotes. The characters will be displayed on the screen exactly as they appear between the quotes. In the second format, a *varname* is a variable name. Any value that your program stores in that variable will be displayed.

To try the first format, let's display a message beginning at row 12, column 40 on the screen. Get to the dot prompt, then enter

```
@ 12,40 SAY "Enter name."
```

This displays the prompt **Enter name.** beginning at row 12, column 40 on the screen.

Now let's try the second format. Enter this:

```
STORE 1200.57 TO AMOUNT
@ 6,30 SAY AMOUNT
```

This stores 1200.57 in the variable AMOUNT and then displays the value at row 6, column 30.

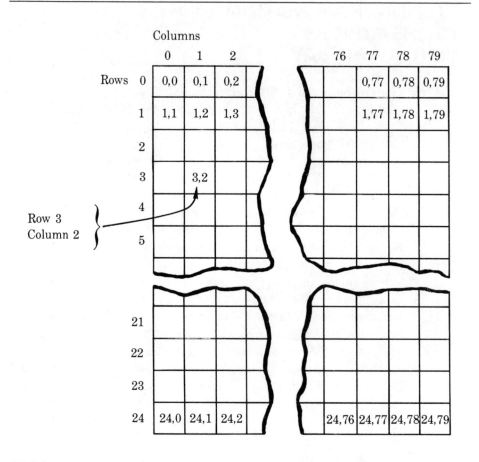

Figure 13-2. Screen coordinates

Keep in mind that when using the @ command and SAY option to design screen displays, the coordinates for the edges of the screen may or may not actually be displayed at your screen's edges. Some monitors may cut off the edges; so to be safe, you may want to stay away from the outer edges of the screen. Because dBASE III PLUS puts system and error messages at the 22nd, 23rd, and 24th lines on the screen, it is a good idea to avoid these lines altogether.

You can erase any part of the screen with the @ command and CLEAR option. The format is @*row,column* CLEAR.

The screen beginning at *row,column* will be erased to the lower-right corner. You use the @ command and CLEAR option in a manner similar to the @ command and SAY option, but don't enter any prompts or variables after the word CLEAR. For example, the following command,

```
@ 12,7 CLEAR
```

would erase the screen beginning at 12,7 to the lower-right corner.

Using GET and READ With @ and SAY

Now that you know how to display information at selected places on the screen, you need a way to store responses to screen prompts. This is done with two new options, GET and READ, which in combination display existing variables or field names and the field length of the record being referenced by the pointer, and store the typed replies to screen messages and prompts. There are two formats: @*row,column* SAY "*prompt*" GET *varname*... READ and @*row,column* SAY "*prompt*" GET *fieldname*... READ.

The GET option tells dBASE III PLUS to get ready to accept information. The information displayed with GET can be either an existing memory variable or any field in the database in use. The READ command then tells dBASE III PLUS to enter *full-screen editing mode*, which, much like APPEND, allows the user to move the cursor around the screen; to accept responses from the keyboard for any of the preceding GET options; and to store the responses in memory. In addition, the READ option lets you edit the displayed information.

A GET option does not have to be immediately followed by a READ option; it can be the last command in a series of GETs. But if you use a GET without READ, you cannot enter any responses from the keyboard. READ options are only used following GET options. You could, for example, create a command file like this one:

```
@ 5,10 SAY "Enter name." GET LASTNAME
@ 7,10 SAY "Enter address." GET ADDRESS
@ 9,10 SAY "Enter city." GET CITY
@ 11,10 SAY "Enter state." GET STATE
READ
```

If you were to use the database containing the field names and run this command file, dBASE III PLUS would provide a screen display that would prompt you for the desired information. The prompts would appear at the screen locations identified by the @ command and SAY option. Once the READ option was encountered, the full-screen edit mode would be entered, and the cursor would be placed at the start of the first field identified by a GET option. As data is entered, dBASE III PLUS stores all of the entries in memory under the field names or variable names used. The name would be stored in LASTNAME, the address in ADDRESS, the city in CITY, and so on.

You could also use the INPUT command along with a prompt to place information on the screen and store a response. But with INPUT, you cannot control where on the screen the information appears. The example that follows will show how the use of the @ command and SAY, GET, and READ options can result in a clear, well-designed menu screen.

Designing a Menu With @, SAY, and GET

You now have a main menu system for the ABC Realty database, but it uses ? and INPUT commands that do not provide much flexibility when it comes to placing the information on the screen. To change this, you must get into the dBASE III PLUS word processor and edit the command file used to display the menu. Enter this:

```
MODIFY COMMAND MENU
```

When the dBASE III PLUS word processor appears, the menu command file you developed in Chapter 8 will appear along with it. Change the file so it looks like this one:

```
USE ABC1
SET TALK OFF
STORE 0 TO CHOICE
DO WHILE CHOICE < 5
* Do while loop will redisplay menu unless 5 is chosen.
    CLEAR
    *Display main menu.
    @ 5,15 SAY "=====ABC Realty Database System Menu====="
    @ 7,18 SAY "Choose a selection shown below:"
    @ 10,5 SAY "1 Add new entries."
    @ 10,34 SAY "3 Produce Reports"
    @ 12,5 SAY "2 Change existing entries."
    @ 12,34 SAY "4 Display Tenant Data"
    @ 15,21 SAY "5 Exit this program."
    @ 19,7 SAY "Enter selection: " GET CHOICE
    READ
    DO CASE
        CASE CHOICE = 1
        DO ADDER
        CASE CHOICE = 2
        DO CHANGES
        CASE CHOICE = 3
        REPORT FORM INCOME
        CASE CHOICE = 4
        DO SHOW
        CASE CHOICE = 5
        RETURN
    ENDCASE CHOICE
ENDDO
```

When you are finished entering the command file, type CONTROL-END to save it. You then might want to try using the system; start it by entering DO MENU. Choose the menu choice for adding a record, and while you are watching the system's operation, you might want to think about ways to improve further on the system design. Perhaps you can modify the command files used by your system, so that other choices from the menu provide easy-to-understand screen displays. When you are finished using the system, the CONTROL-END key combination will get you out of any of the Edit or Append functions and back to the system menu.

Customizing a Data-Entry Screen

One area of the system that could stand improvement is in the adding of data. Currently, the system relies on the APPEND command. With the @ command and the SAY, GET, and READ options, you can display the prompts more neatly than you could with the APPEND command and you can store the data in variables that will be added to the database. Let's create a new command file, called ADDER, that will be used whenever you want to add a record to the database. Enter MODIFY COMMAND ADDER, and enter the following as the command file:

```
USE ABC1
CLEAR
APPEND BLANK
@ 2,3 SAY "Tenant's last name:" GET LASTNAME
@ 3,2 SAY "Tenant's first name:" GET FIRSTNAME
@ 5,14 SAY "Address:" GET ADDRESS
@ 6,17 SAY "City:" GET CITY
@ 7,16 SAY "State:" GET STATE
@ 8,18 SAY "Zip:" GET ZIP
@ 9,16 SAY "Phone:" GET PHONE
@ 11,3 SAY "Number of bedrooms:" GET BEDROOMS
@ 12,2 SAY "Number of bathrooms:" GET BATHROOMS
@ 14,5 SAY "Lease expires on:" GET EXPDATE
@ 15,5 SAY "Type of property:" GET PROPTYPE
@ 17,10 SAY "Rental cost:" GET RENTAMT
@ 18,12 SAY "Unit size:" GET SIZE
@ 19,1 SAY "Parking (true/false):" GET PARKING
@ 20,9 SAY "Sales office:" GET SALESOFF
@ 21,0 SAY "Description of extras:" GET EXTRAS
READ
RETURN
```

Let's examine this command file before saving it. After opening
the file with USE and clearing the screen, you then use the
BLANK option of the APPEND command. Whenever dBASE III
PLUS sees APPEND BLANK as a command, it adds a blank
record to the end of the database, and the record pointer is positioned at the last record. Each @ command and SAY option prints
a query, such as **Tenant's last name:**. The GET option not only
displays the contents of each field listed, but it displays them in
reverse video in the dimensions of the field width. Since the record
pointer is referencing the last record, which is empty, only the
reverse video will be displayed. The READ command toward the
bottom of the file activates the reverse video, or *full-screen entry*
and *editing*, specified by the GET option. When data entry or editing has been completed for the last field, you then return to the
main menu section of the program.

Type CONTROL-END now to save the command file. Now you'll
need to make one change in the main menu command file to inte-
grate the new ADDER command file into the system. Enter MOD-
IFY COMMAND MENU, and change the word APPEND in the
command file to DO ADDER; then press CONTROL-END to save the
file.

Try out the new command file by entering DO MENU. Choose
menu 1 and try entering a rental property description.

Using PICTURE

The PICTURE option is used with the @ command to format data.
Using PICTURE, you can display dollar amounts with both commas and decimal places, or you can display dates in American or
European date formats. PICTURE restricts the way data can be
entered into the system. You can accept numbers only, for dollar
amounts, or a date only, rejecting any other characters.

The PICTURE option is divided into function and template
symbols (Table 13-1). The format is @*row,column* SAY *expression*

Table 13-1. Functions and Templates Used With PICTURE

Functions

Symbol	Meaning
A	Displays alphabetic characters only
B	Left-justifies numeric data
C	Displays letters "CR" for credit, after a positive number
D	Displays American date format
E	Displays European date format
X	Displays letters "DB" for debit, after a negative number
Z	Displays any zeros as blanks
!	Displays capital letters only
(	Surrounds negative numbers with parentheses

Templates

Symbol	Meaning
9	Allows only digits for character data, or digits and signs for numeric data
#	Allows only digits, blanks, and signs
A	Allows only letters
L	Allows only logical data (.T. or .F.; .Y. or .N.)
N	Allows only letters and digits
X	Allows any characters
!	Converts letters to uppercase
$	Displays dollar signs in place of leading zeros
*	Displays asterisks in place of leading zeros
.	Specifies a decimal position
,	Displays a comma if there are any numbers to the left of the comma

PICTURE *"clause"*. You use the PICTURE option by adding the word PICTURE and then the letters or symbols that specify the function or template.

The functions or templates in *clause* are surrounded by quotes. An @ symbol must appear as the first character in a function. Two examples of the PICTURE option are

```
@ 12,40 SAY "Enter efective date-" GET PICTURE "@E"
@ 14,20 SAY "Customer name is: " GET LASTNAME PICTURE"!!!!!!!!!!!!!!!!!"
```

In the first example, the @ symbol defines the *clause* as a function. The letter E defines the function as European date format. A template is used in the second example. The exclamation points in the template will result in a display of uppercase letters regardless of how the letters are stored in the database.

Some of the functions used with PICTURE apply only to certain kinds of data. The C, X, B, (, and Z functions apply only to numeric data. The A and ! functions apply to character data only, but the D and E functions apply to date, character, and numeric data.

You can combine function symbols for multiple functions. For example, the function symbols BZ align numeric data at the left side of the field and display any zero values as blanks.

You can get a better idea of how the PICTURE option is used if you try a few examples. First let's try the X and C functions. The X function will display a DB, for debit after a negative number, while the C function will display a CR, for credit after a positive number. Try the following commands to illustrate these functions:

```
CLEAR
STORE -1650.32 TO A
STORE 795 TO B
@5,0 SAY A PICTURE "@X"
@10,0 SAY B PICTURE "@C"
```

results in:

```
1650.32 DB

795 CR
```

This is useful in accounting.

The ! template is useful when you want character displays to appear in all uppercase letters. Try this:

```
CLEAR
STORE "small words" TO WORDS
@10,10 SAY WORDS PICTURE "!!!!!!!!!!!"
```

The # template reserves space for digits, blanks, or signs, while the comma template specifies where the comma should appear in numeric data. Try these templates with the following example:

```
STORE 1234.56 TO A
@16,0 SAY A PICTURE "#,###.##"

1,234.56
```

When you are using templates, you must use a symbol for each character that is to be displayed with SAY or GET. To display a character field that is 10 characters wide in uppercase, for example, you would need 10 exclamation points in the template. The template would look like this:

```
@20,10 SAY "Name is--"  GET NAME PICTURE "!!!!!!!!!!"
```

Let's try a PICTURE option in the command file for adding a record. Enter MODIFY COMMAND ADDER. Change the line of the program that reads

```
@17,10 SAY "Rental cost:" GET RENTAMT
```

to this:

```
@17,10 SAY "Rental cost:" GET RENTAMT PICTURE "#,###.##"
```

Save the program with CONTROL-END; then run the system with DO MENU. Choose the "Add new entries" option and enter another record; but this time, use a rental amount of $1000 or more. You'll see the new format caused by the PICTURE specification as you enter the rental amount; the comma will automatically be added. You can get out of the system without making changes to the database by pressing the ESC key and then 5 to return to the dot prompt.

USING FORMAT FILES

Let's say that you wanted to enter only last names, first names, and rental cost without being required to step through all of the other fields that normally appear on the screen—addresses, phone numbers, lease expiration dates, parking, and so on. You can limit the amount of information shown on a screen in either append mode or edit mode by using a *format file*. A format file is a special file with the extension .FMT that contains an @ command and SAY and GET options that will display messages and prompts according to your arrangements. Once you have created the format file, you can implement it with the SET FORMAT TO command. For example, create a format file with the word processor by entering

```
MODIFY COMMAND QUICKIE.FMT
```

This will create a file called QUICKIE with the format extension of .FMT. Now enter the following commands:

```
@ 10,10 SAY "The last name is: " GET LASTNAME
@ 12,10 SAY "The first name is: " GET FIRSTNAME
@ 18,20 SAY "The rental amount will be: " GET RENTAMT
```

Press CONTROL-END to save the format file. When the prompt reappears, enter APPEND (be sure that ABC1 is the active file). Notice that what you see is the normal Append screen with all of its fields. Press ESC to get back to the dot prompt.

To use the format file, you must use the SET FORMAT TO *file-name* command (you don't have to supply the .FMT extension). Enter

```
SET FORMAT TO QUICKIE
```

Now enter APPEND. With the new format file in effect, only the fields specified are shown. Press ESC to leave APPEND without making changes.

Now enter GOTO 5. This will move the pointer to record 5. Enter EDIT. Instead of the normal editing screen, you get just those fields specified in the format file that apply to record 5. Press ESC to get out of edit mode without making any changes. To disable a format file when you finish using it, simply enter CLOSE FORMAT without specifying a filename (because only one format file may be opened at a time).

Format files can come in handy when you want to use the same screen format many times in different parts of a program. You can include SET FORMAT TO *filename* anywhere in a dBASE III PLUS command file, and that format file will then take effect for any appending or editing until you use CLOSE FORMAT. Format files can contain only @ commands and SAY options, with or without GET added, or any comment lines that start with a NOTE command or an asterisk. You cannot use any other types of statements or commands in a format file.

An Easier Way

Now that you've learned how to write @-SAY-GET commands to place information on the screen and prompt the user for a response, let's consider why you shouldn't bother writing such files — at least, in some cases, such as for common data-entry screens. The Screen Painter, discussed in Chapter 5, automatically creates format files with all the @-SAY-GET commands you may ever need.

To summarize what was covered in Chapter 5, Screen Painter is a menu-driven feature of dBASE III PLUS that creates data-entry screens, complete with descriptive titles and borders, when desired. The information used by Screen Painter to design a particular screen is stored in a screen file, which is assigned the .SCR extension. The Screen Painter also creates a format file, with a .FMT extension. This file contains the @-SAY-GET commands that would be required if you were to write a command file that would display the same information in the same format as the Screen Painter.

For example, in Chapter 5 you created an entry form called ABCFORM. To see the effects of that form, enter these commands:

```
USE ABC1
SET FORMAT TO ABCFORM
EDIT
```

The screen that appears is the entry form created with the aid of Screen Painter. Press ESC to leave the EDIT function, and enter this command:

```
DIR *.FMT
```

This use of the directory command will cause dBASE III PLUS to display a list of all format files currently on your disk. Among those files, you will see one named ABCFORM.FMT, the file created by Screen Painter for the ABC Realty form.

To see the contents of the file, you can use the TYPE command. (The TYPE command is a command that will cause the contents of any text file to be "typed," or displayed, on the screen.) Enter the command

```
TYPE ABCFORM.FMT
```

and you will see the following:

```
@  1, 20   SAY "ABC REALTY COMPANY DATA ENTRY FORM"
@  3,  0   SAY "LASTNAME"
@  3, 12   GET   ABC1->LASTNAME   FUNCTION "!"  PICTURE "AAAAAAAAAAAAAAA"
@  3, 40   SAY "FIRSTNAME"
@  3, 50   GET   ABC1->FIRSTNAME
@  5,  0   SAY "ADDRESS"
@  5, 12   SAY   ABC1->ADDRESS
@  6,  0   SAY "CITY"
@  6, 12   SAY   ABC1->CITY
@  7,  0   SAY "STATE"
@  7, 12   SAY   ABC1->STATE
@  8,  0   SAY "ZIP"
@  8, 12   SAY   ABC1->ZIP
@  9,  0   SAY "PHONE"
@  9, 12   GET   ABC1->PHONE
@ 10, 40   SAY "EXTRAS"
@ 10, 50   GET   ABC1->EXTRAS
@ 11,  0   SAY "BEDROOMS"
@ 11, 12   GET   ABC1->BEDROOMS
@ 11, 30   SAY "(Control-PgDn to add text; Control-End saves.)"
@ 12,  0   SAY "BATHROOMS"
@ 12, 12   GET   ABC1->BATHROOMS
@ 13, 30   SAY "EXPIRATION DATE"
@ 13, 50   GET   ABC1->EXPDATE
@ 14, 30   SAY "PARKING"
@ 14, 42   GET   ABC1->PARKING
@ 15,  0   SAY "PROPERTY TYPE"
@ 15, 17   GET   ABC1->PROPTYPE
@ 16,  0   SAY "RENTAL AMOUNT"
@ 16, 18   GET   ABC1->RENTAMT   RANGE 400.00, 2000.00
@ 17, 30   SAY "SIZE"
@ 17, 42   GET   ABC1->SIZE
@ 19, 30   SAY "SALES OFFICE"
@ 19, 46   GET   ABC1->SALESOFF
@  0, 18   TO  2, 55     DOUBLE
```

If you wanted to manually create a format file that would display the information in the ABC Realty database in the same manner as the ABCFORM format file, you would be faced with writing a format file that contained all of these commands. Obviously, in many cases, it can be advantageous and time-saving to use the commands generated by Screen Painter instead of writing format files from scratch. A direct example of the time that can be saved is evident if you compare this format file to the manual commands entered previously in the ADDER command file. Enter the command

```
TYPE ADDER.PRG
```

and the command file that you created earlier to display new records appears. Presently, this command file uses 22 lines of programming code to accomplish its task. Now create another command file by entering the command

```
MODIFY COMMAND ADDTWO
```

You will create another program for adding records. Enter the following commands in this program:

```
USE ABC1
SET FORMAT TO ABCFORM
APPEND BLANK
READ
RETURN
```

Save this program with CONTROL-END, then enter DO ADDTWO to try the program. With five lines of programming code, this program has accomplished a function similar to the ADDER program, which uses four times as many lines of programming. That's not to say that the first method of creating format files is necessarily wrong. In some cases, you may want to display just one or two pieces of information. It would be overkill to use the Screen Painter to create an entry form for a single variable that's displayed somewhere in a program. The two methods of creating format files described in this chapter can be likened to the difference between manual and automatic transmission in a car. Neither is necessarily correct; it is up to the driver (in this case, you) to determine the appropriate method.

A Note About Screen Painter And Format Files

If you use Screen Painter to create forms, any modification of the form (with MODIFY SCREEN from the dot prompt, or by selecting the Format option of the Modify menu) will update both the screen (.SCR) file and the format (.FMT) file. If you use the format files along with your programs, and you make any changes manually to the format file using a word processor, you should rename the file with a name different from the corresponding screen file. This will prevent the format file from being accidentally overwritten if you later use Screen Painter to make changes to the screen. If you do use a word processor to make changes manually to a format file, remember that the corresponding screen file is not updated. To update the screen file, you must make your changes within the Screen Painter.

HELPFUL HINTS ON SCREEN DESIGN

Think about these aspects of screen design when you are designing a dBASE III PLUS system:

- Use menus as often as necessary. They should clearly say what choices are available to the person using the system.

- Avoid overly cluttered menus or data-entry screens. It may be better to break the entry screen in half, input half of the information, clear the screen with CLEAR, and then input the other half of the information rather than trying to fit a large number of fields on one data-entry screen. You can apply the same tactic to a menu by grouping a number of choices in a second menu that can be reached by a single choice on the main menu.

- Give users a way out; that is, a way of changing their minds after making a choice from a menu or selecting a particular entry screen.

- Finally, never leave the screen blank for any noticeable period of time. Few things are as unnerving to a computer user as a blank screen. A simple message that states that the computer is doing something (sorting, indexing, or whatever) is reassuring to the user.

More Programming
With dBASE III PLUS

Chapter 14

This chapter describes some additional commands and programming techniques that will be useful when you create more intricate command files to automate your work with dBASE III PLUS.

COMMON FUNCTIONS

dBASE III PLUS offers a number of functions for use within command files. Functions perform numerous tasks that would be difficult or impossible to do with individual commands. For example, you used the EOF function to determine when the pointer was at the end of a file. Functions look almost like commands, each beginning with a key word. Among the more common functions are the date and time functions and the functions used for converting characters from uppercase to lowercase and vice versa. Later in this chapter you will use a special function, called the macro function, to store information to the same variable name.

dBASE III PLUS provides the date and time by means of a clock built into your computer. For this reason, if the date and time set with your computer's DOS are incorrect, the date and time functions of dBASE III PLUS will also be incorrect. The format for DATE is DATE( ), and it provides the current date in the form MM/DD/YY. Dates follow the American date format, month followed by day followed by year, unless you use the PICTURE option (Chapter 13) or the SET DATE command to tell dBASE III PLUS otherwise. The TIME format of the function is TIME( ), and it provides the current time in HH:MM:SS format in the 24-hour system (for example, 23:30:00 is 11:30 P.M.). Note that for either function you do not need to supply anything between the parentheses, as they only serve to identify TIME and DATE as functions.

From the direct command mode, you could display the current date and time by entering this:

```
? DATE()
? TIME()
```

The output of the date and time function can be stored as a variable for use within the program, as in the example shown below:

```
SET PRINT ON
SET FORMAT TO REPORT2
@4,5 SAY "Date of this report is "
@5,5 SAY DATE()
@6,5 SAY "Time of this report is "
@7,5 SAY TIME()
STORE DATE() TO TRANSDAT
? TRANSDAT
```

UPPER

The UPPER function converts lowercase letters to uppercase letters. UPPER can thus be used to display text and variables in a uniform format if consistency is desired. It may be used with a character string or a memory variable that contains a character string. For example:

```
? UPPER ("This is not really uppercase")
THIS IS NOT REALLY UPPERCASE
STORE "not uppercase" TO WORDS
? UPPER(WORDS)
NOT UPPERCASE
```

LOWER

The LOWER function is the reverse of UPPER; it will convert uppercase characters to lowercase characters, as in the following example:

```
STORE "NOT CAPS" TO WORDS
? LOWER(WORDS)
not caps
```

RECNO

The RECNO function provides the current record number. This gives you a way of knowing exactly where in a database the pointer is positioned. The value provided by RECNO can be stored in a variable for further use. The following example program would tell the user how many records are contained in a given database.

```
GO BOTTOM
STORE RECNO() TO TOTAL
@5,5 SAY "There are "
@6,5 SAY TOTAL
@7,5 SAY "records in the database."
```

CTOD and DTOC

CTOD and DTOC are the character-to-date and date-to-character functions, respectively. CTOD converts a string of characters to a value that is recognized as a date by dBASE III PLUS. DTOC performs the opposite function, converting a date into a string of characters. Acceptable characters that can be converted to dates range from "1/1/100" to "12/31/9999." Any character strings that have values that fall outside these values will produce an error message if the CTOD function is used. As an example of the CTOD function, the following command might be used within a program to convert a string of characters to a value that could be stored within a date field:

```
STORE CTOD("05/26/87") TO EXPDATE
```

And as an example of the DTOC function, the following command would convert the contents of a date field to a character string and store that character string to the variable named LEASEOUT:

```
STORE DTOC(EXPDATE) TO LEASEOUT
? "Your lease expires on " + LEASEOUT
```

The DTOC function is particularly useful, because date fields cannot be used with the LIST, DISPLAY, or LOCATE commands. You could not, for example, search for a record containing a given expiration date with commands like these:

```
STORE "12/20/85" TO FINDIT
LIST FOR EXPDATE = FINDIT
```

The commands shown would result in a **data type mismatch** error message. Using the DTOC function as shown in the example that follows, such a search could be performed.

```
STORE "12/20/85" TO FINDIT
LIST FOR DTOC(EXPDATE) = FINDIT
```

TRIM

The TRIM function removes trailing blanks, or spaces that follow characters, from a character string. The TRIM function is useful as part of an expression in reports and labels, to close large gaps of space that often occur between fields. For example, the commands

```
USE ABC1
GO 2
SET PRINT ON
? FIRSTNAME, LASTNAME, ADDRESS
```

result in an unattractive printout that looks like this:

```
Carol           Levy          1207 5th Street S.E.
```

Using the TRIM function, the large gaps between the fields can be eliminated, as shown in the following example:

```
USE ABC1
GO 2
SET PRINT ON
? TRIM(FIRSTNAME), TRIM(LASTNAME), ADDRESS

Carol Levy 1207 5th Street S.E.
```

STR

The STR function is used to convert a numeric value into a character string. This type of conversion lets you mix numeric values with characters within displays and reports. As an example of the STR function, the command

```
? "The name is " + LASTNAME + "and the rent amount is " + RENTAMT
```

will produce a **data type mismatch** error, because RENTAMT is a numeric field, and the rest of the expression contains character values. The STR function can be used to convert the numeric value into a character value, as follows:

```
? "The name is " + LASTNAME + "and the rent amount is " + STR(RENTAMT)
```

MORE ABOUT MEMORY VARIABLES

You've been using memory variables in direct commands and in command files. However, all memory variables that you've used are only temporary: as soon as you turn off the computer they vanish. You can make a memory variable permanent by storing the variable to a memory file on disk. As you might expect, when the values are stored on disk, they can be recalled by a dBASE III PLUS program. dBASE III PLUS's memory lets you store up to 6000 characters and up to 256 memory variables. Each memory variable is assigned a different name.

Get to the dot prompt; then enter the following:

```
STORE 25 TO QUANTITY
STORE "Jefferson" TO NAMES
STORE TIME() TO CLOCK
? QUANTITY, NAMES, CLOCK
```

The previous example displayed the values stored in memory with the STORE command. However, you can use the DISPLAY MEMORY command to take a look at all variables that have been defined in memory. Enter

```
DISPLAY MEMORY
```

to display a listing of variables, a letter designating the type of variable, and what each variable contains.

```
WORDS       pub  C      "NOT CAPS"
QUANTITY    pub  N          25      (    25.00000000)
NAMES       pub  C      "Jefferson"
CLOCK       pub         "22:20:34"
```

You should keep two guidelines in mind. First, it's a good idea not to name variables after a field. If a program encounters a name that can be either a variable or a field, the field name will take precedence over the memory variable.

Second, note that you must store a value to a memory variable before you start using it in a program. This must be done because of dBASE III PLUS's firm rule that some type of value, even if it is a worthless one, must be stored to a dBASE III PLUS variable before you can begin using the variable. If you attempt to use variables in a program before defining them with the STORE command, dBASE III PLUS will respond with a **variable not found** error message.

To save variables on disk, use the SAVE TO command. The format of this command is SAVE TO *filename,* where *filename* is the name of the file that you want the variables saved under. The .MEM extension will automatically be added to the filename.

Right now, you have four memory variables defined from the previous examples—WORDS, QUANTITY, NAMES, and CLOCK. To save them, enter the following:

```
SAVE TO FASTFILE
```

Once the variables have been stored, you can clear the memory of variables with the RELEASE ALL command. Enter the following:

```
RELEASE ALL
DISPLAY MEMORY
```

You'll see that the memory variables no longer exist in memory. To get the memory variables back from FASTFILE, use the RESTORE FROM *filename* command. This command will restore variables from *filename* to memory. You do not have to include the file extension .MEM. Enter

```
RESTORE FROM FASTFILE
```

Then enter DISPLAY MEMORY. The variables are again in the system, ready for further use. When you use the RESTORE

FROM *filename* command, all variables in memory will be removed to accommodate variables from the file.

Getting back to RELEASE, you can select specific variables to remove from memory by including either the EXCEPT or the LIKE option. RELEASE with EXCEPT eliminates all variables except those that you list after EXCEPT. RELEASE with LIKE, on the other hand, removes the variables that you list after LIKE, the opposite of EXCEPT. As an example, enter

```
RELEASE ALL EXCEPT NAMES
DISPLAY MEMORY
```

This causes all memory variables except the variable called NAMES to be erased from memory.

You can use LIKE to erase some memory variables and leave other variables untouched. Try this:

```
RESTORE FROM FASTFILE
RELEASE ALL LIKE QUANTITY
DISPLAY MEMORY
```

This causes the memory variable QUANTITY to be erased from memory (the others will be untouched), or you can remove only those variables that you list with RELEASE *variable-list*.

USING dBASE III PLUS MACROS

dBASE III PLUS has a handy macro-substitution function. Macro substitution works like this: An ampersand (&) is placed in front of a memory variable name. This combination of ampersand and variable name becomes the dBASE III PLUS macro. Then, whenever dBASE III PLUS sees that macro, it will replace it with the contents of the memory variable. If, for example, you had a memory variable NAME, you could store names of people in that variable at different times during a program. When you prefix NAME with an ampersand (&), it is a macro. Each time dBASE III PLUS encounters &NAME, it references the value of &NAME instead of the name of the variable. Try a macro operation in immediate mode by entering the following commands from the dot prompt:

```
USE ABC1
INDEX ON LASTNAME TO NAME
STORE "Levy" TO TEST
FIND &TEST
DISPLAY
```

Commands that list their parameters literally require macros if they are to treat the parameter as a variable. One such command is FIND. With the FIND command, you normally would be required to enter the actual name of the item to be found. But with the macro function, you are able to substitute a variable for the search term. In this example, you could have easily specified the contents of the variable instead of creating the variable to use as a macro; using macros saves time in programming, since the variable will probably have been declared. You can use macro substitution in response to a user's query to search a database selectively for information. And once you have found the item, you can edit or delete it. You'll try these techniques in the next section.

EDITING RECORDS
UNDER PROGRAM CONTROL

You know that you can edit records with the EDIT command, but first you must get to the record before you can change it. Let's use macro substitution for the editing functions of the ABC Realty database system. If you remember where you left that section of the system, the editor program (CHANGES.PRG) displays all records in the database. The system then asks you for the record number to be edited, and the EDIT command is used to edit that record. But if the database has grown beyond a screenful of rentals, you won't be able to see all of the records on a screen at once. Obviously, a better method of editing is needed. The employees of ABC Realty have agreed that it would be best if they could enter the last name of the tenant to have dBASE III PLUS search for the record. When you first think about what must be done, you might draw up this list:

1. Ask for the last name of the tenant whose record is to be edited

2. Store the name to a variable

3. Using the macro function, find the name in the database

4. Edit the record whose number corresponds to that name.

Let's change the EDITOR command file so that it does this task. Enter MODIFY COMMAND CHANGES. Remember, you can use CONTROL-Y to delete an entire line and CONTROL-N to insert a new line. Change the program so it looks like this:

```
CLEAR
@2,10 SAY "Please wait..."
INDEX ON LASTNAME TO TEMPS
@5,10 SAY "Editing a record."
@7,10 SAY "Enter the last name of the tenant whose record"
@8,10 SAY "is to be edited."
@10,10
ACCEPT "Enter last name: " TO TEST
GO TOP
FIND &TEST
     IF EOF()
          CLEAR
          @5,10 SAY "There is no such name in the database."
          @7,10
          WAIT
          RETURN
     ENDIF
EDIT
RETURN
```

Press CONTROL-END to save the file. Try the system again by entering DO MENU, and press 2, "Editing A Record." Try entering the name Levy. If all went well, the selected record will appear on the screen. The FIND &TEST is the key to the solution. Whatever name is entered with the ACCEPT command will be substituted for the macro when the FIND command is executed.

There are a number of additional dBASE III PLUS commands that may come in handy on an occasional basis. Think of these as the more specialized programming tools of dBASE III PLUS.

EXIT

The EXIT command is used when you are within a DO-WHILE programming loop. EXIT lets dBASE III PLUS exit from a DO-WHILE-ENDDO loop to the first command below ENDDO. An EXIT command arbitrarily placed within a DO-WHILE will prevent dBASE III PLUS from ever reaching the commands below EXIT to ENDDO; thus, EXIT only makes sense if it is executed conditionally. For this reason, you will frequently find EXIT commands with IF-ENDIF and CASE statements.

Consider the following example:

```
USE ABC1
SET TALK OFF
GO TOP
ACCEPT "What is the address (street only) " TO CHOICE
DO WHILE .NOT. EOF()
     IF ADDRESS = CHOICE
          SET PRINT ON
          ? LASTNAME, FIRSTNAME
          SET PRINT OFF
          EXIT
     ENDIF
     SKIP
ENDDO
```

If the contents of ADDRESS, a field, match &CHOICE, a variable, the EXIT command will cause the DO-WHILE loop to terminate. If no match is found, the commands below the IF will be executed and finally will drop from the loop when the last record is accessed.

Use EXITs conservatively: a program that is always jumping out of loops, and around the program for that matter, is difficult to follow and debug, contrary to good program design. Most DO-WHILEs that have loops can be redesigned without them.

CHANGE

The CHANGE command is a fast way of editing selected fields and records in a database. CHANGE performs a function that is similar to the EDIT command, but CHANGE displays only those fields that you list with the command. The format of the command is CHANGE FIELDS *fieldnames* [FOR/WHILE *condition*]. The FOR or WHILE is optional; it can be used to specify various conditions during which the CHANGE command takes place.

If you want to edit the first and last name of a tenant in ABC1, try this:

```
CHANGE FIELDS LASTNAME, FIRSTNAME
```

To get out of the edit screen function without making any changes, you can press ESC.

CANCEL

The CANCEL command will exit a dBASE III PLUS command file and return you to the dot prompt. It can be useful when you are testing various commands and program files; however, using CANCEL in a completed dBASE III PLUS program may be unwise. CANCEL will cause the dot prompt to reappear, and the inexperienced user may not know how to exit dBASE III PLUS to DOS or return to the program. QUIT is used more often to exit programs and return to the DOS prompt. You can add a selection at the main menu that allows the user to get out of dBASE III PLUS and back to the computer's operating system when the work is completed.

WAIT

The WAIT command halts execution of a dBASE III PLUS program until a key is pressed. WAIT can optionally display a message, or prompt, and store the value of the key pressed as a character variable. The normal format of the command is

```
WAIT (prompt) TO (memory variable)
```

Both the prompt and the memory variable are options. If a prompt is not specified, dBASE III PLUS supplies the message **Press any key to continue ...** as a default prompt. For example, to display a message, halt execution of a program until a key is pressed, and store that key as a variable named ANSWER, the following command might be used:

```
WAIT "Enter Y to begin processing transactions, any other key to
continue:" TO ANSWER
```

ZAP

The ZAP command is a one-step command for erasing all records from a database while leaving the structure of the database intact. Using ZAP is functionally equivalent to entering DELETE ALL and then entering PACK. However, ZAP operates considerably faster than a DELETE ALL command followed by a PACK command.

RUN

The RUN command is used to leave dBASE III PLUS temporarily, run another program under the computer's operating system, and return to dBASE III PLUS when the program has completed running. Type RUN followed by the name of the program, and dBASE III PLUS will call up that program from DOS. The program must be what is known in DOS terms as an "executable" program; that is, it must have an extension of .COM or .EXE. You can also execute DOS commands such as DIR and ERASE. However, there is one important catch to using RUN. dBASE III PLUS pulls some fancy tricks in using your computer's memory to run an outside program and return from that program. In order for such tricks to work properly, your computer must have additional memory beyond dBASE III PLUS's required 256K. How much additional memory depends on how much memory your outside program requires. If you attempt to run a DOS command, you need no more than an additional 64K for a total of 320K. If you try to run a word processor like Microsoft's Word or MultiMate that demands a significant memory, you will run into problems. If the program that you try to run does not function properly, there is insufficient memory.

HIDING AND SHOWING VARIABLES WITH PRIVATE AND PUBLIC

dBASE III PLUS offers two commands, PRIVATE and PUBLIC, that are used to classify memory variables. The names PRIVATE and PUBLIC refer to how the individual programs within a large dBASE III PLUS program will treat variables. Variables that you create in one program are considered private by default; if you do not use the PUBLIC command, dBASE III PLUS will assume that all the variables you create are private variables. Private variables are available only to the program in which they are created and to all programs called by that program. This means that if you create a variable in a program that is called by another program and then transfer control back to the calling program with the RETURN command, the contents of that memory variable will be lost. You may or may not want those contents to be discarded, so you can use the PRIVATE and PUBLIC commands to specifically tell dBASE III PLUS how to handle your variables.

The PUBLIC command tells dBASE III PLUS that a memory variable is to be made available to all programs, regardless of where the memory variable is created. The PRIVATE command tells dBASE III PLUS that the variable will be available only to the program that created the variable and all programs that are called by that specific program. Declaring a variable public requires two steps: using the PUBLIC command (the format is PUBLIC *variable name*), and declaring the actual variable with the STORE command or with an assignment (=) symbol. An example follows:

```
PUBLIC YearsRents
STORE rentamt * 12 to YearsRents
```

In this example, the variable YearsRents will be available to all parts of the program, even if program control returns from the part of the program containing these commands to a higher-level (or, calling) program. There is normally little need to declare a memory variable as private, since dBASE III PLUS sets all memory variables to private by default. However, there may be times that you want to declare a variable that was previously declared public as private. To do this, you can use the PRIVATE command in a format (PRIVATE *variable name*) similar to that used by the PUBLIC command. For example,

```
PRIVATE Tenant
STORE LASTNAME + FIRSTNAME to Tenant
```

As an example of the problems that can occur if variables are not declared private or public, consider the following programs. The first program, named FIRST.PRG, passes control to the second program, called SECOND.PRG. The second program declares a variable (NAME), and then passes control back to the calling program, FIRST.PRG. The calling program then tries to display the contents of the memory variable, NAME.

```
*FIRST.PRG is first program
CLEAR
? "Hit any key, and this program will call the second program."
WAIT
DO SECOND
CLEAR
? "Control has returned to first program."
? "The name is: " + NAME
? "End of first program."


*SECOND.PRG is second program
CLEAR
STORE "Smith" to name
? "The name is: " + NAME
? "Press any key to return to first program."
WAIT
RETURN
```

When the program is run with DO FIRST, this is the error message that results after program control returns from the second program:

```
Control has returned to first program.
Variable not found.
                        ?
? "The name is: " + NAME
Called from - C:first.prg
```

dBASE reports an error because the variable NAME was private to the second program. When control was passed back to the first program, the contents of the variable were lost. This problem can be solved by declaring the variable public, as in the following example:

```
*SECOND.PRG is second program
CLEAR
PUBLIC NAME
STORE "Smith" to name
? "The name is: " + NAME
? "Press any key to return to first program."
WAIT
RETURN
```

When the FIRST program is run after the change is made, the program completes successfully without an error.

You can use the ALL, LIKE, and EXCEPT options with PRIVATE to cover more than one variable at a time. These options operate in the same manner as was previously described in this chapter. Examples of the use of the ALL, LIKE, and EXCEPT options with PRIVATE would include

```
PRIVATE ALL EXCEPT ???names
PRIVATE ALL LIKE *rent
PRIVATE ALL EXCEPT YearsRents
```

You can use the accepted DOS wildcards, asterisk (*), and question mark (?) as a part of the variable names. Refer to your DOS manual, if needed, for a description of the use of wildcards.

USING THE APPLICATIONS GENERATOR

dBASE III PLUS offers an Applications Generator, an aid in developing a complete menu-driven application. In programming lingo, the Applications Generator is a program generator, or a program that writes other programs. The Applications Generator is contained on the Applications Generator disk, present in your dBASE III PLUS package. The Applications Generator has its limits (which will be detailed), but it can save you some programming time in the development of applications. This program allows you to build simple menu-operated applications, whether you have a programming knowledge of dBASE III PLUS or not. The Applications Generator also provides menu selections that let you create new databases, index files, entry screens, reports, and labels, by opening the appropriate dBASE III PLUS menus for these functions. Before using the Applications Generator, you should copy the program from the Applications Generator disk onto your working disk (if you are using a two-disk system) or onto your hard disk. The Applications Generator is written in the

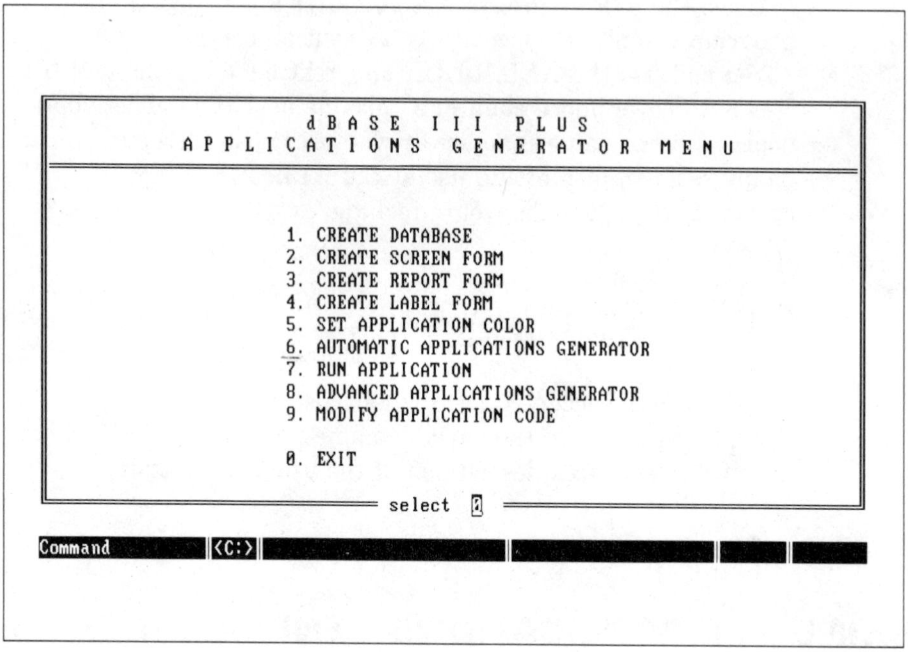

```
                    d B A S E   I I I   P L U S
          A P P L I C A T I O N S   G E N E R A T O R   M E N U


                1. CREATE DATABASE
                2. CREATE SCREEN FORM
                3. CREATE REPORT FORM
                4. CREATE LABEL FORM
                5. SET APPLICATION COLOR
                6. AUTOMATIC APPLICATIONS GENERATOR
                7. RUN APPLICATION
                8. ADVANCED APPLICATIONS GENERATOR
                9. MODIFY APPLICATION CODE

                0. EXIT

                     = select  0  =
Command        <C:>
```

Figure 14-1. Applications Generator main menu

dBASE III PLUS programming language, so you can run the program with the same DO command used to run any dBASE III PLUS program.

Once you have copied the Applications Generator program onto your working disk or hard disk, start dBASE III PLUS in the usual manner. At the dot prompt, use the SET DEFAULT TO command to change the default drive to the drive containing the Applications Generator program. Then enter the command

```
DO APPSGEN
```

In a moment, the program will load, and the Applications Generator's main menu will appear on the screen (Figure 14-1).

The first four choices on the Applications Generator menu (Create Database, Create Screen Form, Create Report Form, and Create Label Form) cause the respective dBASE III PLUS menus for these functions to appear. These menu options on the Applications Generator exist purely as a convenience, to let novice dBASE III PLUS users directly access the CREATE, CREATE SCREEN, CREATE REPORT, and CREATE LABEL commands of dBASE III PLUS without leaving the Applications Generator. Since previous chapters have already covered how to perform these functions, they will not be discussed here. Choice 5, Set Application Color, is used to choose standard and enhanced colors for an application; this option is useful if you are using a color monitor.

If you are using a monochrome monitor, you may wish to read the next five paragraphs to get an idea of how colors can be set. If you have a color monitor, enter 5 now to select this option. The Set Color menu of the Applications Generator will appear (Figure 14-2).

The menu provides options for standard text and background, enhanced text and background, and a border color. You can also specify whether characters displayed will be normal or bright and whether they will be blinking. The enhanced text and background combinations apply to all data that dBASE III PLUS shows in reverse video, such as the contents of fields when in APPEND, EDIT, or BROWSE. Note that among the colors shown, color number 5 is blank, or "secure." If this color is chosen, you will not be able to see the characters that you type. Such an approach is rarely used, but it may be useful if you want to hide the characters being entered from view (such as in the case of entering a user's passwords).

Select and enter a color for each of the options. Once you have entered the numbers for the choices, the cursor will move to the options for "bright" characters and then to the option for "blinking" characters. It is suggested that you leave the blinking options at the default of "N" for "no." Setting any of these options to "yes" results in a visually busy screen that is annoying to most users.

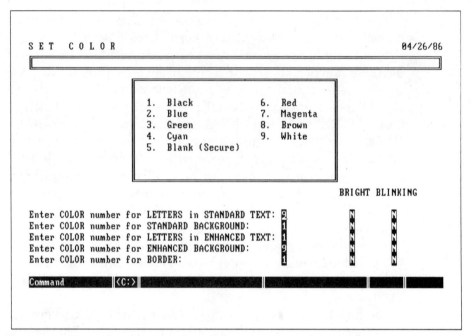

```
S E T   C O L O R                                                    04/26/86
┌──────────────────────────────────────────────────────────────────────────┐
└──────────────────────────────────────────────────────────────────────────┘

              ┌────────────────────────────────────────────────┐
              │   1.   Black            6.   Red                │
              │   2.   Blue             7.   Magenta            │
              │   3.   Green            8.   Brown              │
              │   4.   Cyan             9.   White              │
              │   5.   Blank (Secure)                           │
              │                                                 │
              └────────────────────────────────────────────────┘

                                                      BRIGHT BLINKING

  Enter COLOR number for LETTERS in STANDARD TEXT:  9      N      N
  Enter COLOR number for STANDARD BACKGROUND:       1      N      N
  Enter COLOR number for LETTERS in ENHANCED TEXT:  1      N      N
  Enter COLOR number for ENHANCED BACKGROUND:       9      N      N
  Enter COLOR number for BORDER:                    1      N      N

  Command          <C:>
```

Figure 14-2. Set Color menu

Once you have entered your choice for the final option in the "blinking" column, the following prompt will appear at the bottom of the screen:

```
COMMAND:   (E)xit, (R)edo, (S)ave
```

The (E)xit choice lets you exit the Set Color menu and return to the Applications Generator without saving any of the color changes. The (R)edo choice lets you change your choices of colors, while the (S)ave option tells the Applications Generator to proceed with the color changes as specified. Enter S to save your color choices and return to the Applications Generator menu.

Menu option 6, Automatic Applications Generator, is the choice used to generate a simple application. Before option 6 can be used, a database must exist. It is not necessary that a screen form, report form, or label form exist in advance; however, if such files do exist, the Applications Generator can make use of them.

To demonstrate the use of the Applications Generator, you will use it to build an application using the ABC Realty database, the ABCFORM screen form, the INCOME report format, and the ABCMAIL mailing label format. Select 6 from the menu, and press RETURN.

The Applications Generator first asks for the name of the application author. You can enter your name, or you can press RETURN to bypass this question. If you enter a name, the name will be included in the program code of the application.

Next, the Applications Generator will request the name that will be given to the application. Like all command files, the application name will be assigned a .PRG extension. In this case, enter the name

APPSTEST

and press RETURN. Next, the Applications Generator will request the name of the database file to be used by the application.

Enter ABC1 and press RETURN. The Applications Generator will request the name of an index file associated with the database. If no index file exists, the Applications Generator will create one after requesting the name of a field to index on. In this case, enter ALLNAMES for the name of the index file, and press RETURN.

The Applications Generator will next ask for the name of a screen form file. Enter ABCFORM and press RETURN. (If no form is desired, this option can be bypassed by pressing RETURN without entering a name.)

Next, a name for the report form will be requested. Enter INCOME and press RETURN. The Applications Generator will then ask for a name for a mailing label form. Enter ABCMAIL and press RETURN. As with the screen form prompt, you can press RETURN without entering any names for the report or label forms.

Finally, the Applications Generator will ask for the name of a menu heading that will appear at the top of the application's menu. Enter the heading

```
ABC TEST APPLICATION
```

and press RETURN. Once you have completed the entry of the heading, the Applications Generator will write the program for the application and store the program under the name APPSTEST.PRG. When this process is complete, the Applications Generator menu will reappear.

You can run the completed application from the dot prompt by entering DO APPSTEST or from within the Applications Generator menu by selecting option 7. Choose option 7 now, and enter APPSTEST as the name of the application to run. When the menu for the new application appears, select the Change Information option. Note that the application is written in such a way that you are placed immediately into the edit mode when you select this option. Try the other menu choices in order, to get a feel for the design of this application. When you are finished, choose 0 to exit the application, and return to the Applications Generator menu.

Option 9 of the Applications Generator menu, Modify Application Code, lets you use the dBASE III PLUS word processor to make desired programming changes to the application. (The use of option 8 will be covered shortly.) Option 9 is offered as a convenient way to load the dBASE word processor to modify the program. You could enter the command, MODIFY COMMAND APPSTEST, from the dot prompt and get the same result.

To examine the kind of programming provided by the Applications Generator, select option 9 now. A warning message will appear on the screen, indicating that a part of the program may be lost if the program is too large for the dBASE word processor. In this case, there is more than enough space available to edit the command file, so enter Y to proceed. Since the dBASE word processor can only store files of 4000 characters or less, it is not a wise idea to use the dBASE word processor to edit large command files.

In response to the prompt for the name of an application to edit, enter APPSTEST and press RETURN. You will see the program, APPSTEST.PRG, on your screen.

```
* Program..: APPSTEST.PRG
* Author...: JOHN DOE
* Date.....: 04/24/86
* Notice...: Copyright (c) 1986, JOHN DOE, All Rights Reserved
* Notes....:
* Reserved.: selectnum
*

SET TALK OFF
SET BELL OFF
SET STATUS ON
SET ESCAPE OFF
SET CONFIRM ON
USE ABC1 INDEX ALLNAMES

DO WHILE .T.

     * ---Display menu options, centered on the screen.
     *     draw menu border and print heading
     CLEAR
     @ 2, 0 TO 16,79 DOUBLE
     @ 3,20 SAY [A B C   T E S T   A P P L I C A T I O N]
     @ 4,1 TO 4,78 DOUBLE
     * ---display detail lines
     @  7,30 SAY [1. ADD INFORMATION]
     @  8,30 SAY [2. CHANGE INFORMATION]
     @  9,30 SAY [3. REMOVE INFORMATION]
     @ 10,30 SAY [4. REVIEW INFORMATION]
     @ 11,30 SAY [5. PRINT REPORT]
     @ 12,30 SAY [6. PRINT LABELS]
     @ 14, 30 SAY '0. EXIT'
     STORE 0 TO selectnum
     @ 16,33 SAY " select       "
     @ 16,42 GET selectnum PICTURE "9" RANGE 0,6
     READ

     DO CASE
        CASE selectnum = 0
           SET BELL ON
           SET TALK ON
           CLEAR ALL
           RETURN

        CASE selectnum = 1
        *  DO ADD INFORMATION
           SET FORMAT TO ABCFORM
```

```
          APPEND
          SET FORMAT TO
          SET CONFIRM OFF
          STORE ' ' TO wait_subst
          @ 23,0 SAY 'Press any key to continue...' GET wait_subst
          READ
          SET CONFIRM ON
       CASE selectnum = 2
       *  DO CHANGE INFORMATION
          SET FORMAT TO ABCFORM
          EDIT
          SET FORMAT TO
          SET CONFIRM OFF
          STORE ' ' TO wait_subst
          @ 23,0 SAY 'Press any key to continue...' GET wait_subst
          READ
          SET CONFIRM ON

       CASE selectnum = 3
       *  DO REMOVE INFORMATION
          SET TALK ON
          CLEAR
          @ 2,0 SAY ' '
          ? 'PACKING DATABASE TO REMOVE RECORDS MARKED FOR DELETION'
          PACK
          SET TALK OFF
          SET CONFIRM OFF
          STORE ' ' TO wait_subst
          @ 23,0 SAY 'Press any key to continue...' GET wait_subst
          READ
          SET CONFIRM ON

       CASE selectnum = 4
       *  DO REVIEW INFORMATION
          BROWSE
          SET CONFIRM OFF
          STORE ' ' TO wait_subst
          @ 23,0 SAY 'Press any key to continue...' GET wait_subst
          READ
          SET CONFIRM ON

       CASE selectnum = 5
       *  DO PRINT REPORT
          REPORT FORM INCOME TO PRINT
          SET CONFIRM OFF
          STORE ' ' TO wait_subst
          @ 23,0 SAY 'Press any key to continue...' GET wait_subst
          READ
          SET CONFIRM ON
```

```
           CASE selectnum = 6
         *  DO PRINT LABELS
            LABEL FORM ABCMAIL TO PRINT
            SET CONFIRM OFF
            STORE ' ' TO wait_subst
            @ 23,0 SAY 'Press any key to continue...' GET wait_subst
            READ
            SET CONFIRM ON
     ENDCASE

     ENDDO T
     RETURN
     * EOF: APPSTEST.PRG
```

All programs created by option 6 of the Applications Generator will resemble this one, with choices for adding information (using the APPEND command), changing a database (with EDIT), removing information (with PACK), and viewing a database (using the BROWSE command). If you specified a name for a report and for a label form when creating the application, then appropriate sections of program code for reports and labels are included in the program.

To a new user of dBASE III PLUS, an application created by the Applications Generator may seem like all that is needed to do the job. But an experienced dBASE programmer will spot major shortfalls in such a program. If you have been through all of the exercises in this text up to this point, it is likely that you will spot these flaws. One of the most significant drawbacks is an inability to search for a desired record to edit. Simply entering an EDIT command, as the program does, is fine for a database with 10 or 20 records. Unfortunately, few PC users invest in a program like dBASE III PLUS to manage a database of that size. When your actual database grows to 500 or 3000 records, simply entering EDIT (or BROWSE) and pressing the PG UP and PG DN keys will not be an acceptable way to search for and edit a record.

Another trait lacking in this application is the ability to choose more than one report form or index file. Real-life applications demand the ability to generate a number of reports, indexed on a number of different fields. There are many other features that you might want to see added to an application like this one, such as the ability to find and then delete a given record. The point that should be obvious is that if you are going to develop serious applications with the dBASE programming language, then nothing you've learned up to this point will be wasted, because the Applications Generator will not develop such applications for you. The Applications Generator can save you an hour or two of programming time by quickly developing a clean, bug-free main menu program. It is then up to you to modify that program and to call other programs that will accomplish the rest of the job.

To provide more flexibility to serious dBASE programmers, the Applications Generator offers option 8, the Advanced Applications Generator. Like option 6, this choice causes the program to generate an applications program. But instead of assuming that particular commands like APPEND and EDIT should be used, this option lets you select the commands that will be executed by the menu choices in the application. To see how this works, you'll write an application that uses the programs developed in previous chapters.

Press ESC to leave the dBASE word processor and return to the Applications Generator menu. Enter 8 to choose the Advanced Applications Generator. If desired, enter your name as the application author. For the name of the application, enter NEWTEST. For the database file, again enter ABC1. For the index file, enter ALLNAMES; for the screen format file, enter ABCFORM, and for the application menu heading, enter the following:

```
ABC Realty Test Application
```

Once you have entered the information, a setup screen for the menu you are creating will appear (Figure 14-3).

The setup screen is divided into two halves. The left half will contain the desired menu options, which can be any description you prefer to provide. The right half of the screen will contain the dBASE III PLUS commands that you want the system to carry out, or execute, once the menu choice has been made. Up to nine menu options are allowed by the Advanced Applications Generator.

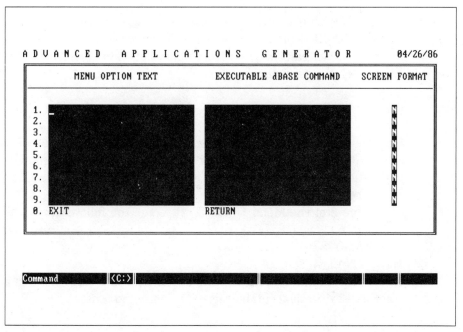

Figure 14-3. Setup screen for menu

The tenth choice is always reserved for exiting the application. By allowing you to specify a dBASE command, the Advanced Applications Generator gives you the flexibility to use any dBASE command or to run other command files. The Applications Generator has no way of knowing whether the commands that you specify are correct; you must check to ensure that the commands you specify can be carried out within the program.

The far right side of the screen also contains "yes/no" selections for screen formats. For these selections, you can cause a screen format to be used if you are using a full-screen command like EDIT or APPEND.

The cursor is now at the first choice for the menu. Adding records is an appropriate first choice. However, instead of using APPEND, you can use the ADDER program developed in Chapter 13. For line 1 of the Menu Option Text, enter the following:

```
Add Records To Database
```

Once you have pressed RETURN, the cursor will move to the Executable dBASE Command half of the screen. In this case, a command that calls another command file, namely ADDER, is desired. Enter the following:

```
DO ADDER
```

Upon pressing RETURN, the cursor moves to the Screen Format column. The ADDER command file uses @-SAY-GET commands to create its own format, so a screen format is not needed in this case. Press RETURN to accept the default value of "no."

For line 2 of the Menu Option Text, enter the following:

```
Edit Current Records
```

Again, a command file has been written for the task of editing records. For the Executable dBASE Command, enter

```
DO CHANGES
```

The CHANGES command file does use an EDIT command, and the use of a screen format would present an attractive screen. Therefore, enter Y for "yes" in response to the Screen Format question.

To complete the menu, enter the information supplied below:

```
    MENU OPTION TEXT        EXECUTABLE dBASE COMMAND     SCR FORMAT

3.  Display Report On Screen    REPORT FORM INCOME              N
4.  Print Report On Printer     REPORT FORM INCOME TO PRINT     N
5.  Display Tenant Data         DO SHOW                        N
6.  List Expiration Dates       LIST LASTNAME,EXPDATE          N
```

Once you have completed the entry of the information, press CONTROL-END to save. A menu for the application will appear, and a prompt asking if you wish to (E)xit, (R)edo, or (S)ave will appear at the bottom of the screen (Figure 14-4).

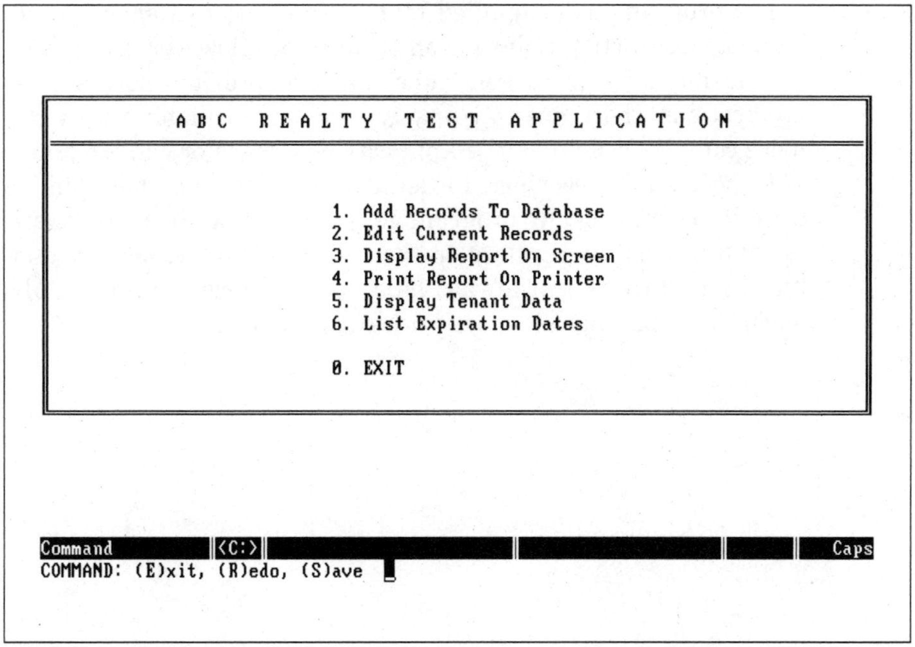

```
        A B C   R E A L T Y   T E S T   A P P L I C A T I O N


                    1. Add Records To Database
                    2. Edit Current Records
                    3. Display Report On Screen
                    4. Print Report On Printer
                    5. Display Tenant Data
                    6. List Expiration Dates

                    0. EXIT




Command        <C:>                                    Caps
COMMAND: (E)xit, (R)edo, (S)ave
```

Figure 14-4. Menu

The (E)xit choice lets you exit from the Applications Generator without saving any of the information. The (R)edo choice lets you change information in the menu choices and executable commands, while the (S)ave option tells the Applications Generator to proceed with writing the application and saving it on disk.

Enter S for "save" and press RETURN, and the Applications Generator will again proceed to write the code for the application. When the Applications Generator menu appears, choose 7 to run the application (enter NEWTEST for the name of the application). Try the various options, and you will see that the programs created in the previous chapters have been used by the new application. When done, choose 0 to exit the program.

The program code supplied by the Applications Generator can be a logical starting point for an application. However, if you have a need for a program generator that can provide more serious applications, there are third-party products available that write more complex code than the Applications Generator can offer. One such product is described in detail in Chapter 20. One point to consider regarding any program generator is that the most sophisticated program generators on the market cannot cover all possibilities, and there will always be a need for programming skills when developing applications with dBASE III PLUS.

Improving Your dBASE III PLUS Programs

Chapter 15

Once you begin implementing dBASE III PLUS programs in your applications, you're likely to find room for improvement. By now, you've probably noticed that dBASE III PLUS does some things faster than others, but any operations that require disk access will slow the program noticeably. You can speed up your programs by limiting the amount of disk drive interaction. Most disk accesses are the result of the main-menu command file calling other command files. This chapter will describe a method by which only one disk access is necessary to execute a series of command files. After designing and then beginning to implement your program file, like as not you will encounter programming errors. dBASE III PLUS offers a variety of commands that should help you isolate most program errors so you can then correct them. These commands and some programming hints will also be discussed in this chapter.

SPEEDING UP YOUR PROGRAMS WITH PROCEDURES

Throughout the development of the ABC Realty database system, you've used separate command files that each perform a specific operation. To perform an operation, the user selects it from the listing on the main menu. This is the recommended way to develop your system for an important reason: it is far easier to design, implement, and debug individual command files that perform one function or a small group of functions than it is to create and debug one large program that performs dozens of functions. But once your program is well tested and thoroughly debugged, it then makes sense to combine the individual program files into a large file. *Procedures* can be used for this purpose.

Procedures are groups of commands, identified by different group names, that are stored in a single command file. An example is the four command files currently in the ABC Realty system: MENU, ADDER, CHANGES, and SHOW. MENU contains the commands that display the menu and *call* (transfer program execution to) one of the other command files. ADDER contains the commands necessary for adding records to the database, CHANGES contains the commands for editing records, and SHOW contains the commands for displaying a record. Each time the user makes a choice from the menu that requires the execution of one of the command files, dBASE III PLUS must load the command file from disk and then execute the commands in it. When the commands in that command file have been executed, dBASE III PLUS exits the file and returns to the MENU command file. This entire process is repeated each time the user makes a menu selection.

In a large system, such use of multiple command files creates noticeable delays (not to mention the wear and tear on your disk drives). However, it's not necessary to rewrite the entire set of programs to function as a single program; instead you can perform a two-step process. In the first step you combine the individual

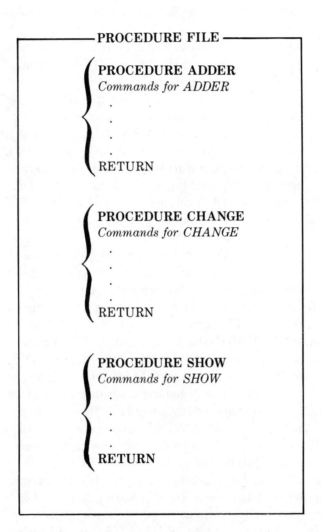

Figure 15-1. Model of a procedure file. Each procedure name consists of the word PROCEDURE, followed by a name, then the commands, and finally the word RETURN

command files into a single command file. Each command file in the new combined file is then enclosed, or bracketed, with a procedure name and the RETURN command. Next, a SET PROCEDURE statement replaces the DO statement in the file that called the command files. Figure 15-1 illustrates the design of command files that use procedures.

The second step is to tell the main file, in this case MENU, that the command files are now located in one file as procedures. The command that does this is SET PROCEDURE. The SET PROCE-DURE *filename* command tells dBASE III PLUS what file will contain all of the procedures. Now when the program encounters a DO command-file statement, such as DO ADDER, instead of accessing the ADDER command file, dBASE III PLUS will jump to the procedure file named in SET PROCEDURE. There is no required placement of the SET PROCEDURE command in the main file other than it be executed before encountering a DO command-file statement. No modifications to the DO command-file statements in the main file are necessary.

To use this example, you would then have to create a command file, called MYFILE.PRG, that will contain all command files referenced by MENU, the main program. With all of the command files combined into a single procedure file, the MYFILE.PRG file is read from disk just once. dBASE III PLUS stores the contents of the procedure file in memory. From that point on, dBASE III PLUS can instantaneously access any procedure in the procedure file rather than having to find the commands in another disk file.

If you want to try speeding up the ABC Realty system with procedures, you'll need to do a little work with your word processing software. But merging files is a job that, unfortunately, is not possible with the simple built-in word processor. You'll need to load a commercially available word processor along with the disk you have been using for dBASE III PLUS files and programs. Create a new file, called MYFILE.PRG, on the data disk. The extension .PRG is necessary so that dBASE III PLUS will recognize the file as a program file. Use your word processor's merge-file commands to read the following files from the disk:

```
ADDER.PRG
CHANGES.PRG
SHOW.PRG
```

Once you have merged the files into a single file, separate the programs into three groups by adding a PROCEDURE *name* command at the beginning of each group and a RETURN command at the end of each group (Figure 15-1). Then add the new procedure at the end of the file:

```
PROCEDURE REPORTER
REPORT FORM INCOME TO PRINT
RETURN
```

This procedure prints the income report for ABC Realty. When you are done, the MYFILE.PRG file should look like this:

```
PROCEDURE ADDER
USE ABC1
CLEAR
APPEND BLANK
@ 2,3 SAY "Tenant's last name:" GET LASTNAME
@ 3,2 SAY "Tenant's first name:" GET FIRSTNAME
@ 5,14 SAY "Address:" GET ADDRESS
@ 6,17 SAY "City:" GET CITY
@ 7,16 SAY "State:" GET STATE
@ 8,18 SAY "Zip:" GET ZIP
@ 9,16 SAY "Phone:" GET PHONE
@ 11,3 SAY "Number of bedrooms:" GET BEDROOMS
@ 12,2 SAY "Number of bathrooms:" GET BATHROOMS
@ 14,5 SAY "Lease expires on:" GET EXPDATE
@ 15,5 SAY "Type of property:" GET PROPTYPE
@ 17,10 SAY "Rental cost:" GET RENTAMT PICTURE "#,###.##"
@ 18,12 SAY "Unit size:" GET SIZE
@ 19,1 SAY "Parking (true/false):" GET PARKING
@ 20,9 SAY "Sales office:" GET SALESOFF
@ 21,0 SAY "Description of extras:" GET EXTRAS
READ
RETURN

PROCEDURE CHANGES
CLEAR
@2,10 SAY "Please wait..."
INDEX ON LASTNAME TO TEMPS
@5,10 SAY "Editing a record."
@7,10 SAY "Enter the last name of the tenant whose record"
```

```
@8,10 SAY "is to be edited."
@10,10
ACCEPT "Enter last name: " TO TEST
GO TOP
FIND &TEST
     IF EOF()
          CLEAR
          @5,10 SAY "There is no such name in the database."
          @7,10
          WAIT
          RETURN
     ENDIF
EDIT
RETURN
PROCEDURE SHOW
USE ABC1
SET TALK OFF
CLEAR
GO TOP
* Begin loop that contains commands to display record.
ACCEPT "Search for what last name?" TO SNAME
DO WHILE .NOT. EOF()
     IF LASTNAME = SNAME
          ? "Last name is "
          ? LASTNAME
          ? "First name is "
          ? FIRSTNAME
          ? "Address is "
          ? ADDRESS
          ? CITY + STATE + " " + ZIP
          ?
          ? "Rent per month is "
          ? RENTAMT
          ? "Unit type is "
          ? PROPTYPE
          ? "Number of bedrooms is "
          ? BEDROOMS
          ? "Number of bathrooms is "
          ? BATHROOMS
          ? "Lease expires on "
          ? EXPDATE
          ?
     ENDIF
     SKIP
ENDDO
WAIT
RETURN

PROCEDURE REPORTER
REPORT FORM INCOME TO PRINT
RETURN
```

Now save the file, and as long as you are still in your word processor, edit the main-menu command file, MENU.PRG. Add one line at the beginning of the file that reads

```
SET PROCEDURE TO MYFILE
```

and change the line that reads REPORT FORM INCOME to

```
DO REPORTER
```

Save the modified command file. Get back into dBASE III PLUS, turn on your printer, and enter DO MENU. Try using various menu choices to move around to different parts of the system. You'll see that the improvement in speed is worth your efforts.

DEBUGGING TECHNIQUES

Debugging is the process of finding out why a program does not operate the way it was designed. Debugging can range from correcting a spelling error to rewriting the entire program. Some program bugs are relatively easy to find and solve, such as a misspelled command, which results in a **SYNTAX ERROR** message displayed on the screen when the command is executed. Other program bugs may cause problems that don't surface until you reach a different part of the program and can be far more difficult to solve. But remember that it is truly a rare experience for a program, written for the first time, to operate without any bugs. In dBASE III PLUS, the bugs that you are likely to see most often are

- Misspelled variable names and commands. The message **SYNTAX ERROR** is usually displayed for commands. The message **VARIABLE NOT FOUND** is usually displayed for variables.

- Missing ENDIF and ENDDO commands. Every DO WHILE loop must end with an ENDDO statement, and every IF command must be matched by an ENDIF command. dBASE III

PLUS will wander off in the wrong direction if you leave out an ENDIF statement.

Errors in loops are a major cause of program bugs. To avoid this problem, verify on paper that your program loops are properly designed to begin with. An example of an improperly designed DO WHILE loop is

```
STORE 0 TO CHOICE
DO WHILE CHOICE < 3
     @4,5 SAY "Enter selection:"
     WAIT TO CHOICE
     IF CHOICE = 1
          SKIP
          DELETE
     ELSE
     IF CHOICE = 2
          SKIP
          ? NAME, CITY, STATE
ENDDO
STORE RECNO() TO LOCATION
ENDIF
(rest of program...)
```

The flaw in this example is that the IF statement begins within the DO WHILE loop but ends outside the DO WHILE loop. Whenever an IF-ENDIF statement is used inside a DO WHILE loop, the IF statement must terminate within the DO WHILE loop. The properly designed loop would look like this:

```
STORE 0 TO CHOICE
DO WHILE CHOICE < 3
     @4,5 SAY "Enter selection:"
     WAIT TO CHOICE
     IF CHOICE = 1
          SKIP
          DELETE
     ELSE
     IF CHOICE = 2
          SKIP
          ? NAME, CITY, STATE
     ENDIF
ENDDO
STORE RECNO() TO LOCATION
(rest of program...)
```

• Character strings mixed with numeric variables. If you tell dBASE III PLUS to store the value of 3 to a variable, and to store the character string "3" to another variable, the two items are interpreted in entirely different ways. dBASE III PLUS recognizes the first entry as a numeric value of 3. The second entry is stored as a string of characters, in this case, the character 3. If you apply a string option to the numeric variable as you try to use the string variable in a calculation, you will get all sorts of errors in your program. Numeric variables and string variables cannot be used interchangeably unless you use functions (like ASC and VAL) that will convert the type.

dBASE III PLUS provides you with debugging tools to help track down those hard-to-find bugs in your programs: SET TALK, SET ECHO, SET DEBUG, SET STEP, SET ALTERNATE, SET HISTORY, SET DOHISTORY, LIST and DISPLAY HISTORY, SUSPEND, and RESUME.

Using SET TALK

You have routinely used the SET TALK command in previous examples. If SET TALK is activated, which it is by default, dBASE III PLUS displays responses to many of its commands. This extra information isn't all that necessary during daily operation of the program, but in debugging it is useful to display results as the command file is being executed. To do this, tack on the command SET TALK ON at the beginning of the command file. You can then watch the screen as the program is run for hints that will help you find the errors in the program. Entering SET TALK OFF will turn off the screen display of processing results.

Using SET ECHO

SET ECHO is similar to SET TALK. The SET ECHO command will cause each command line to be printed on the screen as it is executed. This will enable you to follow the flow of the program.

Since SET ECHO is normally deactivated, enter SET ECHO ON at the top of the program. Entering SET ECHO OFF will disable the display.

Using SET DEBUG

The SET DEBUG command is used along with the SET ECHO command. When SET DEBUG ON is entered, any results that would normally be displayed on the screen with SET ECHO will be routed to the printer instead. This can prevent the screen from being littered with the results of program execution and debugging.

Using SET STEP

dBASE III PLUS programs often execute with such speed that it is difficult to pace the flow of the program. If you enter the command SET STEP ON, dBASE III PLUS will pause after the execution of each command line and display the message **Type any key to stop—ESC to halt.** When you press any key except ESC, the program will proceed to the next command line. But if you press ESC, execution is terminated. You can inspect the results of the program by entering DISPLAY MEMORY or the FIND or SEEK command. SET STEP OFF deactivates the process.

Using SET ALTERNATE

For problems that occur only when you are not around and someone else is using the program, you can use the SET ALTERNATE commands to save a record of operations to a disk file. SET

ALTERNATE TO *filename* creates a file that will store any keyboard entries and most screen displays. The file will have the extension .TXT. When the SET ALTERNATE ON command is used, everything that appears on your screen, with the exception of full-screen editing operations, will be stored in the text file in ASCII format. When you no longer want the information to be stored in the file, you use the SET ALTERNATE OFF command. You can continue to use SET ALTERNATE ON and SET ALTERNATE OFF as many times as desired to add more text to the file. When you are finished with the process altogether, you can close the file with the CLOSE ALTERNATE command.

You can later examine the contents of the text file to see what replies to the program were typed and what program responses occurred as a result. Obviously, using these commands may quickly consume disk space, so consider available disk space before using the SET ALTERNATE commands.

About HISTORY

A highly effective method of debugging programs is to examine the most recent commands issued. dBASE III PLUS offers a HISTORY function, which keeps track of the last 20 commands given. Normally, only those commands given at the dot prompt are stored as HISTORY. However, the SET DOHISTORY command can be used to cause commands executed within a program to be stored as HISTORY. You can also tell dBASE III PLUS to store more than the last 20 commands as HISTORY. The commands used with HISTORY are SET HISTORY, SET DOHISTORY, DISPLAY HISTORY, and LIST HISTORY. In addition to using these commands, you can also use the ↑ and ↓ keys to move back and forth through the history of the last 20 dBASE commands.

As an example, get to the dot prompt, and enter the following commands:

```
USE ABC1
SET INDEX TO ALLNAMES
GO BOTTOM
DISPLAY
LIST ALL FOR LASTNAME = "Mitchell"
```

After entering the commands, try pressing the ↑ key five times, then press the ↓ key five times. As you do this, each of the commands previously entered will be displayed. You can edit any of the commands contained in HISTORY by moving the cursor to the left or right, and using the INS or DEL keys as necessary. This makes the correction of typographical errors within dBASE commands a simple matter.

The LIST HISTORY and DISPLAY HISTORY commands will show all commands stored in HISTORY. The DISPLAY HISTORY command will stop with each screen, while the LIST HISTORY command will continue scrolling up the screen until all commands in HISTORY have been shown. Normally, HISTORY will contain only the last 20 commands, but you can change this number with the SET HISTORY command. The format for this command is SET HISTORY TO X, where X is the number of commands that you want HISTORY to contain. As an example, the command

```
SET HISTORY TO 40
```

will cause dBASE III PLUS to store the last 40 commands in HISTORY.

Normally, commands executed within a program are not stored within HISTORY. You can force all commands executed within a program to be stored in HISTORY with the SET DOHISTORY ON command. For example, enter DO SHOW, and enter the name Hart. When the program completes its execution, enter LIST HISTORY. The display that results,

```
do show
list history
```

demonstrates that the commands in the program are not present in HISTORY. Now enter the command

```
SET DOHISTORY ON
```

and again enter DO SHOW, supplying the name Hart in response to the prompt. Enter LIST HISTORY when the program completes its execution, and you will see a display like this one:

```
list history
        ? BEDROOMS
        ? "Number of bathrooms is "
        ? BATHROOMS
        ? "Lease expires on "
        ? EXPDATE
        ?
    ENDIF
    SKIP
ENDDO
    IF LASTNAME = SNAME
    SKIP
ENDDO
    IF LASTNAME = SNAME
    SKIP
ENDDO
    IF LASTNAME = SNAME
    SKIP
ENDDO
    IF LASTNAME = SNAME
    SKIP
ENDDO
    IF LASTNAME = SNAME
    SKIP
ENDDO
WAIT
RETURN
```

Note that the last 20 commands carried out by the SHOW program are included in the HISTORY after the SET DOHISTORY command is used. This use of HISTORY is a powerful aid in debugging programs, but it does result in the execution speed of a program being slowed down considerably. Once you have found the source of any problems, you can cancel the effects of the SET DOHISTORY ON by entering the command, SET DOHISTORY OFF.

Using SUSPEND and RESUME

When dBASE halts because of an error in your programs, it displays the following message at the bottom of the screen:

```
Cancel, Ignore, or Suspend? (C, I, or S)
```

Entering C for "cancel" halts execution of the program and clears all variables in memory. This option is best when you know the cause of error and want to make changes immediately to the program to cure the problem. If you are not sure why the error occurred, you can use the Suspend option to suspend execution of the program. dBASE III PLUS will return to the dot prompt, but variables will not be cleared from memory. You can then use interactive commands to display the values in memory. Often, seeing these values will provide a clue as to why a particular error occurred. You can change the contents of various memory variables with the STORE command, and then enter RESUME to start execution of the program where it halted.

The Ignore option tells dBASE III PLUS to ignore the error and continue with the program. Use this option at your own discretion; it may or may not make sense to tell dBASE III PLUS to ignore the cause of a program error, depending on the circumstances that led to the error.

CUSTOMIZING dBASE III PLUS PROGRAMS WITH SET COMMANDS

Other SET commands can be used to customize your program and take advantage of various dBASE III PLUS features. This is not a complete list, but it does include the most commonly used SET commands.

SET BELL

Activates the beep that sounds during data entry. The beep is normally on and will sound when you fill a field with data or enter incorrect data into a field (such as character data into a numeric field). SET BELL OFF will deactivate the beep.

SET CARRY

When you use APPEND, the record that appears on the screen is normally blank. SET CARRY ON following the APPEND command causes dBASE III PLUS to copy the entries in the fields of the previous record to the new record. SET CARRY OFF disables this feature.

SET COLOR

Sets color for screen display when using a color monitor, and sets screen highlighting when using a monochrome monitor. The normal format of the command is SET COLOR TO *standard* [*,enhanced*][*,border*], where *standard*, *enhanced*, and *border* are pairs of letters separated by a slash, that represent the desired foreground and background colors or screen highlighting. The values are shown in Table 15-1. If you have a color monitor, try the following:

```
SET COLOR TO B/W, R/GR, BR
```

This results in a standard display of blue letters on white background, an enhanced (reverse video) display of red letters on brown background, and a border color of magenta. On mono-chrome monitors, acceptable values are white, black, and the letter U (for "underline," which causes all lines on the screen to be underlined).

SET CONSOLE

Turns screen displays on or off. SET CONSOLE is normally on, but once a SET CONSOLE OFF command is encountered, no information is displayed on the screen, although commands will still be executed. Only until a SET CONSOLE ON is executed will information again be displayed. Using SET CONSOLE is like turning the monitor screen on or off.

SET DATE

The SET DATE command sets the desired format for date values and expressions. dBASE III PLUS offers any one of six date formats:

Table 15-1. Color Codes for SET COLOR

Color	Letter
black	N
blue	B
green	G
cyan	BG
red	R
magenta	BR
brown	GR
white	W
blank (secure)	X

American (mm/dd/yy), ANSI (yy.mm.dd), British (dd/mm/yy), Italian (dd-mm-yy), French (dd/mm/yy), and German (dd.mm.yy). Unless told otherwise, dBASE III PLUS sets the default value of the date format to American. The format of the command is SET DATE *format*, where *format* is American, ANSI, British, Italian, French, or German.

SET DECIMALS

Sets the number of decimal places that are displayed during calculations involving division, square roots, or exponentiation. The format of the command is SET DECIMALS to *expression*, where *expression* is an integer value limiting the decimal places. Thus, if SET DECIMALS is assigned to 4, then 4 decimal places will be displayed for division, exponentiation, or square root operations until another SET DECIMAL command is executed. The default is 2 digits. SET DECIMAL does not affect other math operations unless the SET FIXED command (*described later*) is also used.

SET EXACT

The SET EXACT command is used to tell dBASE III PLUS to perform (or not to perform) exact comparisons between character strings. The format of the command is SET EXACT ON/OFF. For example, the following commands

```
USE ABC1
LIST FOR LASTNAME = "Rob"
```

will find all records with "Robinson" in the LASTNAME field. On the other hand, the following commands,

```
SET EXACT ON
USE ABC1
LIST FOR LASTNAME = "Rob"
```

will not find any records in the ABC1 database that apply, because "Rob" is not an exact match of "Robinson."

SET FIXED

Fixes the number of decimals shown during a dBASE III PLUS calculation regardless of the type of mathematical operation. When a SET FIXED ON command is encountered, dBASE III PLUS will display the results of all calculations with the number of decimal places specified with the SET DECIMALS command. If the SET DECIMALS command has not been used, dBASE III PLUS will assume a default value of 2 decimal places. For example, to show three decimal places in all numeric displays, enter

```
SET DECIMALS TO 3
SET FIXED ON
? 5 * 3
```

The result

```
15.000
```

shows the effect of the commands. Enter SET FIXED OFF to disable the SET FIXED command for mathematical operations other than exponentiation, division, and square root.

SET FUNCTION

Changes the performance of the function keys. Each function key is assigned to a dBASE III PLUS command (Table 15-2), and when pressed, will execute the command. You can change the function keys, with the exception of F1, to any character expression, 30 characters or fewer, with SET FUNCTION *integer-expression* TO *"character string."*

Character string must be enclosed in quotes. For example, to change F7 from DISPLAY MEMORY to BROWSE enter

```
SET FUNCTION 7 TO "BROWSE;"
```

Remember to include the semicolon to produce a RETURN.

The SET FUNCTION command can be quite useful for reducing the number of repetitive steps during the data-entry process. As an example, by including the following SET FUNCTION commands within the MENU.PRG program for ABC Realty, the function keys would be redefined to enter the names of various cities and states.

```
SET FUNCTION 2 TO "Silver Spring"
SET FUNCTION 3 TO "Rockville"
SET FUNCTION 4 TO "Columbia"
SET FUNCTION 5 TO "Washington"
SET FUNCTION 6 TO "Alexandria"
SET FUNCTION 7 TO "Falls Church"
SET FUNCTION 8 TO "MD"
SET FUNCTION 9 TO "VA"
SET FUNCTION 10 TO "DC"
```

Table 15-2. Default Setting for Function Keys. Semicolon Produces a Carriage Return

Function Key	dBASE III PLUS Command
F1	HELP;
F2	ASSIST;
F3	LIST;
F4	DIR;
F5	DISPLAY STRUCTURE;
F6	DISPLAY STATUS;
F7	DISPLAY MEMORY;
F8	DISPLAY;
F9	APPEND;
F10	EDIT;

When the commands shown in the example have been executed, users can press the respective function keys during the APPEND or EDIT process, to enter the names without typing the actual keystrokes. During large data-entry jobs, reassigning the function keys in this manner can save hours of time in entering records.

SET HELP

Turns the message **Do you want some help? (Y/N)** on or off when a syntax error occurs during keyboard entry of commands. SET HELP ON activates the message; SET HELP OFF deactivates the message.

SET INTENSITY

Turns on or off the reverse video display of fields during full-screen operations such as APPEND. To activate reverse video, enter SET INTENSITY ON; to deactivate reverse video, enter SET INTENSITY OFF. Reverse video is normally on, but you can find out the current state of SET INTENSITY or the status of any SET command by entering

```
DISPLAY STATUS
```

The status of the SET commands along with the function key designations will then be displayed. For example:

```
Currently Selected Database:
Select area:  1, Database in Use: C:abc1.dbf     Alias: ABC1
          Memo file:    C:abc1.dbt

File search path:
Default disk drive: C:
Print destination:  PRN:
Margin =      0
Current work area =      1
```

Press any key to continue...

ALTERNATE	– ON	DELETED	– OFF	FIXED	– OFF	SAFETY	– ON
BELL	– ON	DELIMITERS	– OFF	HEADING	– ON	SCOREBOARD	– ON
CARRY	– OFF	DEVICE	– SCRN	HELP	– ON	STATUS	– ON
CATALOG	– OFF	DOHISTORY	– OFF	HISTORY	– ON	STEP	– OFF
CENTURY	– OFF	ECHO	– OFF	INTENSITY	– ON	TALK	– ON
CONFIRM	– OFF	ESCAPE	– ON	MENU	– ON	TITLE	– ON
CONSOLE	– ON	EXACT	– OFF	PRINT	– OFF	UNIQUE	– OFF
DEBUG	– OFF	FIELDS	– OFF				

Programmable function keys:
```
F2  - assist;
F3  - list;
F4  - dir;
F5  - display structure;
F6  - display status;
F7  - display memory;
F8  - display;
F9  - append;
F10 - edit;
```

SET MEMOWIDTH TO

The SET MEMOWIDTH TO command is used to control the width of a memo field when it is displayed, such as with a LIST or DISPLAY command. The default value is 50 characters wide. Using SET MEMOWIDTH to narrow the default width of a memo field can result in a more pleasing display of information. As an example, these commands:

```
USE ABC1
GO 5
DISPLAY LASTNAME, FIRSTNAME, EXTRAS
```

result in this display:

```
Record#  LASTNAME       FIRSTNAME         EXTRAS
     5   Jones          Jarel             Spectacular lakeside view, r
ec room in basement,

                                          two fireplaces.
```

The display is an unattractive one, because the words in the memo field wrap around the screen and are broken by the right-hand margin. The following commands:

```
SET MEMOWIDTH TO 25
USE ABC1
GO 5
DISPLAY LASTNAME, FIRSTNAME, EXTRAS

Record#   LASTNAME        FIRSTNAME           EXTRAS
      5   Jones           Jarel               Spectacular lakeside
                                              view, rec room in
                                              basement, two fireplaces.
```

provide a much more attractive format for the display of the memo field.

SET MESSAGE TO

The SET MESSAGE TO command is used to display an optional message at the bottom of the screen. Normally, dBASE III PLUS displays the message **Enter a dBASE III PLUS command** on this line. By entering the command, SET MESSAGE TO *character string*, where *character string* is the text you want included in the message, you can display a custom message of your own choice. For example, the command

```
SET MESSAGE TO "ABC Realty System - press F1 for help"
```

would cause that message to be displayed at the bottom of the screen. Note that any message that you enter will be replaced by the Assistant when it is in use. When leaving the Assistant, the message previously entered will appear again.

SET SAFETY ON/OFF

The SET SAFETY command lets you specify whether a prompt will warn you when dBASE III PLUS is about to overwrite an existing file. When SET SAFETY is on and any dBASE III PLUS

command will result in the overwriting of an existing file, dBASE
III PLUS will stop and ask

```
(filename) already exists, overwrite it? (Y/N)
```

and you must confirm this by entering Y to proceed with the operation. SET SAFETY is normally ON with dBASE III PLUS. This
can result in unwanted messages and interruptions within your
programs when you intentionally want to overwrite a file, such as
during the reindexing of a database. In such cases, you can include
a SET SAFETY OFF command in your program, and dBASE III
PLUS will not stop to ask for confirmation before overwriting a
file.

Using the Set Menu

Nearly all SET commands that have been discussed in previous
paragraphs can be executed in one of three ways: from the dot
prompt, as a command within a program, or from the Set menu.
The Set menu is a menu of various commands and options that
appears when you enter SET without specifying any additional
command name. From the dot prompt, enter

```
SET
```

and the Set menu will appear (Figure 15-2). The Set menu offers
seven menu choices: Options, Screen, Keys, Disk, Files, Margin,
and Decimals. The Options menu, which is currently open, contains most of the SET commands. The Screen menu, which performs the equivalent of the SET COLOR TO command, contains
options for color settings for a color display. The Keys menu contains function key settings; this menu performs the equivalent of
the SET FUNCTION command. The Disk menu lets you set the
default disk drive and a DOS path, if used (just as the SET
DEFAULT TO command does). The Files menu lets you choose

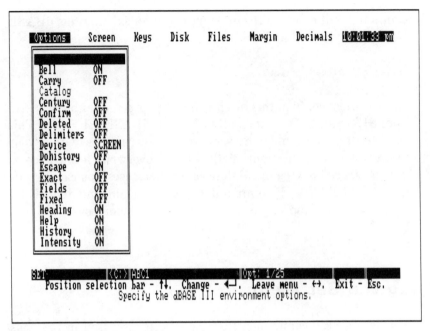

Figure 15-2. Set menu

index files, alternate files, or format files (the equivalent of the SET INDEX TO, SET ALTERNATE TO, and SET FORMAT TO commands). The Margin menu allows you to set the left margin and the memo width margin (the equivalent of the SET MARGIN TO and SET MEMOWIDTH commands). Finally, the Decimals menu lets you set the number of decimal places displayed by dBASE III PLUS (the equivalent of the SET DECIMALS TO command).

When the Options menu is open, you can use the PG UP and PG DN keys to see all available options. In all of the Set menu choices, you can select a desired choice by highlighting that choice and pressing RETURN. If the particular command is an "ON/OFF" type of command (such as SET BELL ON/OFF), then pressing the RETURN key will toggle the selected option between ON and OFF.

If the command requires the entry of a value (such as a margin amount or a name of a file), you will be prompted to enter a value. In the case of the Screen options for foreground, background, and border colors, pressing RETURN for the desired option will cause dBASE III PLUS to toggle through all of the available color choices.

As with other dBASE III PLUS menus, the ← and → keys can be used to move among the menu choices, or you can press the first letter of the desired menu choice. When you have made your desired selections from the Set menu, you can press ESC to leave the menu and return to the dot prompt. The Set menu is not available from the Assistant. Also, note that some SET commands, including SET DATE, SET ECHO, SET MESSAGE TO, and SET RELATION TO, are not available from the Set menu.

You can use the SET command to display the Set menu, as an option within a dBASE III PLUS program. To see how this works, try adding three lines to the menu program for ABC Realty. Enter the command

```
MODIFY COMMAND MENU
```

and add the three lines shown between the lines that read "STORE 0 TO CHOICE" and "DO WHILE CHOICE < 5."

```
USE ABC1
SET TALK OFF
STORE 0 TO CHOICE
? "Press a key to set options first."
WAIT
SET
DO WHILE CHOICE < 5
    CLEAR
    *Display main menu.
    @ 5,15 SAY "=====ABC Realty Database System Menu====="
```

Try running the system with DO MENU. When you press a key to respond to the "WAIT" prompt, the Set menu will appear. Make any desired changes and press ESC, and the ABC Realty program will continue.

For simplicity's sake, we made the use of SET a mandatory part of the ABC Realty program. When designing your actual applications, however, there may be good reasons for not writing a program in that manner. Novice users could get themselves into trouble with some of the SET commands; therefore, you may wish to place such an option in a system configuration menu that is not normally seen by casual users.

USING A CONFIGURATION FILE

You can assign values for the SET commands and the function keys in a disk file, named CONFIG.DB, that will be executed when the dBASE III PLUS program is first started. dBASE III PLUS will initially look for CONFIG.DB. If this file does not exist, dBASE III PLUS will simply proceed to the dot prompt; but if the file does exist, it will be executed and any settings in the file will be carried out. By putting the SET commands in a start-up file, you don't have to enter them into the computer each time you start dBASE III PLUS. That's not all; you can place other commands in the file, and they too will be executed (usually the command is to execute a command file).

Most SET commands, color settings, assignments for function key values, and the name of an optional word processor to be used by MODIFY COMMAND can be placed within the CONFIG.DB file. If you are tired of seeing the famed dBASE dot prompt, you can even change that within the CONFIG.DB file. The CONFIG.DB file is made up of a series of lines, each containing a format of

(KEYWORD) = (VALUE)

where *keyword* is a SET command or other command that is allowed within a CONFIG.DB file, and *value* is the desired value for that command.

For example, if you wanted the ABC Realty menu to appear after dBASE III PLUS was loaded, and you wished to set the screen colors to the values that you used in the SET COLOR command, you would use the dBASE III PLUS word processor (or your favorite word processor) to create a text file named CONFIG.DB (it must have this name) containing the following commands:

```
COMMAND = DO MENU
COLOR = B/W, R/GR, BR
```

The commands in the CONFIG.DB file must use an equal sign in place of the normal SET statement used within dBASE III PLUS. In the previous example, the COMMAND statement is followed by the equal sign, the DO command, and the name of the program that you want dBASE III PLUS to run. The COLOR statement is followed by the equal sign and the desired color values.

To change the type of prompt, enter the line, PROMPT = X, where "X" is the desired replacement for the dot prompt. If you are using a hard disk, you can copy your favorite word processor into the same subdirectory that contains dBASE III PLUS, and then use that word processor in place of the dBASE III PLUS word processor. To do this, simply include two lines in the CONFIG.DB file that read

```
WP = (program name)
TEDIT = (program name)
```

where *program name* is the name of your favorite word processor.

The "WP" specification is used to choose the editor that will be used for editing memo fields, while the "TEDIT" specification is used to choose the editor that will be used to edit programs with MODIFY COMMAND. As an example,

```
WP=ED
TEDIT=ED
```

will cause the program named ED.EXE (actually PC-Write) contained within the dBASE subdirectory to be loaded whenever memo fields or programs are edited from within dBASE III PLUS. Two separate specifications for memo fields and for editing programs give you the flexibility to let users use their favorite word processor to add information to memo fields, while you use a different word processor to make changes to the application programs. The TEDIT and WP specifications require extra memory beyond the 256K needed to run dBASE III PLUS. For example, if your word processor requires 128K, you will need at least 384K of memory to use these options.

The standard CONFIG.DB file that is supplied on the dBASE III PLUS system disk contains these lines:

```
STATUS=ON
COMMAND=ASSIST
```

You can remove the second line, COMMAND=ASSIST, if you want dBASE III PLUS to bypass the Assistant in favor of the dot prompt when the program is loaded. The first line, STATUS=ON, turns on the status bar that is normally displayed at the bottom of the screen. It, too, can be removed at your option.

The CONFIG.DB file must be placed on the dBASE III PLUS system disk or in the hard-disk directory containing the dBASE III PLUS programs, as dBASE III PLUS will look for the file on that disk.

Interfacing
With dBASE III PLUS

Chapter 16

The ability to exchange information with other programs enhances the power of dBASE III PLUS. dBASE III PLUS allows you to transfer files between it and nearly all popular software available for the PC. (dBASE II files can also be transferred by special conversion programs that will be discussed in Chapter 18.) However, there is one main limitation to dBASE III PLUS's ability to transfer information: the other programs must be able to transfer information in a format acceptable to dBASE III PLUS.

FILE FORMATS

You can transfer information between dBASE III PLUS and another program in one of six formats: ASCII, Delimited, System Data Format (SDF), Document Interchange Format (DIF), Symbolic Link format (SYLK), and Lotus worksheet format (WKS). As described shortly, Delimited and SDF files are composed of ASCII text in a special format.

You can also use the IMPORT FROM and EXPORT TO commands to transfer files between dBASE III PLUS and PFS:FILE. The IMPORT FROM and EXPORT TO commands are available from the Assistant menu or from the dot prompt. Other commands throughout this chapter are available only from the dot prompt.

ASCII Format

The term "ASCII format" refers to files that are composed of characters and spaces not necessarily arranged in any particular order. The name "ASCII" stands for the American Standard Code for Information Interchange, an international method of representing information in computers. Text files created by word processors are stored as ASCII text. You'll use ASCII files if you need to merge the contents of a database with a document created by a word processor. If, for example, your database contains a list of names, you can save those names to a text file in ASCII format. You can then use your word processor to call up that text file and use it as part of a document.

Delimited Format

Delimited-format ASCII files are composed of records in which the fields are surrounded by quotation marks and are separated from other fields by commas. Each record occupies a separate line, so each record is followed by a carriage return. Delimited files have the following form:

```
"Robinson","1607 21st Street NW","Washington","DC","20009-0101"
"Morse","4260 Park Avenue","Chevy Chase","MD","20815-0988"
"Westman","4807 East Avenue","Silver Spring","MD","20910-0124"
"Robinson","270 Browning Ave #3C","Takoma Park","MD","20912"
```

As an example, WordStar's MailMerge option uses Delimited format for storing information.

SDF

Like Delimited files, files using SDF store each record as an individual line, so the records are separated from each other by carriage returns. However, the records in an SDF file maintain a preset width for the individual fields. SDF format files are occasionally referred to as *flat files*. dBASE III PLUS has the ability to store files in SDF format for use by other programs. Many spreadsheets can store data on a disk in SDF. dBASE III PLUS can then read those files, using an SDF option of the APPEND command (which will be discussed shortly). The following example shows a file in SDF format created by dBASE III PLUS using the LAST-NAME, CITY, and RENTAMT fields of the ABC Realty database:

```
Robinson      Washington       900.00
Morse         Chevy Chase      750.00
Westman       Silver Spring    570.00
Robinson      Takoma Park      425.00
Jones         Reston          1025.00
Mitchell      Arlington        990.00
Hart          Fairfax          720.00
```

The SDF format uses a fixed number of spaces for each field, regardless of the actual size of the information in the field. Information that is too long to fit in an SDF file will be truncated.

DIF, SYLK, and WKS

In addition to using ASCII text, many programs can transfer data using one of three common file formats: SYLK, DIF, and WKS. The SYLK format (an abbreviation for "Symbolic Link"), developed by Microsoft Corporation, is commonly used by Microsoft products as a means of exchanging files. Microsoft's Chart (graphics), Multiplan (spreadsheet), and File (database manager) all can work with files written in the SYLK format.

The DIF format (an abbreviation for "Document Interchange Format") can be used by a wide assortment of programs, including

VisiCalc (spreadsheet), R:base 5000, and PC-File III (database managers). Internally, the DIF format bears a resemblance to Delimited format files.

Finally, the WKS file format is used by Lotus 1-2-3 and by most other products that can directly read and write Lotus 1-2-3 files. The WKS files that are created by dBASE III PLUS can be used by both versions of Lotus 1-2-3 (version 1.1A and the newer Release 2) and by Symphony. Files with a "WR1" extension created by Symphony and files with a "WK1" extension created by Lotus 1-2-3 Release 2 can be read by dBASE III PLUS.

When transferring data out of dBASE III PLUS, you must decide what format you wish to use. A list of some of the better-known programs and the types of data they can exchange is shown in Table 16-1.

As a general rule, most word processors will transfer ASCII, Delimited, or SDF. Many spreadsheets will transfer data in DIF or SDF format, and most database managers will transfer data in DIF or Delimited format. Lotus 1-2-3 and Symphony can use the WKS file format. If it isn't obvious which format your software package uses, check the owner's manual.

Table 16-1. Software Interchange Formats

Brand	Type of Package	File Type
WordStar	Word processor	ASCII, Delimited, or SDF
MailMerge	Option of WordStar	Delimited
Microsoft Word	Word processor	ASCII, Delimited, or SDF
MultiMate	Word processor	ASCII, Delimited, or SDF
Lotus 1-2-3	Spreadsheet	WKS
PC-File III	Database manager	Delimited
R:base 4000	Database manager	Delimited
R:base 5000	Database manager	DIF or Delimited
Microsoft Multiplan	Spreadsheet	SYLK
Microsoft Chart	Graphics	SYLK

THE DATA SHARING OPTIONS OF THE APPEND AND COPY COMMANDS

Many exchanges of data between dBASE III PLUS and other programs will be accomplished with the aid of certain Type options within the COPY and APPEND commands. Using COPY, you can copy data from dBASE III PLUS to another program; using APPEND, you can append, or transfer, data from another program into a dBASE III PLUS database. The normal format for these commands, when used with a Type option, is

```
COPY TO (filename) (SCOPE) (FIELDS field list) (type)

APPEND FROM (filename) (SCOPE) (FIELDS field list) (type)
```

In this case, *filename* is the name of the file to be transferred between dBASE III PLUS and the other program, and *type* is one of the six acceptable types: SYLK, DIF, WKS, ASCII, Delimited, and SDF. As a brief example, to copy the ABC Realty database into a Lotus-compatible file, you might use this command:

```
COPY TO 123FILE WKS
```

And you might use the following command to transfer a file from Microsoft's Multiplan to dBASE III PLUS:

```
APPEND FROM MPFILE SYLK
```

You can add other options, such as a scope (ALL, NEXT, or a record number) or a list of fields to the COPY and APPEND commands when using these commands to transfer data to other programs. You can also use the FOR condition to specify records that will be transferred.

SOME EXAMPLES

The rest of this chapter will provide working examples of transferring files. Since you may not be using the software packages described, you may not be able to follow along with the examples. If you have the software package mentioned or a similar software package with the ability to use the file formats acceptable to dBASE III PLUS, try using the examples with your software.

Transferring Files From dBASE III PLUS To WordStar and Other Word Processors

Most word processors work with ASCII format, so let's try it first. Suppose you needed to pull names and rent amounts from the database to provide a memo to the staff containing all tenants' rent amounts. You can use SET ALTERNATE to help you perform this task. SET ALTERNATE opens a text file for recording all operations displayed on the screen. In effect, the file is a record of all dBASE III PLUS operations on the screen for a given period.

Using SET ALTERNATE in this way is a two-step operation. First, the file is created with SET ALTERNATE TO *filename*. This file will have an extension of .TXT. When the SET ALTERNATE ON command is used, everything that appears on your screen (with the exception of full-screen editing operations) will be stored in the text file, in ASCII format. When you no longer want to record the commands' operations, use the SET ALTERNATE OFF command to terminate the process. You can use SET ALTERNATE ON and SET ALTERNATE OFF as many times as needed. When you are finished, you can close the file with the CLOSE ALTERNATE command.

Try using SET ALTERNATE and CLOSE ALTERNATE commands by entering the following:

```
USE ABC1
SET ALTERNATE TO RENTERS
SET ALTERNATE ON
LIST LASTNAME, FIRSTNAME, RENTAMT
SET ALTERNATE OFF
CLOSE ALTERNATE
```

Now exit dBASE III PLUS and load your word processor. Enter the command to open a file; and when your word processor asks you for the filename to edit, enter RENTERS.TXT. The file should then appear on your screen. For WordStar the screen should resemble Figure 16-1.

You can use commands in your word processor to delete the LIST that appears at the beginning of the file and the SET ALTERNATE OFF commands that appear at the end of the document.

WARNING: At the bottom of the file that was transferred with dBASE III PLUS there may be a left-pointing arrow or similar graphics character (whether or not there is one depends on what word processor you are using). If you are using WordStar, you may see one or more control-at symbols ($\wedge$ @) at the end of the file. This character represents an end-of-file marker that dBASE III PLUS produced when it was finished writing to the file. You can use the BACKSPACE key or a DELETE command to erase this unwanted character. Different word processors interpret this end-of-file marker in different ways, so you may see a character other than $\wedge$ @.

Get out of your word processor by using its normal exit commands, and reload dBASE III PLUS now.

```
        C:RENTERS.TXT   PAGE 1 LINE 1 COL 01        INSERT ON
                    < < <   M A I N   M E N U   > > >
        --Cursor Movement--      : -Delete- :  -Miscellaneous-  : -Other Menus--
    ^S char left ^D char right :^G  char  : ^I Tab   ^B Reform : (from Main only)
    ^A word left ^F word right :DEL chr lf: ^U INSERT ON/OFF   :^J Help  ^K Block
    ^E line  up  ^X line down  :^T word rt:^L Find/Replce again:^Q Quick ^P Print
        --Scrolling--          :^Y  line  :RETURN End paragraph:^O Onscreen
    ^Z line down ^W line up    :          : ^N Insert a RETURN :
    ^C screen up ^R screen down:          : ^U Stop a command  :
    L----!----!----!----!----!----!----!----!----!----!--------R
    list lastname, firstname, rentamt                                          <
    Record#  lastname       firstname        rentamt                           <
          1  Robinson       William           900.00                           <
          2  Morse          Marcia            750.00                           <
          3  Westman        Andrea            570.00                           <
          4  Robinson       Shirley           425.00                           <
          5  Jones          Jarel            1025.00                           <
          6  Mitchell       Mary Jo           990.00                           <
          7  Hart           Edward            720.00                           <
          8  Jackson        David             570.00                           <
          9  Drummond       Rick              810.00                           <
         10  Andrews        Robin            1010.00                           <
         11  Turner         Mitchell          875.00                           <
    set alternate off                                                          .
    1HELP   2INDENT 3SET LM 4SET RM 5UNDLIN 6BLDFCE 7BEGBLK 8ENDBLK 9BEGFIL 10ENDFIL
```

Figure 16-1. File transfer from dBASE III PLUS to WordStar

Transferring Files From dBASE III PLUS To MailMerge and Other Database Managers

If you need data in Delimited format, you'll use the DELIMITED option of the COPY command. Delimited formats are used by WordStar's MailMerge option and by many other database managers.

First copy the fields from the active database to a separate file used by the other program. The format of the COPY command with the Delimited option is COPY TO *filename* [*scope*] [FIELDS *fieldlist*,] DELIMITED. *Filename* is the name of the file that will contain the fields. You can limit which records to copy by including *scope*, specified by ALL, NEXT, or RECORD. Fields can be limited by the FIELD and *fieldlist* option. When you specify the DELIMITED option, the .TXT extension is automatically appended to *filename*.

As an example, let's say that you need to transfer a list of the names, addresses, and cities from ABC1 to a file named DATA-FILE that will be used by another database manager. Enter the following commands:

```
USE ABC1
COPY TO DATAFILE FIELDS LASTNAME, FIRSTNAME, ADDRESS, CITY DELIMITED
```

The file DATAFILE created by COPY TO will contain one line for each record that was copied from ABC1. Each record includes the tenant's last name, first name, address, and city. Each field is enclosed by quotation marks, and each field is separated by a comma.

The TYPE command can be used to list on the screen the contents of any disk file. Let's examine DATAFILE with the TYPE command to see the Delimited file format. With TYPE you are required to supply the file extension, in this case .TXT, and you are not allowed to view an open file (in that case use LIST instead). From the dot prompt enter

```
TYPE DATAFILE.TXT
```

and the following will be displayed:

```
"Robinson","William","1607 21st Street NW","Washington"
"Morse","Marcia","4260 Park Avenue","Chevy Chase"
"Westman","Andrea","4807 East Avenue","Silver Spring"
"Robinson","Shirley","270 Browning Ave #3C","Takoma Park"
"Jones","Jarel","5203 North Shore Drive","Reston"
"Mitchell","Mary Jo","617 North Oakland Street","Arlington"
"Hart","Edward","6200 Germantown Road","Fairfax"
"Jackson","David","4102 Valley Lane","Falls Church"
"Drummond","Rick","9030 Jacob Way","Detroit"
"Andrews","Robin","417 State Plaza","Highland Park"
"Turner","Mitchell","117 Coral Drive","Detroit"
```

```
.op
.df b:datafile.txt
.rv lastname,firstname,address,city
```

                    May 1, 1985

&firstname& &lastname&
&address&
&city&

Dear Mr./Ms. &lastname&:

 Our records indicate that your lease will be expiring
within the next 90 days. We welcome the opportunity to
continue to be of service to you. If you plan on remaining
in your home, please contact our offices by phone or by
mail so that we may extend your current lease.

Sincerely,

O. J. Springs, Manager
ABC Realty, Inc.

Figure 16-2. WordStar form letter for use with MailMerge and dBASE III
        PLUS

        This file can be used by almost all other database managers,
including PC-File III, R:base 4000, and R:base 5000, or it can be
used by WordStar's MailMerge option to create a form letter. In
such cases, you must use the appropriate commands of the particular database manager or MailMerge to import a file in the Delimited format. MailMerge works very well with Delimited files; and
with a few MailMerge commands inserted within a WordStar file,
you can create form letters that gather information from a Delimited file. An example of a template for a form letter, written with
WordStar for use with MailMerge, is shown in Figure 16-2.

May 1, 1985

David Jackson
4102 Valley Lane
Falls Church

Dear Mr./Ms. Jackson:

Our records indicate that your lease will be expiring
within the next 90 days. We welcome the opportunity to
continue to be of service to you. If you plan on remaining
in your home, please contact our offices by phone or by
mail so that we may extend your current lease.

Sincerely,

O. J. Springs, Manager
ABC Realty, Inc.

Figure 16-3. Letter produced by using the form in Figure 16-2 and
MailMerge

The template letter uses a number of WordStar and MailMerge
commands. The .op command tells WordStar not to use page
numbers when printing the form letter. The .df command identifies the Delimited file that will be used by MailMerge. The .rv
command identifies the names and order of the fields in the
Delimited file. The ampersands surrounding the field names in the
form letter will be replaced by the data contained in the appropriate fields of the Delimited file. When the MailMerge option of
WordStar is used, it generates a form letter similar to the one that
is shown in Figure 16-3.

For database managers and other programs that accept data in
the DIF format, use the DIF option with the COPY and APPEND
commands, as demonstrated in the following examples:

```
COPY TO B:STOCKS.VC1 FIELDS LASTNAME, FIRSTNAME, CITY, STATE DIF

APPEND FROM C:MAILER DIF
```

The first example will copy the contents of the named fields within a database in use to a file named STOCKS.VC1 on drive B. The file will be stored in DIF format. In the second example, records will be copied from a DIF file called MAILER into the database in use. Remember that when importing data into dBASE III PLUS with the APPEND command, the database structure must match the structure of the records within the file that contain the data.

Transferring Files Between dBASE III PLUS and PFS:FILE

Databases from PFS:FILE can be converted to dBASE III PLUS format, and dBASE III PLUS databases can be converted to PFS:FILE format. PFS:FILE is a special case and does not use the COPY TO and APPEND FROM commands used with other software packages. Instead, dBASE III PLUS provides two commands, IMPORT and EXPORT, to perform the task of sharing files with PFS:FILE. These commands can be used from the dot prompt or from the Tools menu of the Assistant.

The IMPORT command reads a PFS:FILE database and creates a dBASE III PLUS database with a matching database structure. The IMPORT command also creates a screen format file that matches the screen format of the PFS:FILE database. In addition, a view file is created that, when used, will link the database and screen format files together. The format of the IMPORT command, when used from the dot prompt, is

```
IMPORT FROM D:(filename) TYPE PFS
```

where *filename* is the name of the PFS:FILE database, and D: is the drive designator of the disk drive containing the database. As an example, to import a PFS:FILE database named PATIENTS, you would use a command like this one:

```
IMPORT FROM B:PATIENTS TYPE PFS
```

To use IMPORT from the Assistant, open the Tools menu and select IMPORT. Choose a disk drive that will be used to load the PFS:FILE database. The Assistant will prompt you for the name of the database to import (Figure 16-4). Enter the name of the database and press RETURN and the conversion process will take place.

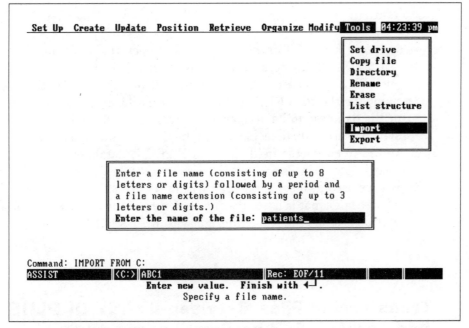

Figure 16-4. IMPORT choice of Tools menu

You can use the converted database separately or with the view file or screen format file created along with the database by the IMPORT command. All field types contained in the converted database will be character fields, as PFS:FILE treats all fields as character fields.

The EXPORT command is the opposite of the IMPORT command, converting a dBASE III PLUS database to a PFS:FILE database. The format of the EXPORT command is

```
EXPORT TO D:(filename) TYPE PFS
```

where *filename* is the name of the PFS:FILE database, and D: is the drive designator of the disk drive containing the database. For example, to export to a database named CLIENTS as a PFS:FILE database, you would use a command like this one:

```
EXPORT TO B:CLIENTS TYPE PFS
```

To use EXPORT from the Assistant, open the Tools menu and select EXPORT. Choose a disk drive that will be used to store the PFS:FILE database. The Assistant will prompt you for the filename for the PFS:FILE database (Figure 16-5). Enter the name of the database to be created and press RETURN, and the conversion process will take place. All fields in the database are converted to character fields in the PFS:FILE database. If a screen format file is in use when the conversion takes place, that form will be used as a screen design within the PFS:FILE database. If no screen format is used, the file structure of the dBASE database will be used as the screen design within PFS:FILE.

Transferring Files Between dBASE III PLUS And Lotus 1-2-3 or Symphony

Exchanging data between Lotus 1-2-3 or Symphony and dBASE III PLUS is a simple matter. dBASE III PLUS has an important

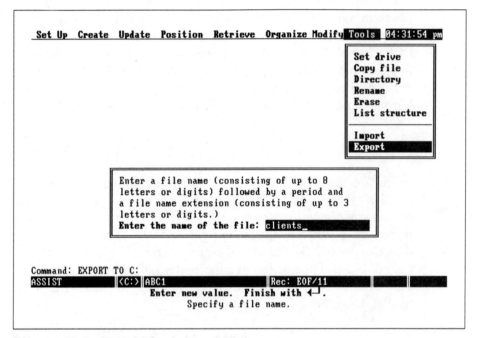

Figure 16-5. EXPORT choice of Tools menu

ability that earlier versions of dBASE lacked: the ability to directly read and write files in Lotus 1-2-3 format. dBASE III PLUS can exchange data between 1-2-3 Release 1.1A and between the newer 1-2-3 Release 2 and Symphony. To transfer data to and from Lotus 1-2-3 or Symphony, you will use the APPEND and COPY commands with the worksheet file type, as shown in the example that follows:

```
APPEND FROM LOTUSFIL WKS
```

```
COPY TO LOTUSFIL WKS
```

The APPEND FROM command, when used in this manner, will read the contents of an existing 1-2-3 or Symphony spreadsheet and add those contents to a database that is in use. (If no database exists to store the data, you must first create a database with a structure that matches the column layout of the spreadsheet.) The COPY TO command will copy the contents of an existing database to a file that can be read by Lotus 1-2-3 or by Symphony. The file will have the .WKS extension. If you have Lotus 1-2-3, try the following commands to create a WKS file for a 1-2-3 spreadsheet:

```
USE ABC1
COPY TO 123FILE FIELDS LASTNAME, FIRSTNAME, CITY, RENTAMT, SIZE WKS
```

The file 123FILE.WKS created by these commands will contain a 1-2-3 spreadsheet, with one record in each row. The individual columns of the spreadsheet represent the fields that were transferred, as specified by the list of fields in the example. Enter QUIT to leave dBASE III PLUS and return to the DOS prompt. If your copy of 1-2-3 is in a different subdirectory of a hard disk, then use the DOS COPY command to copy the file, 123FILE.WKS, to that directory.

Load Lotus 1-2-3 in your usual manner. When the opening 1-2-3 screen appears, press any key to get a blank spreadsheet on the screen. The FILE LOAD command of Lotus 1-2-3 can be used to load the file. Once you are in the spreadsheet, type a slash (/) to bring the 1-2-3 commands to the top of the screen. Then, press F (for "file"), which will display the 1-2-3 file transfer menu, and press R (for "retrieve file"). 1-2-3 will respond by displaying the names of any spreadsheets on your disk.

Highlight the correct filename (123FILE.WKS) and press RETURN. The spreadsheet will be loaded and will appear on the screen (Figure 16-6).

To read Lotus 1-2-3 files into dBASE III PLUS, no special preparation in 1-2-3 is needed. Simply store a 1-2-3 file in the usual manner, and use the APPEND command of dBASE III PLUS to add the contents of the file into a dBASE III PLUS database. To import a 1-2-3 spreadsheet named FINANCE, created by 1-2-3 Release 1A, you would use the following command from the dot prompt:

```
APPEND FROM FINANCE WKS
```

```
A1: 'LASTNAME                                              READY

          A               B                C         D    E     F
  1  LASTNAME        FIRSTNAME        CITY        RENTAMTSIZE
  2  Robinson        William          Washington      900 1400
  3  Morse           Marcia           Chevy Chase     750 1600
  4  Westman         Andrea           Silver Spring   570 1250
  5  Robinson        Shirley          Takoma Park     425  870
  6  Jones           Jarel            Reston         1025 2230
  7  Mitchell        Mary Jo          Arlington       990 2350
  8  Hart            Edward           Fairfax         720 1670
  9  Jackson         David            Falls Church    570  980
 10  Drummond        Rick             Detroit         810 1412
 11  Andrews         Robin            Highland Park  1010 2020
 12  Turner          Mitchell         Detroit         875 1850
 13  Johnson         Larry            Asheville         0    0
 14  Mills           Jeanette         Pheonix           0    0
 15  Simpson         Charles          New York          0    0
 16
 17
 18
 19
 20
```

Figure 16-6. Lotus 1-2-3 spreadsheet

To import a spreadsheet named FINANCE, created by Lotus 1-2-3
Release 2, you would use this command:

```
APPEND FROM FINANCE.WK1 WKS
```

And to import a Symphony worksheet named FINANCE, you
would use the following command:

```
APPEND FROM FINANCE.WR1 WKS
```

The only difference between the commands shown is the addition of the .WK1 extension to the filename in the second example,
and the .WR1 extension to the filename in the third example.
These are the extensions used by Release 2 of 1-2-3 and by Symphony, respectively. dBASE III PLUS, however, expects the extension of a file loaded with the WKS type specified to be .WKS
unless told otherwise.

Transferring Files
From dBASE III PLUS
To Other Spreadsheets

Users of Microsoft's Multiplan can transfer a dBASE III PLUS database to a Multiplan spreadsheet by using the SYLK option of the COPY command. The SYLK file format is used for transfer of data to Multiplan and other Microsoft products. The normal format for the COPY command, when used with this option, is

```
COPY TO (filename) (SCOPE) (FIELDS field list) SYLK
```

As an example, the following commands could be used to create a spreadsheet that could be read by Microsoft's Multiplan:

```
USE ABC1
COPY TO MPFILE2 FIELDS LASTNAME, CITY, STATE, RENTAMT, SIZE SYLK
```

The spreadsheet would contain columns for each of the fields named. Multiplan users should note that when loading the file into Multiplan, the Transfer Options choice should be selected from the main Multiplan menu, and Symbolic should then be chosen from the menu that appears. This will tell Multiplan to load Symbolic Link type, or SYLK, files.

If you need to save a file in SDF format, you'll use the SDF option of the COPY command. The SDF format is used for transferring data from dBASE III PLUS to spreadsheets that cannot read SYLK or WKS format files. Try this variation of the COPY command to create an SDF file:

```
COPY TO CALCFILE FIELDS LASTNAME, CITY, RENTAMT SDF
```

The file CALCFILE created by this command will contain one line for each record, with each record containing LASTNAME, CITY, and RENTAMT fields. Instead of being surrounded by quotes and separated by commas, each field is allotted space according to its width. To see the file in SDF format, enter

```
TYPE CALCFILE.TXT
```

and the following will be displayed on your screen:

```
Robinson      Washington       900.00
Morse         Chevy Chase      750.00
Westman       Silver Spring    570.00
Robinson      Takoma Park      425.00
Jones         Reston          1025.00
Mitchell      Arlington        990.00
Hart          Fairfax          720.00
Jackson       Falls Church     570.00
Drummond      Detroit          810.00
Andrews       Highland Park   1010.00
Turner        Detroit          875.00
```

How you will load the file into your spreadsheet will depend on what spreadsheet you are using. It would be impossible to explain the file-loading command for all spreadsheets, but in every case, you will need to perform two steps to import the dBASE III PLUS file into your spreadsheet. First, you must set your spreadsheet's load command so that the spreadsheet is ready to receive files in the SDF format. Second, you must use your spreadsheet's external load or import command to load the SDF file.

Transferring Files From Other Spreadsheets To dBASE III PLUS

Most spreadsheets provide an option for printing a file onto disk. The resulting disk file matches the SDF format. Different spreadsheets use different commands to create such files, so check your spreadsheet manual for instructions. Listed in Figure 16-7 are methods for creating dBASE-compatible files with some of the more popular spreadsheets.

Before transferring an SDF file into a database, be sure that the database field types and field widths match the SDF format precisely. You can use the APPEND FROM command with the SDF option to transfer the data into dBASE III PLUS. The format of APPEND FROM with the SDF option (less the conditional option, discussed in Chapter 4) is APPEND FROM *filename* SDF. The APPEND FROM with SDF operates exactly like APPEND FROM with DELIMITED. *Filename* is the name of the file that will be transferred and appended to the active database file.

Lotus 1-2-3 Users:

1. Press the slash key (/) to display Lotus 1-2-3 commands.
2. Press F (for "file").
3. Press S (for "save").
4. Specify a name for the file you will create.
5. Press the slash key.
6. Press Q (for "quit").

NOTE: Lotus 1-2-3 Release 2 saves all files with an extension of .WK1. You must include this extension when naming the file in the dBASE III PLUS APPEND TO command.

Multiplan Users:

1. Press ESC to highlight Multiplan commands.
2. Press T (for "transfer").
3. Press O (for "options").
4. Press S (for "symbolic"), then RETURN.
5. Press T (for "transfer").
6. Press S (for "save").
7. Specify a name for the file you will create.

NOTE: Use the SYLK option of the APPEND command to read a Multiplan file into a dBASE III PLUS database.

SuperCalc 2 and 3 Users:

1. Press the slash key (/) to display SuperCalc commands.
2. Press O (for "output").
3. Press D (for "display option").
4. Specify a range of the spreadsheet to be transferred to the file.
5. Press D (for "disk").
6. Specify a name for the SDF file.

NOTE: SuperCalc saves all non-SuperCalc files with an extension of .PRN. You must include this extension when naming the file in the dBASE III PLUS APPEND TO command.

Figure 16-7. Procedures for creating dBASE III PLUS-compatible files for Lotus 1-2-3, Multiplan, and SuperCalc 2 and 3

The fields in the database must be as wide as or wider than the fields in the SDF file. If the database fields are narrower, the incoming data will be truncated to fit the field. An alternate method for transferring data from a spreadsheet is to convert the SDF file to a Delimited file. This is done by using your word processor to edit the file, removing extra spaces between fields, and adding commas and quotation marks to separate the fields. You can then transfer the data with the DELIMITED option of the APPEND FROM command, but this time you need not be concerned that the field widths precisely match the width of the SDF files.

Transferring Files From WordStar And Other Word Processors to dBASE III PLUS

Transferring data from other programs into a dBASE III PLUS database may take just a little more work than the process of sending dBASE III PLUS data to other programs (particularly to word processors). This is because files brought into a dBASE III PLUS database must follow a precise format, such as an SDF or Delimited format. So when you send data from your word processor to a dBASE III PLUS database, you must edit the file from your word processor until it matches the format of a Delimited or an SDF file.

After your word processor creates a file in Delimited or SDF format, you can use the APPEND command of dBASE III PLUS to load the file. At first glance it may seem easier to use SDF format instead of Delimited format because you don't have to type all of the quotes and commas. But if you choose the SDF format, you must keep track of the size of each field. Each field must have the same width as the database field in which you will be transferring data, and the fields must be in the same order as those in the database. For this reason, it is often easier to use Delimited format.

When transferring files created by your word processor (or any other program) to dBASE III PLUS, you must also create or use a dBASE III PLUS database with a structure that matches the design of the files you wish to transfer. For purposes of simplicity, the following examples assume that the files created by other software match the structure of the ABC Realty database.

Let's try a transfer using a Delimited file. Suppose you have created a mailing list with a word processor and you now want to use that mailing list with dBASE III PLUS. If you have a word processor that can create files in ASCII text, follow along.

Use your word processor to create the following Delimited file and give it the name MAIL2.TXT. (**NOTE**: If you are using WordStar or NewWord, press N from the No-File menu to create a document that does not contain WordStar formatting codes.)

```
"Johnson","Larry","4209 Vienna Way","Asheville","NC","27995"
"Mills","Jeanette","13 Shannon Manor","Phoenix","AZ","87506"
"Simpson","Charles","421 Park Avenue","New York","NY","10023"
```

Save the file with your word processor's save commands. Now load dBASE III PLUS. You'll use the DELIMITED option of the APPEND FROM command to append the file to ABC1. The format of the APPEND command when used to import a Delimited file (without conditions, which is discussed in Chapter 4) is APPEND FROM *filename* DELIMITED.

To transfer MAIL2.TXT to dBASE III PLUS, enter the following from the dBASE III PLUS dot prompt:

```
USE ABC1
APPEND FROM MAIL2.TXT DELIMITED
```

dBASE III PLUS will respond with the message **3 records added**. To examine the database enter GO TOP and then LIST, and at the bottom of the database you will see that the names and addresses from the mailing list have been added to the database.

In this example, fields are in order of last name, first name, address, city, state, and ZIP code. Fortunately, this is the same order as the fields in ABC1. In real life, though, things may not be as simple. If, for example, the list of tenants were ordered by first name and then last name, you would have to transpose the names before transferring the file to dBASE III PLUS. When the fields in the database used by the other program do not match the database used by dBASE III PLUS, you will need to perform whatever work is necessary to make them match. You can do this in one of two ways: either change the order of the data in the other file, or design a new database in dBASE III PLUS that matches the order of the data in the other file.

Transferring Databases
Between dBASE III PLUS and Framework II

Users of Ashton-Tate's Framework II integrated software will find that databases can be easily exchanged between dBASE III PLUS and Framework. (This is not surprising, considering that the same company is behind both packages.) No changes are needed for a dBASE database that is to be transferred to Framework II. Framework users should load the dBASE database onto the Framework desktop in the usual manner, highlight the frame, and press F5 (RECALC). Framework II will proceed to convert the database to a Framework database.

To export a Framework database to dBASE III PLUS, employ the usual Framework commands to highlight the frame containing the database. Then, open the Disk menu of Framework with CONTROL-D, and choose the Export option. From the next menu that appears, choose dBASE Delimited (Figure 16-8). Framework will proceed to create a delimited file, which can be read into dBASE III PLUS using the Delimited type option of the COPY command, as described earlier in this chapter.

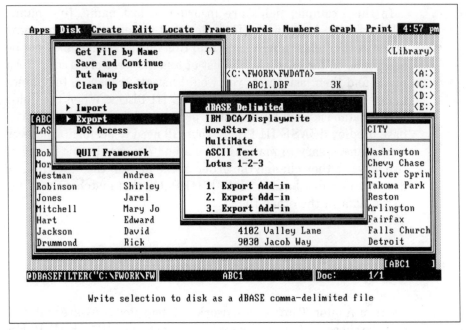

Figure 16-8. Framework's Export option

   One caution for users of Framework II: the maximum size of a
Framework database is limited by the amount of memory in your
PC. dBASE III PLUS, on the other hand, is in practice limited
only by disk space. If a dBASE III PLUS database is too large to
fit within a Framework II database, Framework II will import as
much of the file as it can handle and will display a warning message indicating the number of records that are present in the
Framework database. If this becomes a problem, an option is to
break the dBASE database into smaller pieces with the Scope
option of the COPY command. As an example, you could copy the
contents of a 550-record dBASE database into three separate files
with the following commands:

```
USE MAILDATA
COPY NEXT 200 TO FWONE
GO 201
COPY NEXT 200 TO FWTWO
GO 401
COPY NEXT 150 TO FWTHREE
```

These commands would create three files, each containing specific records in the dBASE database. The files could be brought onto the Framework desktop and used on an individual basis.

Sample dBASE III PLUS Programs

Chapter 17

This chapter contains three sample dBASE III PLUS programs: a mailing list, an inventory system, and a payroll system. You will want to try these programs and modify and expand on them to meet your own needs. When commands within the programs set the default drive to B:, hard-disk users will want to substitute the appropriate drive designator.

A MAILING LIST

The Mailer program maintains a mailing list. It lets you add new names to the list, edit existing names in the list, and delete names that are no longer needed. It also contains a print program designed to print names and addresses from the mailing list (in alphabetical order). You will print the names and addresses on mailing labels.

Before using the Mailer program, you must create a database for the records. The database should be assigned the name MAILLIST.DBF; so enter CREATE MAILLIST and specify the fields and their characteristics listed in Table 17-1.

Table 17-1. Database Structure for a Mailing-List System

Field name	Type	Width	Dec
LASTNAME	char/text	20	
FIRSTNAME	char/text	15	
COMPANY	char/text	20	
ADDRESS1	char/text	25	
ADDRESS2	char/text	15	
CITY	char/text	15	
STATE	char/text	2	
ZIP	char/text	10	

After saving the structure, return to the dot prompt and use either the dBASE III PLUS word processor or another one to create the following main-menu command file for the mailing-list system. Name it MAILER.PRG.

```
*Displays Main menu and calls other programs.
SET SAFETY OFF
SET TALK OFF
SET DEFAULT TO B:
STORE 0 TO CHOICE
DO WHILE CHOICE < 5
    *Loop displays menu unless 5 is chosen.
    CLEAR
    @2,5 SAY "Mailing List System"
    @3,5 SAY "Choose a selection."
    @6,0
    TEXT
    =========================================
    1. Enter a new name and address.
    2. Edit an existing name and address.
    3. Delete an existing name and address.
    4. Print mailing labels.
    5. Exit this program.
    =========================================
    ENDTEXT
    INPUT "Enter a number:" TO CHOICE
    IF CHOICE > 5
        CLEAR
        @2,2 SAY "Please try a number from 1 to 5."
        @3,2
        INPUT "Enter a number now." TO CHOICE
```

```
        ENDIF
        DO CASE
             CASE CHOICE =1
             DO NEW
             CASE CHOICE =2
             DO CHANGE
             CASE CHOICE =3
             DO REMOVER
             CASE CHOICE =4
             DO PRINTS
             CASE CHOICE =5
             QUIT
        ENDCASE CHOICE
        STORE 0 TO CHOICE
ENDDO
```

This command file displays the menu, which calls four command files in the system or terminates the program.

The following command file (call it NEW) allows the addition of new entries to the mailing list. The APPEND BLANK command adds an empty record to the database, and the @ command with SAY and GET options will prompt the user for the information for the new record. (The .PRG extension will automatically be included if the file is created by dBASE III PLUS's word processor.)

```
*Routing adds new names to the list.
USE MAILLIST
*Put names in alphabetical order.
INDEX ON LASTNAME TO ORDER
CLEAR
@3,5 SAY "Add a name to the mailing list."
GO BOTTOM
APPEND BLANK
@7,5 SAY "Enter last name-" GET LASTNAME
@9,5 SAY "Enter first name- " GET FIRSTNAME
@11,5 SAY "Enter company name- " GET COMPANY
@13,5 SAY "Enter 1st address line- " GET ADDRESS1
@15,5 SAY "Enter 2nd address line- " GET ADDRESS2
@17,5 SAY "Enter city- " GET CITY
@17,50 SAY "Enter state- " GET STATE
@19,5 SAY "Enter Zip- " GET ZIP
READ
CLEAR ALL
RETURN
```

The next command file allows you to edit the mailing list. The command file first asks for the last name in the record you want to edit. The LOCATE command then begins a search for the name by advancing the pointer to each record until a match has been found; and when it is found, the EDIT command is used to edit the record. Enter the following and save it under the name CHANGE.PRG:

```
*Routine edits existing records.
USE MAILLIST
CLEAR
@5,10 SAY "Enter Last Name for the record to be edited."
ACCEPT TO TEST
LOCATE FOR LASTNAME=TEST
IF LASTNAME <> TEST
     *The name wasn't found, so return to menu.
     @7,10 SAY "This person is not in the mailing list."
     @8,10 SAY "Return to the menu to add new names, or"
     @9,10 SAY "to try a different name."
     @10,10
     WAIT
     RETURN
ENDIF
*The name was found, so enter edit mode.
CLEAR
@7,1 SAY "Make necessary changes; press CONTROL-END when done."
WAIT
EDIT
CLEAR ALL
RETURN
```

If you are searching for a last name that occurs in more than one record, only the first encounter will be edited, even if it is not the record you want. Asking for the first name along with the last helps avoid duplication, so try including this feature in your CHANGE command file.

The third command file prints each record in the database in mailing-label format. A DO WHILE loop contains commands to print each record and move the record pointer to the next record. This process is repeated until the last record has been printed. Enter the following and save it under the name PRINTS.PRG:

```
*Routine prints the records.
CLEAR
SET TALK OFF
SET PRINT ON
USE MAILLIST
DO WHILE .NOT. EOF()
```

```
     *Loop prints one label for each record.
     ? TRIM(FIRSTNAME)+" "+LASTNAME
     ? COMPANY
     ? ADDRESS1
     ? ADDRESS2
     ? TRIM(CITY)+" "+STATE+" "+ZIP
     ?
     ?
     ?
     SKIP
ENDDO
SET PRINT OFF
CLEAR
@5,5 SAY "A total of"
@5,17 SAY RECNO()-1
@6,5 SAY "labels have been printed."
@10,5 SAY "To return to the menu:"
@12,5
WAIT
RETURN
```

The fourth and final command file deletes records from the mailing list. The command file will first ask for the last name in the record to be deleted. The LOCATE command is then used to search for the last name, and if it is found, the DELETE and PACK commands are used to remove the record. Enter the following and save it under the name REMOVER.PRG:

```
*Routine deletes unwanted records.
USE MAILLIST
CLEAR
@5,10 SAY "Enter Last Name for the record to be edited."
ACCEPT TO TEST
LOCATE FOR LASTNAME=TEST
IF LASTNAME <> TEST
     *The name wasn't found, so return to menu.
     @7,10 SAY "This person is not in the mailing list."
     @8,10 SAY "Return to the menu to add new names, or"
     @9,10 SAY "to try a different name."
     @10,10
     WAIT
     RETURN
ENDIF
*Name found, so display and confirm deletion.
CLEAR
@5,5 SAY "The record chosen is as follows:"
@7,5 SAY FIRSTNAME
@7,22 SAY LASTNAME
@8,5 SAY COMPANY
@9,5 SAY ADDRESS1
@10,5 SAY ADDRESS2
```

```
@11,5 SAY CITY
@11,22 SAY STATE
@11,26 SAY ZIP
@13,5 SAY "Delete this record? Enter 1 to delete record, or"
@14,5 SAY "press any other key to return to menu."
@16,5
WAIT TO NUMB
IF NUMB="1"
     DELETE
     PACK
     CLEAR ALL
     RETURN
ENDIF
RETURN
```

The same problem that occurred in CHANGE occurs again in REMOVER with greater consequences: you might delete the wrong record if you are searching for a last name that occurs more than once.

To use the system from the dot prompt, enter DO B:MAILER.

Improvements to the System

Some mailing labels come three-up (three labels on each row of label paper). If you wish to use these types of labels, you could try adding more print statements to PRINTS.PRG. And if you really want to get fancy, try adding routines that let you print by selected ZIP codes or by last names beginning with certain letters. Once the separate command files are operating properly, you can combine them into a procedure file.

AN INVENTORY SYSTEM

The following inventory system keeps track of part numbers, product descriptions, costs, and stock. Menu choices ask you to add items to the inventory, reduce inventory, and create new inventory items. There is also a print program designed to print a list of the items and their quantities.

Table 17-2. Database Structure for an Inventory System

Field name	Type	Width	Dec
PNO	numeric	4	
NAME	char/text	20	
QUAN	numeric	3	
COST	numeric	7	2

Before using the inventory program, a database with the name INVENTOR should be created. So enter CREATE INVENTOR and specify the fields and their characteristics listed in Table 17-2.

After saving the structure, return to the dot prompt and then use the dBASE III PLUS word processor to create the main menu for the inventory system.

The following command file displays the main menu and evokes the other command files. Enter the following and save it under the name INVENT.PRG:

```
*Displays inventory menu and calls other programs.
SET SAFETY OFF
SET TALK OFF
SET DEFAULT TO B:
STORE 0 TO CHOICE
DO WHILE CHOICE < 4
    *Loop displays menu unless 5 is chosen.
    CLEAR
    @2,5 SAY "Inventory System"
    @3,5 SAY "Choose a selection."
    @6,0
    TEXT
    =================================================
    1. Add parts to the inventory.
    2. Add or subtract quantity of a part.
    3. Print all items in the inventory.
    4. Exit this program.
    =================================================
    ENDTEXT
    INPUT "Enter a number:" TO CHOICE
    IF CHOICE > 4
        CLEAR
        @2,2 SAY "Please try a number from 1 to 4."
        @3,2
```

```
            INPUT "Enter a number now." TO CHOICE
    ENDIF
    DO CASE
        CASE CHOICE =1
        DO ADDINV
        CASE CHOICE =2
        DO QUAN
        CASE CHOICE =3
        DO PRINTINV
        CASE CHOICE =4
        QUIT
    ENDCASE CHOICE
ENDDO
```

The first command file adds new parts and their names to the inventory. This command file uses an infinite loop created by the DO WHILE .T. statement near the beginning of the command file to allow new inventory items to be added, one after another, until a part number of 9999 is requested, which causes the DO WHILE loop to end. In this case, part number 9999 acts as a *flag* to terminate the DO WHILE loop. It is not a part. Enter the following and save it under the name ADDINV.PRG:

```
*Routine adds new items, descriptions to the inventory.
SET TALK OFF
USE INVENTOR
DO WHILE .T.
    *Loop until 9999 is entered.
    STORE 0 TO SPNO
    CLEAR
    @2,1 SAY "Add items to inventory."
    @10,1 SAY "Enter part number to be added." GET SPNO
    @12,1 SAY "Enter a part number of 9999 to exit."
    READ
    IF SPNO=9999
        CLEAR ALL
        RETURN
    ENDIF
    LOCATE FOR PNO=SPNO
    IF PNO = SPNO
        *User is trying to add part no. that's already in database.
        @15,5 SAY "That part number already exists."
        STORE 1 TO TIMES
        *Delay so user can read message.
        DO WHILE TIMES <50
            STORE 1+TIMES TO TIMES
        ENDDO
        *Return to beginning of Loop; try another part number.
        LOOP
    ENDIF
    IF PNO <> SPNO
        *New part number, so enter required information.
```

```
        CLEAR
        *Create variables for storage of new values.
        STORE "                    " TO RNAME
        STORE 0 TO RQUAN
        STORE .00 TO RCOST
        STORE SPNO TO RPNO
        CLEAR
        @10,5 SAY "Part number is "
        @10,22 SAY RPNO
        @11,5 SAY "Enter name: " GET RNAME
        @12,5 SAY "Enter current quantity on hand: " GET RQUAN
        @13,5 SAY "Enter item cost: " GET RCOST
        READ
        APPEND BLANK
        REPLACE PNO WITH RPNO, NAME WITH RNAME
        REPLACE QUAN WITH RQUAN, COST WITH RCOST
    ENDIF
ENDDO
```

The second command file lets the user increase or decrease the quantity of an existing part. The user inputs the part number, and the LOCATE command finds the record containing the part number. Once the record has been found, the program asks how much the part has increased or decreased (express decreases with a negative number). The REPLACE command is used to replace the current quantity with the new quantity. Enter the following and save it under the name QUAN.PRG:

```
*Routine changes inventory quantity.
SET TALK OFF
USE INVENTOR
STORE 0 TO TEST
STORE 0 TO RQUAN
CLEAR
TEXT
=========================================
Enter the part number you wish to
change quantity of.
=========================================
ENDTEXT
INPUT TO TEST
LOCATE FOR PNO=TEST
IF PNO <> TEST
    *No such part no., so back to menu.
    @20,10 SAY "This part number does not exist in the inventory."
    @22,10 SAY "Return to the main menu to choose another selection."
    @23,10
    WAIT
    RETURN
ENDIF
*Part no. exists, so change quantity.
CLEAR
@3,5 SAY "For part no.- "
@3,22 SAY PNO
```

```
@4,5 SAY "Description- "
@4,20 SAY NAME
@5,5 SAY "Current stock level-"
@5,30 SAY QUAN
@6,5 SAY "Add or subtract how many items?"
@8,5
INPUT TO RQUAN
REPLACE QUAN WITH RQUAN + QUAN
RETURN
```

The last command file prints a listing of all part numbers in the inventory with corresponding names, quantities, and costs. Enter the following and save it under the name PRINTINV.PRG:

```
*Prints the inventory.
SET TALK OFF
USE INVENTOR
CLEAR
@15,10 SAY "Make sure your printer is ready, then"
@16,10
WAIT
LIST PNO, NAME, QUAN, COST TO PRINT
RETURN
```

To use the system from the dot prompt, enter DO INVENT.

Improvements to the System

This is a "bare-bones" inventory system with room for a number of additions. For example, it would be useful to add a method for editing a record to change the part name or number. If the part number remains the same but the name or cost of the item changes, you could easily modify both by this same method. You also could try adding a routine that calculates the cost of a group of items removed from the inventory. That cost could then be printed as part of an invoice to a customer. Other routines could search the inventory database by product name and part number. Once the command files operate properly, you can combine them into a procedure file.

Table 17-3. Database Structure for a Payroll System

Field name	Type	Width	Dec
EMPNAME	char/text	30	
SSNUMB	numeric	9	
SALRATE	numeric	5	2

AN EMPLOYEE PAYROLL SYSTEM

This payroll system prints a weekly payroll based on hours worked and rate of pay. There are menu choices for adding new employees, removing former employees, adjusting employee pay rates, and printing the weekly payroll. The database will be called PAY-RECS, so enter CREATE PAYRECS and specify the database structure listed in Table 17-3.

Save the structure, get back to the dot prompt, and then use the dBASE III PLUS word processor to create the payroll system menu. Enter the following and save it under the name PAYROLL:

```
*Displays menu and calls other programs.
SET SAFETY OFF
SET TALK OFF
SET DEFAULT TO B:
STORE 0 TO CHOICE
DO WHILE CHOICE < 5
    *Loop displays menu unless 5 is chosen.
    CLEAR
    @2,5 SAY "Payroll System"
    @3,5 SAY "Choose a selection."
    @6,0
    TEXT
    ==========================================
    1. Run the weekly payroll.
    2. Add new employee to payroll.
    3. Change an employee's name/salary.
    4. Delete employee from payroll.
    5. Exit this program.
    ==========================================
```

```
            ENDTEXT
            INPUT "Enter a number:" TO CHOICE
            IF CHOICE > 5
                 CLEAR
                 @2,2 SAY "Please enter a number from 1 to 5."
                 @3,2
                 INPUT "Enter a number now." TO CHOICE
            ENDIF
            DO CASE
                 CASE CHOICE =1
                 DO PAYER
                 CASE CHOICE =2
                 DO PAYRUN
                 CASE CHOICE =3
                 DO SALJUST
                 CASE CHOICE =4
                 DO EMPDEL
                 CASE CHOICE =5
                 QUIT
            ENDCASE CHOICE
         STORE 0 TO CHOICE
ENDDO
```

The following command file prints the weekly payroll. A DO WHILE loop first calculates each employee's salary by asking the user to enter the number of hours worked and then multiplying hours worked by the hourly rate. The result is written to a text file with the SET ALTERNATE command. After all employees' salaries have been stored in the text file, the text file is then displayed on screen and printed. Enter the following and save it under the name PAYER:

```
*Routine runs weekly payroll.
SET TALK OFF
SET SAFETY OFF
USE PAYRECS
STORE 0 TO HOURS
STORE 0 TO WEEKSAL
SET ALTERNATE TO PAYPRINT.TXT
DO WHILE .NOT. EOF()
    *This loop writes employees' salaries to a text file.
    CLEAR
    @3,5 SAY "For employee "
    @3,19 SAY EMPNAME
    @5,5 SAY "How many hours were worked?"
    @6,5
    INPUT TO HOURS
    STORE HOURS*SALRATE TO WEEKSAL
    SET CONSOLE OFF
    SET ALTERNATE ON
    DISPLAY EMPNAME, SSNUMB, WEEKSAL
    ?
```

```
       SET ALTERNATE OFF
       SET CONSOLE ON
       SKIP
ENDDO
*Print the text file now.
CLEAR
@5,5 SAY "Processing completed.  Printing payroll."
@6,5 SAY "Turn printer on then press any key."
WAIT
CLOSE ALTERNATE
SET PRINT ON
TYPE B:PAYPRINT.TXT
EJECT
SET PRINT OFF
CLEAR
@5,5 SAY "To return to the menu,"
WAIT
CLEAR ALL
RETURN
```

The second command file adds new employees to the payroll. @ commands with SAY and GET store the information about the new employee to memory variables. The APPEND BLANK command is then used to add a blank record to the database. Finally, the REPLACE command moves information from the memory variables into the fields of the new record. Enter the following and save it under the name PAYRUN:

```
*Routine adds new employees.
SET TALK OFF
SET SAFETY OFF
USE PAYRECS
STORE "                   " TO NEMPNAME
STORE 0.00 TO NSALRATE
STORE 999999999 TO NSSNUMB
CLEAR
@2,5 SAY "This part of the program allows the addition"
@3,5 SAY "of new employees to the payroll database."
@5,5 SAY "Enter the following information:"
@7,5 SAY "Employee Name: " GET NEMPNAME
@9,5 SAY "Social Security Number: "GET NSSNUMB PICTURE "999999999"
@11,5 SAY "Hourly pay rate: "GET NSALRATE
READ
APPEND BLANK
REPLACE EMPNAME WITH NEMPNAME
REPLACE SSNUMB WITH NSSNUMB
REPLACE SALRATE WITH NSALRATE
CLEAR ALL
RETURN
```

The third command file makes any changes to employee data, such as salary rates or employee names. LOCATE finds the Social

Security number of the employee, and since every employee has a unique Social Security number, duplication won't be a problem. The EDIT command makes the necessary changes. Enter the following and save it under the name SALJUST:

```
*Routine used to change salary history
USE PAYRECS
CLEAR
@5,10 SAY "Enter Social Security Number of employee."
INPUT TO TEST
LOCATE FOR SSNUMB=TEST
IF SSNUMB <> TEST
     *Soc. Sec. number not found, so return to menu.
     @7,10 SAY "This employee is not in the salary database."
     @8,10 SAY "Return to the menu to try a different name."
     @10,10
     WAIT
     RETURN
ENDIF
*Soc. Sec. number found, so edit the record.
CLEAR
@2,1 SAY "Make the necessary changes; press CONTROL-END when done."
WAIT
EDIT
RETURN
```

The last command file removes employees from the payroll. The user is prompted to enter the Social Security number in the record to be deleted. The LOCATE command locates the employee record matching the number, and then the DELETE and PACK commands remove it from the database. Enter the following and save it under the name EMPDEL:

```
*Routine used to delete former employees.
USE PAYRECS
CLEAR
@5,10 SAY "Enter Social Security Number of employee."
INPUT TO TEST
LOCATE FOR SSNUMB=TEST
IF SSNUMB <> TEST
     *Soc. Sec. number not found, so return to menu.
     @7,10 SAY "This person is not in salary database."
     @8,10 SAY "Return to the menu to try a different name."
     @10,10
     WAIT
     RETURN
ENDIF
*Soc. Sec. number found, so confirm and delete.
CLEAR
```

```
@5,5 SAY "The record chosen is as follows:"
@7,5 SAY EMPNAME
@8,5 SAY SSNUMB
@9,5 SAY SALRATE
@11,5 SAY "Delete this employee? Enter 1 to delete employee, or"
@12,5 SAY "press any other key to return to menu."
@13,5
WAIT TO NUMB
IF NUMB="1"
     DELETE
     PACK
     RETURN
ENDIF
CLEAR
RETURN
```

To run the system from the dot prompt, enter DO PAYROLL.

Improvements to the System

This payroll system ignores the myriad of taxes and deductions that should be calculated for each employee's paycheck. A routine to handle Social Security and state and federal taxes could be included in the program. You might also want to add a routine that records each week's total salaries in a disk file. For faster operation, combine the command files into a procedure file.

A PERSONNEL TRACKING SYSTEM

The prior programs are simple by design in order to provide a basis for further development. To offer an example between such programs and a more complex one that provides the features desired in a typical working application, the following example is given. The command files are designed to provide an orderly method of managing personnel records. The system uses a PER-SONNL database, which contains fields for names and addresses, Social Security numbers, departments, EEO classifications, and insurance data. The structure for the database is shown in Table 17-4.

Table 17-4.   Database Structure for a Personnel System

Field name	Type	Width	Dec
SOCSEC	Numeric	9	
LASTNAME	Character	20	
FIRSTNAME	Character	15	
MIDNAME	Character	10	
ADDRESS	Character	30	
CITY	Character	15	
STATE	Character	2	
ZIP	Character	9	
PHONE	Character	10	
SEX	Character	1	
DEPART	Character	15	
BIRTHDATE	Date	8	
EEOCLASS	Character	1	
DATEHIRED	Date	8	
INSPOLICY	Logical	1	
NUMBDEPN	Numeric	2	

The command files for the system consist of a main menu that calls one of five procedures. One of the five files, used for printing reports, calls one of three command files. This design is illustrated in Figure 17-1.

The main menu is generated by the file PERSONNL.PRG. This command file displays the menu and uses CASE...ENDCASE choices to call one of five procedures. The personnel system makes use of the SET DELETED ON/OFF command to provide a method of moving employees to and from an inactive employment status. Inactive employees are deleted from the database, but the database is never PACKed. With SET DELETED ON, deleted employees are hidden from view and not included in any reports. If an inactive employee rejoins the company, a menu choice uses the RECALL command to restore the employee record to full view. When the command file PERSONNL.PRG is started, the database PERSONNL.DBF is opened and indexed by Social Security number. A WAIT command stores a character string that indicates whether the user wishes to update the database index. If so,

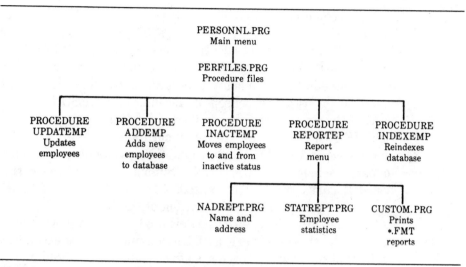

Figure 17-1. Personnel system design

this is done with the INDEX ON SOCSEC TO SOCIAL statement, rather than with the REINDEX command. This method allows the user of a new (empty) database to run the program for the first time, by choosing "Y" when the question appears. If REINDEX were used instead, the program would crash when used for the first time, because the index file would not exist. You may want to consider creating the database and creating an index file with the command INDEX ON SOCSEC TO SOCIAL. You could then use REINDEX in place of the INDEX ON SOCSEC TO SOCIAL statement, as using REINDEX would be slightly faster than recreating the entire index file.

The main section of the PERSONNL command file, contained within the DO WHILE .T. loop, displays the menu and calls one of five procedures contained in a procedure file. The DO CASE and CASE statements offer seven choices; five of the choices call the procedures, one calls the Assistant menus, and one choice exits from dBASE III PLUS by invoking the QUIT command. Placing the menu display and the menu choices inside of an endless loop (DO WHILE .T.) ensures that an invalid entry will result in a re-display of the menu with no action taken.

The procedures called by PERSONNL.PRG are contained in the procedure file PERFILES.PRG. The procedures are named UPDATEMP, ADDEMP, INACTEMP, REPORTEP, and INDEXEMP. UPDATEMP is used to update the personnel records of existing employees. When this procedure is used, a SEEK command performs a fast search of the indexed PERSONNL database. If the Social Security number is not found, a test of end-of-field (IF EOF( )) causes a **number not found** message to appear on the screen. A RETURN statement then causes program control to pass back to the PERSONNL command file. If the correct Social Security number is located, a series of @...SAY...GET commands permits full-screen editing of the record.

A similar procedure, ADDEMP, is used to add employees to the database; in this procedure, a SEEK command is first executed to verify that the new employee has not already been entered into the database. If the Social Security number already exists in the database, a test for a matching Social Security number (IF TEMP = SOCSEC) causes an **employee already exists** message to appear on the screen. A RETURN statement then causes program control to pass back to the PERSONNL command file. If the program verifies that the Social Security number does not exist in the database, an APPEND BLANK command then adds a new record, and the @...SAY...GET commands allow data entry.

The INACTEMP procedure moves employees to and from inactive employment status. First, the TEST variable is set to 1 or 2, corresponding to whether an employee record is to be moved to or from inactive status. Then, SET DELETED is turned off if an inactive employee is to be moved back to active status. A SEEK command then locates the desired record. A series of @...SAY...GET commands displays the data, so that the user can verify that the chosen record is the desired one. Depending on the previously-stored value of TEST, a pair of IF...ENDIF statements will delete or recall the chosen employee.

The INDEXEMP procedure is used to reindex the database. This provides the user with an option for updating the index at any time.

The REPORTEP procedure displays another menu that offers the user a choice of reports to be printed, by calling one of three command files: NADREPT.PRG, STATREPT.PRG, or CUSTOM .PRG. These three command files allow the user to select either of two standard reports or a custom report option. (Custom reports are created with the dBASE III PLUS Report Generator.) Both standard reports, NADREPT.PRG and STATREPT.PRG, are columnar reports that turn on a printer's compressed print mode to fit the necessary information on a single line. The compressed print modes assume the use of standard Epson printer codes and are executed with the statement ? CHR(15). The compressed print modes are turned off when no longer needed with the statement ? CHR(18). If your printer cannot respond to Epson codes, you will need to omit some fields (which you can place in another report), or you can let the command file print more than one line for each record printed. If the custom report option is selected, the command file CUSTOM.PRG causes a directory of all report format files to be displayed. From the menu, a user can then select a previously created report form or choose to create a new custom report form by entering a new name for the report form. If a name for a new report form is chosen, the dBASE III PLUS Report Generator is called by the program.

```
*Personnl.prg
SET SAFETY OFF
SET DEFAULT TO B:
SET BELL OFF
SET DELETED ON
SET PROCEDURE TO PERFILES
USE PERSONNL
CLEAR
@5,5 SAY "Shall I update the index? Y/N:"
WAIT " " TO INDEXER
IF UPPER(INDEXER) = "Y"
   @7,5 SAY "Please wait while I update the index."
   INDEX ON SOCSEC TO SOCIAL
ENDIF
SET TALK OFF
DO WHILE .T.
    CLEAR
    @2,5 SAY "==Personnel Database Master Menu=="
    @3,5 SAY "===Your Company Name Here=="
    @5,10 SAY "Enter Selection:"
    @6,0
TEXT
```

```
============================================================
       1. Update Existing Employees

       2. Add New Employees

       3. Move Existing Employees To/From Inactive Status

       4. Generate Personnel Reports

       5. Reindex Personnel Files

       6. Use dBASE III Manually With ASSIST

       7. Quit Using Personnel System

Your Choice?
============================================================
ENDTEXT
    INPUT TO CHOICE
    DO CASE
        CASE CHOICE = 1
            DO UPDATEMP
        CASE CHOICE = 2
            DO ADDEMP
        CASE CHOICE = 3
            DO INACTEMP
        CASE CHOICE = 4
            DO REPORTEP
        CASE CHOICE = 5
            DO INDEXEMP
        CASE CHOICE = 6
            ASSIST
        CASE CHOICE = 7
            QUIT
    ENDCASE CHOICE
ENDDO
*Perfiles.prg
*contains procedures
PROCEDURE UPDATEMP
*Routine used to update existing employees.
USE PERSONNL
SET INDEX TO SOCIAL
CLEAR
STORE 999999999 TO TEMP
@5,5 SAY "Enter Social Security number of employee to be updated."
@6,5 GET TEMP PICTURE "@R ###-##-####"
READ
GO TOP
SEEK TEMP
IF EOF()
    CLEAR
    @5,5 SAY "This employee does not exist in the database."
    @6,5 SAY "return to the menu to choose a function."
    WAIT
    RETURN
ENDIF
CLEAR
@1,1 SAY "Enter the necessary corrections now."
@2,5 SAY "Social security number: "
@2,31 GET SOCSEC PICTURE "@R ###-##-####"
@4,5 SAY "Last Name: " GET LASTNAME
@5,5 SAY "First name: " GET FIRSTNAME
@6,5 SAY "Middle name: " GET MIDNAME
@8,5 SAY "Address: " GET ADDRESS
@9,5 SAY "City: " GET CITY
@10,5 SAY "State: " GET STATE
@10,40 SAY "Zip Code: " GET ZIP PICTURE "@R #####-####"
@12,5 SAY "Phone: " GET PHONE PICTURE "@R ###-###-####"
```

```
@13,5 SAY "Sex (M/F): " GET SEX
@14,5 SAY "Department: " GET DEPART
@15,5 SAY "Date of birth: " GET BIRTHDATE
@16,10 SAY "Date hired: " GET DATEHIRED
@17,5 SAY "EEO Classification: " GET EEOCLASS
@18,10 SAY "[M]inority  [F]emale  [H]dcp  [V]eteran"
@19,10 SAY "Number of dependents: " GET NUMBDEPN
@20,10 SAY "Optional insurance: " GET INSPOLICY
READ
CLEAR
RETURN
PROCEDURE ADDEMP
*Routine used to add new employees to the database."
USE PERSONNL
SET INDEX TO SOCIAL
CLEAR
STORE 999999999 TO TEMP
@5,5 SAY "Enter Social Security number of new employee."
@6,5 GET TEMP PICTURE "@R ###-##-####"
READ
GO TOP
SEEK TEMP
 IF TEMP = SOCSEC
     CLEAR
     @10,10 SAY "This employee is already in the personnel data file."
     @12,5 SAY "Return to the menu to add new employees."
     WAIT
     RETURN
 ENDIF
GO BOTTOM
APPEND BLANK
CLEAR
@3,1 SAY "Enter data for new employee."
@5,10 SAY "Social Security Number: " GET SOCSEC PICTURE "@R ###-##-####"
@6,10 SAY "Last Name: " GET LASTNAME
@7,10 SAY "First name: " GET FIRSTNAME
@8,10 SAY "Middle name: " GET MIDNAME
@10,10 SAY "Address: " GET ADDRESS
@11,10 SAY "City: " GET CITY
@12,10 SAY "State: " GET STATE
@12,40 SAY "Zip Code: " GET ZIP PICTURE "@R #####-####"
@13,10 SAY "Phone: " GET PHONE PICTURE "@R ###-###-####"
@14,10 SAY "Sex (M/F): " GET SEX
@15,10 SAY "Department: " GET DEPART
@16,10 SAY "Date of birth: " GET BIRTHDATE
@17,10 SAY "Date hired: " GET DATEHIRED
@18,10 SAY "EEO Classification: " GET EEOCLASS
@19,15 SAY "[M]inority  [F]emale  [H]dcp  [V]eteran"
@20,10 SAY "Number of dependents: " GET NUMBDEPN
@21,10 SAY "Optional Insurance (Y/N): " GET INSPOLICY
READ
CLEAR
RETURN
PROCEDURE INACTEMP
*Routine moves employees to/from "Inactive" work status.
USE PERSONNL
SET INDEX TO SOCIAL
STORE 0 TO TEST
CLEAR
@10,10 SAY "Choose a selection."
@12,10 SAY "(1)- Place current employee on inactive status."
@14,10 SAY "(2)- Place Inactive employee back on current status."
@16,5 SAY "Enter choice, press RETURN."
@16,32 GET TEST RANGE 1,2
READ
*Enter the socsec no. and find the record.
STORE 999999999 TO TEMP
CLEAR
```

```
@5,5 SAY "Enter Employee Social Security number."
@6,5 GET TEMP PICTURE "@R ###-##-####"
READ
IF TEST = 2
    SET DELETED OFF
ENDIF
GO TOP
SEEK TEMP
IF EOF()
    CLEAR
    @5,5 SAY "This employee does not exist in the database."
    @6,5 SAY "return to the menu to choose a function."
    WAIT
    RETURN
ENDIF
CLEAR
@1,1 SAY "The employee record is as follows:"
@2,5 SAY "Social security number: "
@2,31 GET SOCSEC PICTURE "@R ###-##-####"
@4,5 SAY "Last Name: " GET LASTNAME
@5,5 SAY "First name: " GET FIRSTNAME
@6,5 SAY "Middle name: " GET MIDNAME
@8,5 SAY "Address: " GET ADDRESS
@9,5 SAY "City: " GET CITY
@10,5 SAY "State: " GET STATE
@10,40 SAY "Zip Code: " GET ZIP PICTURE "@R #####-####"
@12,5 SAY "Phone: " GET PHONE PICTURE "@R ###-###-####"
@13,5 SAY "Sex (M/F): " GET SEX
@14,5 SAY "Department: " GET DEPART
@15,5 SAY "Date of birth: " GET BIRTHDATE
@16,5 SAY "Date hired: " GET DATEHIRED
@17,5 SAY "EEO Classification: " GET EEOCLASS
@18,10 SAY "[M]inority  [F]emale  [H]dcp  [V]eteran"
@19,5 SAY "Number of dependents: " GET NUMBDEPN
@20,5 SAY "Optional Insurance: " GET INSPOLICY
@21,0
IF TEST = 1
    *Move employee to inactive status.
    @22,5 SAY "Press 1 to remove employee from active status."
    @23,5 SAY "Press any other key to return to menu."
    WAIT TO TEST2
    IF TEST2 <>"1"
        RETURN
    ENDIF
    DELETE
ENDIF
IF TEST = 2
    *Move employee off inactive status.
    @22,5 SAY "Press 1 to remove employee from inactive status."
    @23,5 SAY "Press any other key to return to menu."
    WAIT TO TEST2
    IF TEST2 <>"1"
        RETURN
    ENDIF
    RECALL
SET DELETED ON
ENDIF
RETURN
PROCEDURE REPORTEP
DO WHILE .T.
CLEAR
@5,0
TEXT
```

```
==========================================================

Choose A Report:

              1.   Employee Name and Address Report

              2.   Employee Vital Statistics Report

              3.   Custom Reports Created With dBASE III

              4.   Return To Main Menu

==========================================================
Enter A Selection:
ENDTEXT
INPUT TO CHOOSE
DO CASE
   CASE CHOOSE = 1
         DO NADREPT
   CASE CHOOSE = 2
         DO STATREPT
   CASE CHOOSE = 3
         DO CUSTOM
   CASE CHOOSE = 4
         RETURN
ENDCASE CHOOSE
ENDDO
RETURN

PROCEDURE INDEXEMP
*Reindex the database
USE PERSONNL
SET INDEX TO SOCIAL
CLEAR
@10,10 SAY "Please wait while I reindex the database."
SET TALK ON
REINDEX
SET TALK OFF
RETURN
*Nadrept.prg
*Prints name and address report
USE PERSONNL
SET TALK OFF
CLEAR
@4,5 SAY "Printing will be in alphabetical order based on name index."
@5,5 SAY "Shall I update the index? Y/N:"
WAIT " " TO INDEXER
IF UPPER(INDEXER) = "Y"
   @7,5 SAY "Please wait while I update the index."
SET TALK ON
INDEX ON LASTNAME + FIRSTNAME + MIDNAME TO NAMES
SET TALK OFF
ENDIF
CLEAR
SET PRINT ON
? CHR(15)
? "==============Employee Listing of Names And Addresses=============="
?
? "Last Name           First Name      Mid. Name  Address"
?? "                              City            State  Zip      Phone"
? "================================================================="
?? "================================================================="
GO TOP
```

```
DO WHILE .NOT. EOF()
    ? LASTNAME + " " + FIRSTNAME + " " + MIDNAME + " " + ADDRESS
    ?? CITY + "   " + STATE + "    " + ZIP + "   " + PHONE
    SKIP
ENDDO
EJECT
? CHR(18)
SET PRINT OFF
RETURN
*Statrept.prg
*Prints employee status listings
USE PERSONNL
CLEAR
@4,5 SAY "Printing will be in alphabetical order based on name index."
@5,5 SAY "Shall I update the index? Y/N:"
WAIT " " TO INDEXER
IF UPPER(INDEXER) = "Y"
   @7,5 SAY "Please wait while I update the index."
SET TALK ON
INDEX ON LASTNAME + FIRSTNAME + MIDNAME TO NAMES
SET TALK OFF
ENDIF
CLEAR
SET PRINT ON
? CHR(15)
? "=============Employee Listing of Employee Statistics============="
?
?
? "Lastname            Firstname       Mid. Name      Soc. Sec. "
?? " Sex  Birthdate  Date Hired  Insured?  No.Dep.   EEO Class"
?? "  Dept."
? "================================================================="
?? "================================================================="
GO TOP
DO WHILE .NOT. EOF()
    ? LASTNAME + "  " + FIRSTNAME + "  " + MIDNAME + "    "
    ?? SOCSEC
    ?? "   " + SEX + "    "
    ?? BIRTHDATE
    ?? "    "
    ?? DATEHIRED
    ?? "    "
    IF INSPOLICY
       ?? "Insured."
       ELSE
          ?? "          "
    ENDIF
    ?? "    "
    ?? NUMBDEPN
    ?? "          " + EEOCLASS + "     " + DEPART
    SKIP
ENDDO
EJECT
? CHR(18)
SET PRINT OFF
RETURN
*Custom.prg
*Prints reports created with dBASE III report generator.
USE PERSONNL
CLEAR
@4,5 SAY "Printing will be in alphabetical order based on name index."
@5,5 SAY "Shall I update the index? Y/N:"
WAIT " " TO INDEXER
```

```
IF UPPER(INDEXER) = "Y"
    @7,5 SAY "Please wait while I update the index."
    SET TALK ON
    INDEX ON LASTNAME + FIRSTNAME + MIDNAME TO NAMES
    SET TALK OFF
ENDIF
CLEAR
? "Custom report files on this disk are listed below:"
?
DISPLAY FILES LIKE *.FRM
?
?
? "Enter the name of the desired report (DO NOT INCLUDE EXTENSION)"
? "or enter a new report name to create a new report."
ACCEPT TO NAME
STORE NAME + ".FRM" TO NAME
IF FILE('&NAME') = .T.
    REPORT FORM &NAME TO PRINT
    EJECT
    RETURN
ENDIF
CREATE REPORT &NAME
RETURN
```

The dBASE II
To dBASE III PLUS
Connection

Chapter 18

If you have files formatted in dBASE II, you can still use them by converting them to dBASE III PLUS format. This chapter discusses dCONVERT, the conversion program included with dBASE III PLUS. dCONVERT can convert dBASE II files to dBASE III PLUS format and reconvert dBASE III PLUS files to dBASE II format.

To convert files from dBASE II to dBASE III PLUS, you will need a copy of the disk containing the dCONVERT program. dCONVERT is on the Sample Programs and Utilities disk. You will also need the disk containing the dBASE II files that you wish to convert and a blank DOS-formatted disk, which will be used to store the converted programs.

dCONVERT can convert six types of files: database, memory variable, report format, index, command, and screen format files. dCONVERT performs a complete conversion of dBASE II database files (extension .DBF) to dBASE III PLUS format.

dCONVERT also performs most or all of the necessary work to

convert dBASE II command files to dBASE III PLUS format. Some dBASE II commands differ from those used in dBASE III PLUS, so you will have to replace foreign dBASE II commands with dBASE III PLUS commands. Be sure to check the converted program file for exclusive dBASE II commands (more on this topic later).

dCONVERT doesn't actually convert a dBASE II index file. Instead it creates a command file containing the commands necessary to create the new index file. From the dot prompt you then execute the command file, and a new index file is created. You can manually perform the same task without dCONVERT by simply creating the required new indexes for the converted database with the INDEX ON command.

USING dCONVERT

To start the conversion process, insert the Sample Programs and Utilities disk into drive A, and type

```
DCONVERT A: B:
```

Hard-disk system users enter the following instead:

```
DCONVERT A: C:
```

The conversion program will be loaded into memory. Once the program is ready to be used, you will see the menu shown in Figure 18-1.

As soon as the menu appears, you should remove the disk containing dCONVERT, and place the disk with the dBASE II files in drive A and the disk that will contain the converted dBASE III PLUS files in drive B. (Hard-disk users can ignore the drive B step.)

```
        dBASE CONVERT - dBASE III File Conversion Aid   v2.01   11/19/85
              (c) 1984 By Ashton-Tate    All Rights Reserved

                      dBASE II --> dBASE III

                   1 - Database File          <.DBF>_
                   2 - Memory Variable File   <.MEM>
                   3 - Report Format File     <.FRM>
                   4 - Command File           <.PRG>
                   5 - Screen Format File     <.FMT>
                   6 - Index File Help        <.NDX>
                   7 - Un-dCONVERT III->II    <.DBF>

                   9 -         Instructions
                   0 -            EXIT




       < Use cursor arrows to move between choices;  hit RETURN to select choice >
```

Figure 18-1. Main menu for dCONVERT program

The menu offers six types of file conversion plus a reconversion option and instruction. You can choose one of the selections in the menu by pressing the ↑ or ↓ key to move the highlight to the selection. When you choose the type of file to be converted, dCONVERT will then list all files of that type and the amount of space available on the disk. You are then prompted to enter the name of the file to be converted.

After you enter a filename, dCONVERT performs the conversion and, by slowly printing a row of periods on the screen, indicates that progress is being made. After the conversion the dBASE II file will retain the same name and extension except that B (for "backup") will replace the last letter of the extension; that is, dBASE II database files will now have extensions of .DBB instead of .DBF as before. Index files will have the same name as the original index file and a new extension of .NDX. This new file is *not* an index file; instead it is a dBASE III PLUS command file that will be used to recreate an index file once you are using dBASE III PLUS.

Once the conversion of database files is complete, no additional work is necessary. In the case of index files, one additional step must be performed from within dBASE III PLUS: after creating the index command file and activating the parent database with the USE command, you build the new index file by entering DO *Index-name.NDX*. For example, if you had a dBASE II database named MAILER with an index file named ZIP, you would first convert the database file, which would be called MAILER.DBF. Then you would "convert" the index file, which would be called ZIP.NDX. To rebuild the index file, you would have to get into dBASE III PLUS and then issue the following commands (assuming the disk with the database is in drive B):

```
USE B:MAILER
DO ZIP.NDX
```

The proper index file will be rebuilt automatically. When this process is completed, the dot prompt will reappear.

An alternative method is to perform the entire index-file creation process without dCONVERT and use the INDEX ON command.

Converting Command Files

To convert a dBASE II command program file to run under dBASE III PLUS, select 4, "Command File." After the command files are displayed, you will be prompted for the name of the command file to be converted. Enter the name and the conversion process will begin. Again dCONVERT will, by slowly printing a row of periods on the screen, indicate that progress is being made.

When the conversion process is complete, you will see the message

```
Conversion complete...
        Press a key to continue
```

Press a key and the dCONVERT menu will reappear. If you have more programs to convert, you can again select choice 4 and enter the names of the additional dBASE II command files to be converted. When you are done converting programs, enter 0 in the dCONVERT menu and the program will return to the DOS prompt. The converted command file has the same name as the original dBASE II command file, but will have a new extension of .PRB; the last letter in the .PRM extension will be replaced with B (for "backup").

At this point you may be anxious to load dBASE III PLUS and begin running your converted dBASE II programs, but this would not be a good idea. Most converted programs will not run without errors because there are some differences between dBASE II and dBASE III PLUS commands. dCONVERT transfers dBASE II commands to dBASE III PLUS format but does not translate them. For this reason, the conversion may not be completely automatic.

Fortunately, dCONVERT provides help in this area. Whenever a line includes a dBASE II command that is unrecognizable to dBASE III PLUS or syntactically different from dBASE III PLUS, dCONVERT will transfer the line prefixed by an asterisk (*) and two exclamation points (!!). Before operating a converted command file, you should print it (or at least examine it on the screen with the TYPE command) to look for any occurrences of the asterisk and exclamation points. When you find such commands, you must analyze the logic behind the command and decide on a suitable substitute that will work with dBASE III PLUS.

Even after you modify marked command lines, there may still be some incompatible operations that dCONVERT simply cannot detect. Most often these are subtle differences between the operation of various dBASE II and dBASE III PLUS commands. An example is the status of the record pointer after FIND fails to locate a character string. In dBASE III PLUS the pointer is then positioned at the bottom of the database; in dBASE II the pointer is set to a value of 0, because dBASE II programs test for zero to indicate an unsuccessful FIND operation. After such a program is converted to dBASE III PLUS, it will not run properly until the program is rewritten to follow the style of the dBASE III PLUS FIND command. This type of program modification is, unfortunately, beyond the capabilities of dCONVERT.

Converting Memory Variable, Report Format, and Screen Format Files

You can use dCONVERT to convert memory variable files, report format files, and screen format files. Like other dCONVERT operations you convert, this choice is made from the dCONVERT menu. You select 2 for memory variable files, 3 for report format files, and 5 for screen format files. Before making a selection, load drive A with the disk containing the dBASE II files to be converted, and load drive B with another formatted disk with space for the converted files. You then select the appropriate choice from the menu. When dCONVERT prompts you for a filename, enter the name of the file to be converted. When the process is complete, you will see the **Conversion completed** message. At that time you can press any key to return to the dCONVERT menu.

When conversion of the files is complete, you can use them in dBASE III PLUS without further modification.

Converting Databases From dBASE III PLUS to dBASE II

Within limits, dBASE III PLUS databases can be converted to dBASE II format by using option 7, "Un-dCONVERT III->II", from the dCONVERT menu. The limitations of this type of conversion are due to the less powerful capabilities of dBASE II, when compared with dBASE III PLUS. dBASE II can have only 32 fields per record. Thus, if your dBASE III PLUS database contains more than 32 fields per record, dCONVERT will display a **too many fields** error and will abort the conversion process. The conversion process will also be aborted if the dBASE III PLUS database contains memo fields. Memo fields have no equivalent in dBASE II.

To "unconvert" a database file from dBASE III PLUS to dBASE II, select 7, "Un-dCONVERT III->II", from the dCONVERT menu. All files with the .DBF extension will be displayed, and you will be prompted to enter the name of the database to be unconverted. During the conversion process, dCONVERT again displays its progress by printing a row of periods on the screen. When the message **Conversion complete** appears on the screen, the dBASE II database is ready for use. The dBASE III PLUS database is left with the same name as the unconverted dBASE II database, but the extension of the dBASE III PLUS database will be .BAK.

USING dCONVERT FROM DOS

You can use the dCONVERT program directly from DOS, bypassing the menu entirely. The format for using dCONVERT directly from DOS is DCONVERT [A:]*filename.ext*[B:].

The disk drive identifiers A and B (surrounded by brackets) are optional. If you don't include them, the program will use the default drive as both the source (dBASE II file) and the destination (dBASE III PLUS file). dCONVERT determines the type of file conversion from the file extension (dCONVERT will not ask you for the type of file), so give the full filename when using the command. For example, if you wanted to convert a database called MAILER to dBASE III PLUS format, you could enter this command:

```
DCONVERT A:MAILER.DBF
```

dCONVERT would convert the program and store it on the disk in drive A.

Using dCONVERT in DOS allows you to use DOS *wildcards* to save time. Wildcards are symbols that replace part or all of a filename in a command. When the command is executed, the symbols are interpreted as files on the disk. A frequently used wildcard is the asterisk (*). The asterisk serves as a global replacement for both filename and extension; thus, specifying *.DBF as the filename for dCONVERT will cause dCONVERT to convert all database files, the asterisk being expanded to mean all files with the .DBF extension. For example, the command used to convert all database files from dBASE II format on a disk in drive A to dBASE III PLUS format on a disk in drive B would be

```
DCONVERT A:*.DBF B:
```

This command converts all files with the .DBF extension to dBASE III PLUS format and stores the new files on the disk in drive B. Remember, a copy of dCONVERT should reside on the disk and in the drive from which the program will be invoked. If you use the asterisk (*) wildcard with dCONVERT directly from DOS, you can quickly convert a large number of dBASE II files in one command. Consult your DOS manual for further details on wildcards.

dBASE II users who have upgraded to dBASE III PLUS may be tempted to begin anew and recreate their database and program files instead of converting them. But converting database files is easily worth the effort since it is a simple task. In most cases, you will find it much easier to convert command files and make the necessary post-modifications than to rewrite the command files from scratch.

Using dBASE III PLUS
On a Local Area Network

Chapter 19

This chapter provides information that you will need if you intend to use the network version of dBASE III PLUS. The first half of this chapter provides an overview of local area networks, requirements for using dBASE III PLUS on a network, instructions for installing and using dBASE III PLUS on a network, and general hints for effective network use. The second half of this chapter explains the use of the PROTECT utility to provide security to a dBASE system, along with considerations for programmers who write applications that will be used on a network.

The complexity of local area networks requires that this chapter be written at a higher level than most other chapters in this book. It is assumed that the reader is already familiar with the use of dBASE III PLUS, with the use of basic DOS commands including the use of DOS subdirectories, and with the use of the network commands for the particular network that dBASE III PLUS will be installed on. The appropriate manuals for network operation should be referred to for any questions regarding the use of the network operating system commands.

dBASE AND NETWORKS

A local area network, or LAN, is a system of computer communications that links together a number of personal computers, usually within a single building, for the transfer of information between users of the computers. In its minimal configuration, a local area network consists of two PCs connected together by some type of wire that allows information transfer between the two machines. A local area network allows the sharing of printers, modems, hard disks, and other devices that may be attached to computers on the network. Files (such as databases) and commonly-used software can also be shared among the users of a local area network. Figure 19-1 shows how computers can be linked together using a local area network.

There are differing designs for local area networks, but all LANs are made up of the same basic components: servers, work stations, and the physical cable linking the components together. Servers are computers that provide devices that can be employed by all users of the network. Most servers are one of three types: file servers, which provide shared hard disks; print servers, which provide shared printers; and communications servers, which provide shared modems. Servers can simultaneously provide more than one of these functions; a single server, for example, may have a hard disk and a printer attached, making that server both a file server and a print server.

Work stations are computers attached to the network that do not normally provide shared resources for other users. Work stations are used by the individual users of the network, to run software that may be present on a work station or on the file server. Some types of networks allow the simultaneous use of the same computer for a file server and a work station, although this practice is not recommended because network performance suffers as a result. When dBASE III PLUS is used on a network, the file server must not be used as a work station, because Ashton-Tate recommends that dBASE Administrator (which normally resides on the file server) and dBASE ACCESS (which normally resides on the work station) never be installed on the same computer.

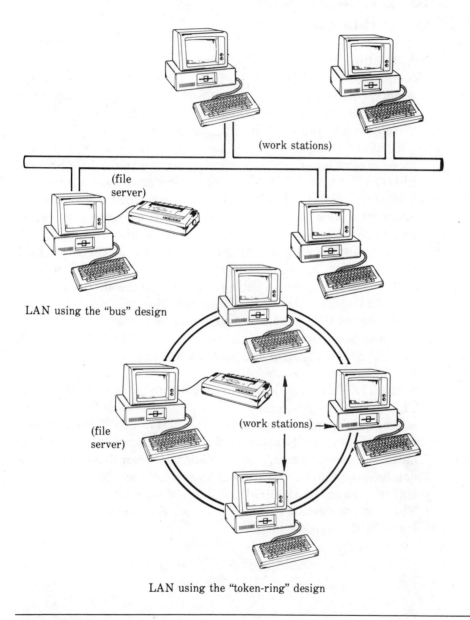

(work stations)

(file
server)

LAN using the "bus" design

(file
server)

(work stations) →

LAN using the "token-ring" design

Figure 19-1. Local area network (LAN)

dBASE III PLUS and
Compatible Networks

At the time of this writing, a number of local area networks are compatible with dBASE III PLUS. The IBM PC Network, the 3Com 3+ network, and the Novell S/Net Network can be operated with dBASE III PLUS installed on any of the file servers. Each of these networks must use DOS 3.1 or above.

dBASE III PLUS, when used on a local area network, consists of three programs: dBASE Administrator, dBASE ACCESS, and PROTECT. dBASE Administrator is the network-compatible version of dBASE III PLUS. dBASE Administrator contains the necessary operational and programming features to provide file and record locking. dBASE Administrator also recognizes any security limitations outlined through the use of the PROTECT program. dBASE Administrator can be installed on one or more file servers throughout a network. Figure 19-2 illustrates the use of dBASE Administrator on file servers throughout a network.

dBASE ACCESS is the program used at a work station to gain access to the dBASE Administrator. Each work station that will use dBASE III PLUS on the network must have a copy of dBASE ACCESS.

PROTECT is a stand-alone program, run outside of dBASE III PLUS, that lets you control access to the dBASE Administrator and to databases residing on the file server. The PROTECT program lets you specify authorized users, passwords, whether databases will be encrypted, and whether users can make changes to databases or can only view (read) those databases. PROTECT is an optional feature of dBASE III PLUS; you do not have to use PROTECT on your network. However, if security is an issue, the use of PROTECT is recommended.

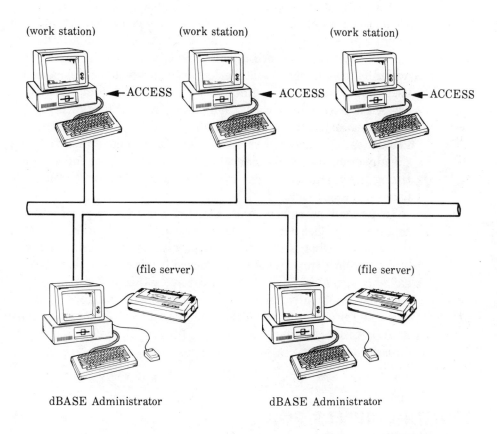

Figure 19-2. dBASE programs residing on a network

About Database Integrity

Users of database software on any local area network must consider database integrity. Database integrity, or the completeness of the database, is threatened whenever two users attempt to modify the same database record at the same time. If the software is not designed to operate on a network, serious problems can occur. One user may write over the other user's changes, or in more extreme cases, the network operating software may "crash" and bring the entire network down. In network lingo, such a potential disaster is known as a collision. Another common problem, known as a "deadly embrace," can occur when programs execute endless loops trying to provide exclusive use of the same file to more than one user on the network.

To prevent such problems, dBASE Administrator offers two features: file locking and record locking. File locking causes a database file that is in use by one user to be made unavailable to any other users on the network. Record locking is the same type of safeguard, but for an individual record within a file. dBASE III PLUS will normally perform file locking on any database that you use. In addition to the file locking that is set by default, you can use specific programming commands to turn off file locking and turn on record locking.

REQUIREMENTS FOR NETWORK USE

To run dBASE III PLUS on a network, you will need a minumum hardware configuration of one file server and one work station. The work station can be any IBM PC, XT, or AT, or 100% compatible computer, with one or two floppy disk drives. The file server can be an IBM PC or XT with hard disk, an IBM PC/AT with hard disk, or a 100% IBM-compatible computer with hard disk. (Some network vendors also manufacture dedicated file servers that are compatible with dBASE III PLUS: the Novell S/Net

Server is an example of such a file server.) If more than three work stations are to make regular use of the network, an IBM PC AT or AT-compatible is recommended instead of a PC-compatible or XT-compatible. Serious speed degradation usually occurs when a large number of work stations use a server that is a PC- or XT-compatible.

If the network is the IBM PC Network, you must have the IBM PC Network Program, version 1.0 or above. If you are using a Novell network, you must have Novell Advanced Netware/86, Version 1.01 or above. 3Com networks require any version of 3+ software.

File Server Requirements

File servers on IBM-PC and Novell networks must contain a minimum of 640K of memory and a hard disk drive. File servers on 3Com networks must contain a hard disk drive; memory requirements will vary, depending on the network configuration (see your 3Com documentation for more details). If you are using a Novell network, an expanded memory board meeting the joint Intel/Lotus memory specification (such as the Intel Above Board) is not mandatory, but it is recommended. The presence of an expanded memory board will speed network performance considerably. A CONFIG.SYS file should also be present in the hard disk root directory, or on the start-up disk that is used to start the file server. (See Chapter 3 for details on how to create a CONFIG.SYS file.) The CONFIG.SYS file for network use should contain the following statements:

```
FILES = 24
BUFFERS = 20
FCBS = 16,8
LASTDRIVE = X
```

Note that "X" in the LASTDRIVE statement refers to the valid drive letter (A through Z) that is the last available drive on your network. See your network operator's manual, if necessary, to determine the last drive for your particular network.

Work Station Requirements

Work stations that will use dBASE III PLUS on the network should contain a minimum of 384K of memory (on Novell networks) or 512K of memory (on IBM PC and 3Com networks). Each work station will require a copy of the dBASE ACCESS program to use the network.

INSTALLING dBASE III PLUS ON A NETWORK

Installation of dBASE III PLUS on a network consists of two major tasks: installing dBASE Administrator on one or more file servers, and installing ACCESS on all work stations that will use dBASE III PLUS. Every copy of dBASE III PLUS contains a copy of dBASE Administrator, on two disks marked Administrator #1 and Administrator #2. Each dBASE III PLUS system disk #1 contains a copy of ACCESS. The INSTALL program, also present on system disk #1, is used to install the dBASE Administrator or the dBASE ACCESS programs on the respective file servers or work stations. These programs are copy-protected; therefore, you cannot install Administrator or ACCESS simply by copying the programs onto a hard disk. You must use the INSTALL program to install the software on a hard disk. If the ACCESS program is to be used on a work station with no hard disk, you must use the INSTALL program to activate the ACCESS program on system disk #1. (Until it is activated, the ACCESS program is hidden from view on a directory of the disk.) Once activated, the work station user can employ system disk #1 to use the network version of dBASE III PLUS.

Installing dBASE Administrator
On the File Server

Before installing dBASE Administrator on the file server, you should create a subdirectory that will contain the dBASE Administrator and make that subdirectory the default directory by using the DOS "change directory" command. Consult your DOS manual, if necessary, for instructions on creating subdirectories. If you are using any memory-resident software on the file server, it may be a good idea to remove such software from memory before installing dBASE Administrator. Certain memory-resident software packages will cause the INSTALL program for dBASE Administrator to lock up, requiring a restart of the file server.

WARNING: Do *not* attempt to install a single-user version of dBASE III PLUS and the network version, dBASE Administrator, on the same file server (even if the programs are to reside in different subdirectories). If you do this, one version of the program may display erroneous "unauthorized duplicate" error messages and fail to operate.

Installing dBASE Administrator

To install dBASE Administrator on a file server, perform the following steps, after making the dBASE subdirectory your default directory:

1. Insert system disk #1 in drive A, and select drive A by entering A: and pressing RETURN.

2. Assuming that your hard disk is drive C, enter the following command. Substitute the appropriate letter if your hard disk uses a drive designator other than C.

```
INSTALL C: DBA
```

3. When prompted, insert the dBASE Administrator disk #1 into drive A, and press any key. Files contained on the Administrator disk #1 will be copied into the hard disk subdirectory.

4. When prompted, insert the dBASE Administrator disk #2 into drive A, and press any key. Files contained on the Administrator disk #2 will be copied into the hard disk subdirectory.

5. When the message **dBASE Administrator has been successfully installed** appears and the DOS "A" prompt reappears, enter C: and press RETURN to switch back to your hard disk, and then remove the Administrator disk #2 from drive A. dBASE Administrator is now ready for use on the network. Each user must have an installed copy of dBASE ACCESS (see the next section for details). If you wish to add security features, including password protection, you should also use the PROTECT utility. Use of the PROTECT utility is covered later in this chapter.

Installing ACCESS
On the Work Station

The dBASE ACCESS program must be installed for use on every work station that will use dBASE Administrator on the network. (Additional copies of ACCESS are also available in sets of three copies, called "LAN Packs," from your software dealer.) dBASE ACCESS can be installed in one of two ways. The program can be installed on system disk #1 and used from the floppy disk; or you can install ACCESS onto a hard disk that is a part of the work station system. Ashton-Tate recommends that you not install ACCESS on a file server that also contains dBASE Administrator. Installation of ACCESS on a file server that contains dBASE

Administrator risks damage to dBASE program files and a possible loss of the dBASE III PLUS program.

The system disk #1 that you use to install ACCESS should not have been used previously to install the single-user version of dBASE III PLUS onto a hard disk. Because both the single-user version and the network version use the same hard disk installation program, you are limited to one installation of either type. If you have installed the single-user version of dBASE III PLUS onto a hard disk, use the UNINSTAL procedure outlined in your dBASE documentation to remove that version from the hard disk before attempting to install ACCESS. You should also be aware that, once you install ACCESS, you will not be able to use that system disk to run the single-user version of dBASE III PLUS. If you wish to use the single-user version of dBASE III PLUS, you must use the UNINSTAL procedure to remove ACCESS first.

To install ACCESS onto system disk #1 for use on a floppy-disk system, insert system disk #1 in drive A, and enter the following command at the DOS "A" prompt:

```
INSTALL A: ACCESS
```

When the installation process is complete, you will see a confirmation message indicating that ACCESS has been installed, and the DOS prompt will reappear.

To install ACCESS onto a work station with a hard disk, insert system disk #1 in drive A. Assuming that your hard disk is drive C, enter the following command at the DOS "A" prompt. (If your hard disk is a letter other than C, substitute the appropriate designation.)

```
INSTALL C: ACCESS
```

Follow any additional prompts that appear on the screen. When the installation process is complete, you will see a confirmation message indicating that ACCESS has been installed, and the DOS prompt will reappear.

STARTING dBASE ON A NETWORK

To use dBASE on the network, you must first ensure that the file server and work stations to be used are turned on and started in the usual manner. See your network operator's manual for instructions on starting work stations and file servers on the network.

Using the ACCESS Command

Once the file server and work station are running, log onto the network at the work station. The manner used to start the ACCESS program will vary, depending on whether you are using ACCESS from a floppy or hard disk. Follow the instructions shown for your particular type of work station.

1. If dBASE ACCESS is installed on your work station hard disk, enter the following command:

   ```
   ACCESS M=x:\path
   ```

   where "x" represents the disk drive designator that you normally use to access the hard disk on the file server containing dBASE Administrator. "Path" represents the name of the file server subdirectory containing dBASE Administrator.

2. If dBASE ACCESS is installed on your system disk #1, insert system disk #1 in drive A and enter the following command:

   ```
   A:ACCESS M=x:\path
   ```

   where "x" represents the disk drive designator that you normally use to access the hard disk on the file server containing dBASE Administrator. "Path" represents the name of the file server subdirectory containing dBASE Administrator.

Once the proper ACCESS command has been entered, the program will load, and the dBASE Administrator copyright notice will appear, followed by the dot prompt. Unlike the single-user version, the network version does not automatically call up the Assistant (although it is available at any time by entering the ASSIST command).

NOTE: If the dBASE Administrator has been protected with the PROTECT utility, you will be prompted for a user name and password. See the subheading entitled "Using PROTECT" for additional details regarding user names and passwords.

You can load dBASE III PLUS and run a command file by including the name of the desired command file following the word ACCESS in the command. For example, to start dBASE III PLUS and run a command file named MENU, you would enter the following command from the work station:

```
ACCESS MENU M=x:\path
```

If you make use of command files of your own design on a network, there are programming considerations that apply only to command files running on a network. See the latter half of this chapter for additional details.

Storing the ACCESS Command Within Batch Files

You can make the process of starting dBASE easier by storing the appropriate ACCESS command within a DOS batch file. (A *batch file* is a text file of commands that are carried out just as if you had typed them from the DOS prompt; see your DOS manual for more details.) As an example, you can use any word processor that creates text files (including the dBASE Word Processor) to create a file called DBSTART.BAT. The file should be stored on the same disk or drive subdirectory that contains the ACCESS program. The file should contain the appropriate command for starting ACCESS, as in the following examples:

```
ACCESS M=x:\path

A:ACCESS M=x:\path

ACCESS MENU M=x:\path
```

Once the batch file has been created, you can carry out the stored command by entering the name of the batch file from the DOS prompt, in this example, DBSTART. The dBASE Administrator will then be loaded at the file server, just as if you had manually entered the ACCESS command.

Using dBASE III PLUS on a network is in most respects identical to using it in a single-user environment. Users should remember to use proper disk drive designators, as most network work stations have a confusingly large number of available disk drives. As an example, a work station may have available drives A and B (dual floppies in the work station), drive C (a hard disk attached to the work station), and drives D, E, F, and G (four hard disks at the file server). The SET DEFAULT command should be used, when appropriate, to select the desired drive for storage of files and programs on a network.

NETWORK COMMANDS

There are some additional commands available to network users of dBASE III PLUS; these commands provide information and control certain functions within dBASE Administrator. The new commands include DISPLAY/LIST STATUS, DISPLAY/LIST USERS, and SET PRINTER.

DISPLAY STATUS/LIST STATUS

The DISPLAY STATUS and LIST STATUS commands provide the same information in dBASE Administrator as they do in the single-user versions of dBASE III PLUS (the name of the database in use, the status of most SET commands, and the status of the programmable function keys). In addition to this information, the DISPLAY STATUS and LIST STATUS commands also indicate whether database files and individual records within a file are locked. An example of the display resulting from the DISPLAY STATUS or LIST STATUS command follows:

```
DISPLAY STATUS

Currently Selected Database:
Select area:  1, Database in Use: C:ABC1.dbf    Alias: ABC1
            Memo file:   C:ABC1.dbt
          Lock:      record     5 is locked


Select area:  2, Database in Use: C:WORLDWID.dbf   Alias: WORLDWID
          Lock:      database is locked


Alternate file: C:stat.txt
File search path:
Default disk drive: C:
Print destination:  PRN:
Margin =      0
Current work area =      1


ALTERNATE  - ON    DELETED     - OFF  EXCLUSIVE  - ON   PRINT       - OFF
BELL       - ON    DELIMITERS  - OFF  FIELDS     - OFF  SAFETY      - ON
CARRY      - OFF   DEVICE      - SCRN FIXED      - OFF  SCOREBOARD  - ON
CATALOG    - OFF   DOHISTORY   - OFF  HEADING    - ON   STATUS      - OFF
CENTURY    - OFF   ECHO        - OFF  HELP       - ON   STEP        - OFF
CONFIRM    - OFF   ENCRYPTION  - ON   HISTORY    - ON   TALK        - ON
CONSOLE    - ON    ESCAPE      - ON   INTENSITY  - ON   TITLE       - ON
DEBUG      - OFF   EXACT       - OFF  MENU       - ON   UNIQUE      - OFF


Programmable function keys:
F2  - assist;
F3  - list;
F4  - dir;
F5  - display structure;
F6  - display status;
F7  - display memory;
F8  - display;
F9  - append;
F10 - edit;
```

Both commands operate in an identical manner, with the exception that LIST STATUS will display the information without pausing, while DISPLAY STATUS will pause every 24 lines. The TO PRINT option can be added to either command, to cause the status to be printed on your printer.

DISPLAY USERS/LIST USERS

The DISPLAY USERS and LIST USERS commands show all users currently sharing dBASE Administrator on the file server. The names shown by the commands are the names assigned through the use of the network operating system software. An example of the DISPLAY USERS command follows:

```
DISPLAY USERS

Server Phoenix
--------------
  STA-ALLEN
> STA-JUDIE
  STA-BILL
> STA-LARRY
  STA-CATHY
```

In the above example, the > sign indicates the users who are currently logged on the network and using dBASE Administrator. Both commands operate in an identical manner, with the exception that LIST USERS will display the names of all users without pausing, while DISPLAY USERS will pause every 24 lines. The TO PRINT option can be added to either command, to cause the list of users to be printed on your printer.

SET PRINTER

The SET PRINTER command is used to specify whether print output should be sent to a "local" printer (one attached to a work

station) or to a printer attached to a server. The normal syntax of
the command is

```
SET PRINTER TO \\(computer name)\(printer name) = (destination)
```

where *computer name* is the name of the work station as assigned
by the network operating software, and *printer name* is the network name assigned to the desired printer. *Destination* is the DOS
device that identifies the printer (example: LPT1, LPT2, and so
on). If no destination is specified, the default destination will be the
first parallel port (LPT1). As an example, to redirect printer output to the parallel printer port #1 (LPT1) connected to the work
station named "Chicago," where an attached laser printer has been
named "LASER" by the network operating system software, you
would use the following command:

```
SET PRINTER TO \\CHICAGO\LASER = LPT1
```

To redirect output to a printer attached to a file server that has
been named "PUBLIC" by the network software, enter

```
SET PRINTER TO \\PUBLIC
```

To redirect output to a printer attached to your work station and to
choose LPT1 for the printer port, enter

```
SET PRINTER TO LPT1
```

GENERAL NETWORK HINTS

Some points should be kept in mind to make the most effective use
of dBASE III PLUS on a network. In any multiuser environment,
large numbers of files tend to clutter the working space on the file
server. To hold such clutter to a minimum, heavy users should be
provided with individual subdirectories on the file server. The
dBASE SET PATH command can be used to cause all dBASE

commands that read files to search private subdirectories. (See Appendix A for information on the SET PATH command.) If users are going to create smaller files that will not be used by other users of the network, encourage those users to store such files at their work stations, rather than on the file server. Back up all databases regularly to floppy disk or tape backup. Create new applications and databases at a work station, in a single-user mode, and thoroughly test those applications before placing the files in shared space on the file server. A multiuser environment is not the best place to get all of the "bugs" out of a system's design.

INTRODUCING PROTECT

The next section of this chapter describes the use of PROTECT, a menu-driven program that builds a security system around the dBASE Administrator and the databases present on the file server. PROTECT should be used by the network administrator, to assign security procedures and levels of file access to users of the network. PROTECT controls access only to the dBASE Administrator and to dBASE databases; to establish security for other files on a network, you should continue to use the security features available within your version of network operating system software. Three kinds of security are provided by PROTECT. They are log-in access, file access and field access levels, and database encryption.

About Log-In Access

Log-in access requires users to enter names and passwords before the system can be used. The names and passwords for each user are stored in a file that is read by the dBASE Administrator when a user attempts to use the system. Log-in access will require three items from the users: a group name, a user name, and a password. Each item is entered on a separate line of a log-in screen presented by dBASE Administrator. If valid names and passwords are provided by the user, access to the dBASE Administrator is granted.

About File and Field Access

File access and field access levels are used to assign privilege access levels to each user, restricting changes that can be made to a database in varying degrees. (Privilege access levels are also referred to as the file privilege scheme.) Such privilege access levels are optional; as the network administrator, you can choose to allow all users unrestricted access to all fields in all databases. Access to databases and to the fields present in the databases is controlled by the matching of file and field access levels with user access levels. User access levels are varying levels granted to users, on a sliding scale of 1 (the least restrictive) to 8 (the most restrictive). The network administrator controls what privileges are available at the varying user access levels.

At the database file level, privileges can control the ability to read (read privilege), edit (update privilege), append (extend privilege), and delete (delete privilege) records within a database. At the field level, privileges can control whether users have full access (FULL), read-only access (R/O), or no access (NONE) to particular fields within a database.

When creating a file privilege scheme, some points should be kept in mind. First, the file access controls that you specify within PROTECT cannot override any read-only limitations set by the network operating system software. In general, limitations set by network operating system security commands will take priority over limitations set by the PROTECT program. Secondly, you can specify the most restrictive access level for each type of privilege (read, extend, update, and delete). When you do this, all levels that are less restrictive than the specified level will be given the privilege, while all levels that are more restrictive than the specified level will be denied the privilege. As an example, if you choose level 5 as the level to grant delete privileges, then all users with access levels of 1 through 5 will have the ability to delete records, while users with access levels of 6 through 8 will not be able to delete records.

About Database Encryption

Database encryption causes each database identified by PRO-TECT to be encrypted. Encrypted databases cannot be read unless proper user names, group names, and passwords are supplied. PROTECT automatically creates encrypted versions of database files. Whenever you specify privileges while using the PROTECT program, the database file will be encrypted. An encrypted file is a file that has been encoded to protect that file from unauthorized access. Once a database has been encrypted, it cannot be used without proper entry of the user name, group name, and password when ACCESS is initially started. The PROTECT program creates a copy of the original database file; the copy is encrypted, while the original file remains in its original condition. Encrypted database files have an extension of .CRP. For maximum security following the use of PROTECT, you should delete the database file with the .DBF extension, and rename the database file with the .CRP extension to a .DBF extension.

About User Groups

Each user is assigned a security profile when you add a user to the file of user names and passwords with the PROTECT program. In addition to the user name and password, the security profile will also contain the name of a group to which the user is assigned.

Various users should be assigned to various groups in a logical order (such as TAX group, LEGAL group, PERSONNL group, and so on). Each group will be associated with a set of database files. Once the files have been encrypted by PROTECT, a user must belong to a qualified group to access a database. You give groups the ability to access various database files through a menu selection within the PROTECT program. Users can belong to more than one group. However, to gain access to a database that belongs to a different group, a user must log out with the QUIT command and log back in as a member of the other group.

Introducing **DBSYSTEM.DB**

The PROTECT program stores the security profile information in a special file named DBSYSTEM.DB. The file is a special form of database, containing a record for each user with user name, group name, password, and assigned access level. The file is encrypted, so you cannot use dBASE III PLUS to directly read the DBSYS-TEM.DB file. User names, group names, passwords, and access levels should be written down and stored in a safe place so that if the DBSYSTEM.DB file is accidentally erased, the network administrator will have a copy of the information. It is also a good idea to copy the DBSYSTEM.DB file created by PROTECT to a backup disk for safekeeping.

When a user attempts to gain access to the dBASE Administrator by using his or her copy of the ACCESS program, the dBASE Administrator will first attempt to read a file called DBSYS-TEM.DB. If no such file is present, no log-in sequence will be required by the dBASE Administrator. However, the database encryption codes are stored within the database files. Thus, if the DBSYSTEM.DB file is missing, users will not be able to open encrypted databases until the missing file has been restored by the network administrator.

USING PROTECT

The PROTECT program is located on the dBASE III PLUS Administrator disk #1. To use PROTECT, you should first copy the program from the disk to the subdirectory containing the dBASE Administrator on the file server. To do so, place the Administrator disk #1 in drive A of the file server. Change the default directory to the directory containing the dBASE Administrator. Then, assuming that your hard disk on the file server is drive C, enter the following command from the DOS prompt. (Substitute the appropriate drive designator if your hard disk is not drive C.)

```
COPY A:PROTECT.EXE C:
```

To run the PROTECT program, enter PROTECT from the DOS prompt. A copyright screen will appear, and in a moment, that screen will be replaced by a network administrator log-in screen (Figure 19-3).

NOTE: Before entering a password, make a note of the password in a safe place. Once you have defined a password for the network administrator, you must know that password to use the PROTECT program. There is no way to retrieve a network administrator password from the system; therefore, do not lose the password!

You must enter a password of eight or fewer characters for use by the network administrator. The first time that you use PROTECT, the program will ask for the password to be entered twice for verification of spelling. Thereafter, the program will ask for the password just once when starting. An incorrect password entry will result in the program displaying an **unauthorized log-in** message, and the user will be returned to the DOS prompt.

Once the password has been entered correctly, the Protect menu appears (Figure 19-4). The Protect menu is similar in design to other menus used throughout dBASE III PLUS. The menu bar

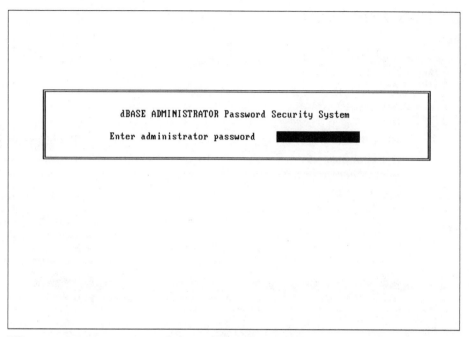

Figure 19-3. Network administrator log-in screen

offers three choices: Users, Files, and Exit. The Users menu is used to specify user names, passwords, group names, account names, and access levels of network users. You can also delete existing users from a group of dBASE III PLUS users through the Users menu.

The Files menu lets you identify file and field access privileges for a specific database file. Varying levels of privileges let you identify whether groups of users can read, edit (update), append to (extend), or delete records in the specified database.

The Exit menu lets you save changes made while in the User or Files menus. You can also abandon any changes made without saving the changes.

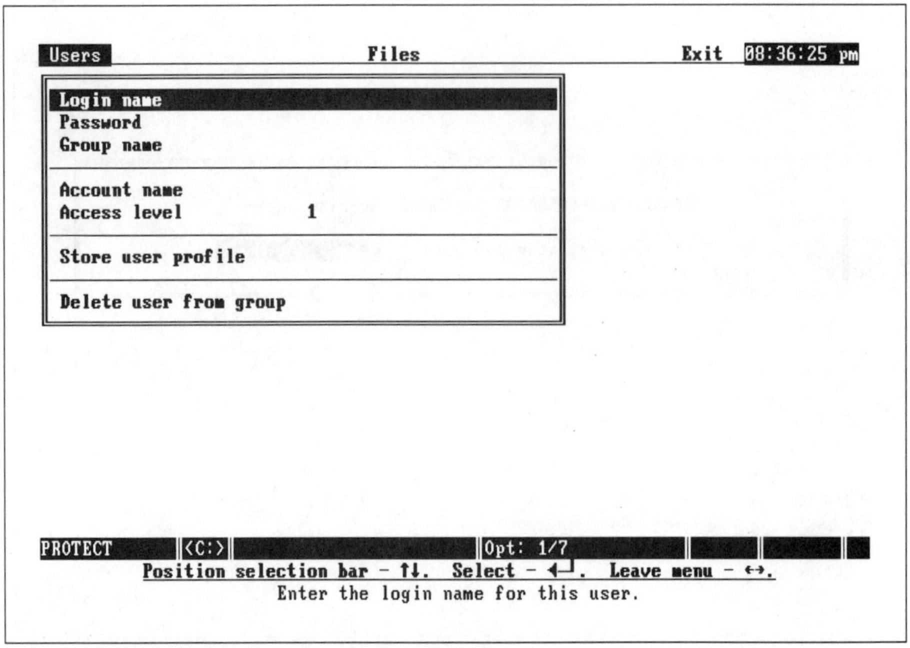

```
┌──────────────────────────────────────────────────────────────────────┐
│ ▌Users            │        Files            Exit  ▌08:36:25▐ pm        │
│ ┌──────────────────────────────────────┐                              │
│ │▌Login name                          ▐│                              │
│ │ Password                             │                              │
│ │ Group name                           │                              │
│ │──────────────────────────────────────│                              │
│ │ Account name                         │                              │
│ │ Access level              1          │                              │
│ │──────────────────────────────────────│                              │
│ │ Store user profile                   │                              │
│ │──────────────────────────────────────│                              │
│ │ Delete user from group               │                              │
│ └──────────────────────────────────────┘                              │
│                                                                        │
│                                                                        │
│                                                                        │
│                                                                        │
│                                                                        │
│ ▌PROTECT     ▐ ▌<C:>▐              ▌Opt: 1/7  ▐  ▌     ▐ ▌      ▐       │
│     Position selection bar – ↑↓.  Select – ◄┘.  Leave menu – ↔.        │
│          Enter the login name for this user.                           │
└──────────────────────────────────────────────────────────────────────┘
```

Figure 19-4. PROTECT menu

Adding Users

The first step in creating a security system with PROTECT is to add authorized users. To do this, you normally perform the following steps:

1. Open the Users menu.

2. Enter a user's log-in name of eight or fewer characters.

3. Enter a user password of eight or fewer characters.

4. Enter a group name of eight or fewer characters.

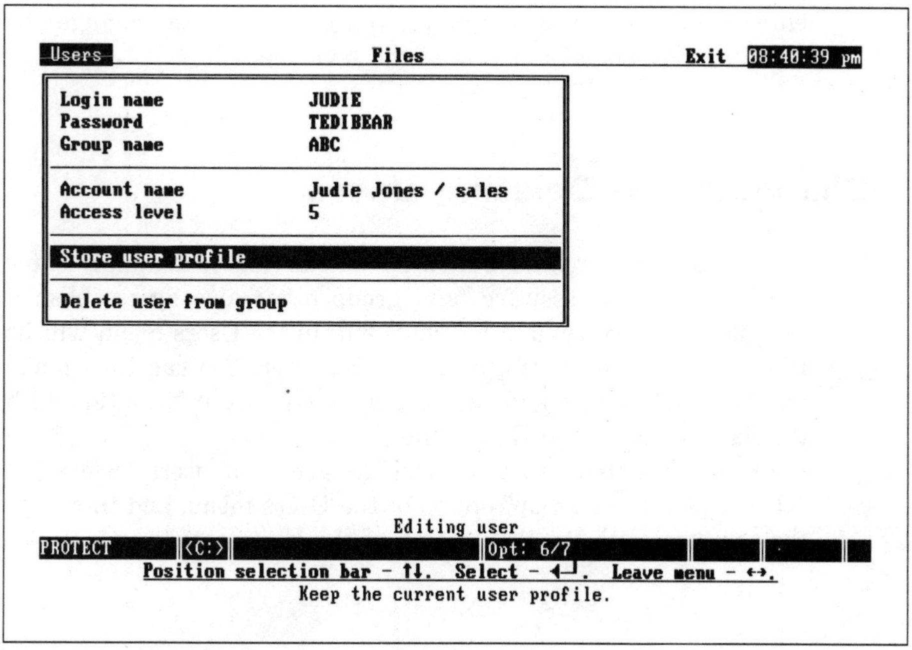

```
┌─────────────────────────────────────────────────────────────────────┐
│  ▓Users▓                          Files                Exit  08:40:39 pm│
│  ┌────────────────────────────────────────────────────────────┐     │
│  │ Login name            JUDIE                                  │     │
│  │ Password              TEDIBEAR                               │     │
│  │ Group name            ABC                                    │     │
│  │                                                              │     │
│  │ Account name          Judie Jones / sales                    │     │
│  │ Access level          5                                      │     │
│  │ ▓Store user profile▓                                         │     │
│  │                                                              │     │
│  │ Delete user from group                                       │     │
│  └────────────────────────────────────────────────────────────┘     │
│                                                                       │
│                                                                       │
│                                                                       │
│                           Editing user                                │
│ ┌PROTECT┐ ┌<C:>┐░░░░░░░░░░░░░░░░░░░░░│Opt: 6/7│░░░░░░░░░░░░░░░░░▓ │     │
│        Position selection bar - ↑↓.   Select - ◄┘.  Leave menu - ↔. │
│                    Keep the current user profile.                     │
└─────────────────────────────────────────────────────────────────────┘
```

Figure 19-5. Filled-in Users menu

5. Enter an account name. This is an option; you can use account names to give further definition to the user names.

6. Select a user access level from 1 (least restrictive) to 8 (most restrictive). This access level will be matched to privileges that you specify when using the Files menu.

7. Select "Store user profile" to store the data for this user.

8. Repeat steps 1 through 7 for each additional user.

Figure 19-5 shows a filled-in Users menu for a sample user on a network. If you decide that you do not wish to save the information

entered during any of the steps, you can cancel the changes by
selecting the Abandon option of the Exit menu.

Changing and Deleting Users

To change the user information for an existing user, simply enter
the log-in name, password, and group name already established
for that user. The remaining fields within the Users menu will be
filled in with the existing data for that user. You can then make
any desired changes and save the updated user information with
the Save option of the Exit menu.

To delete a user from a specified group of users, select the
"Delete user from group" option of the Users menu, and then save
the selection with the Save option of the Exit menu.

Creating File Privileges

The Files menu (Figure 19-6) is used to assign file and field access
privileges to a database file. You can assign any combination of
read, update (or edit), extend (or append to), and delete privileges
to a specific group of users. You can specify up to eight access levels, and you control precisely what privileges are available at each
level. You may choose to use one, two, or all of the available access
levels. If you do not use the Files menu to specify privileges, all
users of the network can read and write to all database files.

By using the "Field access privileges" section of the Files menu,
you can specify access to individual fields. Such access can be
FULL (read/write), R/O (read-only), or NONE (no access) to a
particular field. The default value is FULL, so if you do not specify
field privileges, all users of the network can access all database
fields.

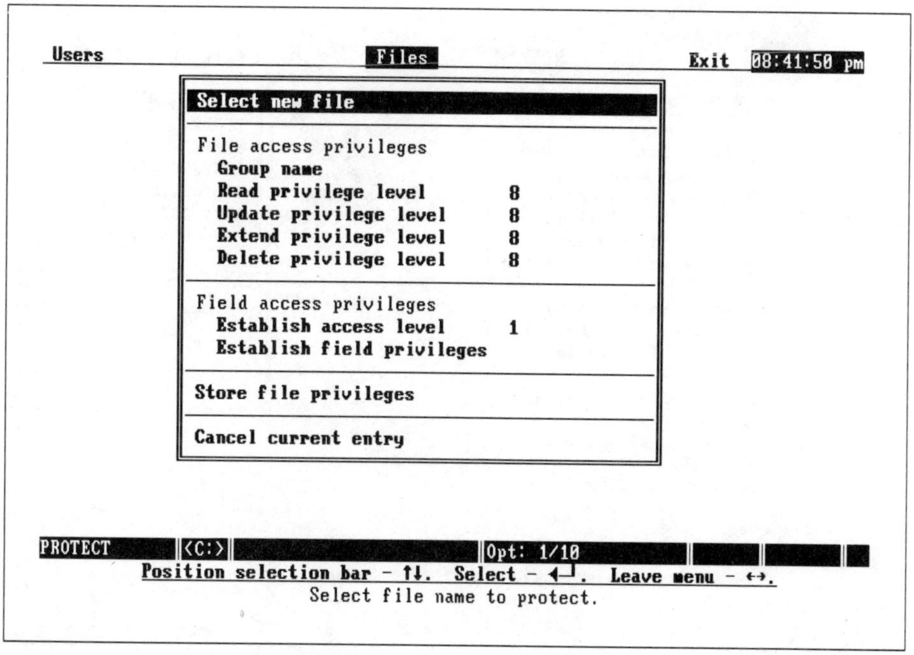

```
 Users                         Files                    Exit  08:41:50 pm
          ┌──────────────────────────────────────────┐
          │ Select new file                           │
          │                                           │
          │ File access privileges                    │
          │   Group name                              │
          │   Read privilege level       8            │
          │   Update privilege level     8            │
          │   Extend privilege level     8            │
          │   Delete privilege level     8            │
          │                                           │
          │ Field access privileges                   │
          │   Establish access level     1            │
          │   Establish field privileges              │
          │                                           │
          │ Store file privileges                     │
          │                                           │
          │ Cancel current entry                      │
          └──────────────────────────────────────────┘



 PROTECT      ‖<C:>‖               ‖Opt: 1/10‖
      Position selection bar - ↑↓.  Select - ◄┘.  Leave menu - ↔.
                  Select file name to protect.
```

Figure 19-6. Files menu

To identify file privileges with the Files menu, perform the following steps:

1. Open the Files menu.

2. Choose the "Select new file" option. A menu of files will appear, as shown in the example (Figure 19-7).

3. Highlight the desired database, and press RETURN.

4. Select "Group name," and enter the name of a group that will have access to the file.

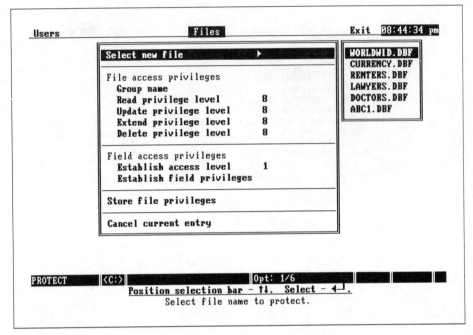

Figure 19-7. Files menu with available database files

5. Using a number of your choice from 1 (least restrictive) to 8 (most restrictive), specify the access level for the read, update, extend, and delete privilege levels.

6. If field access privileges are also desired, select an access level, and enter the desired field privileges for that access level. When you enter a number (from 1 to 8) for the access level and then select the "Establish field privileges" option, a list of fields will appear (Figure 19-8).

   Choose the desired field privilege for each field by highlighting the field and pressing RETURN to display the available options. As you press RETURN, the field privilege will switch between FULL (full access), R/O (read-only), and NONE (no access to the field). When the desired option

```
 Users                        Files                  Exit  08:49:53 pm
                                                        ┌──────────────────┐
          ┌─────────────────────────────────────┐      │ LASTNAME    FULL │
          │ Select new file         C:RENTERS.DBF│      │ FIRSTNAME   FULL │
          │ ─────────────────────────────────────│      │ ADDRESS     R/O  │
          │ File access privileges                │      │ CITY        R/O  │
          │    Group name            ABC          │      │ STATE       R/O  │
          │    Read privilege level  8            │      │ ZIP         R/O  │
          │    Update privilege level 5           │      │ PHONE       FULL │
          │    Extend privilege level 4           │      │ BEDROOMS    R/O  │
          │    Delete privilege level 1           │      │ BATHROOMS   R/O  │
          │ ─────────────────────────────────────│      │ EXPDATE     R/O  │
          │ Field access privileges               │      │ PARKING     R/O  │
          │    Establish access level 5           │      │ PROPTYPE    R/O  │
          │ ▐ Establish field privileges ▶        │      │ RENTAMT     R/O  │
          │ ─────────────────────────────────────│      │ SIZE        FULL │
          │ Store file privileges                 │      │ EXTRAS      FULL │
          │ ─────────────────────────────────────│      │ SALESOFF    NONE │
          │ Cancel current entry                  │      └──────────────────┘
          └─────────────────────────────────────┘

 PROTECT      <C:>                      Opt: 1/16
                      Select - ◄┘.  Leave menu - ↔.
         Define individual field privileges for the access level displayed above.
```

Figure 19-8. List of fields

appears, use the ↑ or ↓ key to move to the next field. After all desired privileges have been set, press the ← or → key to leave the list of fields.

You can repeat step 6 for each access level desired. Doing so lets you set individual field privileges for all access levels that you have specified for groups of users. Note that when you specify field privileges as any choice other than the default value (FULL), all field privileges for more restrictive user access levels are changed to NONE unless you specify otherwise.

7. Select the "Store file privileges" option from the Files menu. The privileges will be stored in memory, and the "Select new file" option will be highlighted at the top of the menu.

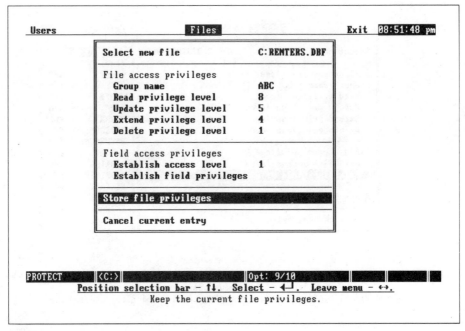

```
 Users                          Files                          Exit  08:51:48 pm
┌─────────────────────────────────────────────────────────────┐
│  Select new file                    C:RENTERS.DBF            │
│                                                               │
│  File access privileges                                       │
│    Group name                       ABC                       │
│    Read privilege level             8                         │
│    Update privilege level           5                         │
│    Extend privilege level           4                         │
│    Delete privilege level           1                         │
│                                                               │
│  Field access privileges                                      │
│    Establish access level           1                         │
│    Establish field privileges                                 │
│ ┌───────────────────────────────────────────────────────┐   │
│ │ Store file privileges                                  │   │
│ └───────────────────────────────────────────────────────┘   │
│  Cancel current entry                                         │
└─────────────────────────────────────────────────────────────┘

 PROTECT      │<C:>│                    │Opt: 9/10
        Position selection bar - ↑↓.  Select - ↵.  Leave menu - ↔.
                  Keep the current file privileges.
```

Figure 19-9. Filled-in Files menu

8. Repeat steps 1 through 7 for each additional database that you wish to assign privileges for. You can also choose to assign different privileges for the same database to different groups. To do so, simply specify a different group name while giving the same filename when in the Files menu. Note that you can only enter privileges for up to ten databases at a time. You must save all changes with the Save option of the Exit menu to select privileges for more than ten database files.

Figure 19-9 shows a filled-in Files menu for a sample database on a network. If you decide that you do not wish to save the information entered during any of the steps, you can cancel the operation by selecting the "Cancel current entry" option of the Files menu.

To change the file and field privileges for an existing group, open the Files menu and enter the name of the database file and the name of the group. The rest of the information previously entered will then be accessible through the menu selections. Make the required changes, and choose the "Store file privileges" option to save any changes.

Exiting From the PROTECT Program

The Exit menu (Figure 19-10) contains choices for saving changes, abandoning changes, and exiting from the PROTECT program. To save any entries while within PROTECT and continue using the PROTECT program, choose the Save option. To cancel any entries and continue using PROTECT, choose the Abandon option. To save your entries and exit from the PROTECT program, choose the Exit option. Once you select Exit, appropriate databases will be encrypted; and user, password, and access level information will be stored in the DBSYSTEM.DB file. With large databases, the encryption process may take a few moments. When the process is complete, the DOS prompt will reappear.

Once the dBASE Administrator has been protected with the PROTECT program, any attempt to load dBASE with a copy of ACCESS will result in the log-in screen (Figure 19-11) being presented to the work station user.

The user must enter a valid user name, group name, and password before the dBASE Administrator will display a dot prompt or run a program. The user name and group name are displayed during the entry process, but the password remains hidden as it is entered. If the entries match valid entries specified during the use of PROTECT, the user will be allowed access to the system. If the entries are invalid, the user will be given a maximum of three

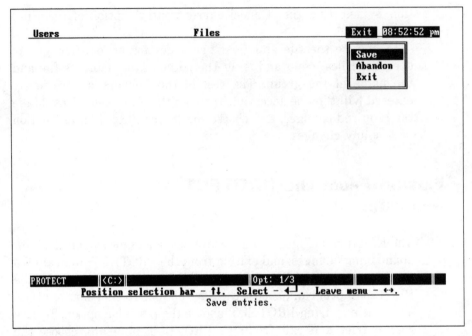

Figure 19-10. Exit menu

chances to enter valid information. If valid information is not entered, the message

```
Unauthorized Login
 ***End Run    dBASE III PLUS
```

will appear, and the user will be returned to the DOS prompt.

GENERAL SECURITY HINTS

Network administrators should keep some general hints in mind when implementing security for dBASE III PLUS on a network. A record of user names and passwords should be kept in a safe

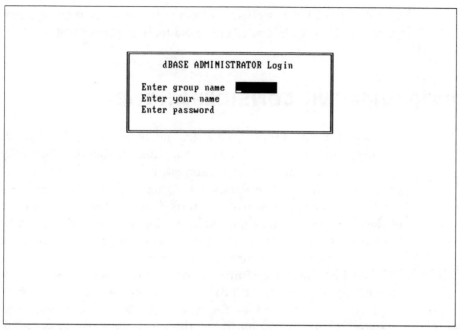

dBASE ADMINISTRATOR Login
Enter group name
Enter your name
Enter password

Figure 19-11. Log-in screen

place. A fast way to do this is to use SHIFT-PRTSCR to print copies of the User menus and Files menus while creating the security system with the PROTECT program. Users should be encouraged to memorize passwords and to avoid using easy-to-decipher passwords (like the name of a spouse). Only the network administrator and a responsible backup administrator should have access to the PROTECT program password. If encryption of databases is important in your application, remember to delete the unencrypted (.DBF) database files once the encrypted versions have been created, and rename the encrypted (.CRP) files to files with .DBF extensions. Any security system is only as strong as its weakest link; and in most large organizations, the network administrator (this probably means *you*) is usually held responsible for any breach of security due to carelessness. The network version of dBASE III PLUS has effective tools to increase security on a network, but it is up to you to put those tools to proper use.

PROGRAMMING CONSIDERATIONS

Additional programming tools are made available by dBASE Administrator that are designed to maintain database integrity and security in a network environment. Effective use of these tools calls for an in-depth discussion of programming for networks, which is beyond the scope of this book. The purpose of this section of the chapter is to make the reader aware of the existence of these tools and to suggest additional resources that can provide more information for the network programmer.

The additional programming tools, which consist of various commands and functions, are needed to prevent potential problems when users share files. Collisions between users, caused when users try to use the same file at the same time, can cause additional problems for the network programmer, because the program must be provided with enough "intelligence" to sense such problems and find a solution. Certain commands and functions can be used to provide a program with routines that test for activity on the network. Included in these programming tools are the SET EXCLUSIVE and the UNLOCK commands and the LOCK, FLOCK, and RLOCK functions. These are not all of the available programming commands and functions that can be used for control of dBASE programs on a network. However, they do provide important features and serve as an introduction to programming for network use.

Using SET EXCLUSIVE

The SET EXCLUSIVE command controls whether files are available on a shared basis or are available only for the exclusive use of the first user to access the file. The format for the command is

```
SET EXCLUSIVE ON/OFF
```

If SET EXCLUSIVE is ON, only one user can access a database file at a time. Until the file is closed, no other user can gain access. If SET EXCLUSIVE is OFF, a database file can be accessed simultaneously by multiple users. Once a program opens a file with SET EXCLUSIVE turned OFF, it is the responsibility of the program to guard against potential collisions, by checking the status of files and records with the locking functions (FLOCK, RLOCK, and LOCK).

Using Locking Functions

In dBASE Administrator, locking functions can be used to prevent collisions and occurrences of the "deadly embrace." Locking functions let a program test to see if a file or a record is locked by another user on the network. Locking functions operate in a slightly different manner from other functions. Where other dBASE functions usually return a value (such as TRUE or FALSE), the locking functions can perform an action (the locking of a file or a record) as well as returning a value. There are three locking functions within dBASE Administrator: FLOCK( ), RLOCK( ), and LOCK( ). The RLOCK( ) and LOCK( ) functions perform identical tasks; both are used to check the status of a record and to lock that record (if it is presently unlocked). The FLOCK( ) function checks the status of a file and locks the file if it is not already locked. Like all functions, the locking functions can be used in an interactive mode (from the dot prompt) or from within a command file. For example, the following commands,

```
USE ABC1
? FLOCK()
```

will cause dBASE Administrator to respond with TRUE (.T.), assuming that no other users are using the file, ABC1. The use of the FLOCK( ) function causes the ABC1 file to be locked and the file lock status to then be reported as TRUE. If another user then logs onto the system and enters the same commands, the dBASE Administrator will respond with FALSE (.F.), which indicates that the ABC1 file is already locked.

Within a program, you can combine IF expressions with various locking functions and pass program control to appropriate parts of a program, depending on the status reported by the locking functions. As an example of a simple method of protection against collisions, a program might include a SET EXCLUSIVE command and the FLOCK( ) function, as shown in the following example:

```
ON ERROR DO ERRFIND
SET SAFETY OFF
SET TALK OFF
SET EXCLUSIVE ON
USE ABC1
*test for file lock.
IF .NOT. FLOCK()
     *file not locked, so exit program.
     CLEAR
     ? "Another user is using the ABC database right now."
     ? "try your choice again later."
     RETURN
ENDIF
*file lock successful, so continue.
DO MAINMENU
(rest of program...)
```

The UNLOCK Command

Once your program has completed operations with a record or a file, the UNLOCK command can be used to clear all locks. The format of the command is simply

```
UNLOCK
```

As an alternative method of clearing a lock, you can lock a different record or file or close the database with a CLEAR ALL, USE, or QUIT command. Any of these operations will release a previous lock on a record or file.

WATCH OUT
FOR THE DEADLY EMBRACE...

Many programs written for the single-user environment must be rewritten to contend adequately with the demands of a network environment. A common fault of single-user dBASE programs running on a network is an inability to guard against the "deadly embrace" condition, which results when programs executed by two or more users contend for the same files and become locked in an endless loop. Even with the simple type of file locking shown in the previous program example, a deadly embrace can occur. Consider the example shown in Figure 19-12, when two users run the same program and one user happens to start the program an instant before the other user.

In the deadly embrace illustrated by the example, what occurs is this: the first user's program opens ABC1 in work area 1, locking the file. Then, the WORLDWID file is opened in work area 2, releasing the lock on ABC1 and locking WORLDWID. At exactly the same time, the second user's program opens ABC1, locking the file. The first user's program now tries to open ABC1 with the SELECT 1 command, but it is unsuccessful because ABC1 is now locked by the second user's program. The second user's program is trying to open WORLDWID, but it is unsuccessful because WORLDWID is locked by the first user's program. Normally, both users would get **file in use** error messages at this point. But because the programs contain an ON ERROR RETRY statement, the dBASE Administrator gets caught in an infinite loop of trying to give both users exclusive access to the same files. The example is provided to demonstrate the planning necessary when programming applications that will be used on a network. In this case, bet-

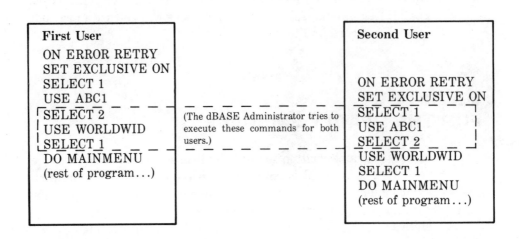

Figure 19-12. The deadly embrace

ter use of the ON ERROR command would be to transfer control to a part of the program that would use the locking functions to test the status of the desired files. Depending on the results, the program could then take appropriate action.

WHERE DO I GO FROM HERE?

As stated earlier, this section is intended to provide a brief introduction to the need for undertaking additional considerations when programming applications for a network environment. Programmers who plan to develop serious applications on a network should take advantage of all available resources, including the network operator's manual for the particular network in use, the network programming concepts section of the dBASE documentation, and various programmers reference guides for dBASE III PLUS, such as *Advanced dBASE III PLUS Programming and Techniques*, by Miriam Liskin (Osborne/McGraw-Hill, available October 1986).

Utility Programs
For dBASE III PLUS

Chapter **20**

As you continue to build your database system, you will look for ways to automate tasks that you do frequently, such as producing complex reports, writing detailed menu command files, and checking command files for errors. Various programs, called utilities, have been designed by independent software manufacturers to perform these and other functions. This chapter will briefly examine popular utilities used with dBASE III PLUS: dUTIL III PLUS, QUICKCODE III, QUICKREPORT, CLIPPER, and dBASE III-Compilers.

dUTIL III PLUS

dUTIL III PLUS is a utility program distributed by Fox & Geller, Inc., of Elmwood Park, New Jersey. dUTIL III PLUS is best described as a programmer's aid that accomplishes the following:

- Automatically capitalizes dBASE III PLUS commands and functions, and converts all filenames, fields, and variables to lowercase.

- Indents all commands between DO WHILE and ENDDO statements, IF and ENDIF statements, and CASE and END-CASE statements. If you nest any of these statements within loops, dUTIL III PLUS will use multiple levels of indentation.

- Prints maps showing the relationships between command files. For example, dUTIL III PLUS will print a diagram (called a map) showing that a main-menu command file calls five other command files and two of those command files call two more command files. The map will show the name of each command file as well as the names of the calling command files.

- Tests IF-ENDIF statements to ensure that they end with ENDIF; tests DO WHILE-ENDDO loops.

- As an option, creates an error file containing a list of all errors in program coding detected by dUTIL III PLUS, along with the line number of the program containing the error.

dUTIL III PLUS is useful for debugging, as the following example will show.

```
set talk off
use abcl index lastname
set alternate to BALANCE.TXT
do while .not. eof()
store 0 to NEWBAL
@7,10 say "Last name is:" LASTNAME
@8,10 say "First name is :" FIRSTNAME
@9,10 say "Enter balance due" get NEWBAL
set alternate on
set console off
list lastname, firstname, newbal
set alternate off
set console on
skip
if newbal=0
? "Processing complete."
enddo
clear
endif
enddo
```

This portion of a command file contains programming errors and lacks indentation: the ENDIF and ENDDO statements have been transposed, no commands are capitalized (they need not be capitalized, but it makes for easier reading), and none of the commands between the DO WHILE and ENDDO statements or the IF and ENDIF statements are indented. After dUTIL III PLUS processes the file, it creates a new one.

```
SET TALK OFF
USE abcl INDEX lastname
SET ALTERNATE TO balance.txt
DO WHILE .not. eof()
    STORE 0 TO newbal
    @7,10 SAY "Last name is:" lastname
    @8,10 SAY "First name is :" firstname
    @9,10 SAY "Enter balance due" GET newbal
    SET ALTERNATE ON
    SET CONSOLE OFF
    LIST lastname,firstname,newbal
    SET ALTERNATE OFF
    SET CONSOLE ON
    SKIP
    IF newbal=0
        ? "Processing complete."
        ENDDO

        *** WARNING - illegal structure closing ***          ENDDO
        CLEAR
    ENDIF newbal=0
ENDDO WHILE .not. eof()
```

The new file contains comments indicating that the ENDDO and ENDIF statements are mismatched. All dBASE III PLUS commands have been converted to uppercase, and statements between the IF-ENDIF and DO WHILE-ENDDO loops have been properly indented. One operation of dUTIL III PLUS may or may not be appealing to your taste: the program converts field names to lowercase.

dUTIL III PLUS comes in a ready-to-use format for the IBM PC and most compatibles, so no preparations are necessary. When you load dUTIL III PLUS by entering DUTIL, a copyright screen

```
                        d U T I L   I I I   P L U S

     ┌──────────────────────────────────────────────────────────────┐
     │        INPUT FILES                     OUTPUT FILES            │
     │        ‾‾‾‾‾‾‾‾‾‾‾                      ‾‾‾‾‾‾‾‾‾‾‾‾            │
     │   (1) SOURCE   -  LESSPRO.prg      (4) SOURCE -   PRETTY.new    │
     │   (2) KEYWORDS -  KEYWORDS.key     (5) TREE   -   DTREE.tre     │
     │   (3) UNITLIST -  .unt             (6) BATCH  -   DTREE.bat     │
     ├──────────────────────────────────────────────────────────────┤
     │   (10) MAIN DRIVE     -  A:       (14) SOURCE EXTENSION -  prg,new │
     │   (11) ALTERNATE DRIVE -  B:      (15) BATCH TYPE        -  TYPE   │
     ├──────────────────────────────────────────────────────────────┤
     │   (12) SOURCE TAB SIZE -  4       (16) MAX DEPTH DO      - 7    │
     │   (13) TREE TAB SIZE   -  5       (17) MAX DEPTH INCLUDE - 7    │
     ├──────────────────────────────────────────────────────────────┤
     │   (20) include  (21) skip    (22) caps    (23) tree   (24) code  │
     │   (25) display  (26) do      (27) process (28) page   (29) batch │
     │   (30) nounit   (31) return  (32) comment (33) use    (34) xref  │
     │   (35) list     (36) errfile                                     │
     └──────────────────────────────────────────────────────────────┘
       (0) EXECUTE    (37) SAVE      (99) EXIT
     * * * Please Enter Selection Number -->  _
```

Figure 20-1. dUTIL III main menu

appears momentarily, and then the main menu listing various tasks performed by the program (Figure 20-1) appears.

dUTIL III PLUS is mainly a menu-driven program; that is, most commands and procedures are executed by menu selections. The commands and operations are fully explained in the dUTIL III PLUS documentation.

QUICKCODE III

QUICKCODE III is a program generator, a program that can create databases and programs for dBASE III or for dBASE III

```
                    Q U I C K C O D E   III
┌──────────────────────────────────────────────────────────────────┐
│  To Design Your Screen  :  Q         │      To Exit:  E            │
├──────────────────────────────────────┴─────────────────────────────┤
│                     SCREEN SELECTION                               │
│            NEW Name For Your Screen:        N                      │
│            Get an OLD Screen From Disk:     O                      │
│            Get a TEXT File From Disk:       T                      │
├────────────────────────────────────────────────────────────────────┤
│                      CUSTOMIZATION                                 │
│      Customize Your Screen Design Commands:             C          │
│      Customize Your Screen Settings (widths,lengths,etc.):  S      │
│      Turn on the QUICKMENU Menu Generator:              M          │
│      Change Your Output Options (see list below):       X          │
├────────────────────────────────────────────────────────────────────┤
│              GENERATE dBASE-III PROGRAMS                           │
│      Generate ALL Programs:      ESC   Generate just one:  G       │
│              ADD          DBF    ED    FAU     GET                 │
│                    IO     LBL    OUT   PRG     PRN                 │
│                    RPT    SCR    VAL   WS                          │
└────────────────────────────────────────────────────────────────────┘
CURRENT SCREEN IS:     NONAME     (AUTO PILOT ON)
                  ENTER COMMAND        -
```

Figure 20-2. QUICKCODE III main menu

PLUS. This utility is also provided by Fox & Geller. With QUICK-CODE III you create the database structure on an input screen by entering the names and statistics of the fields that you wish to use in the database. QUICKCODE III then relies on the information contained in this input screen to create a database and various programs for editing records and creating reports.

When you load QUICKCODE III, it displays a menu like that shown in Figure 20-2.

The QUICKCODE III menu offers you the option of selecting a new or existing input screen, customizing the design of your input screen, and changing various output options (which are detailed in the QUICKCODE III documentation). Once an input screen has been designed, the same menu offers you the choice of generating various dBASE programs, compatible with dBASE III or with dBASE III PLUS. QUICKCODE III can generate the following dBASE programs for your database:

- Main-Menu Program: This program lets you choose options for adding new records, editing existing records, displaying data, running reports, creating mailing labels, and creating data files that are compatible with WordStar and MailMerge software.

- Input/Output Screen Display: This program lets you display and enter data, as well as display titles, lines, and boxes formed with graphics characters.

- Output-Only Screen Display: This program lets you display all of the fields in the database along with various messages concerning those fields.

- Add Program: This program lets you add records to the database and automatically updates any indexes.

- Report Program: This program lets you run reports. The reports run by this program must have been created with the dBASE III PLUS report generator.

- WordStar Program: This program creates data files that are compatible with WordStar and MailMerge software.

- Label Program: This program creates mailing labels or forms based on the fields that you specified on the screen when you ran the QUICKCODE III program.

- Get Program: This program lets you find a particular record in the database and display it on the screen. Once you have found the record, this program will let you print, edit, or delete the record.

- Edit Program: This program lets you edit a particular record (which has been retrieved with the Get program).

QUICKCODE III has its limitations; it performs best with an application that does not use more than one database at a time. If your application calls for the use of multiple files, QUICKCODE III becomes difficult to use without a lot of programming effort on your part; you must modify the programs that QUICKCODE III creates so they can be used with your multiple files. But QUICK-CODE III also offers significant advantages. QUICKCODE III will quickly write all of the command files necessary for a basic database system, with easy-to-read, well-designed menus and clear, easy-to-understand commands. You can use these command files as is or "fine-tune" them by modifying the command files until they suit your purposes. The basic system that can be constructed with QUICKCODE III can prove to be an excellent base on which to build a complete database system for your particular application.

QUICKREPORT

Quickreport is a program that lets you produce reports using dBASE III PLUS databases. Quickreport is also provided by Fox & Geller. The basic function of Quickreport is similar to that of the report generator within dBASE III PLUS; however, Quickreport provides many styles of reports that cannot be created with the report generator. Quickreport can create reports that use data contained in up to six databases, and you can provide "breakpoints" (sub-subtotals) on up to 16 fields, as opposed to the two-field limitation posed by the report generator. Quickreport uses a combination menu and blackboard system, similar in basic design to the Screen Painter feature of dBASE III PLUS. When you start the program, it displays a menu like the one shown in Figure 20-3.

Various menu options within Quickreport let you select the names of databases to be used by the report, names of fields within those databases that will be used in the report, relations between

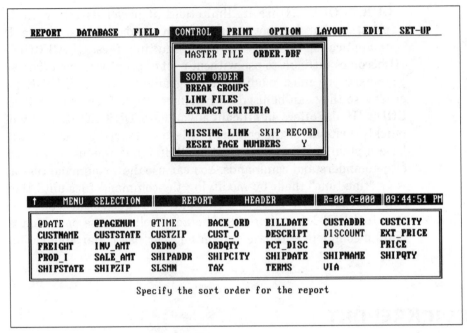

Figure 20-3. Quickreport main menu

databases, whether data will be sorted and in what order, and settings of margins and page sizes. A number of flexible options let you control the ways in which data is displayed or printed within the report. You can also select special printer options, such as boldface, italic, compressed, and emphasized print, if your printer supports such features. The actual report design is drawn on a blackboard (Figure 20-4). You switch back and forth between the various Quickreport menus and the blackboard by pressing F2.

Once you have drawn a report on the screen, you can switch back to the Quickreport menus with F2 and save the report. After the report has been saved, it can be produced with a Run option within the Quickreport program. A noticeable feature in Quickreport's favor is that the design of the program imitates many of the menu

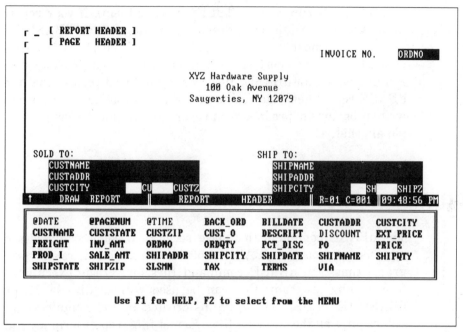

Figure 20-4. Quickreport blackboard

screens available in dBASE III PLUS. Once you are familiar with the way selections are made within the report, label, and Screen Painter menus of dBASE III PLUS, you will find it simple to grow accustomed to the menus and commands of Quickreport.

The only noticeable disadvantage of the program is that you must use it to produce reports that have been created. You cannot use Quickreport to create a report and then run that report using dBASE III PLUS. You must use the Quickreport program, which means either juggling floppy disks to change programs or taking up more space on your hard disk with the addition of the Quickreport software. (The program is not copy-protected, so it is a simple matter to add it to your hard disk.) For developers of applications, Fox & Geller also provides a lower-cost "runtime" version that lets users run reports (but not modify them). If your report needs are met in full by the report generator within dBASE III PLUS, you probably have no need for Quickreport. The reports created by Quickreport could also be created with custom programming within dBASE. However, if you need reports that the dBASE report generator cannot handle and you have no desire to write programs to produce such reports, then Quickreport is a viable alternative.

COMPILERS

The dBASE compilers that have recently become available are very useful tools for dBASE programmers. Compilers are programs that take dBASE command files and create executable, freestanding programs that can be used without dBASE III or dBASE III PLUS. The programs created by the compilers will still require all the database files, format files, report formats, and label formats that were required by the program when it was used with dBASE III PLUS. But since these files are not copyrighted programs (as is dBASE III PLUS), any databases and associated files can be freely copied along with the compiled version of the dBASE program.

A compiler offers two major advantages: speed and the ability to legally share a dBASE application among multiple users without purchasing additional dBASE III PLUS software packages. Compilers are faster than programs running under dBASE III PLUS, because of the way that compilers operate. Computer programming languages fall into the categories of *interpreted* and *compiled*. The dBASE programming language is an interpreted language. With an interpreted language, each command within a program is read by the computer one at a time and broken down into a series of operating instructions in a language closer to the computer's "natural" language (known as *machine language*). A compiler, by comparison, digests an entire program in a single step and translates the program into the basic instructions of the computer, or machine language. Because a compiled program is not read a line of commands at a time (or a single command at a time), the execution speed of the program is greatly increased.

Along with the advantages of compilers come disadvantages. The most notable disadvantage is the lack of access to the "interactive" method of using dBASE III PLUS. Once an application has been compiled, users do not have the flexibility of performing operations that are not available from the menus of that particular application. Interactive commands like EDIT and BROWSE are not available, although the effects of these commands can usually be imitated through various programming schemes. The dot prompt and the ASSIST menus are not available within a compiled program. As a result, such programs must be carefully planned to ensure that users of the program will have all needed functions available through the program's design.

The most popular compilers at the time of this writing are Clipper, from Nantucket, and the dBIII Compiler, from Wordtech Systems. Both compilers take command files and create executable files, normally with the same first name as the command file but with extensions of .COM or .EXE. There is no need to worry about which programs are called by other programs when using one of the compilers; as long as the main program in an application is compiled, all programs called by that program will be compiled in the order necessary for the compiled program to run.

dBASE programmers should remember that some commands are unsupported by the compilers. Clipper, for example, does not support the BROWSE, EDIT, CHANGE, or APPEND commands. (You can, however, use APPEND BLANK to add records, and you can use the @...SAY...GET commands to add or edit data within an existing database.) The programmer may also have to do some clean-up work with the program before it can be compiled without any errors from the compiler. Programs that run without error under dBASE III PLUS will not necessarily run without error when compiled, because of minor differences in the way the compilers handle certain dBASE commands.

As an example, Clipper was used to compile an employer applicant tracking system, very similar in design to the personnel system outlined in Chapter 17. The system was running without error under dBASE III PLUS. Using Clipper consists of two steps. The first step is to run Clipper, which reads the command (.PRG) file and produces a single object code file with an .OBJ extension. The second step is to run a "linker" package, called PLINK86, on the object file. This step produces an executable file that can then be run like any program, without using dBASE III PLUS. The half dozen procedures, main menu, and single format file contained in the sample program are compiled in just under two minutes. Clipper reported eight errors, four of which resulted from its inability to recognize the Single and Double options of the @...SAY commands used to draw borders on the screen in dBASE III PLUS. Once these errors were resolved and the program (.PRG) files recompiled, the program then ran without a problem, with significant increases in operating speed.

In summary, not everyone who uses dBASE III PLUS will need the added power of a compiler. However, professional programmers, developers, and dBASE users who must support the needs of larger corporations will find that a dBASE compiler is an invaluable tool.

Glossary
Of dBASE III PLUS
Commands

This appendix contains a listing of dBASE III PLUS commands. Each command name is followed by the syntax of the command and a description of how the command works. Examples of applications are provided for some commands. Most you will recognize from the tutorial section; others will be introduced here.

GLOSSARY SYMBOLS
AND CONVENTIONS

1. All commands are printed in UPPERCASE, although you can enter them in either upper- or lowercase letters.

2. All parameters of the command are listed in *italics*.

3. Any part of a command or parameter that is surrounded by left and right brackets—[and]—is optional.

4. When a slash separates two choices in a command, such as ON/OFF, you specify one choice but not both.

5. Ellipses (. . .) following a parameter or command mean that the parameter or command can be repeated "infinitely"— that is, until you exhaust the memory of the computer.

6. The parameter *scope*, which is always an option, can have three different meanings depending upon the command: ALL—for all records; NEXT *n*—for *n* number of records beginning at the current position of the record pointer; and RECORD—for only one record beginning at the current position of the record pointer.

Command: ? or ??

Syntax: *? expression* or *?? expression*

The ? command displays the value of a dBASE III PLUS expression. If a single question mark (?) is used, the cursor executes a carriage return and linefeed, and then the value of the expression is displayed. If the double question mark (??) is used, the cursor is not moved before the value of the expression is displayed.

Command: @

Syntax: @ <*row,col*> [SAY *expression*] [GET *variable*] [PICTURE *expression*] [RANGE exp, exp]] [CLEAR][DOUBLE]

The @ command places the cursor at a specific screen location, which is identified by *row,col*. The @ command can be used with one or more of the following options. The SAY option displays the expression following the word SAY. The GET option allows full-screen editing of *variable*. The PICTURE option allows the use of templates, which specify the way data will be displayed or accepted in response to the GET option. The RANGE option is used with the GET option to specify a range of acceptable entries.

Example: To place the message "Enter shareholder name:" at
screen location 12,2 and to allow full-screen editing of
the value contained in the variable SHN, enter

```
@ 12,2 SAY "Enter shareholder name:" GET SHN
```

When used with the TO and DOUBLE options, the @ command
draws single or double lines or borders (or a combination) on the
screen. The first value represents the upper-left screen coordinate,
and the second value represents the lower-right screen coordinate.
If both coordinates share a horizontal or vertical coordinate, a line
is drawn; otherwise, a rectangular border is drawn. The CLEAR
option can be used to clear a line or border that was drawn
previously.

Example: To draw a single line from row 3, column 5 to row 3,
column 50, enter the following:

```
@ 3,5 TO 3,50
```

To draw a double-line box, with the upper-left corner at row 4,
column 1, and the lower-right corner at row 18, column 70, enter

```
@ 4,1 TO 18,70 DOUBLE
```

To erase the border drawn in the previous example, enter

```
@ 4,1 CLEAR TO 18,70
```

Command: ACCEPT
Syntax: ACCEPT [*prompt*] TO *memvar*
The ACCEPT command stores a character string to the memory
variable *memvar*. ACCEPT can be followed by an optional character string. If this string is included, it will appear on the screen
when the ACCEPT command is executed.

Example: To display the prompt "Enter owner name:" and store to the memory variable OWNER the character string that the user enters in response to the prompt, enter

```
ACCEPT "Enter owner name: " TO OWNER
```

Command: APPEND
Syntax: APPEND [BLANK]
The APPEND command appends records to a database. When the APPEND command is executed, a blank record is displayed, and dBASE III PLUS enters full-screen editing mode. If the BLANK option is used, a blank record is added to the end of the database, and full-screen editing mode is not entered.

Command: APPEND FROM
Syntax: APPEND FROM *filename* [FOR/WHILE *condition*] [SDF/DELIMITED]
APPEND FROM copies records from *filename* and appends them to the active database. The FOR/WHILE option specifies a condition that must be met before any records will be copied. If the *filename* containing the data to be copied is not a dBASE III PLUS database, the SDF or Delimited options must be used.

Command: ASSIST
Syntax: ASSIST
The ASSIST command lets you operate dBASE III PLUS with a series of menus. You enter dBASE III PLUS commands by selecting menu choices. To select menus from other menus within ASSIST, press the ← or → key until the desired menu is highlighted and then press RETURN.

Command: AVERAGE
Syntax: AVERAGE *field-list* [*scope*][FOR/WHILE *condition*] [TO *memvar-list*]
The AVERAGE command computes an average of a specified numeric field listed in *field-list*. If the TO option is not used, the average is displayed on screen. If TO is used, the average of the first field is assigned to the first memory variable, the average of the second field to the second memory variable, and so on down the

list; and the average is stored as the memory variable specified. If the *scope* option is not used, the quantifier of ALL is assumed, meaning all records in *field-list* will be averaged. The FOR/WHILE option can be used to specify a condition that must be met for the fields to be averaged.

Command: BROWSE
Syntax: BROWSE [FIELDS *field-list*]
The BROWSE command displays a database on screen. If the database is too large for the screen, BROWSE displays only the fields that will fit on the screen. More fields can be viewed by scrolling to the left or right, by holding the CONTROL key and pressing the ← or → key. The contents of any field can be edited while in BROWSE mode. To save changes made during BROWSE, press CONTROL-END; to exit BROWSE, press CONTROL-ESC. The FIELDS option will display only the fields listed in *field-list*.

Command: CANCEL
Syntax: CANCEL
The CANCEL command halts execution of a command file and returns dBASE III PLUS to the dot prompt.

Command: CHANGE
Syntax: CHANGE [*scope*][FIELDS *field-list*][FOR/WHILE *condition*]
The CHANGE command permits full-screen editing of fields listed in *field-list*. If the *scope* option is absent, the quantifier ALL is assumed. The FOR/WHILE option allows editing to only those records satisfying the *condition*.

Example: To edit the RENTAMT and EXPDATE fields in the ABC1 database, enter

```
CHANGE FIELDS RENTAMT,EXPDATE
```

Command: CLEAR
Syntax: CLEAR
The CLEAR command erases the screen and returns the cursor to

location 0,0 (the upper-left corner). CLEAR can also be used as an option of the @ command, to clear the screen below and to the right of the location specified by the @ command.

Examples: To erase the entire screen, enter

```
CLEAR
```

To erase the screen below and to the right of the cursor at 12,20, enter

```
@12,20 CLEAR
```

Command: CLEAR ALL
Syntax: CLEAR ALL
The CLEAR ALL command closes all open database, memo, index, and format files. The current work area is set to 1.

Command: CLEAR FIELDS
Syntax: CLEAR FIELDS
Clears the list of fields specified by the SET FIELDS command. The CLEAR FIELDS command has no effect if SET FIELDS was not previously used to specify fields (see SET FIELDS).

Command: CLEAR GETS
Syntax: CLEAR GETS
The CLEAR GETS command clears values from variables provided by the GET that were accessed with a READ command.

Example: The following CLEAR GETS command would permit the user to clear previous responses to various GET commands.

```
ACCEPT "Enter Y to store entries, N to delete" TO ANS
IF ANS = "N"
     CLEAR GETS
ENDIF
```

Command: CLEAR MEMORY
Syntax: CLEAR MEMORY
The CLEAR MEMORY command erases all current memory variables.

Command: CLEAR TYPEAHEAD
Syntax: CLEAR TYPEAHEAD
The CLEAR TYPEAHEAD command clears the contents of the typeahead buffer (see SET TYPEAHEAD).

Command: CLOSE
Syntax: CLOSE *file-type*
The CLOSE command closes all file types listed in *file-type*. *File-type* can be one of five: ALTERNATE, DATABASES, FORMAT, INDEX, or PROCEDURE.

Command: CONTINUE
Syntax: CONTINUE
The CONTINUE command resumes a search started by LOCATE. After LOCATE finds the record matching the criteria specified in the command, you can find additional records that meet the same criteria by entering CONTINUE. Using CONTINUE saves you from having to re-enter the LOCATE command. (*See* LOCATE.)

Command: COPY
Syntax: COPY TO *filename* [*scope*] [FIELDS *field-list*]
               [FOR/WHILE *condition*][SDF/DELIMITED
               [WITH *delimiter*]]
The COPY command copies all or part of the active database to *filename*. If *scope* is not listed, ALL is assumed. The FIELDS option is used to pinpoint the fields to be copied. The FOR/WHILE option copies only those records meeting the *condition*. Specifying SDF will copy the file in System Data format; specifying DELIMITED will copy the file in Delimited format.

Example: To copy LASTNAME, RENTAMT, and EXTRAS fields

from the active database ABC1 to WORLDWID, enter

```
COPY TO WORLDWID FIELDS LASTNAME, RENTAMT, EXTRAS
```

Command: COPY FILE
Syntax: COPY FILE *source-file* TO *destination-file*
The COPY FILE command creates an identical copy of a file. You
must supply the extension in both *source-file* and *destination-file*.

Example: To copy a file named REPORTER.FRM, to a new file
named TESTER.FRM, enter

```
COPY FILE REPORTER.FRM TO TESTER.FRM
```

Command: COPY STRUCTURE
Syntax: COPY STRUCTURE TO *filename* [FIELDS *field-
                  list*]
The COPY STRUCTURE command copies the structure of an
active database to *filename*. Specifying FIELDS with *field-list* will
copy only those fields to the structure.

Command: COUNT
Syntax: COUNT [*scope*][FOR/WHILE *condition*]
                  [TO *memvar*]
The COUNT command counts the number of records in the active
database that meet a specific condition. The *scope* option quantifies
the records to be counted. The FOR/WHILE option can be used to
specify a condition that must be met before a record will be
counted. The TO option can be used to store the count to the
memory variable *memvar*.

Example: To count the number of records containing the letters
MD in the STATE field, and to store that count as the
memory variable MTEMP, enter

```
COUNT FOR STATE = "MD" TO MTEMP
```

Command: CREATE
Syntax: CREATE *filename*
The CREATE command creates a new database file and defines

its structure. If CREATE is entered without a filename, dBASE III PLUS will prompt you for one. If CREATE is followed by a filename, a database with that filename will be created. The filename extension .DBF is added automatically to the filename unless you specify otherwise.

Command: CREATE LABEL
Syntax: CREATE LABEL *filename*
The CREATE LABEL command creates a label form file. This file can be used with the LABEL FORM command to produce mailing labels.

Command: CREATE QUERY
Syntax: CREATE QUERY *filename*
Creates or modifies a query file to filter a database of records that do not meet specified conditions. The specified filename is assigned an extension of .QRY. Upon entry of the command, the Query menu appears on the screen. Options within the Query menu allow design of the filter. If a catalog is open when CREATE QUERY is used, the resultant query file will be added to the catalog.

Example: To create a query file named PASTDUE, enter

```
CREATE QUERY PASTDUE
```

Command: CREATE REPORT
Syntax: CREATE REPORT
The CREATE REPORT, or as an alternative, MODIFY REPORT, command creates or allows the user to modify a report form file for producing reports. Once the report has been outlined with the CREATE REPORT command, the report can be displayed or printed with the REPORT FORM command.

Command: CREATE SCREEN
Syntax: CREATE SCREEN *filename*
Creates or modifies a custom screen form that is used for the display and editing of records. Two files are created by the CREATE SCREEN command. One file is assigned the .SCR extension, and the other file is assigned the .FMT extension. Upon entry of the

command, the Screen Painter menu appears. Options within the Screen Painter allow design of the custom screen form. If a catalog is active when CREATE SCREEN is used, the resultant .FMT and .SCR files will be added to the catalog.

Example: To create a custom screen format named PARTS, enter

```
CREATE SCREEN PARTS
```

Command: CREATE VIEW
Syntax: CREATE VIEW *filename*
Creates or modifies a view file to group related databases and associated index, format, and filter files into what appears to be a single file. View files can contain database files open in chosen work areas along with associated index files, one format file, and one filter file. Relations between the open databases are also contained within the view file. The view file is assigned the .VUE extension. Upon entry of the CREATE VIEW command, the View menu appears. Options within the menu allow the selection of databases and associated files that will be contained within the view file. If a catalog is active when CREATE VIEW is used, the view file and its contents will be added to the catalog.

Example: To create a view file named CLIENTS, enter

```
CREATE VIEW CLIENTS
```

Command: CREATE VIEW FROM ENVIRONMENT
Syntax: CREATE VIEW *filename* FROM
                ENVIRONMENT
Creates a view file based upon the databases, index files, relations, and associated format file in use at the time the command is entered. The view file created by the CREATE VIEW FROM ENVIRONMENT command will contain all open database files and associated index files; all existing relations between databases; and one format file, if a format file is open. The current work area number and field list (if a field list is active) are also saved within the view file.

Command: DELETE
Syntax: DELETE [*record-number*][*scope*]
[FOR/WHILE *condition*]
The DELETE command marks specific records for deletion. If DELETE is used without a record number, the current record is marked for deletion. The *scope* option is used to identify the records to be deleted. The FOR/WHILE option can be used to specify a condition that must be met before a record will be deleted. DELETE marks a file for deletion; the PACK command actually removes the record.

Example: To mark 24 records for deletion beginning with the current record and specifying that they have an entry of VA in the STATE field in order to be deleted, enter

```
DELETE NEXT 24 FOR STATE = "VA"
```

Command: DIR
Syntax: DIR [*drive:*][*filename*]
The DIR command displays the directory of all database files or files of a specific type if a file extension is specified. *Drive* is the drive designator (A:, B:, or C: for hard-disk users), and *filename* is the name of a file with or without an extension. Wildcards, which are asterisks or question marks, can be used as part of or as a replacement for *filename*. In the case of database files, the display produced by DIR includes the number of records contained in the database, the date of the last update, and the size of the file (in bytes).

Example: To display all index files from the current default drive, enter

```
DIR *.NDX
```

Command: DISPLAY
Syntax: DISPLAY [*scope*][*field-list*][FOR/WHILE *condition*]
[OFF]
The DISPLAY command displays a record from the active database. You can display more records by including the *scope* option.

The FOR/WHILE option limits the display of records to those satisfying *condition*. Only the fields listed in *field-list* will be displayed; if *field-list* is absent, all fields will be displayed. The OFF option will prevent the record number from being displayed.

Example: To display the LASTNAME, FIRSTNAME, RENT-AMT, and EXPDATE fields for ten records beginning with the current record, enter

```
DISPLAY NEXT 10 LASTNAME, FIRSTNAME, RENTAMT, EXPDATE
```

Command: DISPLAY HISTORY
Syntax: DISPLAY HISTORY [LAST *number*][TO PRINT]
Displays all commands stored in HISTORY, unless the LAST option, where *number* equals the number of commands to display, is used to specify a certain number of commands. The TO PRINT option will cause the displayed commands to be printed on the printer.

Example: To print the last ten commands entered, enter the following:

```
DISPLAY HISTORY LAST 10 TO PRINT
```

Command: DISPLAY MEMORY
Syntax: DISPLAY MEMORY [TO PRINT]
The DISPLAY MEMORY command displays all active memory variables, their sizes, and their contents. From a total of 256 variables the numbers of active variables and available variables are listed along with the numbers of bytes consumed and bytes available. These statistics will be displayed on the printer as well as the screen if TO PRINT is included.

Command: DISPLAY STATUS
Syntax: DISPLAY STATUS
The DISPLAY STATUS command displays the names and aliases of all currently active work areas and active files. Any key fields used in index files, the current drive designator, function-key settings, and settings of SET commands are also displayed.

Command: DISPLAY STRUCTURE
Syntax: DISPLAY STRUCTURE
The DISPLAY STRUCTURE command displays the structure of the active database. The complete filename, along with the current drive designator, number of records, date of last update, and name of fields, including their statistics (type, length, and decimal places), are listed.

Command: DO
Syntax: DO *filename* [WITH *parameter-list*]
The DO command starts execution of a dBASE III PLUS command file. The filename extension of .PRG is assumed unless otherwise specified. If the WITH option is specified and followed by a list of parameters in *parameter-list*, those parameters are transferred to the command file.

Command: DO CASE
Syntax: DO CASE
                CASE *condition*
                    commands...
                [CASE *condition*]
                    commands...
                [OTHERWISE]
                    commands...
                ENDCASE
The DO CASE command selects one course of action from a number of choices. The conditions following the CASE statements are evaluated until one of the conditions is found to be true. When a condition is true, the commands between the CASE statement and another CASE, or OTHERWISE and ENDCASE, will be executed. If none of the conditions in the CASE statements are found to be true, any commands following the optional OTHERWISE statement will be executed. If the OTHERWISE statement is not used and no conditions are found to be true, dBASE III PLUS proceeds to the command following the ENDCASE statement.

Example: In the following DO CASE commands, dBASE chooses

from among three possible alternatives: (1) executing a command file named MENU, (2) appending the database, or (3) exiting from dBASE III PLUS.

```
DO CASE
   CASE SELECT = 1
   DO MENU
   CASE SELECT = 2
   APPEND
   CASE SELECT = 3
   QUIT
ENDCASE
```

Command: DO WHILE

Syntax: DO WHILE *condition*

      commands...

    ENDDO

The DO WHILE command repeatedly executes commands between DO WHILE and ENDDO as long as *condition* is true. When dBASE III PLUS encounters a DO WHILE command, the condition following the command is evaluated: if *condition* is false, dBASE III PLUS proceeds to the command following the ENDDO command; but if *condition* is true, dBASE III PLUS executes the commands following the DO WHILE command until the ENDDO command is reached. When the ENDDO command is reached, the condition following the DO WHILE command is again evaluated. If it is still true, the commands between DO WHILE and ENDDO are again executed. If the condition is false, dBASE III PLUS proceeds to the command below the ENDDO command.

Example: To print LASTNAME, CITY, STATE, RENTAMT, and EXPDATE fields for each record until the end of the file (actually, the end of the database), enter

```
DO WHILE .NOT. EOF()
       ? LASTNAME, CITY, STATE, RENTAMT, EXPDATE
       SKIP
ENDDO
```

Command: EDIT
Syntax: EDIT [RECORD *n*]
The EDIT command allows full-screen editing of a record in the database. If no record number is specified by RECORD (*n* being the record number), the current record, which is identified by the current position of the record pointer, will be edited.

Command: EJECT
Syntax: EJECT
The EJECT command causes the printer to perform a formfeed.

Command: ERASE
Syntax: ERASE *filename.ext*
The ERASE command erases the named file from the directory. The name must include the file extension. You can also use the command DELETE FILE *filename.ext* to erase a file. If the file is on a disk that is not in the default drive, you must include the drive designator.

Command: EXIT
Syntax: EXIT
The EXIT command exits a DO WHILE loop and proceeds to the first command below the ENDDO command.

Example: The following command-file portion uses EXIT to exit the DO WHILE loop if a part number of 9999 is entered.

```
? "Enter part number to add to inventory."
? "Enter 9999 to exit."
DO WHILE .T.
INPUT TO PARTNO
IF PARTNO = 9999
    EXIT
ENDIF
```

Command: EXPORT
Syntax: EXPORT TO *filename* TYPE PFS

Creates a PFS:FILE database file and PFS-compatible screen format, based on a dBASE III PLUS database in use. If a format file is active, that format file will be used as the screen format within the PFS:FILE database.

Example: To export a file, PARTS, to a PFS:FILE database to be named INVPARTS, enter

```
USE PARTS
EXPORT TO INVPARTS TYPE PFS
```

Command: FIND
Syntax: FIND *"character-string"*
The FIND command positions the record pointer at the first record containing an index key that matches *"character-string"*. If there are leading blanks in *character-string, character-string* must be surrounded by single or double quotes; otherwise no quotes are necessary. If the specific character string cannot be found, the EOF( ) value is set to true, and a **NO FIND** message is displayed on the screen (if dBASE III PLUS is not executing a command file). An index file must be open before you use the FIND command.

Command: GO or GOTO
Syntax: GO or GOTO BOTTOM/TOP/*expression*
The GO and GOTO commands position the record pointer at a record. GO TOP will move the pointer to the beginning of a database, while GO BOTTOM will move it to the end of a database.

Command: HELP
Syntax: HELP *command-name*
The HELP command provides instructions on using dBASE III PLUS commands and functions as well as other information. If you enter HELP without specifying a command or function, a menu-driven system of Help screens allows you to request information on various subjects. If HELP is followed by a command or function, information about it will be displayed.

Command: IF
Syntax: IF *condition*
                commands . . .
            [ELSE]
                commands . . .
            ENDIF

IF is a decision-making command that will execute commands when certain conditions are true. If *condition* for the IF statement is true, the commands between the IF and ENDIF will be executed. Should *condition* be false, and there is an ELSE, the commands will be executed between ELSE and ENDIF. On the other hand, if *condition* for IF is not true and there is no ELSE, dBASE III PLUS will drop to the ENDIF statement without executing any commands.

Command: IMPORT
Syntax: IMPORT FROM *filename* TYPE PFS

Creates a dBASE III PLUS database, format file, and view file from a PFS:FILE database. The format file created will mimic the design of the PFS:FILE screen form. The resultant dBASE III PLUS database can be used separately from the format file, or both files can be used, with or without the accompanying view file. The imported file will be assigned the same filename as the PFS file.

Example: In order to create a dBASE III PLUS database, from a PFS:FILE database named ILLNESS, enter

```
IMPORT FROM ILLNESS TYPE PFS
```

Command: INDEX
Syntax: INDEX ON *field-list* TO *filename*

The INDEX command creates an index file based on a field from the active database. Depending on the field, the index file will be indexed alphabetically, numerically, or chronologically. If the index based on the first field has duplicate entries, the duplicates are indexed according to the second field in *field-list*, provided a second field has been listed.

Example: To create an index file called RENTS based on the values in the RENTAMT field, enter

```
INDEX ON RENTAMT TO RENTS
```

Command: INPUT
Syntax: INPUT [*prompt*] TO *memvar*
The INPUT command stores a numeric entry assigned to a memory variable by the user. An optional *prompt* can display a message to the user during keyboard entry. *Prompt* can be a memory variable or a character string.

Example: To display the prompt "Enter name to search for:", and store the response to the memory variable NEWNAME, enter

```
INPUT "Enter name to search for:" TO NEWNAME
```

Command: INSERT
Syntax: INSERT [BLANK][BEFORE]
The INSERT command adds a new record below the record pointer's position and renumbers the records below the insertion. Specifying BEFORE causes the record to be inserted at the record pointer; thus, if the pointer is at record 3, the new record will be 3 and the records below it renumbered. If the BLANK option is omitted, dBASE III PLUS allows full-screen editing of the new record; otherwise the record will be blank.

Example: To insert a new record at position 10 in the active database, enter

```
GO 10
INSERT BEFORE
```

Command: JOIN
Syntax: JOIN WITH *alias* TO *filename* FOR *condition*
            [FIELDS *field-list*]

The JOIN command creates a new database by combining specific records and fields from the active database and the database listed as *alias*. The combined database is stored in *filename*. You can limit the choice of records from the active database by specifying a FOR *condition*. All fields from both files will be copied if you do not include a *field-list*; but if you do, only those fields specified in *field-list* will be copied. Specify fields from the nonactive database by supplying *filename, —> field name*.

Example: To join ABC1 and ABC2 to create a new file named NEWFILE including only the LASTNAME field from ABC2 and records from ABC1 with RENTAMT less than $400, enter

```
JOIN WITH ABC2 TO NEWFILE FOR RENTAMT < 400 FIELDS ABC2-> LASTNAME
```

Command: LABEL FORM
Syntax: LABEL FORM *label-filename* [*scope*][SAMPLE][TO PRINT][FOR/WHILE *condition*][TO FILE *filename*]

The LABEL FORM command is used to print mailing labels from a label form file (extension .LBL). The SAMPLE option allows a sample label to be printed. The FOR/WHILE option can be used to specify a condition that must be met before a label for a record will be printed. The TO PRINT option sends output to the printer, while the TO FILE option sends output to a named disk file.

Example: To print mailing labels, using the label form named MAILERS, for records with STATE fields containing NM, and to restrict printing to the next 25 records beginning at the current record-pointer position, enter

```
LABEL FORM MAILERS NEXT 25 FOR STATE = "NM" TO PRINT
```

Command: LIST
Syntax: LIST [OFF][*scope*][*field-list*]FOR/WHILE *condition*][TO PRINT]

The LIST command provides a list of database contents. The *scope* option is used to quantify the records to be listed. If *scope* is absent,

ALL is assumed. The FOR/WHILE option specifies a condition that must be met before a record will be listed. The OFF option will prevent the record number from being listed. If the TO PRINT option is used, the listing will be printed on the printer.

Command: LIST MEMORY
Syntax: LIST MEMORY [TO PRINT]
The LIST MEMORY command lists the names, sizes, and types of memory variables. If the TO PRINT option is used, the listing will be printed on the printer.

Command: LIST STATUS
Syntax: LIST STATUS [TO PRINT]
The LIST STATUS command lists information on currently open work areas, the active file, and system settings. All open files and open index filenames are displayed, along with work area numbers, any key fields used in index files, the default disk drive, function-key settings, and settings of the SET commands. If the TO PRINT option is used, the listing will be printed on the printer. LIST STATUS does not pause during the listing, which is the only difference between LIST STATUS and DISPLAY STATUS.

Command: LIST STRUCTURE
Syntax: LIST STRUCTURE [TO PRINT]
The LIST STRUCTURE command lists the structure of the database in use, including the name, number of records, all names of fields, and the date of the last update. If the TO PRINT option is used, the listing will be printed on the printer. LIST STRUCTURE does not pause during the listing, which is the only difference between LIST STRUCTURE and DISPLAY STRUCTURE.

Command: LOCATE
Syntax: LOCATE [*scope*] FOR *condition*
The LOCATE command finds the first record that matches *condition*. The *scope* option can be used to limit the number of records that will be searched; but if *scope* is omitted, ALL is assumed. The LOCATE command ends when a record matching *condition* is found, after which dBASE III PLUS prints the location of the record but not the record itself.

Example: To locate a record containing the character string Smith in the LASTNAME field, enter

```
LOCATE FOR LASTNAME = "Smith"
```

Command: LOOP
Syntax: LOOP
The LOOP command causes a jump back to the start of a DO WHILE loop. The LOOP command is normally executed conditionally with the IF statement.

Example: The following portion of a command file uses the LOOP command to return to the start of the DO WHILE loop if the RENTAMT field equals 800.

```
DO WHILE .NOT. EOF()
    IF RENTAMT = 800
        SKIP
        LOOP
    ENDIF
    SET PRINT ON
    LIST LASTNAME,FIRSTNAME,RENTAMT
    SKIP
    SET PRINT OFF
ENDDO
```

Command: MODIFY COMMAND
Syntax: MODIFY COMMAND *filename*
MODIFY COMMAND starts the dBASE III PLUS word processor, which can be used for editing command files or any ASCII text files. *Filename* will be given the extension .PRG.

Command: MODIFY LABELS
Syntax: MODIFY LABELS *filename*
The MODIFY LABELS command creates or allows editing of a label form file. This file can be used with the LABEL FORM command to produce mailing labels. *Filename* will be given the extension .LBL.

Command: MODIFY QUERY
Syntax: MODIFY QUERY *filename*
Modifies an existing query file to filter a database of records that

do not meet specified conditions. (To create a new query file, use CREATE QUERY.) Upon entry of the command, the Query menu appears on the screen. Options within the Query menu allow changes to the filter design. If a catalog is open when MODIFY QUERY is used, the modified query file will be added to the catalog.

Command: MODIFY REPORT
Syntax: MODIFY REPORT *filename*
The MODIFY REPORT command allows you to use a menu-assisted, full-screen editor to create or modify a report form file for producing reports. *Filename* will be given the extension .FRM.

Command: MODIFY SCREEN
Syntax: MODIFY SCREEN *filename*
Modifies an existing custom screen form. (To create a new custom screen form, use the CREATE SCREEN command.) Upon entry of the command, the Screen Painter menu appears. Options within the Screen Painter allow modifications to the design of the custom screen form. If a catalog is active when MODIFY SCREEN is used, the modified .FMT and .SCR files will be added to the catalog.

Command: MODIFY STRUCTURE
Syntax: MODIFY STRUCTURE *filename*
The MODIFY STRUCTURE command allows you to alter the structure of a database. The filename extension .DBF is given to *filename* unless specified otherwise.

A backup copy is created to store the data from *filename*. The data is later returned to the modified file; the backup file remains on disk with the same *filename* but with a different extension of .BAK.

Command: MODIFY VIEW
Syntax: MODIFY VIEW *filename*
Modifies an existing view file that groups related databases and associated index, format, and filter files into what appears to be a single file. (To create a new view file, use the CREATE VIEW

command.) Upon entry of the MODIFY VIEW command, the View menu appears. Options within the menu allow desired changes to the selection of databases and associated files that will be contained within the view file. If a catalog is active when MODIFY VIEW is used, the modified view file will be added to the catalog.

Command: NOTE or *
Syntax: NOTE or *

The NOTE or * command is used to insert comments in a command file. Text after the * or the word NOTE in a command file will be ignored by dBASE III PLUS.

Command: ON
Syntax: ON ERROR *command*
ON ESCAPE *command*
ON KEY *command*

Causes a branch within a command file, specified by *command*, to be carried out when the condition identified by ON (an error, pressing the ESC key, or pressing any key) is met. If more than one ON condition is specified, the order of precedence is ON ERROR, and then ON ESCAPE, and then ON KEY. All ON conditions remain in effect until another ON condition is specified to clear the previous condition. To clear an ON condition without specifying another condition, enter ON ERROR, ON ESCAPE, or ON KEY without adding a command.

Example: To cause program control to transfer to another program called ERRTRAP if an error occurs, enter

```
ON ERROR DO ERRTRAP
```

To cause the program to display a customized error message if an error occurs, enter the following:

```
ON ERROR ? "A serious error has occurred.  Call J.E.J.A. Tech
Support for instructions."
```

To cause the program to call another program, named HELP-ER.PRG, containing customized help screens if the ESC key is pressed, enter

```
ON ESCAPE DO HELPER
```

To halt processing within a program and transfer program control to a program named HALTED.PRG if any key is pressed, enter

```
ON KEY DO HALTED
```

Use of the ON KEY syntax of the command will result in the key that is pressed being stored in the keyboard buffer. The routine that is called by the ON KEY command should use a READ command or INKEY( ) function to clear the buffer.

Command: PACK
Syntax: PACK
The PACK command removes records that have been marked for deletion by the DELETE command.

Command: PARAMETERS
Syntax: PARAMETERS *parameter-list*
The PARAMETERS command is used within a command file to assign variable names to data items that are received from another command file with the DO command. The PARAMETERS command must be the first command in a command file; the parameter list is identical to the list of parameters included with the WITH option of the DO command that called the command file.

Example: The following portion of a command file shows the use of the PARAMETERS command to receive four parameters, SALARY, FEDTAX, STATETAX, and FICA, sent from the command file that called this command file.

```
NOTE This is the calculations command file.
PARAMETERS SALARY, FEDTAX, STATETAX, FICA
STORE SALARY - (FEDTAX + STATETAX + FICA) TO NET
RETURN
(rest of program...)
```

Command: PRIVATE

Syntax: PRIVATE [ALL[LIKE/EXCEPT*skeleton*]][*memory variables list*]

Sets named variables to private, hiding values of those variables from all higher-level parts of a program. *Skeletons* are the acceptable DOS wildcards of asterisk (*) and question mark (?). Memory variables are private by default.

Examples: To hide all variables, excluding BILLPAY, from higher-level parts of the program, enter

```
PRIVATE ALL EXCEPT BILLPAY
```

To hide all variables with eight-character names that end in "TEST" from higher-level parts of the program, enter

```
PRIVATE ALL LIKE ????TEST
```

To hide only the variable named PAYOUT from higher-level parts of the program, enter

```
PRIVATE PAYOUT
```

Command: PROCEDURE

Syntax: PROCEDURE

The PROCEDURE command identifies the start of each separate procedure within a procedure file.

Although using a one-line procedure is inefficient (procedures should be at least three lines long), the following example demonstrates a simple procedure.

Example:

```
PROCEDURE ERROR1
@2,10 SAY "That is not a valid date.  Please try again."
RETURN
```

Command: PUBLIC
Syntax: PUBLIC [*memory variables list*]
Sets named variables to public, making the values of those variables available to all levels of a program.

Example: To make the variables named BILLPAY, DUEDATE, and AMOUNT available to all modules of a program, enter

```
PUBLIC BILLPAY, DUEDATE, AMOUNT
```

Command: QUIT
Syntax: QUIT
The QUIT command closes all open files, leaves dBASE III PLUS, and returns you to the DOS prompt.

Command: READ
Syntax: READ [SAVE]
The READ command allows full-screen data entry from an @ command with GET option. Normally, a READ command clears all GETs when all data entry or editing is completed. The SAVE option is used to avoid clearing all GETs after completion of data entry or editing.

Command: RECALL
Syntax: RECALL [*scope*] [FOR/WHILE *condition*]
The RECALL command unmarks records that have been marked for deletion. If *scope* is not listed, ALL is assumed. The FOR/WHILE option can be used to specify a condition that must be met before a record will be recalled.

Command: REINDEX
Syntax: REINDEX
The REINDEX command rebuilds active index files. If any

changes have been made to the database while its index file was closed, you can update the index file with REINDEX.

Command: RELEASE
Syntax: RELEASE *[memvar-list]*[ALL [LIKE/EXCEPT
                         wildcards]]
The RELEASE command removes all or specified memory variables from memory. Wildcards, which are asterisks or question marks, are used with the LIKE and EXCEPT options. The asterisk can be used to represent one or more characters, the question mark to represent one character.

Example: To release all memory variables except those ending with the characters TAX, enter

```
RELEASE ALL EXCEPT ???TAX
```

Command: RENAME
Syntax: RENAME *filename.ext* TO *new-filen: ne.ext*
The RENAME command changes the name of a file. The name must include the file extension. If the file is on a disk that is not in the default drive, the drive designator must also be included.

Command: REPLACE
Syntax: REPLACE *[scope] field* WITH *expression* *[...field2*
                         WITH *expression2]* [FOR/WHILE *condition*]
The REPLACE command replaces the contents of a specified field with new values. You can replace values in more than one field by listing more than one *field* WITH *expression;* be sure to separate each field replacement with a comma. The FOR/WHILE option can be used to specify a condition that must be met before a field in a record will be replaced. If the *scope* or FOR/WHILE options are not used, the current record (at the current record-pointer location) will be the only record replaced.

Example: To replace the contents of the field RENTAMT at the current record with a new amount equal to the old amount multiplied by 1.05, enter

```
REPLACE RENTAMT WITH RENTAMT * 1.05
```

Command: REPORT FORM
Syntax: REPORT FORM *filename* [*scope*][FOR *expression*]
[PLAIN] [HEADING *character-string*]
[NOEJECT][TO PRINT][TO FILE *filename*]

The REPORT FORM command uses a report form file (previously created with the CREATE REPORT command) to produce a tabular report. A *filename* with the extension .FRM is assumed unless otherwise specified. The FOR *condition* option can be used to specify a condition that must be met before a record will be printed. If *scope* is not included, ALL is assumed. The PLAIN option omits page numbers and the system date. The HEADING option (followed by a character string) provides a header in addition to any header that was specified when the report was created with CREATE REPORT. The NOEJECT option cancels the initial formfeed.

Command: RESTORE
Syntax: RESTORE FROM *filename* [ADDITIVE]

The RESTORE command reads memory variables into memory from a memory variable file. RESTORE FROM assumes that *filename* ends with .MEM; if it does not, you should include the extension. If the ADDITIVE option is used, current memory variables will not be deleted.

Command: RESUME
Syntax: RESUME

The RESUME command is a companion to the SUSPEND command. RESUME causes program execution to continue at the line following the line containing the SUSPEND command (see SUSPEND).

Command: RETRY
Syntax: RETRY

The RETRY command returns control to a calling program and executes the same line that called the program containing the RETRY command. The function of RETRY is similar to the function of the RETURN command; however, where RETURN executes the following line of the calling program, RETRY executes the same line of the calling program. RETRY can be useful in error recovery situations, where an action can be taken to clear the cause of an error and the command repeated, as shown in the following example:

```
*Main Menu program
ON ERROR DO FIXIT
USE ABC1 INDEX NAMES
*rest of program follows...


*FIXIT.PRG
CLEAR
? "Cannot find ABC database and index files on disk."
? "please insert the disk with the databases in drive B,"
? "and press a key to continue."
WAIT
RETRY
```

Command: RETURN
Syntax: RETURN [TO MASTER]
The RETURN command ends execution of a command file or procedure. If the command file was called by another command file, program control returns to the other command file. If the command file was not called by another command file, control returns to the dot prompt. If the TO MASTER option is used, control returns to the highest-level command file.

Command: RUN
Syntax: RUN *filename*
The RUN command executes a non-dBASE III PLUS program from within the dBASE III PLUS environment. The program must have an extension of .COM or .EXE. When the program completes its execution, control is passed back to dBASE III PLUS. You can also execute DOS commands with RUN, provided there is enough available memory.

Command: SAVE
Syntax: SAVE TO *filename* [ALL LIKE/EXCEPT *wildcard*]

The SAVE command copies memory variables to a disk file. Wild-cards, which are asterisks or question marks, are used with the LIKE and EXCEPT options. The asterisk can be used to represent one or more characters, the question mark to represent one character.

Example: To save all existing six-letter memory variables ending in the letters TAX to a disk file named FIGURES, enter

```
SAVE TO FIGURES ALL LIKE ???TAX
```

Command: SEEK
Syntax: SEEK *expression*
The SEEK command searches for the first record in an indexed file whose field matches a specific *expression*. If *expression* is a character string, it must be surrounded by single or double quotes. If *expression* cannot be found and dBASE III PLUS is not execut-ing a command file, the EOF( ) value is set to true and a **No find** message is displayed on the screen. An index file must be open before you can use the SEEK command.

Command: SELECT
Syntax: SELECT *n* or SELECT *alias*
The SELECT command chooses from among ten possible work areas for database files. When dBASE III PLUS is first loaded into the computer, it defaults to a work area of 1. To use multiple files at once, you must select other work areas with the SELECT command; other files can then be opened in those areas. Accepta-ble work areas are the letters A through J for *alias* or the numbers 1 through 10 for *n*.

Example: To open a file named TAXES in work area 5, enter

```
SELECT 5
USE TAXES
```

Command: SET
Syntax: SET
Causes Set Menu to be displayed. Set Menu can then be used to select most available SET parameters within dBASE III PLUS.

Command: SET ALTERNATE
Syntax: SET ALTERNATE ON/OFF and SET ALTER-
                NATE TO *filename*
The SET ALTERNATE ON command creates a text file with extension .TXT, and when actuated by SET ALTERNATE ON stores all keyboard entries and screen displays to the file. The SET ALTERNATE OFF command halts the process.

Example: To store the actions of the LIST command to a text file, enter

```
SET ALTERNATE TO CAPTURE
SET ALTERNATE ON
LIST LASTNAME, FIRSTNAME
SET ALTERNATE OFF
```

Command: SET BELL
Syntax: SET BELL ON/OFF
The SET BELL command controls whether audible warnings will be issued during certain operations.

Command: SET CARRY
Syntax: SET CARRY ON/OFF
The SET CARRY command controls whether data will be copied from the prior record into a new record when APPEND or INSERT is used.

Command: SET CATALOG
Syntax: SET CATALOG ON/OFF
Causes or does not cause files that are opened to be added to an open catalog (see SET CATALOG TO).

Command: SET CATALOG TO
Syntax: SET CATALOG TO *catalog filename*
Opens a catalog, or if the named catalog does not exist, creates a new catalog. Any catalog previously opened will be closed when the SET CATALOG TO command is used.

Command: SET CENTURY
Syntax: SET CENTURY ON/OFF
Causes or does not cause the century to be visible in the display of dates. For example, a date that appears as 12/30/86 will appear as 12/30/1986 after the SET CENTURY ON command is used.

Command: SET COLOR
Syntax: SET COLOR TO *standard* [,*enhanced*][,*border*]
The SET COLOR command is used to select screen colors and display attributes. *See* Chapter 15 for more on SET COLOR.

Command: SET CONFIRM
Syntax: SET CONFIRM ON/OFF
The SET CONFIRM command controls the behavior of the cursor during full-screen editing.

Command: SET CONSOLE
Syntax: SET CONSOLE ON/OFF
The SET CONSOLE command turns output to the screen on or off. SET CONSOLE does not control output to the printer.

Command: SET DATE
Syntax: SET DATE AMERICAN/ANSI/BRITISH/
ITALIAN/FRENCH/GERMAN
Sets the display format for the appearance of dates. American displays as mm/dd/yy; ANSI displays as yy.mm.dd; British displays as dd/mm/yy; Italian displays as dd-mm-yy; French displays as dd/mm/yy; and German displays as dd.mm.yy. The default value is American.

Command: SET DEBUG
Syntax: SET DEBUG ON/OFF
The SET DEBUG command routes the output of the SET ECHO command to the printer instead of the screen.

Command: SET DECIMALS
Syntax: SET DECIMALS TO *n*
The SET DECIMALS command, which applies only to division, SQRT( ), LOG( ), and EXP( ), changes the minimum number of decimal places that are normally displayed during calculations.

Command: SET DEFAULT
Syntax: SET DEFAULT TO *drive:*
This command changes the default drive used in file operations. Usually, *drive:* is A or B; it is usually C for hard-disk drives.

Command: SET DELETED
Syntax: SET DELETED ON/OFF
With SET DELETED ON, all records marked for deletion will be displayed when commands such as LIST are used. With SET DELETE OFF, delete markers are turned off, even though they are still present.

Command: SET DELIMITER
Syntax: SET DELIMITER TO [*character-string*][DEFAULT]
                SET DELIMITER ON/OFF
The SET DELIMITER command assigns characters other than the default colon (:), to be used to mark the field area. Once assigned, SET DELIMITER ON activates the delimiters, and SET DELIMITER deactivates the delimiters. DEFAULT restores the colon (:) as the delimiter.

Example: To mark the beginning of a field with a left curly bracket ({) and end the field with a right bracket (}), enter

```
SET DELIMITER TO "{}"
```

Command: SET DEVICE
Syntax: SET DEVICE TO PRINTER/SCREEN
The SET DEVICE command controls whether @ commands are sent to the screen or printer. SET DEVICE is normally set to SCREEN, but if PRINTER is specified, output will be directed to the printer.

Command: SET DOHISTORY
Syntax: SET DOHISTORY ON/OFF
Causes or does not cause the commands executed by a command file to be stored within HISTORY (see SET HISTORY TO).

Command: SET ECHO
Syntax: SET ECHO ON/OFF
The SET ECHO command determines whether instructions from command files will be displayed or printed during program execution. It is mostly used with SET DEBUG. The default for SET ECHO is OFF.

Command: SET ESCAPE
Syntax: SET ESCAPE ON/OFF
The SET ESCAPE command determines whether the ESC key will interrupt a program during execution. The default for SET ESCAPE is ON.

Command: SET EXACT
Syntax: SET EXACT ON/OFF
The SET EXACT command determines how precisely two character strings will be compared. With SET EXACT deactivated, which is the default case, comparison is not strict: a string on the left of the test is equal to its substring on the right if the substring acts as a prefix of the larger string. Thus, "turnbull"="turn" is true even though it is clearly not. SET EXACT ON corrects for this lack of precision.

Command: SET FIELDS
Syntax: SET FIELDS ON/OFF
Respects or overrides a list of fields specified by the SET FIELDS TO command.

Command: SET FIELDS TO
Syntax: SET FIELDS TO [*list of fields* [ALL]]
Sets a specified list of fields that will be available for use. The ALL option causes all fields present in the active database to be made available.

Command: SET FILTER
Syntax: SET FILTER TO *condition*
The SET FILTER command displays only those records in a database that meet a specific condition.

Example: To display only those records in a database that contain the name Culver City in the CITY field during a DISPLAY or LIST command, enter

```
SET FILTER TO "Culver City" $ CITY
```

Command: SET FIXED
Syntax: SET FIXED ON/OFF
The SET FIXED command activates the SET DECIMAL command for all calculations; thus, when used with SET DECIMAL, SET FIXED specifies the number of decimal places to be displayed with all numeric output.

Command: SET FORMAT
Syntax: SET FORMAT TO *filename*
The SET FORMAT command lets you select *filename* for the format of screen displays. If *filename* has the extension .FRM, you need not supply the extension.

Command: SET FUNCTION
Syntax: SET FUNCTION *n* TO *character-string*
The SET FUNCTION command resets a function key to a command of your choice (30 characters maximum). You can view the current settings with the DISPLAY STATUS command.

Example: To change the function of the F5 key to open a file named ABC1 and enter APPEND mode, enter

```
SET FUNCTION 5 TO "USE ABC1;APPEND;"
```

The semicolon (;) executes a carriage return.

Command: SET HEADING
Syntax: SET HEADING ON/OFF
The SET HEADING command determines whether column headings appear when the LIST, DISPLAY, AVERAGE, or SUM command is used.

Command: SET HELP
Syntax: SET HELP ON/OFF
If SET HELP is ON, the **Do you want some help?** prompt appears if dBASE cannot understand the command you entered.

Command: SET HISTORY
Syntax: SET HISTORY TO *numeric expression*
Identifies the maximum number of commands that will be stored within HISTORY. The default value provided if the command is not used is 20.

Command: SET INDEX
Syntax: SET INDEX TO *filename*
The SET INDEX command opens the index file *filename*. If your file has the .NDX extension, you do not need to include it in the command. You can list more than one index file in the command line, but remember that only seven index files can be opened simultaneously.

Command: SET INTENSITY
Syntax: SET INTENSITY ON/OFF
The SET INTENSITY command determines whether reverse video is on or off during full-screen operations. SET INTENSITY is ON when you begin a session with dBASE III PLUS.

Command: SET MARGIN
Syntax: SET MARGIN TO *n*
The SET MARGIN command resets the left printer margin from the default of 0.

Command: SET MEMOWIDTH
Syntax: SET MEMOWIDTH TO *numeric expression*
Controls the width of columns containing the display or printed

listings of contents of memo fields. The default value provided if this command is not used is 50.

Command: SET MENUS
Syntax: SET MENUS ON/OFF
The SET MENUS command determines whether cursor-movement-key menus appear during full-screen commands. SET MENU is ON when you begin a session.

Command: SET MESSAGE
Syntax: SET MESSAGE TO *character-string*
Identifies a user-definable message that appears on the message line at the bottom of the screen.

Example: To display the message **Press F1 for assistance** on the message line, enter

```
SET MESSAGE TO "Press F1 for assistance."
```

Command: SET ORDER
Syntax: SET ORDER TO *index number*
Makes the index file in the sequence indicated by number the active index without changing the open or closed status of the other index files.

Example: If three index files, NAME, CITY, and STATE, are open and STATE is the active index, to keep the three index files open while changing the active index to CITY, enter

```
SET ORDER TO 3
```

Command: SET PATH
Syntax: SET PATH TO *pathname*
The PATH command identifies a DOS path that will be searched for files if a file is not found in the current directory.

Example: To change the path from the default or root path to a path named DBASE on drive C, enter

```
SET PATH TO C:\DBASE
```

For more information on pathnames, read your DOS manual (version 2.0 or later).

Command: SET PRINT
Syntax: SET PRINT ON/OFF
The SET PRINT command directs output to the printer as well as the screen. The default for SET PRINT is OFF.

Command: SET PRINTER
Syntax: SET PRINTER TO *LPT1, COM1, COM2,...other*
              DOS device
Reroutes printer output to the DOS device specified.

Command: SET PROCEDURE
Syntax: SET PROCEDURE TO *procedure-filename*
The SET PROCEDURE command opens the procedure file named. SET PROCEDURE is placed in the command file that will reference the procedures in a procedure file. Only one procedure file can be open, and up to 35 procedures can be in a procedure file.

Command: SET RELATION
Syntax: SET RELATION [TO *key-expression/numeric-*
              expression] INTO *alias*
The SET RELATION command links the active database to an open database in another area. If the *key-expression* option is used, the active file must contain that key, and the other file must be indexed on that key.

Example: To set a relation between the active database and a database named PARTS, using a key field named CUSTNO, enter

```
SET RELATION TO CUSTNO INTO PARTS
```

Command: SET SAFETY
Syntax: SET SAFETY ON/OFF
The SET SAFETY command determines whether a confirmation

message will be provided before existing files are overwritten. SET SAFETY is normally set to ON.

Command: SET STATUS
Syntax: SET STATUS ON/OFF
Turns on or turns off the display of the dBASE III PLUS status line.

Command: SET STEP
Syntax: SET STEP ON/OFF
This is a debugging command that determines whether processing will stop each time a command in a command file is executed. The default of SET STEP is OFF.

Command: SET TALK
Syntax: SET TALK/ON/OFF
The SET TALK command determines whether responses from dBASE III PLUS commands are displayed on the screen. The default for SET TALK is ON.

Command: SET TITLE
Syntax: SET TITLE ON/OFF
Turns on or turns off the prompt for file titles that appear when files are added to an open catalog.

Command: SET TYPEAHEAD
Syntax: SET TYPEAHEAD TO *numeric expression*
Sets the size, in number of keystrokes, of the typeahead buffer. The default value provided if this command is not used is 20. The size of the typeahead buffer can be increased to prevent fast typists from outrunning the keyboard. Acceptable values are any number between 0 and 32,000.

Command: SET UNIQUE
Syntax: SET UNIQUE ON/OFF
This command is used with the INDEX command to create lists of items with no duplicates. The list may not be indexed adequately if there are duplicates. The default setting for SET UNIQUE is OFF.

Command: SET VIEW

Syntax: SET VIEW TO *filename*/[?]

Selects the view (.vue) file specified by *filename*. If the question mark option is used in place of a valid filename, a menu of all available view files will appear. If a catalog is open, the named view file will be added to the catalog.

Command: SKIP

Syntax: SKIP *expression*

The SKIP command moves the record pointer. SKIP moves one record forward if no value is specified. Values can be expressed as memory variables or as constants.

Example: To skip two records back, enter

```
SKIP -2
```

Command: SORT

Syntax: SORT TO *filename* ON *field name* [A/D] [*field name*[A/D]][*scope*]

The SORT command creates a rearranged copy of a database. The order of the new copy depends on the fields and options specified.

Example: To sort a database on the LASTNAME and then FIRSTNAME fields for duplicate entries in LAST-NAME, both in descending order, and output the sorted file to a file named NEWNAME, enter

```
SORT TO NEWNAME ON LASTNAME/D, FIRSTNAME/D
```

Command: STORE

Syntax: STORE *expression* TO *memvar-list*

This command creates a memory variable and stores a value to that variable.

Example: To multiply the field RENTAMT value for the current record by 1.05 and store it in the new memory variable named NEWAMT, enter

```
STORE RENTAMT*1.05 TO NEWAMT
```

Command: SUM

Syntax: SUM *[scope][field-list]*[TO *memvar-list*] [FOR/
        WHILE *condition*]

This command provides a sum total of *field-list* involving numeric fields. If the TO option is not used, the sum is displayed. If the TO option is used, the sum is stored as the memory variable specified. If the *scope* option is not used, ALL is assumed by dBASE III PLUS. The FOR/WHILE option can be used to specify a condition that must be met before an entry in a field can be summed.

Example: To total the contents of two specified fields (SALARY and TAXES) and store those sums to the memory variables A and B, enter

```
SUM SALARY, TAXES TO A,B
```

Command: SUSPEND

Syntax: SUSPEND

Suspends execution of a command file or procedure and returns program control to the dot prompt while leaving current memory variables intact. Execution of the command file or procedure can be restarted where it was interrupted with the RESUME command.

Command: TEXT

Syntax: TEXT
        text to be displayed
        ENDTEXT

This command displays blocks of text from a command file.

Example:

```
TEXT
Press the RETURN key to run the payroll.
Or press the ESCAPE key to exit.
ENDTEXT
```

Command: TOTAL

Syntax: TOTAL TO *filename* ON *key* [*scope*] [FIELDS *field list*] [FOR/WHILE *condition*]

This command adds the numeric fields in a database and creates a new database containing the results.

Example: To total the SALARY, FEDTAX, STATETAX, and FICA fields in a database named PAYROLL, and store those totals to a second database named RECORDS, enter

```
USE PAYROLL
TOTAL TO RECORDS ON SALARY, FEDTAX, STATETAX, FICA
```

Command: TYPE

Syntax: TYPE *filename.ext* [TO PRINT]

The TYPE command displays the contents of a disk file on screen. If the TO PRINT option is used, the file will be printed.

Command: UPDATE

Syntax: UPDATE [*RANDOM*] ON *key-field* FROM *alias* REPLACE *field* WITH *expression* [,*field2* WITH *expression2*...]

The UPDATE command uses data from a specified database, *alias*, to make changes to the database in use.

Example: To update the RENTAMT field in a database named WORLDWID, based on the contents of the RENTAMT field in a database named CURRENCY, enter

```
SELECT 2
USE CURRENCY
SELECT 1
USE WORLDWID
UPDATE ON LASTNAME FROM CURRENCY REPLACE RENTAMT
  WITH CURRENCY -> RENTAMT
```

Both files must be sorted or indexed on the key field unless RAN-DOM is included, in which case only *alias* need be indexed. *Alias* must be in a work area.

Command: USE
Syntax: USE [*filename*] [INDEX *file-list*][ALIAS *alias*]
This command opens a database file and related index files in a work area.

Command: WAIT
Syntax: WAIT [*prompt*] [TO *memvar*]
The WAIT command halts operation of a command file until a key is pressed. If a prompt is included, it will be displayed on the screen. If the TO option is used, the key pressed will be stored as a memory variable.

Command: ZAP
Syntax: ZAP
The ZAP command removes all records from the active database file. The ZAP command is equivalent to a DELETE ALL command followed by a PACK command.

Trademarks

AboveBoard™	Intel Corporation
Cheshire™	Xerox Corporation
Clipper™	Nantucket
COMPAQ™	COMPAQ Computer Corporation
Corona®	Corona Data Systems
dBIII™	Wordteck Systems, Inc.
dBASE®	Ashton-Tate
dBASE II®	Ashton-Tate
dBASE III®	Ashton-Tate
dUTIL™	Fox & Geller, Inc.
Framework II™	Ashton-Tate
IBM®	International Business Machines Corporation
MailMerge®	MicroPro International
Microsoft®	Microsoft Corporation
MS-DOS®	Microsoft Corporation
MultiMate®	MultiMate International Inc.
Multiplan®	Microsoft Corporation
Netware/86™	Novell Corporation
NewWord™	Rocky Mountain Software
Novell™	Novell Corporation
1-2-3®	Lotus Development Corporation
PC-File III™	Button Ware
pfs®	Software Publishing Corporation
QUICKCODE™	Fox & Geller, Inc.
R:base®	Microrim, Inc.
S/Net™	Novell Corporation

SuperCalc™	Sorcim Corporation
Symphony®	Lotus Development Corporation
3Com™	3Com Corporation
3+™	3Com Corporation
VisiCalc®	VisiCorp
WordStar®	MicroPro International
Xerox®	Xerox Corporation

Index

* command, 487
→ symbol, 247
? command, 34, 213, 466
@ command, 213, 279, 466
@ SAY option, 213

Abbreviated form of commands, 35
ACCEPT command, 210, 230, 467
ACCESS command, 424-426
Active files, 241-245
Adding fields, 100
Adding files to a catalog, 273
Adding information to the database, 48
Administrator disks, 25
ALIAS option, 245
APPEND BLANK command, 285, 381
APPEND command, 48, 357, 468
APPEND FROM command, 246, 367
Applications Generator, 25, 311-324
ASCII format, 354
Ashton-Tate, 11
ASSIST command, 41, 468
Assistant, 30, 84
    options, 56
AT command, 279
Attributes, 16
AVERAGE command, 212, 468

BACKUP command, 29
Batch files, 425
Binary operators, 204
Blackboard, Screen Painter, 91
Blanks, removing, 298
BOF function, 207
Boxes and lines, drawing, 110
BROWSE command, 68-73, 178, 469
BROWSE FIELDS, 71
BROWSE from the ASSISTANT, 73
Bus design, 415

C programming language, 12
Calculator, using dBASE III PLUS as a, 34
CANCEL command, 306, 469
Canceling a menu option, 32
Capabilities of dBASE III PLUS, 12
CASE...ENDCASE choices, 394
CASE statement, 232
Catalog, 271
    adding files to a, 273
    closing a, 274

CHANGE command, 78, 306, 469
Changing your database, 65-86
Character strings, 299
    searching for, 61
Character/text fields, 42
CLEAR ALL command, 245
CLEAR command, 214, 469
CLOSE ALTERNATE command, 358
CLOSE command, 471
CLOSE INDEX command, 134
Color codes, 340
Colors, setting, 313
Columns, report, 153
Combining files, 245
Command abbreviations, 35
Command file, definition of, 195
Command files
    converting, 408
    creating, 197
Command line, 33
Commands, definition of, 8
Commands and Functions menu, 37
Comment lines in programs, 223
Comparison operators, 181
Conditional processing, 177
Conditional statements, 225
Conditionals, using with report commands, 157
Conditions, multiple, 59
CONFIG.DB file, 350
CONFIG.SYS file, 27-28, 275, 419
Configuration file, 350
Constants, 200
CONTINUE command, 471
Control characters, 359
Conventions used in this book, 35
COPY command, 116, 237-241, 357, 471
Copy protection, 29
COPY STRUCTURE command, 250
COUNT command, 211, 472
CREATE command, 40, 472-474
CREATE LABEL command, 169
CREATE QUERY command, 178
CREATE REPORT command, 145
CREATE SCREEN command, 88
CREATE VIEW command, 263
Creating a database, 40-48
CTOD function, 297
Customizing dBASE III PLUS, 338

Data, 16
    definition of, 17

Data encryption, 416
Data entry, 48
    form, 88
    screen, customizing a, 284
Data refinement, 18
Data type mismatch, 129, 203
Database
    active, 243
    changing your, 65-86
    creating and displaying a, 25-64
    definition of, 1
    modifying the structure of a, 81
    sorting and indexing the, 113-138
    viewing a, 55
Database design, 15-24
Database encryption, 432
Database integrity, 418
Database management, definition of, 1
Database managers, transferring files from other, 360
Database structure, displaying a, 48
Databases
    linking, 260
    relational, 4-7
Date conversion, 159
Date fields, 42
Date format, European, 287
Date formats, 341
dBASE ACCESS, 414
    installing, 422
dBASE Administrator, 414
    installing, 421
dBASE II files, converting, 25
    to dBASE III PLUS, 405-412
dBASE III PLUS disks, 25
    customizing with SET commands, 338
    history of, 12
    improvements of, 12
    installing, 26
    installing on a network, 420
    starting, 30
DBF extension, 239
DBMS, 4
DBSYSTEM.DB file, 433
dCONVERT program, 405-412
Deadly embrace, 449
Debugging, 326, 331-338
Decimal numbers, 45
Decimal places, 341
Decision making within programs, 225-236
Default drive, specifying the, 33
DEL command, 116, 383, 475
DELETE RECORD command, 76
Deleting
    fields, 102
    files, 78
    records, 74
Delimited format, 354

DELIMITED option, 360
Designing the database, 15-24
DIF format, 355
DIR command, 475
Directory option, 47
Disk access speed, 325
Disk drive requirements, 13
Disk space, displaying available, 47
Disks, dBASE III PLUS, 25
Display characteristics of a field, changing the, 103
DISPLAY command, 55, 475-476
DISPLAY FOR command, 61
DISPLAY HISTORY command, 336
DISPLAY MEMORY command, 202, 300
DISPLAY options, 57
DISPLAY STATUS command, 427
DISPLAY USERS command, 428
Displaying a database, 25-64
    structure, 48
Displaying database files, 47
DO CASE command, 477
DO CASE-ENDCASE commands, 233
DO WHILE command, 226, 478
DO WHILE loop, 382
DO WHILE statement, 386
DOS commands, executing from dBASE III PLUS, 308
DOS files, 275
DOS programs, running from within dBASE III PLUS, 308
Dot prompt, 33
Double spacing, 150
DTOC function, 129, 159, 297
dUTIL III PLUS, 453

EDIT command, 65-68, 177, 478
Editing functions with APPEND, 51
Editing information, 68
Editing keys used with word processor, 199
Editing with the Append screen, 51
Editor, specifying your own, 351
EJECT command, 142, 478
Employee payroll system, 389-393
Encryption, 432
ENDDO command, 226
Entry forms, creating with Screen Painter, 87-112
EOF function, 207
Epson printer codes, 397
ERASE command, 479
Errors, programming, 331
EXCEPT command, 302
EXCEPT option, 302
EXIT command, 305, 479
Expanded memory, 419
EXPORT command, 354, 366, 479
Expressions, 202

Field
   changing the display characteristics of a, 103
   primary and secondary, 120
   searching within a, 61
Field access, 431
Field types, 42
Field widths, 43
   calculating, 19
   changing from Screen Painter, 97
Fields, 2
   adding, 100
   copying, 238
   creating the, 43
   deleting, 102
   hiding, 265
   moving, 93
   viewing specific, 59
File
   configuration, 350
   procedure, 327
File access, 431
File alias, 244
File extensions, 112, 124, 146, 197, 239, 241,
   358, 369
File formats, 353
File locking, 418
File management, 237-258
   commands, 258
File managers, 5
File names, 41
File privileges, 438
File server, 414
   requirements for, 419
Files
   active, 241-245
   batch, 425
   combining, 245
   converting dBASE II, 405-412
   deleting, 78
   displaying, 47
   DOS and open, 275
   flat, 355
   linking, 260
   merging, 328
   open, 131, 241
   transferring, 353
Filing system, 2
FIND command, 135, 303, 480
Flat files, 355
FLOCK function, 446
Floppy disk system, 26, 423
FOR statement, 121
Form design, 88
Format file, 269, 289
Fox & Geller programs, 453-464
Framework II, 375
Function keys, defining, 343
Functions, 206, 296
   and templates used with PICTURE, 107, 286

GET option, 281
Glossary, 465-507
GO command, 480
GO TOP command, 64
GOTO command, 66, 480
Graphics characters, 111
   in files, 359
Grouping data, 152
Groups menu, 151

Hard disk, 27
Headings, 155
HELP, main menu for, 36
HELP command, 480
HELP files, 36
HISTORY function, 335
History of dBASE database managers, 11

IBM Extended Graphic Character set, 111
IF command, 481
IF...ELSE, and ENDIF, 228
Immediate mode, 10
IMPORT command, 354, 364, 481
INDEX command, 124, 395, 401
Index file, 123
Index key, 125
Indexing, 113-138
   and sorting, differences of, 137
   on fields of different types, 128
   on multiple fields, 125
   on multiple fields with the Assistant, 128
INPUT command, 210, 282, 482
Input requirements, 216
INS (INSERT) key, 92
INSERT command, 482
Insert mode, 52
Installing dBASE III PLUS, 26
   on a network, 420
Intel Above Board, 419
Interfacing with dBASE III PLUS, 353-378
Inventory system, 384-389

JOIN command, 247, 482

LABEL command, 483
LABEL FORM command, 174
Labels, mailing, 168
LAN, 413-452
LASTDRIVE command (DOS), 419
LIKE option, 302
Limitations of dBASE III PLUS, 13
Line spacing, 150
Lines and boxes, drawing, 110
LIST command, 55, 483
   using with the Assistant, 141
LIST HISTORY command, 336
LIST options, 57
LIST STATUS command, 427
LIST STRUCTURE command, 47, 144

LIST USERS command, 428
Local area network, 413-452
    starting dBASE on a, 424
Local area networks
    reference guides for, 450
    requirements for, 418
LOCATE command, 64, 75, 382, 484
Locate menu, 162
LOCK functions, 446
LOCK option of the BROWSE command, 72
Locking functions, 447
Logical fields, 43
Logical operators, 205
Log-in access, 430
LOOP command, 484
Loops, 227, 305
    errors in, 332
Lotus 1-2-3, 356, 366
    worksheet format, 353
LOWER function, 297
Lowercase letters, converting, 296

Macros, 302
Macro-substitution function, 302
Mailing labels, 168
Mailing list program, 379-384
MailMerge, 356
Margin settings, 142
Mathematical operators, 35, 204
Memo field, 345
    entering data in a, 49
    files, 241
Memo fields, 43, 62
    including in a report, 167
Memory requirements, 13
Memory resident software, 276
Memory variables, 201, 300
Menu, designing with @, SAY, and GET, 282
Menu options, selecting, 32
Menu-driven system, 196
Microcomputers, 16-bit, 12
Microsoft software, 356
MODIFY command, 485-486
MODIFY COMMAND command, 197, 304
MODIFY LABEL command, 175
MODIFY QUERY command, 185
MODIFY REPORT command, 161
MODIFY SCREEN command, 98
MODIFY STRUCTURE command, 81, 100, 251
Modifying the database with Screen Painter, 100
Modules, 217
Moving fields, 93
MS-DOS version, 13
MultiMate, 356
Multiplan, 355
Multiuser environment, 429

Nesting expressions within a query, 185
Network, starting dBASE on a, 424
Network commands, 426
Network requirements, 418

Networks, compatible, 416
NOTE command, 487
Novell network, 419
Numeric fields, 42

On-Disk Tutorial, 25
Open files, 131, 241, 275
Operators, 180, 204
Output requirements, 215

PACK command, 383, 488
Page eject, 142
Page headings, 155
Page options, 148
PARAMETERS command, 488
Parentheses, using with query form, 190
Passwords, 416, 434
PC-DOS version, 13
PC-File III, 356
Personnel tracking system, 393-404
PFS:FILE, 364
PICTURE command, 285
Picture Function option, 105
PICTURE option, 285
Picture Template option, 105
Pointer, 62
Primary field, 120
Print servers, 414
Printer codes, 397
Printing graphic characters, 111
PRIVATE command, 308, 489
PROCEDURE command, 489
Procedures, 326-331
Program
    documenting the, 223
    verifying the, 222
Program control, editing records under, 303
Program design, 214
Programmed mode, 10
Programming, 195-224, 295-352
    concepts, 200-208
    errors, 331
    functions, 296
    language, definition of, 8
    local area network, 446
Programs, sample, 379-404
PROTECT program, 416, 425, 430-444
Pseudocode, 221
PUBLIC command, 308, 490

Qualifiers, sorting with, 121
Queries, nested, 185
Query files, 177-194
Query filter, 186
Query menu options, 178
QUICKCODE III, 456
QUICKREPORT, 459
QUIT command, 64, 490

R:base 5000, 356
Range option, 108

READ command, 490
READ option, 281
RECALL command, 76, 490
RECNO function, 297
Record locking, 418
Record numbers, 297
Records, 2
    deleting, 74
    keeping track of, 62
REINDEX command, 133, 395, 490
Relational commands, 259-276
Relational databases, 4-7
Relational operators, 205
Relations, building, 268
Relationships, establishing the, 20
RELEASE ALL command, 301
RELEASE command, 491
REPLACE command, 79, 255, 387, 491
Report
    definition of, 16
    displaying text within a, 166
    editing a, 161
    planning the, 143
REPORT command, 492
Report commands, using conditionals with, 157
Report generator, 143-168
Reports
    creating, 139-176
    producing from the Assistant, 160
RESTORE command, 29, 301, 492
RESUME command, 492
RESUME option, 338
RETRY command, 492
RETURN command, 209, 309, 493
RLOCK function, 446
RUN command, 308, 493

Sample programs, 379-404
Sample Programs and Utilities Disk, 25
SAVE command, 493
SAY and GET options, 381
SAY option, 279
Screen coordinates, 280
Screen design, hints on, 294
Screen displays, 277-294
Screen Painter
    and format files, 293
    creating entry forms with the, 87-112
SDF format, 355
Search conditions, 58-59
Searches, 177-194
Searching for character strings and expressions, 135
Secondary field, 120
Security hints, general, 444
SEEK command, 135, 396, 494
SELECT command, 243-244, 494
Selecting a menu option, 32
Selective data, viewing, 57
Self-booting disk, 26
Servers, 414

SET ALTERNATE command, 334, 358, 495
SET BELL command, 339, 495
SET CARRY command, 339, 495
SET CATALOG command, 271, 495
SET CENTURY command, 496
SET COLOR command, 339, 496
SET command, 495-504
SET commands, customizing dBASE III PLUS with, 338
SET CONFIRM command, 496
SET CONSOLE command, 340, 496
SET DATE command, 159, 340-341, 496
SET DEBUG command, 334, 496
SET DECIMALS command, 341, 497
SET DEFAULT command, 33, 497
SET DELETED command, 77, 394
SET DELIMITER command, 497
SET DEVICE command, 497
SET DOHISTORY command, 336, 498
SET DRIVE option, 34
SET ECHO command, 333-334, 498
SET ESCAPE command, 498
SET EXACT command, 341, 498
SET EXCLUSIVE command, 446
SET FIELDS command, 498
SET FIELDS option, 265
SET FILTER command, 499
SET FILTER option, 184
SET FIXED command, 342, 499
SET FORMAT command, 499
SET FUNCTION command, 342, 499
SET HEADING command, 500
SET HELP command, 344, 500
SET HISTORY command, 335, 500
SET INDEX command, 130, 500
SET INTENSITY command, 344, 500
SET MARGIN command, 142, 500
SET MEMOWIDTH command, 345, 500
SET MENUS command, 347, 501
SET MESSAGE command, 346, 501
SET ORDER command, 501
SET PATH command, 429, 501
SET PRINT command, 139, 502
SET PRINTER command, 428, 502
SET PROCEDURE command, 328, 502
SET RELATION command, 260-263, 502
SET SAFETY command, 346, 502
SET STATUS command, 503
SET STEP command, 334, 503
SET TALK command, 209, 333, 503
SET TITLE command, 503
SET TYPEAHEAD command, 503
SET UNIQUE command, 503
SET VIEW command, 504
SideKick, 276
SKIP command, 209, 504
Software interchange formats, 356
SORT command, 114, 504
Sorting, 113-138
    and indexing, 137
    on multiple fields, 118

MODIFY COMMAND Prog Name

516 Using dBASE III PLUS

Spacing, line, 150
Spreadsheets, transferring files to, 370
Starter Command menu, 38
Starting DBASE III PLUS, 30
STORE command, 201, 300, 504
STR function, 129, 299
String operators, 206
Subtotals, 152
SUM command, 212, 505
Superlok, 29
SUSPEND command, 505
SUSPEND option, 338
SYLK format, 355
Symphony, 366
System requirements, 13

Text, displaying in a report, 166
TEXT command, 213, 505
Token ring design, 415
Tools menu, 239
TOTAL command, 506
Trailing blanks, removing, 298
Transferring files, 353
TRIM function, 298
Truth table, 206
TYPE command, 506

Unary operators, 204
UNINSTAL procedure, 423
UNLOCK command, 446, 448
UPDATE command, 256, 506

UPPER function, 296
Uppercase letters, converting, 296
USE command, 66, 507
User groups, 432
Users
    adding, 436
    changing and deleting, 438
Utility programs, 453-464

Variables
    hiding and showing, 308
    memory, 201
View files, 263-271
Viewing a database, 55
VisiCalc, 356
Vulcan, 11

WAIT command, 307, 394, 507
Wildcards, 311
WKS format, 355
Word processor, 198
Word processors
    transferring files from, 373
    transferring files to, 358
WordStar, 356, 458
    Mailmerge option, 354
Work areas, 241-245
Work station requirements, 420
Work stations, 414

ZAP command, 307, 507

P.3" DO c: APPS GEN

DO c:\DBASE\ APPSGEN